CHRISTIAN HOME COOKBOOK

Traditional Family Recipes Collected
by the Church of God in Christ Mennonite,
from Canada, United States and Mexico

Hearth
PUBLISHING

135 North Main
Hillsboro, KS 67063

A family can't live on bread alone,
I thought as I prepared the meal
Hearts thrive on love that's shown,
And souls grow when we kneel.

The food we eat will feed our bodies
And give us strength to perform our tasks.
The time we share will feed our hearts
And build a family that will last.

My prayer is that each meal will be
Food for body, mind and soul.
May God be honored in this family
Today, tomorrow, and for eternity.

Carol Duerksen

FIRST EDITION
Copyright © 1991 by Hearth Publishing

ISBN 0-9627947-2-4
Library of Congress Catalog Number 91-71447

FOREWORD

Can a cookbook be a legend? If legend is defined as "a story or body of stories handed down for generations and popularly believed to have historical basis," then perhaps this collection of recipes qualifies for legend status. After all, mothers have handed this cookbook to daughters and daughters-in-law for years. Friends have given it to each other and acquaintances have asked to buy it. Certainly a church cookbook in its 9th printing, with 49,000 copies "out there" somewhere, has something unique going for it, something legendary.

The *Christian Home Cook Book* was printed for the first time in 1966 by the Church of God in Christ, Mennonite. The first printing of 2000 books was followed only a year later by another 5000. These Mennonites weren't into marketing plans. No other fanfare surrounded the book. It sold simply because it stood the test of the kitchen. It sold because people found it practical, useful, and the recipes turned out well. It sold because users told others it was "their favorite cookbook." It sold because it was a wonderful, practical gift. Including its eighth printing in 1985, the *Christian Home Cook Book* has sold 49,000 copies. Not bad for a denomination of less than 15,000 members that never marketed the book at all!

The committee of nine Mennonite women in Central Kansas that compiled and tested the recipes in this book never dreamed so many people would benefit from their many hours of work. Elsie Holdeman, one of the original committee members, still remembers the days upon days they donated to put the book together. She also remembers seeing more spellings for "macaroni," and "Worcestershire," than she thought possible. And although she would never have predicted the cookbook's success, she understands why.

"Our married granddaughters have all kinds of other cookbooks, but they tell me they still go back to this one," she said. "I do too. It has such a large variety of easy-cooking recipes — something many other cookbooks just don't have."

For 25 years, the *Christian Home Cook Book* sold itself through word of mouth and satisfied users. We believe this success story deserves the opportunity to reach many more homes. So, with a new cover and convenient spiral binding, but the same tried and true recipes, the *Christian Home Cook Book* is now available in bookstores across the nation.

Perhaps you're curious about the Mennonite group responsible for this cookbook. The Church of God in Christ Mennonite have large settlements throughout the United States as well as Canada, Latin and South America. In terms of lifestyle and appearance, this group of Mennonites drives cars and have electricity in their homes, but televisions and radios are not used. The men grow beards and the women wear black prayer coverings.

There are other characteristics that are uniquely Church of God in Christ Mennonite, but this is a cookbook, not a religious encyclopedia. One belief, though, relates directly to this cookbook, and that is the importance of family, and a family mealtime together.

"We feel very strongly about family life," member Dale Koehn said. "We believe in a good sound meal for a family to share together. There aren't any TV dinners in this cookbook. Neither do the recipes call for anything exotic — just common ingredients you would have at home or can easily buy. I guess I'd call it simply good home cooking."

In this day and age, home is often a place where family members meet each other at the microwave. Not so in these Mennonite homes. Family life is highly valued; and while good meals feed their bodies, food for the soul takes highest priority.

So you see, although food in itself is not a part of faith, the *Christian Home Cook Book* grew out of a deep commitment to families sharing their meals and their lives together. I invite you to make this cookbook a part of your life, or to share it with someone else. I invite you to enjoy the legend of the *Christian Home Cook Book*.

Stan Thiessen
General Manager
Hearth Publishing

TABLE OF CONTENTS

Abbreviations and Measurements

Abbreviations Commonly Used

tsp. = teaspoon
tbsp. = tablespoon
pt. = pint
qt. = quart
pk. = peck
bu. = bushel
oz. = ounce or ounces
lb. = pound or pounds
sq. = square
min. = minute or minutes
hr. = hour or hours
mod. = moderate or moderately
doz. = dozen
pkg. = package
choc. = chocolate
med. = medium
in. = inches

Standard Syrups Used in Canning

Thin Syrup: 1 part sugar—3 parts water
Medium Syrup: 1 part sugar—2 parts water
Thick Syrup: 1 part sugar—1 part water
Combine sugar and water. Boil 5 min.

Simplified Measures

pinch and dash = $\frac{1}{8}$ teaspoon
3 teaspoons = 1 tablespoon
16 tablespoons = 1 cup
1 cup = $\frac{1}{2}$ pint
2 cups = 1 pint
2 pints (4 cups) = 1 quart
4 quarts (liquid) = 1 gallon

8 quarts (solid) = 1 peck
4 pecks = 1 bushel
16 ounces = 1 pound
$5\frac{1}{2}$ tablespoons = $\frac{1}{3}$ cup
4 tablespoons = $\frac{1}{4}$ cup
8 tablespoons = $\frac{1}{2}$ cup
$10\frac{2}{3}$ tablespoons = $\frac{2}{3}$ cup

12 tablespoons = ¾ cup   14 tablespoons = ⅞ cup
2½ tbsp. cornstarch added to 1 cup flour less 2½ tbsp. flour
    equals 1 cup cake flour
For 1 sq. of choc., substitute 3 tbsp. cocoa plus 1 tbsp. fat.

Contents of Cans

Size	Weight	Contents
8 oz.	8 oz.	1 cup
Picnic	10½ to 12 oz.	1¼ cups
12 oz.	12 oz.	1½ cups
No. 300	14 to 16 oz.	1¾ cups
No. 303	16 to 17 oz.	2 cups
No. 2	1 lb. 4 oz. or 1 pt. 2 fl. oz.	2½ cups
No. 2½	1 lb. 13 oz.	3½ cups
No. 3 cyl. or 3 lb. 3 oz. or 46 fl. oz.	1 qt. 14 fl. oz.	5¾ cups
No. 10	6½ to 7 lbs. 5 oz.	12 to 13 cups

Oven Temperatures

Slow ....250 to 300 degrees
Slow moderate ....325 degrees
Moderate ....350 degrees
Quick moderate ....375 degrees
Moderately hot ....400 degrees
Hot ....425 to 450 degrees
Very hot ....475 to 500 degrees

Common Food Equivalents

	Unit	Approximate Measure
Apples	1 ℔.	3 medium (3 cups sliced)
Bananas	1 ℔.	3 med. (2½ cups sliced)
Butter and Other Fats.	1 ℔.	2 cups
Cheese, Cheddar	1 ℔.	4 cups grated
Cheese, Cottage	1 ℔.	2 cups
Cheese, White Cream	3-oz. pkg.	6 tbsp.
	½-℔. pkg.	16 tbsp. (1 cup)

Chocolate Unsweetened ½-lb. pkg.		8 1-oz. squares
Coconut, Shredded	1 lb.	5 cups
Coffee, Ground	1 lb.	80 tbsp.
Cream, Whipping	1 pt.	2 cups (4 cups whipped)
Flour		
All-purpose	1 lb.	4 cups (sifted)
Cake	1 lb.	4½ cups (sifted)
Whole Wheat	1 lb.	3½ cups
Rye	1 lb.	4½ to 5 cups
Lemon, Medium		
Juice	1	2 to 3 tbsp.
Rind, lightly grated	1	1½ to 3 tsp.
Marshmallows	¼ lb.	16
Orange, Medium		
Juice	1	⅓ to ½ cup
Rind, lightly grated	1	1 to 2 tbsp.
Sugar		
Granulated	1 lb.	2 cups
Brown	1 lb.	2¼ cups (firmly packed)
Confectioners	1 lb.	3½ cups (sifted)

Substitutions for Emergencies

1 tbsp. cornstarch (for thickening)	2 tbsp. flour (approximately)
1 whole egg	2 egg yolks plus 1 tbsp. water (in cookies, etc.)
1 whole egg	2 egg yolks (in custards and such mixtures)
1 cup fresh whole milk	½ cup evaporated milk plus ½ cup water
1 cup fresh whole milk	1 cup nonfat dry milk plus 2 tbsp. butter
1 cup fresh whole milk	1 cup sour milk or buttermilk plus ½ tsp. soda (decrease baking powder 2 tsp.)
1 cup sour milk or buttermilk	1 tbsp. lemon juice or vinegar plus enough fresh whole milk to make 1 cup
1 cup honey	1¼ cups sugar plus ½ cup liquid
1 cup canned tomatoes	about 1⅓ cups cut-up fresh tomatoes, simmered 10 min.

BEVERAGES

Beverages

Delicious Hot Milk Steamers

Coffee Cocoa Steamer:

Mix ⅓ cup instant coffee, ⅓ cup instant cocoa, and ⅓ cup sugar. Stir in 2 qts. hot milk. Serve in mugs, top with whipped cream.

Butterscotch:

Add ¼ cup butter and ½ cup brown sugar to 2 qts. hot milk. Serve hot sprinkled with cinnamon or nutmeg.

Other Flavors:

Stir 1 or 2 tbsp. of any of these into 1 cup hot milk. Maple syrup, molasses, or honey. A dab of butter may be added for richer flavor.

Spicy Steamer:

Mix 2 qts. hot milk, 1 cup spiced syrup, ⅛ tsp. salt. Serve in mugs; top with marshmallow or whipped cream. Spiced syrup: Mix in saucepan 2 cups water, 1½ tbsp. cloves, ½ cup red cinnamon candies and ½ cup sugar. Simmer for 15 min., stirring occasionally. Strain. Use 2 tbsp. syrup for each cup of milk.

Lois Boeckner, Moundridge, Kans.

Holiday Punch

½ cup sugar
½ tsp. allspice
½ tsp. cinnamon
2 cups ginger ale (chilled)

1 qt. cider, chilled
1 6-oz. can frozen orange juice

Mix sugar and spices. Stir over low heat until sugar is dissolved; cool. Add cider and orange juice, chill again. Add ale slowly just before serving. Serves 8 to 10.

Mrs. Earl Wiggers, Hesston, Kans.

Fruit Punch (1)

1 pkg. cherry flavor Kool-Aid
1 pkg. fruit punch flavor Kool-Aid
1 6-oz. can pineapple juice
1 6-oz. can lemonade
1 6-oz. can orange juice
2 cups water, and sugar to taste
1 large bottle of ginger ale may be added before serving

Martha Hiebert, Middleton, Mich.

Fruit Punch (2)

1 pkg. raspberry Kool-Aid
8 cups water
2 cups sugar
1 small can frozen orange juice
1 large can pineapple juice
⅓ can frozen lemon juice

Mix all together. Just before serving, add 1 or 1½ quarts of ginger ale.

Mrs. Melvin Koehn, Greensburg, Kans.

Punch

1 gal. strong tea (boil and strain)
1 small can lemon juice
1 large can pineapple juice
2 cups sugar dissolved in tea
1 qt. grape juice
1 qt. ginger ale (added last)

Mrs. Howard Corbin, Newton, Kans.

BREADS

13

Bread

Anadama Bread

1 cup yellow corn meal
1 cup milk, scalded
1 cup boiling water
3 tbsp. shortening
½ cup molasses
2 tsp. salt
2 pkg. yeast
½ cup lukewarm water
6 cups sifted flour (more or less)

Stir corn meal slowly into combined hot milk and water. Add shortening, molasses and salt, let stand until lukewarm. Sprinkle yeast into warm water, stir until dissolved. Stir into corn meal mixture, alternately with flour. Turn out on a lightly floured board and knead about 7 min. until smooth and elastic. Place dough in a greased bowl, turn once to bring greased side up. Cover and let rise in warm place until doubled in bulk, about 1½ hrs. Form into 2 loaves, let rise. Bake 350 to 375 degrees 40 to 50 min.

Mrs. Frances Becker, Galva, Kans.

Brown and White Potato Bread

1 cake yeast (soaked in ½ cup warm water)
¾ cup sugar
1 tbsp. salt
⅔ cup shortening (Swift and lard mixed is best)
6 cups potato water (lukewarm)

Mix all together and sponge with 6 cups of sifted flour. Place in warm place to rise. Stir down slowly after rising a little. This improves the raising power.

Take 10 large spoonsful of mixture for Brown Bread. Knead out with 3½ cups of 100% whole wheat flour. Let rise 4 to 5 times. This dough should be soft. Loaf and place in greased pans. Makes 2 loaves.

Knead the rest sponge mixture with 9 to 10 cups white flour. Roll out and knead about 10 min. Let rise in a warm place. Continue to knead down 4 to 5 times. Let rise higher the last couple of times. Makes 6 to 8 loaves.

Potato bread cannot be very warm. Keep it on the cool side just so it keeps rising.

Mrs. Sam J. Unruh, Copeland, Kans.

Dark Bread

6 cups milk, scalded and cooled	½ to ⅔ cup sugar (molasses may be used)
2 cups water	4 cups all-bran cereal
8 tsp. salt	1½ cups wheat germ

Mix all ingredients. Add 4 pkg. yeast softened in 1 cup luke-warm water. Gradually stir in white flour to form soft dough. Place on floured board and knead well, adding as much flour as necessary. Thoroughly work in ¾ cup very soft shortening in small amounts. Place in greased bowl. Let rise for three 45 min. periods, punching down after each 45 min. Place in greased breadpans. Let rise 1 hr. Bake in moderate oven (350°) for 1 hr. or until done.

Mrs. Wilbur L. Koehn, Cimarron, Kans.

Dilly Casserole Bread

1 pkg. dry yeast	1 tbsp. butter
¼ cup warm water	2 tsp. dill seed
1 cup creamed cottage cheese, heated to luke-warm	1 tsp. salt
	¼ tsp. soda
	1 unbeaten egg
2 tbsp. sugar	2¼ to 2½ cups all-purpose
1 tbsp. instant minced onion	flour

Soften yeast in water. Combine cottage cheese, sugar, onion, butter, dill seed, salt, soda, egg, and softened yeast in mixing bowl. Add flour to form stiff dough, beating well after each addition. Cover. Let rise in warm place (85-90°) until light and double in size (50 to 60 min.) Stir dough down. Turn into well-greased 8 in. round 1½ to 2 qt. casserole. Let rise in warm place until light, 30 to 40 min. Preheat oven. Bake at 350° for 40 to 50 min. until golden brown. Brush with soft butter and sprinkle with salt. Makes 1 round loaf.

Nelda Litwiller, Ithaca, Mich.

French Bread (1)

1 tbsp. sugar	1 generous tsp. shortening
1 tsp. salt	1 cup boiling water

Let cool. Then add ¼ cup warm water, 1 tsp. sugar, sprinkle in 1 pkg. dry yeast. Let dissolve. Knead in 3 cups flour. Work down every 10 min. 4 or 5 times. Let rest 10 min. Roll to less than ½ in. thick. Roll up as for jelly roll, rolling toward you. Place on greased pan. Let rise until double and slit surface 3 or 4 times. Bake 25 min. at 400°.

Mrs. Dale G. Koehn
Mrs. Calvin Koehn, Montezuma, Kans.

French Bread (2)

¼ cup sugar
1⅓ tbsp. salt

¼ cup shortening

Combine the ingredients, add 1 qt. boiling water and let cool. Dissolve 4 cakes yeast in 1 cup warm water. Add 1½ tbsp. sugar and 12 cups flour. Work in flour with spoon. Work down with spoon every 10 min. for about 4 or 5 times. Divide into 4 balls. Let rest 10 min. Roll out to less than ½ in. thickness. Roll as for jelly roll. Place on greased pans, well apart. Let rise until double in bulk. Slash with sharp knife 3 or 4 times on each loaf. If desired can be brushed with milk and egg yolk. 1 egg yolk and 2 tbsp. milk. Bake at 400° about 25 min. Serve hot with butter.

Martha Ensz, Inman, Kans.

French Bread (3)

1 pkg. yeast
1½ cups warm water

2 tbsp. sugar

Dissolve yeast in water and add 2 tbsp. shortening, melted (corn oil for dieters), 1 scant tbsp. salt, add 2 cups sifted flour and beat well. Add 2 more cups sifted flour and beat well. If not stiff enough add more flour. Let rise in warm place for 10 min. and spoon through dough and work with spoon. Work through dough in this way every 10 min. for 5 consecutive times. After the last 10 min. turn dough on lightly floured surface and divide into 2 loaves. Let rise 10 min. Roll each loaf in 12x9 rectangle. Then roll firmly as for jelly roll, starting with long side, seal edge. Place rolls on greased baking sheet. Score top diagonally 6 times. Grease tops and let rise in warm place about 1½ hrs. or until ready to bake. Bake at 350° 30 min. Yields 2 loaves. Brush top with oleo when taken from oven.

Mrs. Obed Johnson, Halstead, Kans.

French Bread (4)

2½ cups warm water
(or potato water)
2 cakes yeast
2½ tsp. salt

7 cups sifted flour
2 tbsp. sugar
2 tbsp. shortening
Sesame Seed

Measure water into large mixing bowl and crumble in yeast. Stir until dissolved. Add salt, shortening and sugar, then stir in flour. Turn dough out on a lightly floured board and knead 8 to 10 min. Place in a greased bowl, brush with melted shortening and cvver with cloth. Let rise until double in bulk, about 40 min., punch down and let rise again until almost double, about 30 min. Punch down and divide into 2 parts, roll each into an oblong about 8x10 in. Begin with wide side, roll up tightly and seal edges by rolling firmly and tapering ends. Make swift slashes with razor blade ¼ in. deep and 1½ in. apart in top of loaf. Brush with cornstarch glaze, sprinkle with sesame seed, and let rise uncovered about 1½ hrs. Brush again with glaze. Bake in 400° oven 40 min.

Cornstarch Glaze

1 tsp. cornstarch   ½ cup water

Combine and cook, stirring constantly till thickened.

Mrs. Harold Nichols, Greensburg, Kans.

French Bread (Perfect)

4 cups warm water or
4 cups scalded milk, cooled
2 pkg. yeast
2 tbsp. salt

4 tbsp. sugar
2 tbsp. shortening
9 to 10 cups flour

Combine the water or milk with yeast, salt, sugar, and shortening. Stir until dissolved. Add 4 cups of sifted flour and beat until smooth. Add 5 to 6 more cups of sifted flour to make a stiff dough. Turn onto floured board. Let rest 5 to 10 min. then knead until elastic (about 5 min.) Place in greased bowl, cover and let rise in warm place until double in bulk. Knead down and rise again until double. Divide dough into 4 equal parts and pat each part flat to about ¼ in. thickness. Roll like a jelly roll and pinch ends together. Place on greased cooky sheet (two to a sheet) and cut three shallow diagonal slashes in top of each loaf. Let rise until light (about 2 hr.) Bake loaves in preheated (400°) oven about 40 min.

Mrs. Donald Unruh, Greensburg, Kans.
Mrs. Leah Dirks, Greensburg, Kans.

Golden Wheat Bread

2 cups milk (scalded and cooled to lukewarm)
2 cups lukewarm water
⅓ cup honey
4 tsp. salt
3 cakes or pkg. yeast
⅓ cup shortening
7 cups whole wheat flour
3 cups white flour

Dissolve yeast in warm water. Measure flour into pan and make a well, add liquid and yeast, part of shortening and salt. Stir. Let rise until spongy. Then add white flour and knead well. Let rise until double in bulk. Knead lightly again. Cover and let stand again until almost doubled in bulk. Shape into loaves and place in greased bread pans, or if baked in greased 46 oz. orange juice cans, it makes nice slices for toaster, sandwiches, etc. Let stand in warm place until doubled again. Then bake at 375° for 40 min.

Mrs. Heber Good, Dalton, Ohio

Health Bread

2 pkg. dry yeast
3 cups lukewarm water
2 cups cracked whole wheat flour
2 cups white flour
½ cup Wesson oil
½ cup crushed nuts (optional)
1 cup raisins
1½ cups finely grated carrots
½ cup honey
3 tsp. salt

Soak the yeast in a little warm water with 1 tsp. sugar. Mix in the other ingredients. Mix together like usual sponge. Let rise about 45 min. then add white flour, until stiff enough like white bread. Let rise, knead, rise again and knead. After risen again, form into 4 or 5 loaves, and let rise an hour or more. Bake for 1 hr. and 15 min. in slow oven (300°). (Cook the raisins in 1 cup of water, use the liquid as part of the 3 cups of water. This makes the raisins soft, and the liquid adds flavor to the bread.)

Mrs. Sylvester Unruh, Bancroft, S. Dak.

Home-made Twin Loaves

Add 1 pkg. dry yeast to 2¼ cups warm water in mixing bowl and mix well, add 3½ cups flour, 3 tbsp. sugar, 1 tbsp. salt, 2 tbsp. soft shortening. Beat until smooth, add more flour, a little at a time. Let rise and punch down. Let rise again. Form into 2 loaves and let rise. Bake about 45 min. at 350°.

Mrs. Menno Dirks, Halstead, Kans.

Raisin Bread

2 cups hot water
½ cup shortening
1 cup sugar
2 tsp. salt
2 eggs, beaten
2 pkgs. yeast
½ cup lukewarm water
7 cups sifted flour
1 cup raisins; chopped if desired
½ tsp. cinnamon

Mix together hot water, sugar, salt, and shortening. Cool to lukewarm. Dissolve yeast in lukewarm water. Add to above mixture. Add beaten eggs, flour, raisins and cinnamon. Stir until well blended. Let rise in warm place about 50 min. Punch down. Knead ½ min. Turn into 2 greased loaf pans. Bake at 375° for 35 to 40 min.

Mrs. Rueben Ensz, Windom, Kans.

Rich Raisin Bread

⅔ cup milk
⅓ cup sugar
1 tsp. salt
½ cup butter or margarine
½ cup warm water
2 pkgs. yeast
3 eggs, beaten
¼ tsp. nutmeg
6 cups sifted flour
1½ cups seedless raisins

Scald milk; add sugar, salt and butter. Cool to lukewarm Measure water into large bowl. Sprinkle yeast over water, stir until dissolved. Add lukewarm milk mixture, eggs, nutmeg, and one half of the flour. Beat until smooth. Add raisins and re-maining flour to make soft dough. Turn out on lightly floured board. Knead until smooth, about 15 min. Place in greased bowl, turning to grease all sides. Cover and let rise in warm place, free from draft, until doubled in bulk, about 1 hr. Punch down, let rise until doubled in bulk about 30 min. Turn out in lightly floured board and divide in half. Cover. Let rest 10 min. Shape into loaves, place in two greased 9x5 in. loaf pans. Cover and let rise until tops of loaves are slightly higher than pan edges about 45 min. Bake at 350° for 40 to 45 min.

Mrs. Willard Dirks, Mullinville, Kans.

Rye Bread

⅓ cup shortening
3 cups warm water
3 tbsp. molasses
1 pkg. yeast dissolved in ½ cup warm water and 1 tsp. sugar

3 cups rye flour
6 cups white flour
1 tbsp. salt
1 tsp. Caraway seed (optional)

Mix in usual manner. Let rise until double in bulk. Make into loaves. Let rise about 30 min. Bake at 350° for 45 min. or 1 hr. depending on size of loaves

Mrs. Russell Wilson, Almena, Wisc.

Buns and Zwieback

Bun Recipe

10 cups flour
2 tbsp. salt
4 cups water

½ cup sugar
1½ cups soft lard or shortening

Dissolve 1 pkg. yeast, 1 tsp. sugar in 1 cup water, let rise. Measure flour into a six quart container, make a well on the side, then add all ingredients. Add yeast which has risen and the very warm water. Stir batter until all ingredients are mixed, then add the rest of the flour until dough is medium hard. Let rise, then punch down and let rise again. Make the zwieback. Let rise again. Bake at 450° until brown.

Mrs. Agnes Barkman, Steinbach, Man.

Corn Meal Buns

1 pkg. yeast
¼ cup water
½ cup butter or oleo
¼ cup shortening
1½ cups corn meal

½ cup sugar
1 tbsp. salt
3 cups sifted flour
2 beaten eggs
2 cups milk

Soften yeast in warm water. Scald milk, add butter, shortening, sugar and salt. Cool. Add flour, yeast and eggs. Beat. Add corn meal and enough flour to make dough right thickness. Place in greased bowl and let rise till double in bulk. Shape into rolls, let rise till double. Makes about 2½ doz. Bake at 375° about 15 min.

Mrs. Elmer Diller, Stapleton, Ga.

Hamburger Buns

2 cakes yeast
2 tbsp. sugar
2 cups milk, scalded and
   cooled
7½ cups sifted flour

½ cup shortening
½ cup sugar
½ tsp. salt
2 eggs, well beaten

Dissolve yeast and 2 tbsp. sugar in lukewarm milk. Add 3¼ cups flour to make a sponge. Beat until smooth; cover and let rise in warm place, until light, about 1 hr. Cream shortening and sugar, add salt. Add to yeast mixture. Add eggs and remaining flour. Knead lightly, grease bowl, cover and let rise again until doubled in bulk, about 2 hrs. Shape into med. sized round buns, place in well greased shallow pans. Cover and let rise again until light, about 1 hr. Bake in oven 325° about 20 min. Makes 4 doz.

Mrs. Elton Wenger, Hesston, Kans.

Jam Buns

Mix as for pie dough:
   2 cups flour
   3 tsps. baking powder
   2 tbsp. sugar

   ¼ tsp. salt
   1 cup lard

Add:
   1 egg
   ½ cup milk

   1 tsp. vanilla

Roll out on floured board ¼ in. thick. Cut into squares and put
in muffin tins. Drop 1 tsp. jam or any other filling on dough.
Bake at 450° until light brown.

Mrs. Frank Froese

Zwieback (1)

2 cups scalded milk
1 cup water
½ cup sugar
2½ tsp. salt
2 eggs (optional)
¾ cup shortening

1½ tbsp. yeast or 1½ cake
    yeast, dissolved in 1 cup
    warm water with
1 tbsp. sugar, let stand un-
    til spongy
8 to 10 cups flour

Add sugar and salt to warm milk, then add yeast mixture, shortening, adding flour gradually and mix to med. soft dough. Knead
dough until soft and smooth. Cover and let rise in warm place
until double in bulk. Knead down once more and let rise again.
Pinch off small balls of dough, placing 2 in. apart on greased pans,
put slightly smaller ball on top, pressing down with thumb. Let
rise until double in size. Bake at (400°) 15 to 20 min. (¼ cup
corn oil may be used with the shortening.)

Mrs. G. H. Dyck, Hesston, Kans.

Zwieback (2)

3 cups scalded milk
1 cup water
½ cup cream
1 cup soft shortening

1½ cake yeast
4 tsp. salt
¼ cup sugar
flour

Combine milk, water, cream and soft shortening. Have this
mixture warm, add crumbled yeast. When yeast is dissolved,
stir in as much flour as you can with a spoon. Turn on floured
table and knead enough flour to make a med. stiff dough. Place
in greased bowl and let rise till double in bulk. Knead down, and
let rise again, then knead down and pinch off small pieces, size
of a small egg and put spaced on greased baking pans. Pinch off
more pieces, a little smaller, and place on top of the larger pieces.
Let rise and bake in hot oven till brown (about 400°)

Mrs. Paul E. Hiebert, Hillsboro, Kans.

Zwieback (3)

6 cups milk (scalded)
1 cup hot mashed potatoes
3 cakes yeast or 3 tbsp.
  dry yeast
  Flour

1 tbsp. sugar
4 tbsp. salt
2 cups shortening
  (oleo and lard)

Dissolve yeast in 1 cup water with 1 tbsp. sugar. Combine milk, mashed potato, shortening and salt. Add flour, 2 cups at a time until a soft dough is formed. Let rise until double in bulk. Punch down, let rise again. Pinch off small balls of dough, place 2 in. apart on greased pan. Put slightly smaller ball on the top and press down with the thumb. Let rise 30 min. then start baking at 400°, 15 to 20 min.

Mrs. Dave Giesbrecht, Glenn, Calif.

Coffee Cakes

Christmas Star Coffee Cake

1 pkg. dry yeast
¼ cup lukewarm water
½ cup milk
¼ cup sugar
1 tsp. salt
½ cup raisins or candied fruit

2 tbsp. melted shortening
2½ cups sifted flour
1 egg, beaten
3 tbsp. melted butter
¼ cup sugar

Soften yeast in water. Scald milk, add sugar, salt and shortening. Cool to lukewarm. Add enough flour to make thick batter, mix well. Add yeast and egg, beat well, add enough flour to make soft dough. Turn out on lightly floured board and knead until smooth and satiny. Place in a greased bowl and cover. Let rise in warm place until doubled in bulk (about 1½ hrs.). When light, punch down and let rest 10 min. Roll out to circle 12 in. in diameter. Place rolled-out dough on greased baking sheet. Brush with melted butter. Mix sugar and raisins or fruit and spread evenly over dough. With scissors cut pie shaped sections by cutting from center toward edge, cutting only to within an inch of outer edge. Roll up each section like butter horn roll, starting at center, curve center of each roll toward middle of coffee cake. Pull ends outward to form star. Cover, let raise until doubled, about 45 min. Bake at 375° for 15 to 20 min. Frost with confectioners sugar icing.

Mrs. Don Nightengale, Fairview, Okla.

Coffee Cake (1)

1 cup milk	½ cup sugar
1 pkg. yeast	½ tsp. salt
3 eggs	2 cups raisins
½ cup butter	4 cups flour

Cream butter and sugar, add eggs, well beaten, warm milk and pour ¼ cup over yeast and let stand 5 min. Add remainder of milk to butter and sugar mixture, add salt and yeast. Rub raisins into flour then add this to above mixture. Let dough rise until quite light, spread dough about ½ in. thick in greased 9 in. pan. Spread thick cream over top dough, cover with a mixture of 1 cup brown sugar, 1½ tsp. cinnamon, and ⅔ to ¾ cup chopped nuts. Let rise until light. Bake 20 min. at 400°. Makes enough for three 9 in. pans.

Mrs. Dean Schmidt

Coffee Cake (2)

Sift:

1½ cups flour	3 tsp. baking powder
¾ cup sugar	¼ tsp. salt

Cut in:

¼ cup butter

Add:

1 egg that has been beaten and mix with ½ cup milk and
1 tsp. vanilla

Mix:

½ cup brown sugar	½ cup chopped nuts
2 tbsp. flour	2 tbsp. butter
2 tsp. cinnamon	

Pour one-half of the batter in a greased pan and sprinkle ½ of the nut mixture and bake for 30 min. at 375°.

Coffee Cake (3)

½ cup butter
2 eggs, unbeaten
1 cup white sugar
1 cup sour thick cream add
1 tsp. soda

¼ tsp. salt
1½ tsp. baking powder
1⅔ cups flour

Pour half the batter into pan

Filling:
½ cup brown sugar
1 cup chopped walnuts
1 tsp. cinnamon

Put half the filling in the middle and the other half on top. Bake for 45 min. in a 375° oven.

Mrs. Ben L. Rempel, Morris, Man.

German Coffee Cake

½ cup butter or oleo
2 cups sugar

2 cups sour cream

Cook till it thickens, then cool to lukewarm.
Dissolve 2 pkgs. dry yeast in ½ cup warm water. Add 1 tsp. sugar, 2 cups more lukewarm water, and 2 cups sifted flour. Let stand till spongy. Then add 7 beaten egg yolks or 4 beaten whole eggs and 2 tsp. salt. Add cooked cream mixture and enough flour to make smooth dough (9 or 10 cups). Let rise until double or 1 hour. Knead down, then let rise again until double. Then shape as for coffee cake. Place in cake or pie pans. (Makes six or seven cakes.) Let rise till light and bake 25 or 30 min. in 350° oven or until done. Ice with favorite brown sugar icing. Also makes delicious cinnamon rolls. Mrs. Lloyd Koehn, Lehigh, Kans.

Mother's Quick Coffee Cake

1½ cups flour
⅔ cup sugar
3 tsp. baking powder

½ tsp. salt
¼ cup shortening

Break one egg into one cup and fill with milk and add to dry mixture. Mix with mixer until well blended. Bake 25 to 35 min. at 375°. This is especially good if self-rising flour is used. Omit baking powder and salt. Mrs. Robert Schroeder, Halstead, Kans.
Velma Dyck, Hesston, Kansas

Hawaiian Coffee Cake

Sift:

1½ cups flour

2½ tsp. baking powder

½ tsp. salt

½ cup sugar

Combine:

1 beaten egg

1 cup crushed pineapple

¼ cup melted shortening

Add pineapple mixture to flour mixture; stir till flour is moistened. Pour in greased 6x10 in. cake pan.

Topping

½ cup coconut

½ cup brown sugar

2 tbsp. flour

2 tbsp. butter

Bake at 400° for 25 to 30 min.

Sour Cream Coffee Cake

⅓ cup well packed brown sugar

⅓ cup sugar

¼ cup chopped walnuts

1 tsp. cinnamon

Mix well and set aside

2 cups sifted flour

1 tsp. baking powder

1 tsp. baking soda

½ cup butter at room temperature

¼ tsp. salt

2 eggs

1 tsp. vanilla

1 cup sour cream

1 cup sugar

Combine sifted flour, baking powder, baking soda, and salt in a bowl. Stir lightly with fork and set aside. Beat butter at medium speed of electric mixer until it is creamy. Gradually add 1 cup sugar beating all the time, continue beating until mixture is light and fluffy. Add eggs, one at a time, beating well after each addition. Beat in vanilla. Turn speed down as low as it will go. Add flour mixture and sour cream alternately to butter mixture beginning and ending with dry ingredients. Beat only long enough after each addition to blend ingredients. Spoon half of batter into well-greased 12x8 in. rectangular cake pan; spread evenly with a rubber scraper. Sprinkle half of brown sugar mixture over batter, add remaining batter, spreading it lightly but evenly. Top with remaining brown sugar mixture. Bake in moderate oven 350° for 30 min. until coffee cake is nicely browned.

Mrs. Gladwin Barkman, Steinbach, Man.
Sharon Koehn

Spanish Coffee Cake

2½ cups sifted flour   1 tsp. cinnamon
1 cup brown sugar   ½ tsp. salt
¾ cup white sugar   ¾ cup butter or shortening

Mix above ingredients thoroughly and remove ½ cup of this crumbly mixture to use as the topping and mix with ⅓ cup nuts.

1 cup butter milk   1 tsp. soda
1 egg   1 tsp. baking powder

Mix soda and baking powder with the crumbly mixture. Mix beaten egg and butter milk, add half of this liquid to the crumbly mixture and beat at med. speed 2 min. Add the rest and beat for 2 more min. Bake in two 6"x10" pans or in one larger pan. Before baking sprinkle the topping mixture on. Bake at 350° for 35 min.   Mrs. Jonas Schmidt, Fairview, Okla.

Streusel-filled Coffee Cake

1½ cups flour   ¼ cup shortening
3 tsp. baking powder   1 egg
¼ tsp. salt   ½ cup milk
¾ cup sugar   1 tsp. vanilla

Sift flour once before measuring. Then sift flour, baking powder, salt and sugar together. Cut in shortening with a pastry blender until mixture is like fine cornmeal. Blend in well beaten egg, mixed with milk. Then blend in vanilla, and beat just enough to mix well. Pour half the batter into a well greased and floured 6x10 in. (or an 8 in. square) heavy baking pan. Sprinkle with half the Streusel mixture over top. Bake 25 to 30 min. in a quick moderate oven, 375°.

Streusel Filling

½ cup brown sugar   2 tsp. cinnamon
2 tbsp. flour   2 tbsp. melted butter
                              ½ cup chopped nuts

Mix sugar, flour and cinnamon together. Then blend in the melted butter and stir in the chopped nuts. Mix well and use as described above.   Sharon Friesen, Ithaca, Mich.
                              Mrs. Dave Reimer, Linden, Alberta
                              Mrs. Newell Litwiller, Carson City, Mich.
                              Mrs. Galen Nichols, Greensburg, Kans.

Quick Breads

Banana Bread

3 ripe bananas
1 tsp. soda
1 tsp. water
2 cups flour
¾ cup sugar
⅛ tsp. salt
1 egg
¼ cup butter

Mash bananas with fork. Blend in sugar, salt and beaten egg. Melt butter and stir into banana mixture. Dissolve soda in water and add with sifted flour. Mix and put in loaf pan for 45 min. in 350° oven. Makes one loaf.

Starlyn Jantz, Livingston, Calif.

Banana Nut Bread (1)

½ cup shortening
1 cup sugar
2 eggs
3 or 4 bananas, mashed
2 cups flour
1 tsp. soda
1 tsp. salt
½ cup chopped pecans

Mix shortening and sugar, add eggs, beat well. Add bananas, flour, soda, salt and nuts. Mix. Bake in loaf pan at 350° for 1 hr.

Mrs. F. P. Schmidt, Chickasha, Okla.

Banana Nut Bread (2)

¾ cup butter or oleo
1½ cups sugar
1 tsp. vanilla
1 tsp. soda
½ cup buttermilk
    or sour milk
2 eggs well beaten
1½ cups mashed bananas
2 cups sifted flour
¾ tsp. salt
¾ cup walnuts, chopped

Cream butter and sugar thoroughly. Blend in bananas, eggs and vanilla. Sift flour, soda and salt together. Add to banana mixture, alternately with buttermilk, mixing well after each addition. Add nuts, mix. Pour batter into greased and floured 9x5x3 in. loaf pans. Bake at 325° for 1¼ hours.

Mrs. Vada Johnson, Galva, Kans.

Banana Nut Bread (3)

1/4 cup shortening
3/4 cup sugar
1 egg, beaten
1/2 tsp. soda
1/2 tsp. baking powder
2/3 cup mashed bananas

3 tbsp. sour milk
or buttermilk
2 cups flour
1/4 tsp. salt
1/2 cup nuts

Cream shortening and sugar. Add beaten egg and rest of ingredients. Add nuts. Bake 1 hour at 350°.

Mrs. Don Seiler, Carson City, Mich.

Carrot Bread

2 cups sugar
4 eggs
3 cups sifted flour
2 tsp. soda
1/2 cup nut meats

1 1/2 cups cooking oil
3 cups grated carrots
1 tsp. salt
2 tsp. cinnamon

Combine sugar with oil. Add beaten egg and beat well. Add carrots with sifted dry ingredients. Mix well and add nuts. Pour into 2 greased and floured 9x5x3 in. loaf pans. Bake in 350° oven for 75 min. or until done. Let stand in pans a few min. Remove to cooling rack to cool.

Mrs. Enoch Unruh, Scott City, Kans.
Mrs. Carl Heppner, Conway, Kans.

Date Nut Bread

1 1/4 cups dates (chopped)
1 cup boiling water

1/2 cup brown sugar

Cook dates in boiling water until thick. Add brown sugar. Cool.

1 egg (beaten)
1 tsp. soda
1/4 tsp. salt

1 2/3 cups flour
1 tsp. baking powder
1 cup nuts

Add ingredients to cooled mixture and mix well.
Bake 1 hour in 325° oven.

Mrs. Maynard Litwiller, Ithaca, Mich.
Mrs. Russell Wilson, Almena, Wisc.

Fresh Apple Bread

1 cup sugar
½ cup shortening
2 eggs
1 cup ground or grated apples
½ tsp. salt

2 cups flour
1 tsp. baking soda
½ tsp. vanilla
1 cup pecans (floured)
1½ tbsp. buttermilk

Cream sugar and shortening. Add beaten eggs and apples. Mix in the dry ingredients: vanilla, buttermilk· and floured pecans. Pour into loaf pan. Sprinkle top with mixture of 3 tbsp. sugar and 1 tsp. cinnamon. Bake in 350° oven for 1 hr.

Mrs. Glen Peaster, Bonners Ferry, Ida.

Grape-Nut Bread

1 cup grape-nuts

2 cups sour milk or buttermilk

Mix together and let stand for ½ hr.

1 cup brown sugar
2 tsp. soda
3 cups flour

3 tbsp. melted shortening
½ tsp. salt

Mix. Pour into 9 in. loaf pan. Bake 1 hr. in 350° oven.

Mrs. Amandus Seiler, Mich.

Pumpkin Bread

Beat together:

4 cups sugar
4 cups pumpkin

1 cup wesson oil

Sift together and add to first mixture:

5 cups flour
1 tsp. cinnamon
1½ tsp. salt
1 tsp. cloves

4 tsp. soda
1 cup nut meats
1 egg
1 cup raisins

Bake 1 hr. at 350° in greased bread pans. Makes 3 med. sized loaves.

Mrs. Edwin Dyck, Bonners Ferry, Ida.

Quick Graham Bread

3 cups graham flour
2 cups flour
2/3 cup brown sugar
1 tsp. salt

1 tsp. baking powder
1½ tsp. soda
2 cups rich buttermilk
1 cup warm water

Bake at 350° till done or 45 to 60 min.

Clara Miller, Ithaca, Mich.
Submitted by Mrs. D. G. Boeckner

Round Raisin Nut Bread

2 cups raisins
2 cups water
2 tsp. soda
2 eggs
1½ cups sugar

⅛ tsp. salt
1½ tsp. vanilla
3 cups flour
1 cup nuts

Combine raisins water, and soda; bring to boiling. When mixture begins to foam, remove from heat. Cool. Beat together eggs, sugar, salt and vanilla. Add the raisins alternately with flour to egg mixture. Fold in nuts. Pour into 2 buttered bread pans. Bake at 350° for 1 hr.   Bernice Giesbrecht, Glenn, Calif.

Biscuits and Muffins

Baking Powder Biscuits

2 cups sifted flour
4 level tsp. baking powder
½ tsp. cream of tartar
½ tsp. salt

2 tbsp. sugar
½ cup shortening
1 egg, unbeaten
⅔ cup milk

Sift flour, baking powder, salt, sugar and cream of tartar. Add shortening to the flour mixture and blend together until of corn-meal consistency, then continue with remaining ingredients. Bake at 450° for 20 min. Leona Nichols, Livingston, Calif.

Mrs. Alfred Koehn, Hillsboro, Kans.
Mrs. Herman P. Koehn, Chickasha, Okla.
Mrs. Raymond Wadel, Greensburg, Kans.

Buttermilk Biscuits

2 cups minus 2 tbsp. flour   ¼ tsp. soda
2½ tsp. baking powder   ⅓ cup shortening or lard
1 tsp. salt   ¾ cup buttermilk

Mix dry ingredients, add shortening and mix. Then add buttermilk all at once. Roll and cut. Bake at 400° for 20 min.

Clara Belle Schneider, Moundridge, Kans.

Cream Biscuits for Two

1 cup flour   ⅔ cup heavy cream
2 tsp. baking powder   ⅓ cup milk
¼ tsp. salt

Sift together flour, baking powder and salt into mixing bowl. Stir liquids with fork into flour mixture until well dampened. Scrape on to floured board and knead lightly until dough feels springy. Pat out and cut into six biscuits. Bake on ungreased sheet 12 to 15 min. in oven preheated at 450°. These should be light and fluffy.

Mrs. G. N. Yost, Montezuma, Kans.

Oatmeal Muffins

1 cup sifted all-purpose   ½ tsp. salt
   flour   ½ cup raisins (optional)
¼ cup sugar   3 tbsp. liquid shortening
3 tsp. baking powder   1 egg, beaten
1 cup quick or old fashioned   1 cup milk
   uncooked oatmeal

Sift together flour, sugar, baking powder, and salt. Stir in oatmeal and raisins. Add shortening, egg, and milk. Stir only until dry ingredients are moistened. Fill greased muffin cups ⅔ full. Sprinkle with cinnamon topping. Makes 12 muffins.

Cinnamon Topping

2 tbsp. sugar   1 tsp. cinnamon
2 tsp. all-purpose flour   1 tsp. melted butter

Combine ingredients and sprinkle on unbaked muffins and bake in preheated oven (425°) about 15 min.

Miss Ramonda Toews, Hillsboro, Kans.

Corn Bread

Corn Bread (1)

½ cup cornmeal   ½ tsp. salt
½ cup flour   ½ cup sugar
1 tsp. baking powder   1 egg, beaten
cream

Combine dry ingredients and put through a sieve. Add egg and enough cream until batter is of desired consistency, (to resemble cake batter). Pour into greased pan and bake at 400° about 25 min. or until browned.

Mrs. Wilmer L. Unruh, Galva, Kans.

Corn Bread (2)

1 cup flour   1 cup cornmeal
1 cup sugar   1 cup cream
1 egg   1 tsp. salt
1 tsp. vinegar   1 tsp. soda

Sift dry ingredients together, add cream, egg and vinegar and beat. Bake in 400° oven for 30 min.

Mrs. Eli B. Raber, Dalton, Ohio

Corn Bread (3)

1 egg   ½ cup flour
¼ cup sugar   ½ cup cornmeal
½ cup cream   1 tsp. baking powder
½ tsp. salt

Beat first 3 ingredients. Sift last 4 ingredients all at once to the first mixture. Pour into well greased 8x8x1¾ in. pan. Sprinkle with sugar and bake in 400° oven about 20 min.

Mrs. Pete D. Schmidt, Copeland, Kans.

Golden Cornbread

1 cup yellow cornmeal   4 tsp. baking powder
¼ cup sugar   1 cup milk

1 cup sifted flour   1 egg
½ tsp. salt   ¼ cup shortening or oil

Sift together dry ingredients into bowl. Add egg, milk and shortening. Beat with egg beater or spoon about 1 min. Do not over beat. Bake in greased 8 in. square pan or muffin tins in hot oven 425° for 20 to 25 min.

Mrs. Denton Burns, Hesston, Kans.

Gingerbread

Gingerbread

½ cup shortening   1½ tsp. soda
½ cup sugar   1 tsp. ginger
1 egg   1 tsp. cinnamon
2½ cups flour   ½ tsp. cloves
1 cup molasses   ½ tsp. salt
1 cup hot water

Cream shortening and sugar. Add egg and beat well, Sift together dry ingredients. Mix molasses and hot water, add alternately with dry ingredients to creamed mixture. Bake in 8x12 in. loaf pan in 350° for 45 min.

Mrs. Vernon Peters, McDavid, Fla.

Quick Gingerbread

1 cup sifted flour   ⅓ cup soft shortening
½ tsp. each of salt,   ½ cup molasses
   nutmeg, cloves, allspice   ½ cup warm water
   and baking powder   1 tsp. soda dissolved in
1 tsp. cinnamon   ¼ cup boiling water
2½ tsp. ginger   1 egg
½ cup sugar

Sift flour, spices, baking powder and sugar together into mixing bowl. Add shortening, molasses and warm water, beat 2 min. with electric beater. Add dissolved soda; beat for a few seconds. Add egg and beat 1 min. Turn into greased and floured pan; bake at 350° for 35 to 45 min.

Doughnuts

Angel Food Doughnuts

¾ cup sour cream	1 tsp. vanilla
¼ cup sour milk	½ tsp. baking soda
1 cup sugar	2 tsp. baking powder
3 eggs	¼ tsp. salt
3 cups sifted flour	¼ tsp. nutmeg

Whip the cream and milk until foamy. Add sugar and stir until dissolved. Add eggs one at a time and stir well after each addition. Then add vanilla. Stir the soda, baking powder and sifted flour, salt and nutmeg into the first mixture and blend well. Let the mixture stand at least one hour before rolling out. Fry in deep, hot fat 365°.

Mrs. Levi Giesbrecht, Winton, Calif.

Coffee Dunkers

½ cup milk, scalded	2 tbsp. shortening
½ tsp. salt	⅓ cup sugar

Stir salt, shortening, and sugar into scalded milk and allow to cool to lukewarm. Add 1 pkg. or cake of yeast that has been dissolved in ¼ cup warm water.

2 eggs, well beaten	2½ cups sifted flour

Stir well, Cover and let rise 45 min. or until doubled in bulk. Stir batter down and drop one tsp. at a time into deep hot fat, 365°. Fry about 3 min. or until brown. Roll in granulated sugar.

Mrs. Francis Peters, McDavid, Fla.

Doughnuts (1)

3 cups milk, scald and cool	1 cake yeast (dissolved in 1
4 cups flour	cup lukewarm water)
1 tbsp. sugar	

Mix: let rise until light.

4 eggs   ½ cup shortening
1 tsp. salt   1 tsp. baking powder
1 tsp. vanilla   1 cup sugar

Cream together shortening, sugar, eggs, vanilla, salt, and baking powder. Add to first mixture. Add enough flour and knead to make a soft dough. Let rise until light, roll and cut. Let rise about 1 hr. Fry in deep fat (365°).*

Mrs. Lola Litwiller, Ithaca, Mich.

*(When frying doughnuts, place risen side in hot fat first, brown, and turn once.)

Doughnuts (2)

2 cakes yeast   ¾ cup shortening
1½ cups milk   1 cup sugar
4 eggs   enough flour for soft dough
3 tsp. salt   2 cups warm water

Mix yeast, sugar and water, let rise. Scald milk, add shortening and salt. Cool. Add eggs, yeast and flour. Let it rise, punch down, let rise again. Then roll out ¾ in. thick and cut. Let rise 1 to 1½ hrs. and fry. Glaze immediately with 2 lbs. powdered sugar, vanilla, and hot water.

Mrs. Gene Koehn, Livingston, Calif.

Glazed Doughnuts

1 pkg. yeast   ¼ cup sugar
1 cup milk   1 tsp. salt
3½ cups sifted flour   1 egg
¼ cup shortening   shortening for deep-frying

Dissolve yeast in lukewarm milk. Add 1½ cup flour and beat until smooth. Cover, let rise in warm place until double in bulk (about 2 hrs.) Combine: shortening, sugar, salt, and egg; stir in yeast sponge. Add remaining flour and beat thoroughly. Grease top with shortening. Let rise until double in bulk (about 2 hrs.). Roll ½ in. thick, cut with doughnut cutter. Allow to rise 45 min. Fry in hot deep fat until brown.

Glaze

1 lb. pkg. powdered sugar, 1 tbsp. cornstarch, and 2 tsp. vanilla enough hot water to make heavy glaze.

Marlene Giesbrecht, Winton, Calif.

Dottie's Doughnuts

1 pkg. yeast. (dissolved
   in ¼ cup warm water)
1¾ cups milk, scalded and
   cooled
½ cup sugar

2 tsp. salt
4 egg yolks and 2 tbsp.
   water (mix)
¼ cup shortening
6 to 7 cups flour

Mix well—let rise once (or twice) in warm place—roll out; cut and let rise again and bake in deep hot fat, (365°).

Mrs. Elmer Dyck, Stapleton, Ga.

Potato Doughnuts (1)

1½ cups sugar
3 eggs
2 cups mashed potatoes
1 cup sweet milk
6 tsp. baking powder

5 cups flour
3 tbsp. melted shortening
1 tsp. salt
¼ tsp. nutmeg

Beat mashed potatoes, add melted fat, beaten eggs, and milk. Sift dry ingredients together and add to liquid. Roll out to ¾ in. thickness. Cut and drop into deep fat 365°. Fry until a golden brown on both sides. Drain on absorbent paper. Roll in sugar and cinnamon mixture, powdered sugar, or frost. Makes about 4 doz. doughnuts.

Roberta Toews

Potato Doughnuts (2)

(large recipe)

1 qt. milk scalded
3 cups potato pulp
3 pkgs yeast soaked in
½ cup warm water

2 tsp. salt
1 cup butter or oleo
1½ cups sugar
6 eggs beaten

Enough flour for soft dough. Fry in deep fat 365°.

Glazed Icing

2 lbs. powdered sugar
2 tbsp. cream
3 tbsp. butter

2 tbsp. cornstarch
1 tsp. vanilla

Enough hot milk to make icing to dip doughnuts into. Glaze while hot.

Mrs. Floyd Frank, Copeland, Kans.

Raised Doughnuts (1)

1 pkg. yeast
2 cups milk, scalded
    and cooled
2 cups flour
4 egg yolks
1 whole egg

½ cup sugar
½ cup butter
2 tsp. salt
1 tsp. vanilla
5 cups flour

Dissolve yeast in lukewarm milk. Add 2 cups flour and let rise until light. Then beat egg yolks and whole egg together. Add rest of ingredients and knead lightly and let rise. Then roll dough to ½ in. thickness and cut doughnuts. Then let rise until light, and fry in deep fat 365°. Glaze while still warm. Makes five dozen doughnuts.

Glaze

Combine:
1 lb. powdered sugar
1 tbsp. cream

1 tbsp. cornstarch
1 tsp. vanilla

Add enough water to make a mitxure of medium consistency. Dip doughnuts while still warm.

Mrs. Milton Schmidt, Montezuma, Kans.

Raised Doughnuts (2)

1½ cups lukewarm potato
    water or milk
1 cake yeast
½ cup sugar
1½ tsp. salt

⅓ cup melted shortening or
    butter
4 cups flour (or enough to
    make soft dough)
2 eggs

Dissolve yeast and sugar in lukewarm liquid. Add shortening, and one cup flour, beat well with egg beater. Add salt and eggs, continue beating. Add remainder of flour and knead. Place in greased bowl and let rise in a warm place until double in bulk, (about 2 hrs.). Knead and immediately roll out to about ¾ in. thickness. Cut with doughnut cutter and place on floured board to rise. Fry in deep fat.

Mrs. Ruben Becker, Galva, Kans.

Raised Doughnuts (3)

2 cups potato water	2 eggs, beaten
1¼ sticks or ⅔ cup oleo	½ cup sugar

2 pkgs. dry yeast, soaked in ½ cup warm water and 1 tsp. sugar.

7-8 cups flour	1 tsp. salt

To make potato water, heat 2 cups of water to boiling point, add ⅓ cup of instant mashed potatoes. To hot potato water add oleo, sugar and salt, cool to lukewarm. Add yeast, mix in 3 or 4 cups of flour, beat until smooth. Add eggs, mix well. Add remaining flour or enough to make a medium soft dough, knead well. Cover, let rise in warm place until double in bulk, roll out about ¼ in. thick. Cut with doughnut cutter. Fry in deep fat 350° until golden brown, turning once. Glaze while hot. Makes 4 to 4½ doz.

Glaze

1½ lbs. powdered sugar, enough hot water to make medium glaze. Add vanilla.

Mrs. Harvey Nichols, Montezuma, Kans.

Raised Potato Doughnuts

2 cups milk	¼ cup lukewarm water
1 cup sugar	3 eggs, well beaten
½ cup shortening	½ tsp. lemon extract
1 cup mashed potatoes	½ tsp. cinnamon
1½ tsp. salt	8 cups flour, sifted
1½ pkgs. dry yeast	

Scald milk until film forms on top, (do not boil). Cool to lukewarm. Dissolve yeast in water, let stand for 5 min. Combine with milk. Add mashed potatoes, eggs, extract, and cinnamon; mix well. Add flour, adding a small amount at a time, beat until smooth with a strong spoon, or knead by hand. Let rise until double in bulk. Knead on lightly floured board. Roll out to ¼ in. thickness and cut with doughnut cutter. Place on floured cloth and let rise until doubled in size. Deep fat fry at 375° until golden brown, turning gently once with a fork. Drain on absorbent paper and glaze while still warm. Yield: 6 doz. doughnuts.

Glaze

¼ cup warm water   1½ cups powdered sugar
½ tsp. vanilla

Mix until smooth. Dip each doughnut into glaze and drain on rack.

Mrs. Howard Koehn, Eldorado, Kans.

Doughnut Snowballs

2 eggs   2 cups sifted flour
¾ cup sugar   2½ tsp. baking powder
2 tbsp. salad oil   ⅓ tsp. salt
½ cup milk   ⅓ tsp. nutmeg
1 tsp. vanilla   granulated sugar for
                                    coating

Beat eggs with sugar, salad oil, milk and vanilla until light; stir in flour, baking powder, salt and nutmeg sifted together; blend until smooth. Drop by tsp. into deep hot fat, 375°, fry turning often until golden-brown; drain on absorbent paper; roll in sugar.

Mrs. Lyle Litwiller, Perrinton, Mich.

Pancakes

Egg Pancakes

6 eggs   ½ tsp. salt
2 cups milk   1 cup flour

Beat eggs, add ¼ cup milk and the flour, beat well, and add the rest of the milk, mix well. Pour ½ cup onto hot oiled griddle or skillet, tilting quickly back and forth for batter to cover. (Experiment to determine right amount for your griddle. The pancake should be thin. Serve hot with syrup, jelly, marmalade, or sugar and cream.

Elizabeth Frank, Copeland, Kans.

Feather Light Pancakes

2 cups sifted flour
1 tsp. baking soda

¾ tsp. salt
3 tbsp. sugar

Combine:

2 beaten eggs
¼ cup vinegar

1¾ cups sweet milk
¼ cup melted shortening

Mix well. Add to dry ingredients, stir until smooth. Bake on hot griddle. Yield—20.

Mrs. Lyle Holdeman, Clarksdale, Miss.

Love Puffs

4 eggs, separated
¾ cup all purpose flour
1 cup milk

¼ tsp. salt
⅛ tsp. nutmeg

Separate eggs as soon as taken from the refrigerator. (Cooled eggs are easier separated.) Let stand at least ½ hr. until eggs reach room temp. Add salt to egg whites and beat until stiff but not dry, using electric mixer at high speed. Sift flour and nutmeg, mix with milk until smooth. Beat egg yolks until lemon colored and add to flour mixture. Carefully fold in beaten egg whites, pour ¾ cup of batter into 6 or 7 in. skillet in which ½ tsp. of butter has been melted. As soon as lightly browned on one side turn over and brown other side. Serve immediately on warm plate with syrup and soft butter, thin blueberry or boysenberry syrup. Serve two to four persons.

Mrs. Fred J. Bortz, Bellaire, Kans.

Man Made Pancakes

2 cups milk
1 cup flour
½ cup wheat germ
2 eggs

1 tsp. baking powder
½ tsp. salt
2 tbsp. salad oil

Put all ingredients in order given. Beat with beater until well mixed. Let stand a few minutes. Ladle onto 400° electric griddle that has been greased. When top of pancake is almost dry turn pancake.

R. Boeckner, Moundridge, Kans.

Pancakes

Mix:

3 cups flour	5 tsp. baking powder
3 tbsp. cornmeal	3 tbsp. sugar
1 tsp. salt	

Beat together:

2 eggs	2½ cups milk (more or less)

Add:

½ stick oleo (melted)

Pour over dry ingredients and mix thoroughly.

Mrs. Abe D. Koehn, Galva, Kans.

Sour Dough Hotcakes

½ cup starter	2 tsp. baking soda
1½ cups flour	1 egg
¾ cup milk	3 tbsp. shortening
½ tsp. salt	2 tbsp. sugar

About 12 hrs. before serving, mix first 4 ingredients, let stand in cloth covered bowl in warm place. Just before baking cakes add soda, egg, shortening and sugar. Mix well and bake on hot griddle. (For thinner cakes add more milk.) Makes about 10 large hotcakes.

Starter

½ pkg. dry yeast	2 tbsp. sugar
2 cups unsifted flour	2½ cups water

Combine ingredients in a stone crock or bowl. Beat well, cover with loose cloth and let stand in warm place for 2 days. (Note: to replenish starter, stir in equal amounts of flour and water.)

Caramel Hotcake Syrup

To one cup packed brown sugar, add 4 tbsp. cream. Cook until sugar is melted. Add ⅛ tsp. salt and ½ tsp. vanilla. If thinner syrup is desired, add a little water.

Lois Boeckner, Moundridge, Kans.

Mother's Pancakes

3 eggs   1 cup milk
1 tsp. salt   1 cup flour

Beat eggs add milk and salt. With spoon slowly stir in 1 cup of flour a little at a time until you have a smooth batter. In hot frying pan put 1 tsp. lard. Pour in batter slowly tilting pan to make a very thin pancake. Put in lard for each pancake. Makes 9 thin 8 in. pancakes.

Noah Wiggers, Hesston, Kans.

Delicious Pancakes

1¼ cups flour   ¾ tsp. salt
1 tsp. sugar   1 cup milk
⅓ cup melted butter or   2 eggs
  margarine   1½ tbsp. baking powder

Beat eggs slightly, sift dry ingredients, add margarine and milk to eggs. Add dry ingredients. Beat only till all flour is mixed. Bake on hot griddle.

Irene Nikkel, Inman, Kans.

Pancakes for Two

1 cup sifted flour   ½ tsp. soda
¼ tsp. salt   1 egg
2 tsp. baking powder   1 cup buttermilk
1 tbsp. melted shortening

Sift flour, salt, baking powder and soda onto wax paper. Beat egg yolk in mixing bowl. Add buttermilk and melted shortening. Add flour mixture and stir without using beater. Fold in stiffly beaten egg whites. Let stand 8 min. before baking on an ungreased griddle.

Mrs. G. N. Yost, Montezuma, Kans.

Wesson Oil Pancakes

2 cups flour   ¼ cup sugar
2 cups milk   ⅓ cup Wesson Oil
6 level tsp. baking powder 2 eggs
½ tsp. salt

Sift together dry ingredients. Add eggs, oil, and milk (use warm milk). Beat until smooth and fry on hot griddle.

Mrs. Milton Schmidt, Montezuma, Kans.

Waffles

Waffles

Sift together in large bowl:
 5 tsp. baking powder   3 cups sifted flour
 2 tsp. sugar   1 tsp. salt

Beat in small bowl at high speed for 1 min:
 4 large eggs

Add:
 2¼ cups milk   1½ tsp. vanilla

Add to dry ingredients, beat just until blended. Blend in ⅔ cup melted butter. Bake.

Delma Friesen, Conway, Kans.

Sunbeam Waffles

Sift together:
 3 cups sifted all purpose   1 tsp. salt
  flour   2 tsp. sugar
 4 tsp. baking powder

Melt and cool ⅔ cup butter or margarine. Put into small bowl of mixer, 4 egg whites, beat at high speed about 1 min. Put into large bowl of mixer: 4 egg yolks. Beat at high speed about 1 min. Add 2 cups milk. Add sifted dry ingredients. Beat at med. speed until blended. Scrape bowl while beating. Add melted and cooled butter. Beat only until blended. Fold in beaten egg whites. Bake in preheated waffle iron.

Mrs. Robert Koehn, Montezuma, Kans.

Miscellaneous Breads

French Toast

3 eggs, beaten
1¼ cups cream

⅛ tsp. salt
½ tsp. vanilla

Blend ingredients, grease skillet lightly only once. Then dampen bread on both sides in the liquid and fry to light brown on each side. The cream helps the bread from sticking to the skillet. Serve with your favorite syrup.

Mrs. Marion Jantz, Horton, Mo.

Fried Corn Meal Mush

3 cups yellow corn meal
2 qt. boiling water

1 tsp. salt
½ cup white flour

Sift together corn meal, white flour, and salt. Slowly add dry ingredients to boiling water, stirring constantly to prevent lumps. Cook until it leaves side of sauce pan. Pour into flat pans to mold or use 1 bread pan. Set in refrigerator to chill thoroughly. Cut in slices ¼ in. thick and fry on griddle or skillet until a golden brown on both sides. Delicious with hot maple syrup, or make your own by taking light Karo syrup and adding maple flavor, heat and serve.

Mrs. Marion Jantz, Horton, Mo.

Syrups

Dutch Honey

1 cup white syrup
1 cup sugar

1 cup cream or top milk
1 tsp. vanilla

Cook sugar and syrup together until it strings. Heat cream till hot. Let both cool awhile and then stir together with vanilla. Delicious on pancakes and waffles.

Mrs. Franklin Smith, Hesston, Kans.

Party Pour-on for Pancakes

½ cup Karo syrup (blue label or Karo waffle syrup)

½ cup heavy cream

¼ cup light brown sugar, packed

Combine heavy cream, brown sugar and Karo syrup in small bowl and stir gently until well blended (about 1 min. on electric mixer). Sauce will be of good pouring consistency. Serve on pancakes or waffles. Good on ice cream too. Makes 1¼ cups.

Mrs. Oliver (Ruby) Unruh, Hesston, Kans.

Pancake Syrups

1 cup brown sugar
1 cup white sugar

1 cup water
¼ tsp. Maple flavor (optional)

Bring to a boil. Cook until syrupy.

*   *   *

1 cup brown sugar
1 cup white syrup

1 cup cream

Bring to a boil.

Grace Wenger, Hesston, Kans.

Rolls

Bread Stickers

Recipe for regular bread dough. After first rising, punch down and make into very small buns or biscuits and put in med. roaster or deep pan. Let set to rise to nearly double in size. Take 1 cup sour cream and

¼ cup sweet milk
1 scant cup white sugar

1 rounded tsp. cinnamon
¼ tsp. soda
¼ tsp. baking powder

Mix, pour over biscuits just before putting in oven. Bake about 20 to 25 min. Serve as are or with cold milk poured over each serving. Very delicious.

Mrs. Mary Peters, Pettisville, Ohio

Bran Refrigerator Rolls

1 cup shortening	2 eggs, well beaten
1 cup boiling water	2 cakes compressed yeast
½ cup sugar	1 cup lukewarm water
1 cup whole bran cereal	6 to 7 cups all purpose flour
1½ tsp. salt	

In a large bowl, mix first five ingredients listed. Let stand until mixture is lukewarm in temperature. Using rotary beater, beat eggs until light and foamy. Stir them into the large bowl of lukewarm ingredients. Be sure it is lukewarm. Stir in yeast dissolved in lukewarm water. Add 6 cups of flour, stirring as you add. Beat thoroughly, if dough does not drop from spoon in definite lumps, add a part of the 7th cup of flour, and keep adding until lumps fall from spoon. (No more than 7 cups). Brush over top of dough with melted butter and cover closely with waxed paper. Place in refrigerator for several hours or days. To use; pinch off bits of dough and form balls to fill muffin pans about ½ full. Set in a warm place to rise until double in size. Bake at 450° for 20 min.

Mrs. Dave H. Smith, DeRidder, La.
Mrs. Laurence Toews, Harrison, Mich.

Butter Horn Rolls

Soften: 2 pkgs. granulated or 2 cakes compressed yeast in ½ cup lukewarm water. Add: 1 tbsp. sugar to the yeast. Scald: 1 cup milk, add ½ cup sugar and ½ cup shortening, stir to melt shortening. Cool to lukewarm. Pour into large bowl. Stir in 3 beaten eggs and 2 tsp. salt. Add: 2 cups flour.

Mix at low speed of mixer or by hand. Add yeast and beat 4 to 5 min. more. Add: 2¾ cups sifted flour. Turn on floured board; add enough flour (about 1½ cups) to make a soft dough. Knead just enough to shape into balls. Place in greased bowl; grease top; let rise until doubled in bulk. Punch down and shape into rolls. May be used as cinnamon or butterhorn rolls.

Mrs. Julian Hiebert, Louisville, Ga.

Buttermilk Cinnamon Rolls

Mix and set aside 1½ pkg. yeast in ½ cup warm water and 2 tbsp. sugar. 1 cup buttermilk, heat to lukewarm and add 1 tsp. salt, ¼ cup sugar, ¼ cup fat or oil. Add 1 cup flour, and yeast and mix. Add ½ tsp. soda and 1 egg beaten. Beat well. Add 3 to 4 cups flour to make a real soft dough and knead 5 min. Let rise till double in bulk and make rolls or cinnamon rolls.

Mrs. Jesse Jantz, Montezuma, Kans.

E-Z Rolls

6 tbsp. shortening
½ cup sugar
¾ tsp. salt
½ cup cold water
½ cup boiling water
1 egg, beaten
1 cake yeast
3 cups unsifted flour

Pour boiling water over shortening, sugar and salt, stir and cool. Let yeast stand in cold water 5 min. Stir and add to first mixture. Add beaten egg, then flour. Mix well, cover and chill 4 hrs. Then roll into desired shape. Place in greased pans and let rise until double in size. Bake at 400° for 12 min. Dough keeps in refrigerator a week or 10 days.

Mrs. Marvin Schmidt, Burns, Kans.

Hot Rolls
(cinnamon rolls)

1 pkg. yeast dissolved in
½ cup warm water
1 cup mashed potatoes
1 cup sugar
3 tsp. salt
1 cup shortening
1 qt. scalded milk (let cool)
4 tsp. baking powder
About 11 cups flour

Mix together all ingredients except shortening and flour, let stand for 2 hrs. then add shortening and flour for a soft dough. Let rise and shape into rolls or store in refrigerator until ready to use. Note: If shortening is added before flour it will slightly retard the action of the yeast. When kneaded, shape and place in pan and rise to double in bulk, about 2 hrs. Bake 15 to 20 min. at 375°.

Verda Wedel, Meade, Kans.
Mrs. Howard Miller, Ithaca, Mich.

Caramel Cinnamon Rolls

1 cup milk	¼ cup shortening
¾ cup sugar	2 tsp. salt
¼ cup warm water	2 eggs, beaten
1 pkg. yeast	1 cup mashed potatoes
4½ cups flour	

Scald milk, add ¼ cup sugar. Cool to lukewarm. Measure water into large bowl. Sprinkle yeast into water. Add milk. Add 2 cups flour and beat until smooth. Cover with cloth and let rise in warm place. Cream shortening and remaining sugar; stir in mashed potatoes. Add salt and beaten eggs. Stir into yeast mixture. Add remaining flour. Place in greased bowl, cover and let rise until double in bulk. Roll into rectangle ¼ in. thick. Brush dough with butter and sprinkle with sugar and cinnamon. Roll and cut into 1-in. slices. Melt ¼ cup butter and 1 cup brown sugar in baking dish. Add nuts if desired. Place rolls close together, cut side up, in baking pan. Let rise until double in size. Bake at 350° about 25 min. Invert pan on cooling rack so butterscotch topping will be on top of rolls.

Mrs. Milton Schmidt, Kans.

Chocolate Cinnamon Rolls

¾ cup warm water	⅓ cup cocoa
1 pkg. dry yeast	2¼ cups sifted flour
¼ cup shortening	1 tbsp. soft butter
1 tsp. salt	1½ tsp. cinnamon
¼ cup sugar	3 tbsp. sugar
1 egg	nuts (optional)

In mixer bowl, dissolve yeast in warm water. Add shortening, salt, sugar, egg, cocoa, 1 cup flour. Beat 2 min. on med. speed, or 300 strokes by hand. Scrape sides and bottom of bowl. Stir in remaining flour; blend well. Cover with cloth; let rise in warm place until double in bulk, about 1 hr. Stir down by beating 25 strokes. Turn soft dough out on well floured board. Roll into rectangle, 12x9 in. Spread with melted butter. Sprinkle with sugar and cinnamon mixture. Roll up beginning at wide side. Pinch edge into roll. Cut into 12 pieces. Place in greased 9 in. pan. Let rise in warm place until double in bulk, about 40 min. Heat oven to 350° and bake for 25 min. Remove from pan;

frost immediately with icing of ¾ cup powdered sugar moistened with cream to spreading consistency. Sprinkle with chopped nuts.

Annabel Holdeman, Hesston, Kans.

Cherry Puff Rolls

1 pkg. dry yeast	3¼ to 3¾ cups all-purpose
¼ cup warm water	flour, sifted
⅔ cup milk, scalded	¼ cup butter or margarine,
¼ cup sugar	softened
3 tbsp. butter or margarine	Cherry preserves
1 tsp. salt	Powdered sugar
1 egg	

Soften yeast in warm water. Combine scalded milk, sugar, butter and salt; stir to dissolve sugar; cool to lukewarm. Add softened yeast, egg, and 1 cup flour; beat until very smooth. Add remaining flour or enough to make soft dough. Turn out on lightly floured surface; knead until smooth. Place in greased bowl, turning once to grease surface. Cover; let rise till double in bulk. Punch down; let set 10 min. Roll ½ in. thick on lightly floured surface. Spread with half the soft butter; fold in half, pinch edges together. Roll ½ in. thick; spread with remaining butter; fold, seal, and roll as before. Cut in 2½ in. circles; place on greased cookie sheet. Cover; let rise until double (about 30 min.). Make depression in center of each and fill with cherry preserves. Bake in hot oven 400° about 10 to 12 min. While warm frost with a powdered sugar icing made with 1 cup powdered sugar. 1½ tbsp. milk. Makes 12 rolls.

Mrs. Edwin Ensz, Middleton, Mich.

Sour Cream Rolls

Bring 2 cups sour cream to a boil, remove from heat, and add:

4 tbsp. shortening	2 tsp. salt
6 tbsp. sugar	¼ tsp. soda

Cool to lukewarm, add 1 yeast cake, 2 eggs, 6 cups flour. Mix well. Knead a little if necessary. Let stand 5 min. Roll out dough as for cinnamon rolls. Spread with melted butter, sugar, and cinnamon. Bake in hot oven (375-400°) about 20 or 25 min. till lightly browned. Frost.

Mrs. Laurence Toews, Harrison, Mich.

Cinnamon Twists

1 cup sour cream	⅓ cup warm water
3 tbsp. sugar	3 cups flour
1 tsp. salt	2 tbsp. butter
3 tbsp. shortening	1 tsp. cinnamon
1 egg, beaten	½ cup brown sugar
1 cake yeast	

Warm sour cream, add sugar, salt, shortening and egg. Add yeast that is dissolved in warm water, add flour and mix well. Roll out, spread with butter, cinnamon and brown sugar. Cut in strips, twist each strip two times, lay in pan. Let rise in warm place 1 hr. Bake 375°—15 min. Spread with butter icing.

Mrs. Anna Esau, Winton, Calif

Cinna Swirls

¾ cup milk	¼ cup water
¼ cup sugar	1 egg, beaten
1 tsp. salt	3¼ cups sifted flour (approx.)
¼ cup oil	¾ cup sugar
1 pkg. yeast	1 tsp. cinnamon

Scald milk, stir in ¼ cup sugar, salt and oil. Cool to lukewarm. Dissolve yeast in warm water with 1 tsp. sugar. Stir in lukewarm milk mixture, beaten egg and half the flour. Beat until smooth. Stir in rest of flour to form a soft dough. On lightly floured board knead until smooth and elastic about 8 to 10 min. Place in greased bowl, turning greased side up. Cover. Let rise until doubled in bulk. Work down, let rise again. Divide dough in half, roll into rectangle, sprinkle with sugar-cinnamon mixture. Roll tightly and seal edges. Cut into 9 equal pieces, place on greased baking sheet, flatten, cover and let rise. Deep fat fry in oil 375° for 2 to 3 min. until brown on both sides. Drain on absorbent paper. Frost while warm with powdered sugar glaze.

Mrs. Wilford Holdeman, Halstead, Kans.

Icebox Bran Rolls

2 cakes yeast dissolved in	6 cups flour
½ cup lukewarm water	1 cup all-bran or bran buds
¾ cup sugar	2 tsp. salt
1 cup shortening	2 eggs
1½ cups boiling water	

Mix sugar, shortening, all-bran, salt and boiling water until shortening is melted. Cool to lukewarm. Add beaten eggs, yeast and flour. Mix well. Cover and store in icebox until needed. Shape into rolls, let raise until double in size. Bake at 350° for 25 min.

Mrs. Lawrence Toews, Harrison, Mich.

Kolache

1 pkg. dry yeast	¾ tsp. salt
¼ cup warm water	1 egg
¾ cup milk, scalded	1 tsp. vanilla
3 tbsp. shortening	3½ cups flour
4 tbsp. sugar	

Dissolve yeast in warm, not hot water. Combine milk, shortening, sugar and salt. Cool to lukewarm, add softened yeast. Add beaten egg. Add vanilla and enough flour to make a smooth, soft dough. Use mixer if desired. Knead lightly on floured board. Place in greased bowl, turn to grease on all sides, cover and let rise until double in bulk. Punch down and roll out about ½ in. thick. Cut with biscuit cutter. Place on greased baking sheet 1" apart. Let rise until nearly doubled in size. Then poke your thumb and forefinger into center of each and spread apart about 1½ in. Place about 1 tsp. of your favorite jelly or preserves into each hole. Bake in a med. oven at 375° for 15 min. While still hot, frost with 1 cup powdered sugar mixed with enough cream and 1 tsp. vanilla to spread easily.

Mrs. Loren Becker, Burns, Kans.

Raised Parker House Rolls

Soften 1 cake or soak 1 pkg. dried yeast in ¼ cup water (lukewarm). Combine:

1 cup scalded milk, cooled	1 tsp. salt
2 tbsp. shortening	2 tbsp. sugar

Mix well. Add 1 egg well beaten, stir in gradually 3½ cups flour. Beat vigorously. Place in lightly greased bowl, let rise in warm place about 2 hrs. Roll or pat out. Cut with doughnut (round cutter), grease tops and double over. Let rolls rise on cookie sheet to double in bulk. Bake in preheated oven about 425° for 12 to 15 min. Yield: 3 doz.

Mrs. Noah Leatherman, Hillsboro, Kans.
Mrs. Evelyn Schmidt, Winton, Calif.

Maraschino Cherry Roll

1 pkg. yeast
2 tsp. sugar
½ cup warm water
½ cup milk
¼ cup sugar

½ tsp. salt
3½ cups flour
2 eggs, beaten
3 tbsp. shortening

Dissolve yeast and 2 tsp. sugar in warm water; Scald milk, add shortening, sugar and salt. Cool to lukewarm. Add 1 cup flour to make a batter. Add yeast and eggs, beat well. Add remaining flour or enough to make a soft dough, knead lightly and place in greased bowl. Let rise to double in bulk. Divide dough in half and roll out very thin. Spread each half with ⅓ cup thick sour cream, ½ cup brown sugar, ½ cup chopped maraschino cherries, ½ cup white sugar and ½ cup chopped pecans. Roll up like cinnamon roll; form a circle on greased cooky sheet. Let rise. Bake for 25 min. at 350°. When removed from oven; immediately top with maraschino cherry juice and powdered sugar. Have quite thin for easier spreading.

Annabel Holdeman, Hesston, Kans.

Pineapple Rolls

1 pkg. dry or 1 cake compressed yeast
¼ cup water
1 cup milk scalded
4 tbsp. sugar
4 tbsp. shortening

1 tsp. salt
1 well beaten egg
3½ cups flour or more
(enough flour to make soft dough)

Soften yeast in warm water. Combine milk, shortening, sugar, salt; cool to lukewarm. Add softened yeast and egg. Gradually stir in flour to make soft dough. Beat vigorously; cover and let rise in warm place till double in bulk, about 2 hr. Roll out on lightly greased surface and spread with the following pineapple filling:

Mix ¼ cup sugar   1 tbsp. corn starch   ¼ tsp. salt

Add a 9 oz. can of crushed pineapple. Cook till thick, stirring constantly. It should be slightly cooled before spreading. Roll up as for cinnamon rolls. Give them plenty of room in pans to rise until light. Bake and while hot glaze with powdered sugar icing.

Mrs. Dennis Decker

Pluckets

1 cake yeast dissolved in	⅓ cup melted butter
¼ cup lukewarm water	½ tsp. salt
1 cup scalded milk	3 eggs, well beaten
⅓ cup sugar	Flour about 3¾ cups

Add the sugar, butter and salt to scalded milk. When lukewarm, add dissolved yeast, eggs and just enough flour to make stiff batter. Cover and let rise until mixture is double in bulk. Knead down and let rise again. Roll small balls of dough about the size of walnuts and dip in melted butter. Then roll each ball in a mixture of ¾ cup sugar, ½ cup ground nut meats and 3 tsp. cinnamon. Pile loosely in an ungreased angel food cake pan and let rise again for 30 min. Bake about 40 min. beginning with 400° and decreasing after 10 min. to 350°. Bake until brown. Turn pan upside down and remove immediately. Serve warm.

Mrs. Robert Mininger, Walnut Hill, Fla.
Mrs. LeRoy Schmidt, Moundridge, Kans.
Mrs. Verle Peters, McDavid, Fla.

Sweet Dough With Wheat Germ

2 pkg. dry yeast	¼ cup shortening
¼ cup warm water	2 eggs, beaten
1 cup scalded milk	4 cups sifted flour
½ cup sugar	¾ cup wheat germ
2 tsp. salt	

Soften yeast in warm water. Combine milk, sugar, salt, and shortening. Cool to lukewarm. Mix flour and wheat germ, add 1 cup to milk mixture; Mix well. Add softened yeast and eggs. Beat well. Add remaining flour and wheat germ to make a soft dough. Turn out on floured surface and knead until smooth and satiny—about 5 min. Place in greased bowl, turn dough over to grease surface. Cover with tea towel and let rise in warm place (80°-85°) until doubled (about 1 to 1½ hr.) Punch down. Let dough rest 10 min. Shape into tea ring rolls or coffee cake. Place on lightly greased cooky sheet or baking pans. Let rise until double (about 1 hr.) Bake 30 min. at 350° for coffee cakes, 25 min. for pan rolls, or 20 min. for individual rolls. Makes three coffee cakes or about 3½ doz. rolls.

Mrs. Henry Buller, Montezuma, Kans.

Potato Refrigerator Rolls

1 cup scalded milk	¼ cup sugar
1 cup hot mashed potatoes	2 tsp. salt
½ cup shortening	Mix together and let cool

Mix 1 pkg. yeast (cake or granules) in ½ cup lukewarm water; 3 eggs beaten, 5 to 6 cups flour. Combine milk, potatoes, shortening, sugar and salt in large bowl. Let stand till lukewarm, add softened yeast, eggs and 1½ cups flour, beat well, cover and let stand in warm place 1 hr. or until full of bubbles. Mix in 3½ to 4½ cups flour to make fairly stiff dough. Knead till smooth, on floured table. Return to greased bowl. Grease top and cover and set in refrigerator. About 1½ hrs. before serving time, shape into desired number of rolls on greased pans, let rise 1 to 1½ hrs. or double in bulk. Bake in hot 425° oven 15 to 20 min. Punch down unused portion and return to refrigerator. Makes 3 doz. med. sized rolls.

Mrs. Abe Nichols, Ingalls, Kans.

Raisin Oatmeal Rolls

¾ cup dark, seedless raisins	2 tbsp. soft butter
1 pkg. dry or cake yeast	1 cup boiling water
3 tbsp. warm water	½ cup brown sugar
½ cup quick cooking rolled	(packed)
oats	1 tsp. salt
2½ cups sifted flour	Melted Butter

Chop raisins coarsely. Soften yeast in warm water in bowl. Combine oats, butter, brown sugar, salt and boiling water. When mixture is lukewarm add yeast, raisins and flour. Mix to moderately stiff dough. Turn out on floured board and knead lightly a few minutes. Return to bowl, cover, and let rise about double in size, about 35 to 45 min. Brush tops with melted butter. Bake in moderately hot oven at 375° for 20 to 25 min. or until nicely browned. Makes about one and a half dozen rolls.

Mrs. Noah Koehn, Halstead, Kans.

Refrigerator Rolls

2 cups boiling water	¼ cup shortening
½ cup sugar	¼ cup lukewarm water
1 tbsp. salt	2 cakes yeast

1 tsp. sugar   8 cups sifted flour
2 eggs, beaten

Mix boiling water, sugar, salt and shortening and cool to lukewarm. Soften yeast in lukewarm water, add 1 tsp. sugar and stir
into first mixture. Add beaten eggs and 4 cups flour. Beat thoroughly. Stir in remaining flour and beat to smooth dough. Knead
lightly but not warm the dough. Grease top; place in large
covered bowl and store in refrigerator. When needed, shape into clover leaf or parker house rolls, or any desired shape. Place
in pans to double in bulk, about 2 hrs. Bake 15 to 20 min. at
425°.

Mrs. Wallace B. Decker, Halstead, Kans.

Roanoke Rolls

1 cup milk   1 cup very warm water
½ cup sugar   2 pkgs., or yeast cakes
1 tbsp. salt   3 eggs, beaten
6 tbsp. margarine   9 cups sifted flour (approx.)

Scald milk; stir in sugar, salt and margarine. Cool to lukewarm.
Measure warm water into large bowl. Sprinkle or crumble
in yeast; stir until dissolved. Add lukewarm milk mixture, beaten eggs and half the flour; stir until blended.
Beat until smooth. Add remaining flour until dough cleans sides
of bowl. Turn out onto lightly floured board. Knead until smooth
and elastic, about 10 min. Place in greased bowl, turning to
grease all sides. Cover. Let rise in warm place, free from draft,
until doubled in bulk, about 1 hr. and 15. min. Divide dough in
half. Roll out each half about ⅜" thick. Cut into rounds with
2½" biscuit cutter. Crease heavily through center with dull
edge of knife; brush lightly with melted margarine. Fold over
so edges just meet; seal. Place together with rolls touching in
greased shallow pans. Cover. Let rise in warm place, free from
draft, until double in bulk, about 1 hr. Bake at 350° (mod.) oven
about 20 to 25 min. until golden brown. Remove from oven.
Brush tops with melted margarine immediately. Makes about
5 dozen.

Mrs. Emerson Koehn, Cimarron, Kans.
Edna Giesbrecht, Winton, Calif.

Sour Cream Twists

3½ cups flour
1 tsp. salt
1 cake compressed yeast
1 cup thick sour cream
1 cup shortening(part
   butter)

1 whole egg
2 egg yolks
1 tsp. vanilla
1 cup sugar (for sprinkling
   board and dough)

Sift flour before measuring. Sift flour and salt together in bowl. Cut in shortening with blender leaving some of shortening in lumps size of peas. Add crumpled yeast, sour cream, well beaten eggs and vanilla. Mix thoroughly. Cover bowl with damp cloth and set in refrigerator for at least 2 hrs. (Dough does not rise but becomes cold and firm.) Take half of the dough, sprinkle board with part of sugar. Roll dough into oblong shape about 8x16." Fold two ends to center overlapping. Sprinkle with sugar and roll to same size again. Repeat process a third time. Roll out a little less than ¼" thick. Cut into strips 1x4". Twist ends of each strip in opposite directions, stretching slightly. Bake immediately. When delicate brown remove from oven and cool. Bake at 475° for 15 min. When baked you see layers of dough with sugar in them.   Mrs. D. G. Boeckner, Moundridge, Kans.

Sweet Petals

2 pkg. active dry yeast or 2 cakes compressed yeast in ½ cup warm water
Combine:
   4 cups hot scalded milk   1 tbsp. salt
   6 tbsp. shortening   ½ cup sugar
Combine in large mixing bowl, cool to lukewarm. Stir in softened yeast. Add enough flour to form a stiff dough. Knead until smooth and satiny. Place in greased bowl and cover. Let rise until light. Roll out to ½ in. thick. Cut in strips 3 in. long and ¾ in. wide. Dip strips in 1 cup melted butter, then in cinnamon topping.

Cinnamon Topping
1½ cups sugar   1 tsp. cinnamon
   1 or 2 cups chopped nuts
Mix and dip buttered strips. Place in pan close together. Let rise in warm place until light. Bake at 350° for 25 to 30 min. These rolls come apart easy when ready to serve.
    Letha Holdeman, Wrens, Ga.

Sweet Rolls (1)

2 cakes yeast
1 tbsp. sugar
1 cup lukewarm water
1 cup milk
3 eggs, beaten

7 tbsp. oleo
½ cup sugar
1 tsp. salt
7 cups flour (or enough
    to make a soft dough)

Dissolve yeast and 1 tbsp. sugar in lukewarm water. Scald milk, and oleo, sugar and salt; cool to lukewarm. Add 2 cups flour to make a batter. Add yeast and beaten eggs, beat well. Add remaining flour or enough to make a soft dough. Knead lightly and place in greased bowl. Cover and set in warm place. Let rise until doubled in bulk. Punch down and let rise again. Punch down and shape according to directions for Swedish Tea Ring, Filled Coffee Ring or Cinnamon Rolls. Excellent for freezing.

Mrs. Reuben Koehn, Goltry, Okla.

Sweet Rolls (2)

2 cups scalded milk
Beat together:
    ¾ cup sugar
    2 tsp. salt

¾ cup butter melted in hot
    milk
2 eggs

Add milk mixture. Dissolve 2 pkgs. yeast in ½ cup warm water. Add to above. Add 4 cups of flour and beat about 10 min. at low speed on mixer. Add 3 to 4 more cups of flour and stir with spoon. The dough should not be so hard that you can't stir with a spoon. Let rise till double in bulk and stir down and let rise again. Shape as desired. Let rise and bake in hot oven about 12 min. Do not over bake or rolls are dry.

Mrs. LaVeda Schmidt, Newton, Kans.

Twist Cinnamon Rolls

1½ pts. warm water
1 pkg. dry yeast
¼ cup melted shortening
2 eggs

2 tsp. salt
¾ cup sugar
11 cups flour

Mix until stiff but not sticky. Let rise. Then roll out, spread with 1 stick of oleo. Mix 1 cup sugar and cinnamon together and put on oleo. Roll over top and cut in strips about ½ or ¾ in. wide and of desired length, and roll around as in a circle. Put in pans and let rise again. Bake at 325° until brown.

Mrs. Lincoln Ratzlaff, Johnson, Kans.

Sweet Roll Dough

Measure into mixing bowl:
½ cup lukewarm water

Add, stirring to dissolve:
2 pkgs. active dry yeast

Stir in:

1½ cups lukewarm milk	2 eggs
½ cup sugar	½ cup soft shortening
2 tsp. salt	7½ cups sifted flour (approx.)

Mix with spoon until smooth. Add enough flour to handle easily. Keep dough as soft as possible. Knead until smooth and elastic. Round up in greased bowl and cover. Let rise in warm place until double in bulk, about 1½ hr. Punch down, let rise again, until almost double, about 30 min. Shape as desired, let rise and bake in med. hot oven 375°, 15 to 20 min. This is a key recipe for any shape of rolls or coffee cake. Good for freezing for later use. For doubled recipe: Take two times each ingredient except yeast, not necessary to increase yeast more than 1½ times. Recipe calls for 2 pkg. yeast, use only 3 pkg.

Mrs. Newlin Johnson, Goltry, Okla.

White Bread

4 cups water (or part pota-to water)	1½ tbsp. yeast dissolved in 1 cup water with 2 tsp. sugar and let stand 10 min.
½ cup sugar	
2 tbsp. salt	Flour to make a soft dough
1 tbsp. shortening	

Combine the 4 cups warm water, sugar, salt, shortening, and yeast which has been dissolved in 1 cup water, and add enough flour to make a soft dough. Turn on lightly floured board. Knead until dough is smooth and elastic. Place in greased bowl. Let rest 15 min. Knead down. Let rise in warm place till double in bulk. Punch down and let rise again till double. Form into loaves. Place in well greased bread pans. Bake at 400° for 15 min., reduce heat to 350° for 45 min. longer. Yields 5 loaves.

(2 cups cracked wheat may be added for variation.)

CAKES

Sponge Cakes

Angel Food Cake (1)

1½ cups cake flour
1½ cups granulated sugar
2 cups egg whites
2 tbsp. cold water

⅛ tsp. salt
1 tsp. cream of tartar
1 tsp. vanilla

Sift cake flour six times. Beat egg whites after adding salt. When foamy, add cream of tartar and beat until stiff. Slowly fold in sugar and vanilla. Using sifter, add a little flour at a time; fold in lightly; add water. Bake in tube pan at 350° for 55 min.

Jocelyn Rempel, Morris, Man.

Angel Food Cake (2)

Preheat oven to 375°. Have egg whites at room temperature.
1¼ cups sifted cake flour
1½ cups (about 12) egg whites
¼ tsp. salt

1¼ tsp. cream of tartar
1 tsp. vanilla
¼ tsp. almond extract
1⅓ cups sifted sugar

Measure sifted flour, add ½ cup sugar, sift together 4 times. Combine egg whites, salt, cream of tartar, and flavorings in large bowl. Beat with beater until moist soft peaks form. Add remaining sugar in 4 additions, beating until well blended each time. Sift in flour mixture in 4 additions, folding in with large spoon each time; turn bowl often. Pour into ungreased 10 in. tube pan. Bake at 375° for 35 to 40 min. Invert cake until cool, then loosen from sides and remove from pan.

Cocoa Angel Food Cake

Remove 3 tbsp. flour from cup and add 3 tbsp. cocoa. Proceed as in preceding recipe.

Chiffon Cake

1½ cups sifted flour	5 unbeaten egg yolks
1 cup sugar	½ cup water
2 tsp. baking powder	1½ tsp. vanilla
1 tsp. salt	¾ cup egg whites
⅜ cup salad oil	½ tsp. cream of tartar

Sift together flour, sugar, baking powder and salt. Make a well and add cooking oil, egg yolks, water and vanilla. Beat until smooth. Beat egg whites with cream of tartar until it forms very stiff peaks (stiffer than meringue). Pour egg yolk mixture gradually over beaten egg whites gently folding in. Do not stir. Pour into ungreased 9-in. tube pan. Bake 45 min. at 325°, then increase heat to 350° for 10 or 15 min. Invert pan to cool cake. Remove from pan. Serve with ice cream and fruit or ice with your favorite icing. Serves 12.

Mrs. Frank P. Toews, Steinbach, Man.

Pink Beauty Party Cake

1 cup sifted flour	⅓ cup cold water
1 cup sugar	1 tsp. vanilla
1½ tsp. baking powder	¾ tsp. salt
¼ cup salad oil	½ tsp. cream of tartar
5 eggs, separated	⅛ tsp. red food coloring

Sift flour, ½ cup sugar, and baking powder. Add oil, egg yolks, water and vanilla. Do not beat. Add salt and cream of tartar to egg white, beat until stiff. Gradually blend in the remaining ½ cup sugar in tbsp.. portions, beating constantly until mixture is very stiff. Beat first mixture until smooth and pour over egg whites in a thin stream, gently folding with rubber scraper until blended. Sprinkle food coloring over batter and fold in with few strokes to give marbled effect. Pour into ungreased angel food cake pan. Bake at 350° for 45 min. or until surface of cake springs back when lightly touched. Invert cake to cool.

Linda Wohlgemuth, Greenland, Man.

Mahogany Chiffon Cake

¾ cup boiling water	1¾ cups sifted cake flour
½ cup cocoa	1¾ cups sugar, sifted

1½ tsp. soda
1 tsp. salt
½ cup cooking oil
7 unbeaten egg yolks

2 tsp. vanilla
1 cup egg whites
½ tsp. cream of tartar

Mix and cool water and cocoa. Sift together into bowl; flour, sugar, soda, and salt. Make a well; add oil, egg yolks, cocoa mixture and vanilla. Beat until smooth. Beat egg whites and cream of tartar until very stiff. Pour egg yolk mixture gradually over beaten egg whites, gently folding until blended. Pour into an ungreased 10-in. tube pan. Bake 65 to 70 min. Invert on funnel to cool.

Mrs. Claude Unruh, Durham, Kans.

Spice Sponge Cake

14 egg yolks (egg yolks left from angel food cake)
1 cup sifted granulated sugar
1 tsp. cinnamon
⅔ cup sifted flour

½ tsp. salt
1 tsp. vanilla
½ tsp. cloves
2 tsp. baking powder
3 egg whites

Beat egg yolks. Add sugar gradually and beat mixture 15 min. with rotary beater. Sift flour, salt and baking powder together. Fold into the beaten egg yolks. Add flavoring and fold into stiffly beaten egg whites. Pour into angel food pan and bake at 325° for 65 min.

Jocelyn Rempel, Morris Man.

Yellow Angel Food Cake

11 to 15 egg yolks
½ tsp. salt
1 cup sugar
1½ cups flour, sifted
½ tsp. baking powder

½ tsp. cream of tartar
½ cup ice water
½ tsp. vanilla
½ tsp. lemon

Beat egg yolks, ice water and salt for 5 min. at med. speed, then high speed for 10 min. Fold in sugar and flavoring. Sift together flour, baking powder, and cream of tartar. Fold into the egg yolk mixture. Pour into angel food pan and bake at 375° for 30 to 35 min.

Mrs. Robert Koehn, Montezuma, Kans.

Vanilla Chiffon Cake

4 large or 5 small egg yolks
⅔ cup cold water
2 tsp. vanilla
1 tsp. grated lemon rind
1 cup egg whites

2 cups cake flour
1⅓ cups sugar
1 tsp. salt
2½ tsp. baking powder
½ cup, less 1 tbsp. salad oil
½ tsp. cream of tartar

Sift flour; measure and resift three times with next three ingredients. Make a well in center of flour; pour in salad oil, unbeaten yolks, water, vanilla, and lemon rind. Beat whites and cream of tartar with rotary beater until stiff. Pour yolk mixture over whites cutting and folding in. Do not stir and over mix, as this makes cake tough. Bake 55 min. or until cake springs back when lightly touched.

Norma Froese, Steinbach, Man.

Butter Cakes

Butterscotch Cake

4 eggs
2 cups sugar
2 cups flour
2 tsp. baking powder

⅛ tsp. salt
1 cup milk
2 tbsp. butter or oleo
1 tsp. vanilla

Beat eggs until light, add sugar, continue beating. Add sifted dry ingredients to creamed mixture. Heat milk to boiling. Add butter and pour while hot into batter mixture. Add vanilla; mix thoroughly. Bake in 13x9 in. pan at 350° for 45 min.

Topping

⅔ cup brown sugar
¼ cup cream

3 tbsp. butter, melted
1 cup coconut or nut meats

When cake is baked, spread at once with topping and return to oven. Bake frosting until light brown.

Mrs. G. H. Dyck, Hesston, Kans.
Mrs. Leo Loetkeman, Enderby. B. C.

Fifteen Minute Cake

1 egg
1 cup sugar
⅓ cup shortening
1 cup milk

1 tsp. vanilla
2 cups flour
2 tsp. baking powder
¼ tsp. salt

Cream egg, sugar, shortening; add milk and vanilla. Mix in flour, baking powder and salt. Grease cookie sheet and drop by tablespoons onto sheet and bake at 350° for 8-10 min. Frost each little cake with a powdered sugar frosting.

Roselette Jantz, Livingston, Calif.

Funny Cake

Line a 9 to 10 in. pie plate with pastry—Then make a sauce and let cool while mixing the cake.

1¼ cups sifted cake flour
1 tsp. baking powder
½ tsp. salt
¾ cup sugar
¼ cup shortening

½ cup milk
1 tsp. vanilla
1 egg (unbeaten)
3 tbsp. chopped nuts or coconut for topping

Pour batter into pastry lined pie plate. Pour lukewarm sauce gently over batter, sprinkle with nuts or coconut. Bake in moderate oven (350°) for 50 to 55 min.
Either chocolate or butterscotch sauce may be used.

Butterscotch Sauce

Combine:
¼ cup butter
½ cup brown sugar (packed)

2 tbsp. light corn syrup

Cook and stir over low heat to boiling, add 3 tbsp. water—bring to boil, boil 1 to 2 min. then remove from heat. Stir in ½ tsp. vanilla.

Chocolate Sauce

1½ sq. unsweetened chocolate
½ cup water
⅔ cup sugar

¼ cup butter
1½ tsp. vanilla

Melt chocolate with water, add sugar. Bring to boil, stirring constantly. Remove from heat, stir in butter and vanilla. Set aside.

Mrs. Oliver (Ruby) Unruh, Hesston, Kans.

Easy White Wedding Cake

1½ cups sugar	6 egg whites
3 cups sifted flour	1 tsp. vanilla extract
½ tsp. salt	½ tsp. almond extract
¾ cup shortening	3½ tsp. baking powder
1 cup milk	

Sift sugar, flour and salt together 3 times. Add shortening, blend at med. speed until mixture resembles pastry mix. Add unbeaten egg whites and 4 tbsp. of the milk, cream until smooth, do not over beat. Add vanilla and almond extract and remaining milk gradually, add baking powder and beat ½ min. longer. Bake in preheated oven 375° for 30 min.

Frosting

½ cup butter	½ tsp. vanilla
4 cups powdered sugar	½ tsp. almond

Soften butter, add powdered sugar and mix until creamy. Add flavorings and blend.

Neoma Mayeske, Fredonia, Kans.

Burnt Sugar Cake

To Caramelize sugar:

Melt ½ cup sugar in heavy skillet over low heat, stir as sugar melts. Heat until melted to a golden brown syrup, stirring constantly. Stir in ½ cup boiling water. Use the amount called for in recipe.

1 egg	3 tbsp. burnt sugar syrup
1 cup sugar	2 cups plus 2 tbsp. flour
½ cup butter	2½ tsp. baking powder
1 cup milk	

Cream butter and sugar. Add egg, and burnt sugar. Sift flour and baking powder. Mix alternately with milk. Bake in 350° oven for 30 min.

Mrs. Sarah Unruh, Hesston, Kans.

Georgia Pound Cake

3 cups granulated sugar	3 cups cake flour
1 cup oleo	6 eggs

1 cup sour cream   1 tbsp. vanilla
¼ tsp. soda

Cream butter, add sugar. Beat eggs one at a time; add flour and ½ cup cream. Beat 2 min. add remaining cream with soda and flavoring. Mix only until well blended. Bake in tube pan for 1 ½ hr. at 300°. Cool for 15 min.

Wanda Holdeman, Wrens, Ga.

Short Cake

2 eggs   ¼ tsp. cream of tartar
1 cup sugar   1 tsp. vanilla
1 cup flour   ½ cup hot water
1¼ tsp. baking powder

Beat eggs and sugar until light colored. Sift dry ingredients. Add to creamed mixture alternately with vanilla and water; mix thoroughly. Bake in greased 8"x8" pan at 350° for 30 min.

Mrs. Ransom Wiebe, Durham, Kans.

Italian Cream Cake

1 cup flour   1 tsp. baking powder
4 eggs, separated   ⅛ tsp. salt
1 cup sugar   1 tsp. vanilla
4 tbsp. water

Beat egg whites and set aside. In another bowl beat yolks; add sugar and beat until light. Add water and flour, beating thoroughly. Add baking powder, egg whites and flavoring. Bake in two 8-in. wax paper lined pans at 325° for 25 to 30 min.

Cream Sauce

1 pt. milk   1 tsp. vanilla
¼ cup flour   1 cup sugar
4 egg yolks   chocolate chips

Mix in double boiler; cook until thick. Divide in half; add chocolate chips to one-half. Cool and put between split layers.

Frosting

½ cup sugar   2 egg whites
2 tbsp. water   1 tsp. vanilla
¼ cup light syrup

Cook sugar, water and syrup to 242° or until it spins a thread 6 to 8 in. long. Beat into beaten egg whites.

Betty Haynes

Lemon Golden Dream Cake

1 pkg. yellow cake mix
1 pkg. instant lemon pud-
   ding mix

¾ cup liquid shortening
¾ cup water
4 eggs

Mix ingredients and bake in large loaf pan at 350° 30 to 35 min. When done punch holes in cake with fork. Pour icing over hot cake.

Icing

2 cups powdered sugar
2 tbsp. melted butter

2 tbsp. water
½ cup lemon juice

Blend lemon juice, butter and water. Add sifted powdered sugar. Blend well.

Joan Schneider, Perrinton, Mich.

Modern Method White Cake

Put into mixing bowl:
2¼ cups sifted flour
5 tsp. baking powder
1 tsp, salt

1½ cups sugar
½ cup shortening
¾ cup milk

Beat for 2 min. Add:
4 unbeaten egg whites
¼ cup milk

1 tsp. vanilla

Beat for 2 min. more. Bake in 2 layers at 350° for 35 min.

Mrs. Levi Stutzman, Hydro, Okla.

Lemon Jell-O Cake

1 pkg. lemon jell-o
1 pkg. yellow cake mix
4 eggs
¾ cup salad oil

¾ cup cold water
1 tsp. lemon extract
¼ cup lemon juice
1 cup powdered sugar

Mix all the ingredients except the lemon juice and powdered sugar, beat at med. speed for about 4 min. Bake in oiled pan 45 min. at 350°. Cool in pan. Mix powdered sugar and lemon juice until smooth. Pour this over the warm cake which has cooled about 10 min. It will seep down into the cake, leaving a glaze on top.

Mrs. Jesse Giesbrecht, Glenn, Calif.
Mrs. Dayton, Hibner, Ga.

Hot Milk Butter Cake

2 eggs	1 cup sugar
1 tsp. baking powder	1 cup flour
⅛ tsp. salt	4 tbsp. butter
½ cup milk	

Beat eggs until thick and lemon colored. Add sugar slowly. Fold in all of sifted dry ingredients. Bring butter and milk to simmering point in saucepan; add to first mixture. Bake in greased pan at 375° about 30 min.

Topping

½ cup brown sugar	2 tbsp. cream
3 tbsp. butter	1 cup coconut

Melt butter, add sugar and coconut. Spread on cake and return to oven long enough to brown topping. Add nut meats if desired.

Mrs. Merle Koehn, Ulysses, Kans.

Nut Cake

¾ cup shortening	1 cup milk
3 eggs	2 tsp. baking powder
3 cups flour	1 tsp. vanilla
¾ cup nuts	1½ cups sugar

Sift dry ingredients three times. Cream shortening and sugar. Add egg yolks, and beat until light, and fluffy. Add milk and dry ingredients alternately and beat hard after each addition. Add vanilla, fold in beaten egg whites and nuts. Bake 30 min. at 350°.

Mrs. Clarence Schneider, Moundridge, Kans.

Sour Cream Cake

2 eggs	1 tsp. baking powder
1 cup sugar	½ tsp. salt
1 cup thick sour cream	1 tsp. soda
2 cups flour	1 tsp. vanilla

Beat eggs until light; add sugar and sour cream, continue beating. Add vanilla. Sift baking powder, soda, and salt with flour and beat into first mixture. Pour into oblong buttered pan and bake at 350° 30 to 35 min. (Raisins, nuts or chocolate may be added if desired.)

Mrs. Pete P. Isaac, Moundridge, Kans.

Sour Cream Pound Cake

½ lb. margarine
3 cups sugar
1 cup sour cream
6 eggs, separated
3 cups flour

¼ tsp. soda
1 tsp. vanilla
1 tsp. lemon extract
¼ tsp. salt

Cream butter and sugar. Add egg yolks, cream, dry ingredients, flavoring and mix well. Fold in beaten egg whites. Pour into greased tube pan. Bake at 300° for 1½ hr.

Mrs. Verle Peters, Walnut Hill, Fla.
Mrs. Vernon Peters, Walnut Hill, Fla.

Chocolate Cakes

Chocolate Buttermilk Cake (3 tier)

1 cup oleo
2¼ cups sugar
2 eggs
1 tsp. vanilla
2 cups buttermilk

½ cup cocoa
3 cups sifted flour
2 tsp. baking soda
1 tsp. salt

Cream butter, add sugar gradually and beat until fluffy. Add eggs, one at a time, then vanilla. Sift dry ingredients together, add to creamed mixture, alternately with buttermilk. Pour batter into three 9-in. cake pans which have been greased and lightly floured, lined with wax paper and buttered. Bake at 350° for 25 to 35 min. Cool on racks. Frost with butter icing.

Mrs. Ivan Schmidt, Fredonia, Kans.
Mrs. Harvey Yost, Greensburg, Kans.

Chocolate Cake (1)

1 cup bisquick
1 cup flour
1½ cups sugar
1 tsp. soda
½ tsp. baking powder

½ cup oleo, softened
2 eggs beaten
1 cup milk
2 tsp. vanilla
4 tsp. cocoa

Cream oleo and sugar. Add eggs, dry ingredients, milk, and flavoring, beat until smooth. Bake at 350° for 35 min.

Mrs. Helen Schmidt, Livingston, Calif.

Chocolate Cake (2)

1 cup shortening
2 cups sugar
5 eggs
½ cup cocoa
2½ cups flour

½ tsp. salt
1 tsp. soda
1 cup sour milk
2 tsp. vanilla
1 cup coarsely broken walnuts

Thoroughly cream shortening and sugar; add eggs, one at a time, beating after each addition. Add sifted dry ingredients alternately with sour milk and vanilla. Stir in nuts. Bake in three 9-in. layer pans at 350° for 25-30 min.

Mrs. Franklin Buller, Montezuma, Kans.

Chocolate Cake (3)

1½ cups flour
1½ cups sugar
1½ cups sour cream
1½ tsp. soda

1½ tsp. salt
1½ tsp vanilla
3 eggs
3 tbsp. cocoa

Sift flour, sugar, soda, salt and cocoa together. Add eggs and sour cream. Bake in mod. oven (350°) about 55 min.

Mrs. Dan Smith, Fairview, Okla.
Mrs. Freeman Unruh, Goltry, Okla.

Chocolate Cake (4)

1 cup sugar
¼ cup shortening
2 eggs
1¼ cups flour
1 tsp. vanilla
1 tsp. baking powder

½ cup sour milk
⅛ tsp. salt
1 tsp. soda
¼ cup cocoa
½ cup boiling water

Cream shortening, sugar and eggs. Sift together flour, baking powder, and salt; add to creamed mixture alternately with sour milk. Add water to cocoa and soda, add to batter last, beat until smooth. Bake at 350° for 35-40 min.

Mrs. Linda Regehr, Linden, Alberta

Chocolate Cake (5)

1¾ cups sifted cake flour
1½ cups sugar
¾ tsp. soda
¾ tsp. salt
½ cup shortening

1 cup buttermilk
2 eggs, unbeaten
2 sq. chocolate, melted
1 tsp. vanilla

Sift dry ingredients together into mixing bowl. Add shortening and ⅔ cup of the buttermilk. Beat 2 min. at med. speed. Add the remaining buttermilk, eggs, choc., and vanilla. Beat two min. more. Bake at 350° for 25 min. Makes 2 layers.

Mrs. William Seiler, Carson City, Mich.

Chocolate Chip Cake Mix

1 pkg. white cake mix
Plus ¼ cup salad oil
(or use white cake recipe)

1-6 oz. pkg. chocolate chips

Prepare cake batter according to directions. Reserve 3 table-spoons chocolate chips for frosting. Chop remainder choc. chips. Pour batter alternately with choc. chips into two 8 in. or 9 in. wax paper lined pans. Bake as directed. Frost with Seafoam Frosting.

Mrs. Lyle Litwiller

Chocolate Pudding Cake

¾ cup sugar
1 cup flour
2 tsp. baking powder
⅛ tsp. salt

1 sq. chocolate
2 tbsp. butter
½ cup milk
½ tsp. vanilla

Sift together dry ingredients; add chocolate and butter melted together over hot water. Add milk and vanilla. Pour into buttered 9"x9" pan.

Topping

1 cup cold water
½ cup brown sugar

½ cup white sugar
2 tbsp. cocoa

Mix dry ingredients and spread over top of cake; then pour water over the top. Bake 40 min. at 325°. Cool, serve with whipped cream or ice cream.

Joyleen Nightingale, Sublette, Kans.

Busy Day Chocolate Cake

2 eggs
2 cups sugar
1 cup cocoa
1 cup shortening
2 tsp. soda
1 cup boiling water

1 tsp. baking powder
3 cups flour, sifted
2 tsp. vanilla
1 tsp. salt
1 cup milk

Mix ingredients in order given. Beat at low speed for 3 min. Bake in large loaf pan at 325° for 40 to 50 min.

Mrs. David Holdeman, DeRidder, La.

Chocolate Chip Cake

1½ cups shortening
3 eggs
2½ cups flour
1½ cups chocolate chips
    and nuts

1½ tsp. cocoa
1½ cups sugar
½ tsp. maple flavoring
1½ tsp. soda
1½ cups milk

Cream shortening, eggs, and flavoring. Add flour, cocoa, soda, and milk. Mix well. Pour into oblong greased and floured cake pan and sprinkle chips and nuts over top. Bake at 350° for 55 min.

Mrs. Gary Unruh, Durham, Kans.

Chocolate Chip Date Cake

1 cup dates, chopped
1 tsp. soda
1 cup hot water
1 cup sugar
1 cup oleo
2 eggs

1¾ cup flour
1½ tsp. cocoa
¼ tsp. salt
1 tsp. vanilla
1 cup choc. chips
1 cup chopped nuts

Pour hot water over dates; sprinkle soda over hot water; cover and let cool. Cream oleo, sugar and eggs; add dates, mix thoroughly. Sift together flour, cocoa, and salt; add to creamed mixture. Add vanilla, ½ cup chocolate chips and nuts. Pour batter into greased pans, sprinkle remaining choc. chips over batter and bake at 325° for 35-40 min.

Mrs. James Toews, Yale, S. Dak.

Chocolate Date Cake

1 cup sugar	¼ tsp. salt
¾ cup shortening	1 cup dates
2 eggs, beaten	1¼ cups boiling water
2 tbsp. cocoa	½ cup nuts
1⅓ cups flour	½ cup choc. chips
1 tsp. soda	

Cut up dates, add boiling water, cool. Cream shortening and sugar, add eggs and cocoa, beat well. Add flour mixture and dates alternately. Sprinkle broken nut meats and chocolate chips over the batter. Bake in 9"x13" pan at 350° for 30 min. (Do not overbake, cake should be moist.) Cut in squares and serve with whipped cream or ice cream.

Mrs. Alfred Koehn, Almena, Wisc.

Chocolate Macaroon Cake

Beat: 1 egg white with 1 tsp. vanilla until soft mounds form.
Add: ½ cup sugar gradually, beating until stiff peaks form.
Stir in: 2 cups fine-grated coconut and 1 tbsp. flour; set aside.
Dissolve: ½ cup cocoa in ¾ cup hot coffee.
Beat: 3 egg whites until soft mounds form. Add ½ cup sugar gradually, beating until meringue stands in stiff peaks.
Add: 1 tsp. soda to ½ cup sour cream.
Combine:

1¼ cups sugar	3 egg yolks
½ cup shortening	1 tsp. salt

1 tsp. vanilla, and half of cocoa mixture. Beat until light and creamy, about 4 min.
Add: 2 cups sifted flour, the sour cream and remaining cocoa mixture. Blend well. Fold in the beaten egg whites.
Turn: ⅓ of the chocolate batter into a 10-in. tube pan greased on bottom. Place ½ of coconut mixture on top. Cover with ½ of remaining chocolate batter. Top with remaining coconut, then chocolate batter.
Bake: at 350° for 55 to 65 min. Cool completely; remove from pan. Frost.

Mrs. Oren Koehn, Butler, Mo.

Dark Moist Chocolate Cake

1 cup flour	1 cup sour milk
1 cup sugar	½ cup melted oleo
3 tbsp. cocoa	1 tsp. vanilla
1 beaten egg	1 tsp. soda

Sift flour, sugar and cocoa three times. Add milk in which the soda has been dissolved, add beaten egg, oleo and vanilla. Blend and mix well. Bake in small cake pan at 350° for 20 min.

Mrs. Vincent Barkman, Mt. Lehman, B. C.

Chocolate Oatmeal Cake

2 cups rolled oats	2 cups sifted flour
3 cups boiling water	1 cup cocoa or less
1 cup shortening	2 tsp. baking soda
3 cups sugar	1 tsp. salt
4 eggs	2 tsp. vanilla

Mix rolled oats and boiling water, let cool. Cream sugar, shortening and eggs. Add the oatmeal mixture together with the flour, cocoa, baking soda, salt and vanilla. Beat until smooth. Bake at 350° for 1 hr. Frost with coconut icing on page 224.

Mrs. Oscar Unruh, Fairview, Okla.

Chocolate Upside-Down Cake

Part 1:

1 cup flour	¾ cup sugar
2 tbsp. cocoa	2 tsp. baking powder
¼ tsp. salt	½ cup milk
2 tbsp. melted shortening	1 tsp. vanilla
½ cup nut meats, chopped	

Cream shortening and sugar; sift flour, cocoa, salt and baking powder together. Add to creamed mixture alternating with milk and vanilla, add nuts. Pour into pan.

Part 2:

½ cup white sugar	2 tbsp. cocoa
½ cup brown sugar	

Mix together, sprinkle over top of batter. Pour 1 cup of cold water over top. Bake at 350° for 25-30 min.

Mrs. Dwain Jantz, Elk City, Kans.

Chocolate Pound Cake

3 cups flour	½ tsp. baking powder
1 cup oleo	½ tsp. salt
½ cup shortening	5 tbsp. cocoa
3 cups sugar	1 cup sour milk with
1 tsp. vanilla	½ tsp. soda added
5 eggs	

Cream shortening, oleo, and sugar. Add eggs and beat. Sift dry ingredients. Add alternately with milk and vanilla. Bake in angel food pan at 325° for 80 min.

Viola Harms, Atmore, Ala.

Delicious Chocolate Cake

¾ cup butter	2 cups flour
1 cup sugar	1 tsp. soda, dissolved
3 egg yolks	in small amt. of boiling
1 cup milk	water
1 tsp. vanilla	1 sq. chocolate grated
	or 3 tbsp. cocoa

Mix all ingredients in order given, except ½ cup of the milk and ½ cup of the sugar. Mix ½ cup sugar, chocolate and ½ cup milk in sauce pan, bring to boiling, remove from heat; while hot add slowly to the first mixture, add vanilla, beat until well blended. Bake in layers at 350° for 30-35 min.

Mrs. Fanny Holdeman, Hesston, Kans.

Easy German Chocolate Cake (1)

¾ cup butter or margarine	1 pkg. German sweet
2½ cups sugar	chocolate
1½ tsp. vanilla	3 cups sifted flour
3 eggs	1½ tsp. soda
1½ cups ice water	¾ tsp. salt

Cream butter, sugar, vanilla and eggs until light and fluffy. Blend in melted chocolate, add sifted dry ingredients alternately with ice water to chocolate mixture; beat until well blended. Bake in three 8-in. layers pans or large 9x13" pan at 350° for 30 to 35 min.

Mrs. Henry B. Koehn, Montezuma, Kans.

Easy German Chocolate Cake (2)

1 pkg. white cake mix
1 pkg. instant chocolate
  pudding
2 eggs
2 cups milk

Mix ingredients well; bake slightly longer than a plain cake mix. (Instant Lemon Pudding may be used in place of chocolate.)

Donella Holdeman, Hesston, Kans.
Mrs. Aaron Becker, Rich Hill, Mo.

Fudge Cake

¾ cup butter or margarine
2¼ cups sugar
1½ tsp. vanilla
3 eggs
1½ cups ice water
2½ sq. unsweetened chocolate, melted
3 cups sifted cake flour
1½ tsp. baking soda
¾ tsp. salt

Cream butter, sugar and vanilla. Add eggs, beating until light and fluffy. Add chocolate and blend well. Sift together dry ingredients; add alternatly with water to creamed mixture. Pour batter into three 8 in. layer pans which have been greased and lined with waxed paper. Bake in moderate oven (350°) for 30-35 min. (May also use loaf or cupcake pans).

Mrs. Edwin Ensz, Middleton, Mich.
Mrs. Raymond Becker, Burns, Kans.

Jiffy Chocolate Cake

1 cup brown sugar
¼ cup cocoa
2 cups hot water
1 cup miniature marsh-
  mallows
1 pkg. chocolate cake mix
1 cup broken nut meats

Mix sugar, cocoa and water and pour into 13x9 in. pan. Scatter marshmallows over mixture. Prepare cake mix according to directions on package and spoon over mixture in pan. Top with nut meats and bake at 350° for 45 min. May be served with whipped cream.

Mrs. Henry B. Koehn, Montezuma, Kans.

Jiffy Chocolate Cup Cakes

1 egg	1 cup sugar
1 tsp. vanilla	1½ cups sifted cake flour
½ cup cocoa	½ tsp. salt
1 tsp. soda	½ cup sour milk
½ cup shortening	½ cup hot water

Combine ingredients in order given. Beat 4 min. at med. speed with electric mixer. Fill greased muffin tins ½ full. Bake at 375° for 15-20 min. Makes 18 cup cakes.

Mrs. Dan S. Jantz, Burns, Kans.

Light Chocolate Cake (1)

⅔ cup butter or margarine	2⅓ cups sifted flour
1 tsp. soda	1 tsp. vanilla
½ tsp. salt	1 cup buttermilk
½ tsp. baking powder	1 bar Baker's German's
1½ cups sugar	Sweet Chocolate
	2 eggs

Cream butter and sugar until softened. Sift in dry ingredients and ½ of the buttermilk; add vanilla; mix until flour is dampened. Beat 2 min. at medium speed on mixer, or 300 strokes by hand. Add melted and cooled chocolate, eggs, and remaining buttermilk. Beat one min. Bake in two 9-in. layer pans for 30 min. Cool. Fill and frost layers with seven-min. frosting.

Mrs. Walter Redger

Light Chocolate Cake (2)

(Substitute for German Choc. Cake)

2½ cups plus 2 tbsp. cake flour	3 eggs
	1⅛ tsp. baking soda
2¼ cups sugar	1⅛ tsp. salt
¾ cup shortening	4½ tbsp. cocoa
1½ cups buttermilk	1½ tsp. vanilla

Sift flour, sugar, cocoa, soda, and salt together. Add shortening, vanilla and 1 cup of milk. Beat 2 min. with mixer at med. speed, scraping bowl often. Add eggs and the remaining milk, beat two min. more. Pour into three 8 in. or 9 in. greased and floured pans. Bake at 350° for 30 to 35 min. Frost with German Choc. Frosting.

Mrs. Reno Hibner, Stapleton, Ga.

Miracle Whip Cake

2 cups flour	1 cup warm water
4 tbsp. cocoa	1 cup Miracle Whip
2 tsp. soda	1½ cups sugar

Sift flour twice, add soda and cocoa. Cream Miracle Whip, add sugar and beat. Add flour mixture and water. Bake in two 8x8 in. greased and floured cake pans. Bake 25 to 30 min. in 350° oven.

Mrs. Vernon Decker, De Ridder La.

Never-Fail Mocha Cake

2 cups sugar	1 tsp. soda dissolved in 2 tsp.
¾ cup butter	water
4 eggs	1 cup cold coffee
⅔ cup cocoa	2 cups flour

Cream butter and sugar, add one egg at a time, beat well after each addition; add soda-water and cocoa. Blend in coffee and flour alternately. Beat well and bake in slow oven, (250°-300°.)

Mocha Filling for Cake

2 cups powdered sugar	6 tbsp. cold coffee
½ cup butter	1 tsp. vanilla
6 tbsp. cocoa	

Cream sugar and butter, add cocoa, coffee and vanilla. Beat until creamy and spread cake.

Mrs. Art Koehn, Halstead, Kans.

Quick Cocoa Cake

(Small)

½ cup shortening or butter	1 tsp. soda
1 cup sugar	1 cup warm milk with 1 tbsp.
1 egg	vinegar or buttermilk
4 tbsp. cocoa	1½ tsp. vanilla
1 cup flour	⅛ tsp. salt

Cream shortening and sugar; add egg, cocoa and soda. Beat until smooth. Add flour and salt alternately with warm milk and vanilla to creamed mixture. Bake in 12x7 in. pan at 350° for 20 min.

Mrs. Jacob N. Yost, Durham, Kans.

Quick Mix Chocolate Cake

1 cup sugar
1 cup flour
¼ cup cocoa
½ tsp. baking powder

¼ cup butter, melted
1 egg
½ cup milk
½ cup boiling water with 1 tsp. soda added

Mix all dry ingredients in mixer bowl; add last five ingredients. Blend well. Bake at 350° for 30 min.

Mrs. Ken Reimer, Linden, Alta.

Red Chocolate Cake

1½ cups sugar
½ cup shortening
2 eggs
2 oz. red food coloring
2 tbsp. cocoa
2 tbsp. vinegar

2¼ cups cake flour
½ tsp. salt
1 cup buttermilk
1 tsp. vanilla
1 tsp. soda

Cream together shortening, sugar, and eggs. Make a paste of the food coloring and cocoa. Add to first mixture; add the sifted cake flour and salt alternately with the buttermilk and vanilla. Remove from mixer. Fold in (do not beat) the baking soda and vinegar. Bake in two 8-in. pans at 350° for 30 min. Frost with Butter Icing.

Mrs. Levi Koehn, Barron, Wis.

Rich Cocoa Cake

½ cup cocoa
½ cup cold water
1½ tsp. soda
1¾ cups sugar
⅔ cup shortening

1½ tsp. vanilla
2 eggs
1 cup buttermilk
2½ cups sifted cake flour
1 tsp. salt

Mix cocoa, water, and soda; let stand. Cream together sugar, shortening and vanilla; add well-beaten eggs. Add cocoa mixture, then flour alternately with buttermilk, mix well. Bake at 300° for 25 to 30 min.

Mrs. Levi Plank, Fredericksburg, Ohio

(Red) Cocoa Cake

1½ cups cake flour
2½ tsp. cocoa
⅛ tsp. salt
½ cup shortening
1 cup sugar

1 egg
½ cup milk
1 tsp. vanilla
1 tsp. soda, dissolved in
½ cup hot water

Sift flour once, measure, then sift with cocoa and salt three times. Cream shortening and sugar together until light and fluffy. Add unbeaten egg and mix well. Add flour mixture alternately with milk. Add vanilla and mix until smooth. Dissolve soda in hot water and add to batter; mix quickly and pour batter into the greased loaf pan. Bake 25 min. at 350°. (This cake remains soft and moist.)

Mrs. Jonas Schmidt, De Ridder, La.

Sheath or Chocolate Sheet Cake

2 cups sugar
2 cups flour
½ cup oleo
½ cup shortening
4 tbsp. cocoa
1 cup water

½ cup buttermilk
2 eggs, slightly beaten
1 tsp. soda
1 tsp. cinnamon
1 tsp. vanilla

Sift sugar and flour into large mixing bowl. Combine oleo, shortening, cocoa and water in saucepan bring to a rapid boil; pour over sugar and flour and mix well. Add remaining ingredients in order given and beat thoroughly. Pour into greased cookie sheet (15"x10"). Bake at 400° for 20 min. (Leave cake in pan).

Icing

(Prepare icing before cake has finished baking)

½ cup oleo
4 tbsp. cocoa
6 tbsp. milk

1 box powdered sugar
1 tsp. vanilla
1 cup pecans, chopped

Melt oleo, add cocoa and milk; bring to boiling. Remove from heat and add remaining ingredients. Beat well, spread on cake while still warm.

Delma Friesen, Conway, Kans.
Bernice Giesbrecht, Glenn, Calif.

Schmidt's Favorite Cake

½ cup shortening
1½ cups sugar
2 eggs
1 tsp. vanilla
½ cup hot water
⅓ cup cocoa

1¾ cups flour
1 cup buttermilk
1 tsp. soda
½ tsp. baking powder
½ tsp. salt

Cream shortening and sugar; add eggs and vanilla. Mix hot water and cocoa, add to creamed mixture. Sift dry ingredients and add alternately with buttermilk; beat two min. Bake in two greased, paper-lined pans at 350° for 30-35 min.

Mrs. Wilmer Boehs, Walker, Mo.

Sour Cream Malt Cake

1¼ cups flour
1 cup sugar
1 tbsp. cocoa
¼ tsp. salt
1 tsp. vanilla

2 eggs, unbeaten
1 cup thick sour cream
1 tsp. soda
¼ cup warm water

Sift together the flour, sugar, cocoa and salt 4 times. Stir in the eggs and sour cream. Dissolve soda in warm water and add vanilla. Add to mixture and beat well. Bake in loaf pan at 350° for 30 min.

Mrs. Wilmont Boeckner, Newton, Kans.

Whipped Sour Cream Cake

1 ¾ cups sifted cake flour
1¼ cups sugar
4 tbsp. cocoa
½ tsp. salt
1½ cups sour cream

2 eggs, beaten
2 tsp. soda
4 tbsp. hot water
2 tbsp. butter, melted
1 tsp. vanilla

Whip sour cream, and beaten eggs. Add sifted dry ingredients and mix well. Add soda, dissolved in hot water, melted butter and vanilla. Bake in greased 9 in. layer cake pans at 350° for 25 min. (This cake is light and moist if not overbaked).

Mrs. Emil Koehn, Montezuma, Kans.

1880 Chocolate Spice Cake

1 cup sugar	1½ tsp. cinnamon
½ cup butter	1 tsp. cloves
1 egg	1 tsp nutmeg
1½ cups flour	1 cup buttermilk
½ tsp. salt	1 tsp. soda
1 tbsp. cocoa	1 tsp. vanilla

Cream together sugar, butter and egg. Sift dry ingredients together. Dissolve soda in buttermilk and add alternately with dry ingredients to creamed mixture, beating well after each addition. Pour into greased and floured 8"x12" pan. Bake at 350° for 25-30 min. Spread icing over hot cake.

Icing

5 tbsp. butter	5 tbsp. cream
7 tbsp. brown sugar	½ cup coconut

Mix all ingredients and spread on cake. Return to oven and broil until icing bubbles and is light brown.

Karen Gearig, Ithaca, Mich.

Spice Cakes

Brown Sugar Spice Cake

1 cup shortening	1 tsp. soda
2 cups brown sugar	1 tsp. baking powder
2½ cups sifted flour	1 tsp. cloves
1 cup sour milk	1 tsp. cinnamon
½ tsp. salt	2 egg whites

Cream shortening and sugar together. Sift flour, salt, soda, baking powder and spices three or four times. Add dry ingredients alternately with sour milk to creamed mixture, fold in 2 stiffly beaten egg whites and pour into 13"x9" pan. Spread topping over cake batter and bake in moderate oven 350° for one hr.

Topping

Beat 1 cup brown sugar into 2 stiffly beaten egg whites; fold in ½ cup nut meats.

Mrs. Aaron Koehn, De Ridder, La.

Mocha Spice Cake

(Quick Method)

2 cups flour	1 cup white sugar
3 tsp. baking powder	½ cup brown sugar
1 tsp salt	½ cup shortening, melted
1 tsp. cinnamon	1 cup milk
1 tsp. allspice	2 eggs
½ tsp. cloves	1 tsp. vanilla
½ tsp. nutmeg	

Sift flour and spices; add sugar, shortening and ¾ cup milk. Beat for 2 min. with electric mixer at low speed. Add remaining milk, eggs and vanilla, beat two more min. Bake in two floured 8 in. pans at 350° for 30-35 min. Frost with fluffy Mocha Frosting.

Mamie Schmidt

Quick Fix Spice Cake With Topping

To any white or yellow ready cake mix, add:

½ tsp. nutmeg	½ tsp. cinnamon
½ tsp. cloves	½ cup nut meats

Topping

1 cup graham cracker crumbs	½ cup melted butter
	¾ cup brown sugar

Mix and crumble on top of cake batter, and bake as directed.

Mrs. Barney Smith, Ardmore, Okla.

Nut Spice Cake

1½ cups sugar	1 cup sour milk
½ cup butter or shortening	⅔ cup raisin juice
2 eggs, beaten	1 cup raisins
1 tsp. soda	1 tsp. cloves
1 tsp. baking powder	2 tsp. cinnamon
3 cups flour, sifted	1 tsp. vanilla
½ cup nuts	¼ tsp. salt

Add 1 cup water to raisins and boil 5 min. set aside to cool. Cream shortening, sugar, and beaten eggs. Sift together, flour, baking powder, cloves, cinnamon and salt. Add to creamed mixture alternately with raisin juice and sour milk, to which 1 tsp. soda has been added. Add vanilla, raisins, and nuts, blend thoroughly.

Bake at 350° for 20-30 min.   (Makes a large loaf cake or three layer cakes.)

Mrs. A. R. Toews, Windom, Kans.

Spice Cake (1)

3 eggs
1 cup brown sugar
1 cup white sugar
¾ cup vegetable oil
¼ cup margarine
1 cup buttermilk
½ cup raisins
¾ cup walnuts

2½ cups flour
½ tsp. baking powder
1 tsp. soda
½ tsp. cloves
½ tsp. cinnamon
½ tsp. nutmeg
½ tsp. allspice
½ tsp. salt

Beat eggs, add sugar and shortening, sift flour with baking powder, soda, spices and salt. Add dry ingredients and buttermilk alternately to egg mixture. Add raisins and walnuts. Pour in 8"x13" pan and bake at 300°, 55 min.

Topping

½ cup brown sugar
4 tbsp. butter

3 tbsp. flour

Moisten with cream, spread on baked cake, place in broiler to brown.

Nellie Eck, Winton, Calif.

Spice Cake (2)

Have ingredients at room temperature
Sift into bowl:

2 cups flour
1½ cups sugar
3½ tsp. baking powder
⅛ tsp. salt

1 tsp. cinnamon
¼ tsp. cloves
½ tsp. nutmeg

Add: beat 2 min.

½ cup shortening
1 cup milk

1 tsp. vanilla

Add and beat 2 min. more:

2 eggs

Bake in loaf pan at 350° for 40-45 min.

Mrs. Marvin Koehn, Copeland, Kans.

Spice Surprise Cake

½ cup butter or oleo	1 tsp. cloves
1½ cups brown sugar	½ tsp. nutmeg
2 egg yolks	1½ cups sour cream
2 cups flour	1 cup raisins
1 tsp. soda	½ cup chopped nut meats
½ tsp. salt	2 egg whites
2 tsp. cinnamon	

Cream butter and sugar thoroughly. Add egg yolks one at a time, beating well after each addition. Sift dry ingredients and spices; add to creamed mixture alternately with sour cream. Add raisins and nuts. Beat egg whites until stiff, fold into creamed mixture. Bake at 350° for 30-40 min. Frost with Browned Butter frosting.

Mrs. Melvin Penner, Isabella, Okla.

Miscellaneous Cakes

Apple Cake

2 cups sugar	1 tsp. cinnamon
⅔ cup shortening	½ tsp. salt
2 cups flour	2 eggs
1½ tsp. soda	4 cups apples, peeled and sliced
1½ tsp. nutmeg	½ cup nuts, chopped

Cream shortening and sugar. Sift together dry ingredients and add to creamed mixture. Add beaten eggs, apples and nuts. Beat until thoroughly blended; bake in greased pan at 350° for 35 min.

Sauce

½ cup butter	1 cup sugar
½ cup cream	1 tsp. vanilla

Mix ingredients and boil 1½ min. Serve over cake.

Gwendene Holdeman, Hesston, Kans.
Mrs. Elmer Kane, Winton, Calif.

Applesauce Cake

2 cups flour	1 tsp. cinnamon
1 tsp. soda	½ cup butter or oleo
¼ tsp. salt	1 cup sugar
¼ tsp. cloves	1 egg, unbeaten
½ tsp. nutmeg	1 cup raisins
1 cup nuts, chopped	1 cup thick applesauce

Sift flour, measure. Add soda, salt and spices, sift together three times. Cream butter, gradually adding sugar, beat until light and fluffy. Add egg and beat well. Add nuts and raisins. Add flour alternately with applesauce. Bake at 350° in 8"x4" loaf pan. (For two ten-in. layers take recipe 1½ times).

Mrs. Andy Troyer, Uniontown, Ohio

Autumn Surprise Cake

2 cups unpeeled, chopped apples	1½ cups sifted flour
1 cup sugar	½ cup cooking oil
1 tsp. soda	1 tsp. vanilla
½ tsp. salt	½ cup chopped nuts
1 egg, beaten	1 cup flaked coconut

Mix apples and sugar. Let stand until juice forms. Sift flour, soda, and salt together. Add apples and remaining ingredients; mix thoroughly. Pour into greased, floured 8 in. sq. pan. Bake at 350° for 40-45 min. Frost with caramel frosting.

Mrs. Norman Wenger, Hesston, Kans.

Banana Cake (1)

1½ cups sifted cake flour	¾ cup mashed bananas
¾ cup brown sugar	½ cup buttermilk
¾ tsp. salt	1 tsp. vanilla
¾ tsp. baking powder	2 eggs, separated
¾ tsp. soda	¼ cup brown sugar
¼ cup liquid shortening	

Mix dry ingredients; add shortening, bananas, vanilla and ¼ cup buttermilk. Beat for one min. Add egg yolks and remaining buttermilk; beat for one min. more. Beat egg whites, add brown sugar and fold into first mixture. Bake at 350° for 40 min.

Mrs. Roland Barkman, Steinbach, Man.

Banana Cake (2)

2 cups cake flour
2 tsp. baking powder
1 tsp. soda
¾ tsp. salt
1⅓ cups sugar
½ cup oleo

½ cup sour milk
1 tsp. vanilla
1 cup mashed ripe bananas
½ cup chopped walnuts
2 eggs (unbeaten)

Cream oleo, add sifted dry ingredients, add ¼ cup milk and mashed bananas, beat 2 min. Add eggs, nuts and remaining milk, beat one min. more. Bake at 375° for 25 min. or until done.

Mrs. Dale Schmidt, Plains, Kans.

Banana Nut Cake (1)

2½ cups sifted cake flour
3 tsp. baking powder
¼ tsp. salt
⅔ cup butter
1½ cups sugar

3 eggs
2 bananas
½ cup buttermilk
1 cup nut meats
1 tsp. vanilla

Cream butter, sugar and egg yolks. Sift dry ingredients three times. Add to creamed mixture alternately with mashed bananas; add buttermilk, vanilla and nutmeats. Fold in stiffly beaten egg whites. Bake at 350° for 30 min.

Mrs. Robert Boehs, Goltry, Okla.

Banana Nut Cake (2)

2½ cups flour
1⅔ cups sugar
1¼ tsp. baking powder
1½ tsp. soda
1 tsp. salt

⅓ cup buttermilk
⅔ cup shortening, melted
1¼ cups mashed bananas
2 eggs, beaten
⅔ cup nuts, chopped

Sift together dry ingredients, add buttermilk, shortening and bananas. Beat 2 min. Add eggs and nuts. Beat 2 min. more. Bake at 350° for 30-35 min. in loaf pan.

Mrs. James Koehn, Livingston, Calif.

Banana Nut Cup Cakes

⅓ cup shortening
1 tsp. vanilla

⅔ cup sugar
1⅓ cups flour

1 tsp. baking powder
½ tsp. nutmeg (optional)
½ tsp soda
½ tsp. salt

¼ tsp. cloves (optional)
¾ cup mashed bananas
¼ cup nuts

Thoroughly cream shortening, vanilla and sugar. Add sifted flour, baking powder, salt and spices. Mix well. Add bananas and nuts. Bake at 375° for 20 min. Yields: 1 doz. cup cakes.

Mrs. Eugene Schmidt

Banana Spice Cake

2½ cups flour
½ tsp. soda
⅛ tsp. cloves
½ tsp. nutmeg
1½ cups sugar
1 tsp. vanilla

2½ tsp. baking powder
¾ tsp. salt
1½ tsp. cinnamon
½ cup shortening
2 eggs
1½ cups mashed bananas

Sift together flour, baking powder, soda, salt, and spices. Beat shortening until creamy, add sugar and continue beating. Add eggs one at a time beating after each addition until fluffy, stir in vanilla and add flour alternately with bananas. Pour into two well greased cake pans. Bake at 375° for 25 min.

Mrs. Robert Koehn, Montezuma, Kans.

Carrot Cake (1)

3 cups flour
2 cups sugar
2 tsp. cinnamon
1 tsp. salt
1 tsp. soda

1½ cups Wesson oil
2 cups grated carrots
1—14 oz. can crushed pineapple
1 tsp. vanilla
3 eggs

Sift dry ingredients, add oil, carrots, pineapple, vanilla, and eggs. Pour into 2 greased, floured loaf pans. Bake 40 min. in 350° oven, (325° in pyrex pans). Very good for freezing. Frost with Broiled Icing.

Mrs. Franklin Nichols, Greensburg, Kans.
Mrs. F. P. Schmidt, Chickasha, Okla.

Carrot Cake (2)

2 cups flour
2 tsp. soda
2 tsp. cinnamon
4 eggs
2 cups sugar

1½ cups Wesson oil
2 tbsp. grated orange peel
3 cups grated carrots
1 cup chopped dates
1 cup walnut nut meats
1 tsp. vanilla

Sift dry ingredients, add dates and nuts. Add grated carrots and orange peel. Beat eggs well, gradually add sugar, beat until creamy and add Wesson oil. Gradually add dry ingredients. Mix well, add vanilla. Fold in grated carrots and orange peel. Bake in well greased floured layer pans at 350° for 45 to 55 min.

Mrs. Art Friesen, Atwater, Calif.

Date and Walnut Cake

1 tbsp. butter
1 cup sugar
1 tsp. salt
1 egg
1½ cups flour

1 cup hot water
1 cup chopped dates
1 cup black walnuts
1 tsp. soda

Cream butter and sugar, add egg. Dissolve soda in hot water and pour over dates, which have been cut fine. Combine remaining ingredients. Bake in greased and floured layer pans. Bake at 375° for 25 min.

Mrs. Carl Dirks, Halstead, Kans.

Fresh Apple Cake

1 cup sugar
¼ cup shortening, soft
1 egg
2 or 3 med. unpeeled apples, grated
1 cup flour

1 tsp. baking soda
½ tsp. cinnamon
½ tsp. nutmeg
½ cup coarsely chopped walnuts
½ cup raisins

Mix thoroughly and pour into a greased and floured loaf pan. Bake 30 min. at 350°. Serve warm with whipped cream.

Irene Eicher, Ithaca, Mich.

Date Cake

1 cup butter
1½ cups brown sugar
½ cup walnuts, chopped
½ tsp. soda dissolved in
1 cup hot water

2 tsp. baking powder
3 eggs
1½ cups fine cut dates
2 cups flour

Pour hot water and soda over dates. Cool. Cream butter and sugar; add eggs. Sift baking powder with flour and add alternately with date mixture. Bake at 350° about ½ hr. Top with Brown Sugar Frosting.

1 cup brown sugar
½ cup sweet cream

Butter size of walnut
1 tsp. vanilla

Boil until soft ball forms in cold water. Beat until creamy.

Mrs. Catherine Penner, Giroux, Man.

Mother's Apple Cake

2 apples, cut fine
½ cup lard or oleo
½ cup sugar
½ cup corn syrup

1 cup raisins
1 tsp. cinnamon
1 cup coffee
⅛ tsp. salt

Bring to a boil and cook until apples are done. Cool until lukewarm. Add 2 cups sifted flour, and 1 tsp. soda. Bake at 350° until done, approximately 35 min. Ice with Carmel Icing.

Mrs. Clarence Schneider, Hesston, Kans.

Maraschino Cherry Cake

2¼ cups cake flour
3 tsp. baking powder
½ cup shortening
¼ cup maraschino cherry
  juice
⅔ cup egg whites—unbeaten

1⅓ cups sugar
1 tsp. salt
½ cup milk
16 maraschino cherries (cut
  in pieces)
½ cup nuts, chopped

Sift dry ingredients into mixing bowl; add shortening, juice, and milk. Beat vigorously for 2 min. Add egg whites, beat 2 more min. Fold in nuts. Pour batter into two 9" layer pans. Bake at 350° for 30 min.

Mrs. Glen Wedel, Durham, Kans.
Mrs. Ben Hiebert

Date Oatmeal Cake

1 cup quick cooking rolled
oats
1 cup dates, cut in pieces
1¾ cups boiling water
1 cup firmly packed, brown
sugar
1 cup white sugar

¾ cup shortening
3 eggs
2 cups sifted flour
2 tsp. baking powder
½ tsp. salt
1 tsp. baking soda

Pour hot water over oats and dates; let stand 20 min. Cream shortening, sugar and eggs. Stir in oatmeal mixture. Sift together dry ingredients. Add to creamed mixture. Bake in floured 13"x9" pan for 45 to 50 min. at 350°. Frost with Lemon Butter Cream frosting.

Mrs. Dan P. Koehn, Montezuma, Kans.

Fruit Cocktail Cake

2 eggs
1½ cups sugar
1 lb. can fruit cocktail

2 cups flour
1 tsp. soda
½ tsp. salt

Beat eggs and sugar until lemon colored. Add and mix well; flour, soda, salt, and cocktail. Pour into greased 9"x12" pan. Sprinkle with ½ cup brown sugar and ½ cup nuts. Bake at 350° about 35 min. Frost cake while hot.

Frosting

1 cup sugar
½ cup oleo

½ cup cream or condensed
milk
1 cup coconut

Boil 2½ to 3 min. Add coconut and mix. Let cool and then beat well.

Mrs. Ransom Wiebe, Durham, Kans.
Mrs. Floyd Nightengale, Huron, S. Dak.

Grandma's Applesauce Cake

2½ cups hot applesauce
(fresh)
2 cups sugar
1 cup shortening
1 tsp. each: allspice, cinnamon, and cloves

4 cups sifted flour
1 cup nuts
2 tsp. soda
1 cup raisins
1 cup dates (chopped)
½ tsp. salt

Cream shortening and sugar well. Add soda to hot applesauce and mix to creamed sugar. Slowly beat in other ingredients mixing well. Bake in 325° oven in large loaf pan or Angel Food Cake pan for 1 hr. or slightly longer until straw inserted comes out clean. This makes a wonderful base for fruit cakes. Decorate with cherries and whole nuts. Serves 16-20.

Mrs. Katherine (Mininger) Fricke, Montezuma, Kans.

Nobby Apple Cake

3 tbsp. butter
1 cup sugar
1 beaten egg
½ tsp. cinnamon
½ tsp. nutmeg
1 tsp. vanilla
½ tsp. salt
1 tsp. soda
1 cup sifted flour
3 cups diced apples
½ cup chopped nuts

Cream shortening and sugar. Add egg and beat well. Sift dry ingredients together; add to creamed mixture. Stir in apples, nuts and vanilla. Bake at 350° for 40 to 45 min.

Mrs. William Seiler, Carson City, Mich.

Oatmeal Cake (1)

1 cup rolled oats
1¼ cups boiling water
1 cup sugar
1 cup brown sugar
½ cup margarine
2 eggs
1⅓ cups flour, unsifted
1 tsp. soda
½ tsp. salt
½ tsp. cinnamon
½ cup broken nut meats
1 tsp. vanilla

Stir oats in water, remove from heat, cover; let stand 20 min. Cream sugar, brown sugar, margarine, and eggs. Add sifted dry ingredients and nut meats. Add vanilla. Bake at 350° for 30 or 40 min.

Topping

6 tbsp. oleo
1 cup brown sugar
¼ cup canned milk
½ cup coconut
½ cup broken nut meats

Cook over low heat until it bubbles. Spread on baked cake. Return to oven until it bubbles again.

Mrs. Alonzo Wesenberg, Ithaca, Mich.
Mrs. Georgorene Unruh, Montezuma, Kans.
Mrs. Lee Koehn, Winton, Calif.

Oatmeal Cake (2)

1 cup boiling water
1 cup quick rolled oats
2 unbeaten eggs
1 cup brown sugar
½ cup white sugar
½ cup shortening
½ cup chopped nuts

½ cup chopped dates or
  raisins
1 cup flour, sifted
1 tsp. soda
1 tsp. salt
½ tsp. cinnamon
½ tsp. nutmeg

Pour boiling water over rolled oats, cool to lukewarm. Mix eggs, brown sugar, white sugar, shortening, nuts, and dates. Sift together flour, soda, salt, cinnamon, and nutmeg. Stir the dry ingredients into the date-nut mixture and add the oatmeal. Bake in loaf pan at 350° for 60 min.

Mrs. Clarence Penner, Iroqouis, S. Dak.

Pineapple Upside Down Cake (1)

¼ cup softened oleo
¼ cup light brown sugar
½ cup corn syrup

12 slices well drained pineapple
1 pkg. white or yellow cake
  mix

Blend oleo, sugar, syrup in 13"x9" pan. Arrange pineapple over mixture. Heat in oven for 15 min. Meanwhile, mix cake batter as directed on pkg. Remove pan from oven, pour batter carefully over fruit. Bake 45 to 55 min. at temperature directed on cake mix pkg. Remove from oven; invert onto rack. Let stand 1 min.; remove from pan. May be served with whipped cream.

Evelyn Friesen, Glenn, Calif.

Pineapple Upside Down Cake (2)

½ cup butter
1 cup brown sugar
  sliced pineapple circles
3 eggs, separated

1 cup sugar
5 tbsp. pineapple juice
1 cup flour
1 tsp. baking powder

Melt butter; add brown sugar and heat. Spread evenly into oblong baking pan. Place circles of pineapple over butter and sugar mixture, covering bottom of pan; place half circles all around sides. Beat egg yolks; add sugar and pineapple juice.

Sift flour and baking powder. Fold in stiffly beaten egg whites. Pour batter over pineapple in baking pan and bake at 350° for 45 min to 1 hr.

Mrs. Monroe Holdeman, Harrison, Mich.

Poor Man's Cake

3 cups sugar	2 heaping tsp. soda
3 cups water	2 tsp. cinnamon
1 lb. raisins	2 tsp. nutmeg
1 cup nuts	1 tsp. salt
5 cups flour	1 cup lard

Mix sugar, water, lard, and raisins together and boil 5 min. Cool to lukewarm; add flour, soda, cinnamon, nutmeg, salt and nut meats. Bake in oven 320° for 1¼ hrs.

Mrs. Ben Friesen, Wauseon, Ohio

Pumpkin Cake

1 Box Honey Spice Cake Mix.
Follow directions on box except use ½ as much water as directed.

Add:
    1 cup pumpkin
    1 cup chopped dates
    1 cup chopped nuts
Bake in two 9 in. layer pans.

Mrs. Delton Wedel, Copeland, Kans.

Tomato Fruit Cake

2 cups flour	2 tsp. baking powder
1 cup sugar	½ cup shortening
1 tsp. cinnamon	1 cup walnuts
1 tsp. nutmeg	1 cup raisins
½ tsp. cloves	1 pkg. candied fruit
1 tsp. soda	1 can tomato soup

Mix sugar, shortening and tomato soup. Sift flour, spices, soda, and baking powder. Add to first mixture; add raisins, walnuts, and candied fruit. Bake 45 min, at 350°.

Mrs. Frances Becker, Galva, Kans.

Prune Cake (1)

2 cups sugar	1 tsp. salt
1 cup Mazola oil	½ tsp. cinnamon
3 eggs	½ tsp. cloves
1 cup sour milk	½ tsp. nutmeg
2 cups flour	½ tsp. allspice
2 tsp. soda	

Mix until smooth; add 1 cup chopped nuts (black walnuts preferred), and 1 cup cooked finely cut prunes. Bake in 9x13-in. pan. Bake at 375° for 35 min.

Icing

1 small pkg. Philadelphia Cream Cheese. Blend in powdered sugar until of spreading consistency. Cream until smooth.

Mrs. Carl Dirks, Halstead, Kans.
Mrs. Wanda Unruh

Prune Cake (2)

½ cup shortening	¼ tsp. salt
1 cup sugar	2 tsp. soda
2 eggs	⅔ cup sour milk
1½ cups sifted flour	1 tsp. vanilla
½ tsp. cinnamon	1 cup cooked, pitted, mashed
½ tsp. cloves	prunes

Cream shortening and sugar; add eggs beating well. Sift dry ingredients together and add to creamed mixture alternately with sour milk. Add vanilla and prunes. Bake at 350° for 25 to 30 min.

Mrs. Jake Smith, Walnut Hill, Fla.
Mrs. Jay Diller, Walnut Hill, Fla.

Upside Down Cherry Cake

1 pkg. cake mix, white or yellow	1 can of cherry pie mix
	¾ cup oleo

Spread cherries evenly into 7"x11" floured cake pan; pour prepared cake mix over cherries. Melt oleo and spread over the cake batter. Bake at 350° for 30 min.

Mrs. Eli Johnson, Rich Hill, Mo.

Tomato Soup Cake

¾ cup shortening	2 tsp. baking powder
1½ cups sugar	1 tsp. cloves
1 cup tomato soup	1½ tsp. cinnamon
(condensed)	½ tsp. nutmeg
¾ cup water	¾ tsp. salt
3 cups flour	1 cup raisins or dates
1 tsp. soda	1 cup nuts

Cream sugar and shortening; add soup and water. Mix in remaining ingredients and bake in tube pan for 1 hr. at 350°. (Improved by freezing.) Mrs. Adam J. Schmidt, Montezuma, Kans.

Rhubarb Shortcake

½ cup butter	½ tsp. salt
1 cup brown sugar	2 tsp. baking powder
2 cups rhubarb, chopped	1 tsp. vanilla
¾ cup sugar	1 egg
1½ cups flour	½ cup milk

Melt butter and brown sugar; pour into 13"x9" baking pan, add chopped rhubarb. Mix the remaining ingredients and spoon over rhubarb mixture. Bake at 375° for 40 min.

Mrs. Jacob Hochstetler, Apple Creek, Ohio

Strawberry Cake

1 pkg. white cake mix	½ cup Wesson oil
1-3 oz. pkg. strawberry jello	3 tbsp. flour
½ cup water	4 eggs
½ pkg. (10 oz. size) frozen strawberries	

Blend all ingredients in large mixer bowl. Beat 4 min. at med. speed with electric mixer. Bake at 350° about 30 min.

Frosting

½ pkg. (10 oz. size) frozen strawberries	¼ cup butter or oleo

Blend:
Add powdered sugar until of right consistency to spread.

Mrs. D. C. Buller, Halstead, Kans.

Strawberry Shortcake

1½ cups cake flour	6 eggs
1½ tsp. baking powder	1 cup, plus 2 tbsp. sugar
½ tsp. salt	1 tsp. lemon extract

Beat eggs until foamy, gradually add sugar, beating until mixture is thick and stands in soft peaks, (this is important.) Fold in extract and sifted dry ingredients, adding small amount at a time, folding in carefully each time. Pour into three greased and wax paper lined pans. Bake at 350° for 12-15 min. Remove layers from pans immediately and remove wax paper. May be served with fruits or whipped cream.

Mrs. Mahlon Hostetler, Jeromesville, Ohio

Whipped Prune Cake

1 cup finely cut, cooked prunes	3 tsp. baking powder
2 eggs, separated	1 tsp. salt
1½ cups sugar	¼ cup vegetable oil
2¼ cups cake flour	1 cup milk
	2 tsp. grated lemon rind

Heat oven to 350°. Grease and flour two pans. In small bowl, beat prunes, egg whites and ¼ cup sugar until stiff, to form prune whip. In large bowl, mix flour, remaining sugar, baking powder, and salt. Add vegetable oil, ⅔ cup milk, and lemon rind; beat 1 min, at med. speed on mixer or 150 strokes by hand. Scrape bottom and sides of bowl constantly. Add remaining milk and egg yolks; beat one more min. scraping bowl frequently. Fold in prune whip. Pour into prepared pans. Bake 35 min. Fill and frost with 1½ cups whipping cream, whipped. Decorate with dried prune halves.

May Koehn, Winton, Calif.

Yum Yum Gems or Cake

1 cup shortening	1 tsp. cloves
2 cups brown sugar	2 cups seedless raisins
2 eggs	4 cups flour
2 cups sour milk	2 tsp. soda
2 tsp. cinnamon	1 cup nuts, chopped fine
2 tsp. nutmeg	1 tsp. vanilla

Cream shortening, sugar, and eggs. Sift dry ingredients together and add alternately with sour milk. Add nuts and raisins. Bake in 350° oven for 30 or 35 min.

Mrs. Clarence Schneider, Ithaca, Mich.

Fruit Cakes

Applesauce Fruit Cake

2 cups unsweetened
  applesauce
¾ cup butter
1 egg
2 cups sugar
3 cups flour
2 tsp. soda

1 tsp. allspice
2 cups cooked raisins
20 orange slice candies, cut
  into pieces
2 cups pecan meats
2 cups dates
1 bottle maraschino cherries

Dissolve one teaspoon soda in a little water. Chop fruits and combine all ingredients. Bake 1½ hr. in 250° to 300° oven.

Nina Holdeman, Hesston, Kans.

Brazil Nut Fruit Cake

¾ cup flour
¾ cup sugar
½ tsp. baking powder
½ tsp. salt
1 tsp. vanilla
½ cup dried apricots, if
  desired

3 eggs
3 cups whole Brazil nuts
1 cup Maraschino cherries
  drained
2 cups pitted dates
1 cup mixed black and white
  figs

Grease and line one 9x5x3 in. loaf pan with waxed paper. Measure first four ingredients into sifter. Place all fruits and nuts in large bowl. Sift dry ingredients over fruits and nuts; mix until well coated. Beat eggs until foamy. Add vanilla and stir into fruit mixture until well mixed. Pour into pan. Bake at 300° for 1¾ hr. Cool on wire rack for 15 min. Remove from pan; pull off waxed paper and cool. Wrap in cloth soaked in orange juice and then in foil. Place in refrigerator or freezer.

Mrs. Willard Schmidt, Hesston, Kans.

Christmas Cake

2 cups flour	2 cups rolled oats
1 heaping tsp. soda	1½ cups brown sugar
1 tsp. salt	1 cup melted butter

Mix and press down in 12x8 in pan. Put on topping.

Topping

2 eggs, well beaten	1 cup brown sugar

Beat together until light, than mix in by hand:

1 cup shredded coconut	1 cup finely cut, red and
1 cup crushed walnuts	green cherries

Put on top of first mixture. Bake in slow oven (325°) for 45 min.

Miss Elaine Barkman, Steinbach, Man.

Dark Fruit Cake

2 cups sugar (white or brown)	1 lb. butter
	12 eggs

Cream butter; add sugar. Add eggs one at a time, beating well after each addition.

	¼ cup orange juice
¼ cup strawberry jam	2 tsp. vanilla

Mix together and add to creamed mixture.

3½ cups flour	1 tsp. nutmeg
½ tsp. salt	½ each of all spice, ginger
2 tsp. cinnamon	and cloves

Sift flour, measure, add spices and add to creamed mixture.

2 lbs. raisins (1 lb. light sultanas and 1 lb. dark seedless raisins

½ lb. currants	½ lb. green glazed cherries
½ lb. glazed pineapple	½ cup dates
1 lb. red glazed cherries	½ cup blanched almonds

Wash and thoroughly dry raisins and currants. Flour fruit and nuts with ½ cup flour and add to batter. Line pans with brown buttered paper. Add batter and bake at 275° for 4 to 4½ hrs.

Leanna Friesen, Ste. Anne, Man.

Coconut Fruit Cake

1 lb. dates, chopped
½ lb. candied pineapple
  (diced)
1 pkg. coconut

3 cups pecans
½ lb. candied whole red
  cherries
2 cans sweetened condensed
  milk

Mix fruits, nuts, and coconut. Add milk and mix well. Line two bread pans with wax paper. Pour mixture into pans. Bake at 275° for 1½ hrs.

Mrs. Edward Schneider, Bartow, Ga.

Extra Special Fruit Cake

1 lb. brazil nuts (1¾ cups)
1 lb. walnuts (2¼ cups)
1 lb. dates (3 cups)
1 tsp. baking powder
4 eggs

1½ cups sugar
2 med. bottles (3 or 3¾ oz.)
  of maraschino cherries (1
  red—1 green)
1½ cups cake flour

Pour sugar over nuts, dates, and cherries that have been left whole. Sift together cake, flour, salt, and baking powder. Add cherry juice. Separate the eggs and add beaten egg yolks. Fold in stiffly beaten egg whites last. Bake at 325° for 1 hr. and 15 min. Makes 2 loaf sized cakes.

Adella Jantz, Hesston, Kans.

Holiday Cake

1 cup shortening
2 cups sugar
1½ cups applesauce
1 cup chopped dates
1 cup chopped nuts
½ cup chopped, candied
  cherries
2 cups buttermilk or sour
  milk

1 tsp. salt
2 tsp. cinnamon
2 tsp. allspice
3 tbsp. cocoa
2 tsp. soda
3½ cups flour

Cream shortening and sugar. Add applesauce, fruits and nuts; blend thoroughly. Sift together dry ingredients. Add flour mixture alternately with buttermilk. Bake at 250° to 300°. This cake can be made ahead of time. To improve flavor wrap in Saran or foil, keep a week or two.

Mrs. Frank A. Koehn, Fairview, Okla.

Plain Fruit Cake

1 cup sugar	1 tsp. soda
1 cup water	1 tsp. baking powder
1½ cup shortening	1 tsp. cinnamon
1 cup white raisins	1 tsp. cloves
1½ cup nuts	⅛ tsp. salt
1½ cup mixed, candied fruit	2 cups sifted flour

Combine sugar, water, shortening, raisins, nuts and mixed fruit; boil together five min. Cool. Sift dry ingredients together and stir into cooled mixture. Pour into greased 5x4x9 inch loaf pan and bake 1½ hrs. at 300°.

Mrs. Wilbur L. Koehn, Cimmaron, Kans.

Unbaked Fruit Cake

1½ lbs. graham crackers	18 to 20 marshmallows
2 cups walnuts	12 candy orange slices cut in-
1 can milk (14½ oz.)	to small pieces
½ lb. dates	1 lb. jar mixed candied fruit
	1 lb. raisins

Heat milk and marshmallows in double boiler until melted; add crushed graham crackers. Add fruits and nuts, mix well. Put mixture into loaf pan and refrigerate.

Yvonne Schmidt, Winton, Calif.

White Fruit Cake (1)

¾ lb. butter or oleo	2 cups sifted flour
2 cups sugar	1 lb. white raisins
6 eggs	1 lb. pecans, chopped
2 oz. lemon extract	

Cream butter and sugar; add egg yolks one at a time and lemon extract. Continue beating and gradually add flour. Place raisins in sieve; run hot water over them and dry. Add raisins and nuts to batter. Fold in stiffly beaten egg whites and pour into two wax paper lined loaf pans. Bake in 250° oven for 2 to 2½ hrs.

Mrs. Willard Dirks, Greensburg, Kans.

White Fruit Cake (2)

1 cup butter or margarine
1½ cups white sugar
6 eggs
½ cup light syrup
3 cups flour
1 tsp. soda in ½ cup juice
¾ tsp. salt

1 cup golden raisins
1 cup broken nut meats
1 cup dates, cut up
1 cup pineapple, grapes, red and green maraschino cherries mixed to equal 1 cup
1 diced apple

Cream butter; add sugar, beaten eggs and syrup. Add 1½ cups flour alternately with the juice in which soda has been dissolved. Pour batter over fruit and nuts which have been mixed with part of the flour (1½ cups). Mix well and bake in 250° oven for 1½ hrs.

Mrs. John T. Friesen, Langdon, North Dak.

CANDIES

Candies

Boston Cream Candy

2 cups sugar   ½ cup dark syrup
1 cup cream or evaporated
   milk

Mix and boil about ½ hour to hard boil stage, (250°). Add ½ cup nuts and 1 cup coconut. Pour into greased pan and cut when cool.

Mrs. Herby Wenger, Newton, Kans.

Peanut Brittle Candy

1 cup sugar   1½ cups raw peanuts
¼ cup water   1 tsp. soda
½ cup light corn syrup   1 tsp. vanilla
½ tsp. butter

Combine sugar, syrup and water in a skillet and cook until it forms a hard ball when tested in cold water. Add butter and peanuts; cook until mixture begins to turn a light brown. Continue stirring so that peanuts will cook and to prevent scorching. Remove from heat; add soda and vanilla, stirring rapidly. Pour onto a well buttered cookie sheet. Tip cookie sheet back and forth to spread evenly. Cool, break into pieces.

Peanut Brittle

1 cup sugar   1 tsp. butter
1½ cups white syrup   1 tsp. vanilla
½ cup water   1 tsp. soda
1 cup raw peanuts

Cook first three ingredients to soft ball stage (236°); add peanuts and cook to hard crack (295°). Remove from heat; add butter, vanilla and soda. Stir vigorously and pour onto greased cookie sheet. Cool; break into pieces.

Mrs. Obed Johnson, Halstead, Kans.

Peanut (or Almond) Brittle Deluxe

2 cups sugar
1 cup corn syrup
¼ cup water
1½ cups salted peanuts or almonds

2 tbsp. butter or margarine
1 tsp. vanilla
2 tsp. soda

In a 3-qt. saucepan combine sugar, corn syrup and water; mix well. Cook over medium heat to 285°, stirring often to prevent scorching. Add peanuts and butter. Stir constantly and cook to hard crack stage (295°). Remove from heat. Add vanilla and soda, stirring in well; work quickly. Pour onto large, well-greased cookie sheet. Spread out with spatula as thin as possible. As soon as candy begins to set, loosen, flip it over; stretch and pull thin as possible. When cold, break into pieces. Makes about 2 lbs.

Myrtle Giesbrecht, Winton, Calif.
LaVerna Peaster, Winton, Calif.

Peanut Butter Candy

2 cups sugar
½ cream
½ cup milk
2 heaping tbsp. peanut butter

2 tbsp. white corn syrup
2 tbsp. butter
1 tsp. vanilla

Mix sugar, cream, milk, and syrup in saucepan. Boil to about 236° or 238°. Remove from heat, add butter, vanilla, and peanut butter. Stir. Pour into buttered pan.

Mrs. Verle Peters, McDavid, Fla.

Caramel Pecan Candy

1½ cups white corn syrup
5 cups white sugar
3 cups sweet cream

1 cup pecans, coarsely chopped
2 tsp. vanilla

Cook syrup, sugar, and cream slowly until soft ball stage, when tested in cold water. Remove from heat, add vanilla and beat until no longer glossy. Add nuts and quickly pour into buttered pans, spread and cool. Yield: 3 lbs. candy.

Mrs. Perry Johnson, Galva, Kans.

Very Good Buttermilk Candy

2 cups white sugar
1 cup buttermilk
2 tbsp. butter
1 tsp. vanilla

½ tsp. soda, added to buttermilk
1½ tbsp. white corn syrup
1 cup nuts

Cook together over low heat until it forms a soft ball when tested in cold water (236°). Remove from heat; add butter. Cool 10 min. Add vanilla; beat until it begins to thicken. Add nuts. Drop from teaspoon onto wax paper.

Mrs. Sam Jantz, Walnut Hill, Fla.

Creamy Caramels

2 cups sugar
⅛ tsp. salt
2 cups light corn syrup
1 tsp. vanilla

½ cup butter
2 cups half and half or light
cream

Combine sugar and corn syrup in a large heavy saucepan. Heat to boiling and cook to firm ball stage, (245°) stirring occasionally. Gradually add butter and cream slowly so mixture does not stop boiling. Continue cooking, stirring constantly, until mixture returns to 245°. (Stirring is important since mixture will scorch easily.) Remove from heat; add vanilla and mix well. Pour into buttered 9 in. sq. pan. When cool turn onto waxed paper and cut into ¾ in. squares. Wrap individually in waxed paper. Makes about two pounds.

Evelyn Friesen, Glenn, Calif.

Chocolate Caramels

2 cups sugar
1 cup brown sugar
½ to ¾ cup cocoa
1 cup light corn syrup
1 cup cream

1½ cups milk
½ cup butter
¼ tsp. salt
1½ tsp. vanilla

Combine sugars with cocoa. Add syrup, milk and cream. Cook, stirring constantly, until sugar is dissolved. Then cook slowly, stirring occasionally, until mixture forms a firm ball when tested in cold water (246°). Remove from heat; add butter, salt and vanilla. Mix well. Pour into greased pan. When cool, remove from pan, cut into cubes and wrap each piece in waxed paper.

Joyleen Nightengale, Sublette, Kans.

Caramel Nut Logs

Nougat Cream Center

3 cups sugar
1⅓ cups light corn syrup
1 cup water
2 egg whites, stiffly beaten

¼ cup melted butter
1 tsp. vanilla
⅛ tsp. salt

(For chocolate center melt 2 sq. unsweetened choc. with butter). Combine ¾ cup sugar, ⅔ cup syrup, ¼ cup water in saucepan. Stir over med. heat until sugar dissolves; boil to 238°. Pour syrup over beaten egg whites, beating constantly until cool (5 min.). Spoon into well buttered bowl, making a well in the center. Let stand while making second syrup. Combine 2¼ cup sugar, ⅔ cup syrup, ¾ cup water. Stir over med. heat until sugar is dissolved. Boil to 260°. Pour syrup into center of egg white mixture in bowl. Beat vigorously with wooden spatula until thoroughly mixed. Stir in butter, vanilla and salt; beat well. Let stand, beating occasionally, until mixture is very stiff and holds its shape. With buttered fingers press mixture evenly into 8"x8" sq. wax paper lined pan. Place in refrigerator until very firm (2 or 3 hours). Turn nougat cream out on board, remove wax paper and cut into four squares. Cut each sq. into 4 equal logs.

Caramel Coating

2 cups sugar
1¼ cups light corn syrup
1½ cups light cream

1 tsp. vanilla
¼ tsp. salt
1 lb. broken walnuts or pecans

Combine sugar, syrup and ½ cup cream in saucepan. Stir over med. heat until sugar dissolves. Boil to 236°. Add ½ cup more cream, cook again to 236°. Add remaining ½ cup cream and cook to 242°. Lower heat and stir often as caramel thickens. Remove from heat, stir in vanilla and salt. Pour into double boiler over hot water. Carefully drop log into caramel mixture. With two forks turn log to coat completely; lift and let drain slightly. Roll in shallow dish with layer of nuts, pressing carefully until covered. Wrap immediately into waxed paper, twisting ends. Store in refrigerator for 4 or 5 hrs.; cut into ½ in. slices. Yield: 4 to 5 lbs. candy.

Mrs. Paul Koehn, Halstead, Kans.

Cereal Nut Krunch

½ cup butter or oleo	2 cups Kix
1 tsp. Worcestershire sauce	2 cups Wheat Chex
½ tsp. celery salt	2 cups Rice Chex
½ tsp. onion salt	2 cups pretzels
2 cups Cheerios	1½ cups mixed salted nuts

Melt butter or oleo in 2 qt. heavy aluminum pan or roaster. Add Worcestershire Sauce and salts. Blend thoroughly. Add cereals pretzels, and nuts. Stir carefully with wooden spoon. Place in slow oven 250°. Bake 1 hr. Stirring carefully every 15 min. Remove from oven. Serve hot or cold. May be stored in air tight containers. Reheat before serving if desired.

Carnation Five-Minute Fudge

⅔ cup undiluted evaporated milk	¾ cup marshmallow creme
	½ cup chopped nuts
1⅔ cups sugar	1½ cups semi-sweet chocolate chips
1½ cups miniature marshmallows or	1 tsp. vanilla

Combine milk with sugar in sauce pan; heat to boiling. Cook 8 min., stirring constantly. Remove from heat; add marshmallows, chocolate chips and vanilla. Stir until marshmallows are melted; add nuts. Pour into buttered 8 or 9 in. pan. Cool and cut into squares.

Mrs. Marshall Harms, Atmore, Ala.

Chocolate Marshmallow Balls

4 sq. unsweetened chocolate	7 oz. evaporated milk
2 cups sugar	1 tsp. vanilla
3 tbsp. butter	

Mix and heat until chocolate is melted. Cool thoroughly.

28 graham crackers, crushed	½ cup chopped nuts, optional
½ lb. miniature marshmallows	

Combine cooled mixture with graham cracker mixture and mix well. Drop by tsp. onto wax paper and let stand over night.

Mrs. Curt Wiebe, Hillsboro, Kans.

Divinity Fudge (1)

2⅔ cups sugar
⅔ cup white syrup
½ cup water

2 eggs whites
1 tsp. vanilla
1 cup nuts

Combine sugar, syrup and water; cook together until syrup forms a hard ball when dropped into cold water (about 265°). Pour syrup slowly over the stiffly beaten egg whites. Beat until creamy, add vanilla and chopped nuts. Pour into buttered pans and cut into squares or drop from spoon onto waxed paper.

Mary Ann Friesen, Glenn, Calif.

Divinity Fudge (2)

2 cups sugar
½ cup water
½ cup light corn syrup

2 egg whites
1 tsp. vanilla
1 cup nuts

Boil sugar, water and syrup until light crack stage when tested in cold water. Pour over well beaten egg whites and continue beating. Add vanilla and nuts; drop from teaspoon onto greased waxed paper.

Mrs. Ben Hiebert

Cereal Candy

Measure into big bowl:
  5 cups cornflakes
  5 cups Rice Krispies
  1 lb. salted peanuts

Cook to soft ball stage (236°):
  1 cup white syrup
  1 cup white sugar
  1 cup cream or rich milk
  1 tsp. vanilla

Pour over cereal, and mix well.

Mrs. Noah Holdeman, Wrens. Ga.

Hard Candy

3¾ cups sugar
1¼ cups white syrup
1 cup water

1 tsp. cinnamon oil or peppermint flavoring
red or green food coloring

Boil together sugar, syrup and water until 300°, or hard crack stage when tested in cold water. Add flavoring and coloring; pour into pans dusted with powdered sugar. Cool; break into pieces.

Phyllis Boeckner, Moundridge, Kans.

Never Fail Fudge

⅓ cup butter
4½ cups sugar
1 can (14½ oz.) evaporated milk
1 cup marshmallow creme

1 bar (13 oz.) sweet chocolate, grated
2 cups chocolate chips
2 tsp. vanilla
2 cups walnuts, coarsely chopped

Combine butter, sugar and milk. Boil 5½ min. Remove from heat and add remaining ingredients except nuts. Beat until well mixed. Add nuts. Working fast pour into buttered pan. Cool until firm; then cut. Yield: 5 lbs. candy.

Mrs. Menno Dirks, Halstead, Kans.

Refrigerator Fudge

¾ cup undiluted evaporated milk
2½ cups sugar
1 6 oz. pkg. chocolate chips

⅓ cup white corn syrup
2 tbsp. butter
1 tsp. vanilla
1 cup chopped nuts

Combine milk and sugar in heavy saucepan. Cook over medium heat stirring constantly until mixture boils. Then turn heat low and cook 10 min. stirring to prevent scorching. Remove from heat; add chocolate chips, syrup, butter and vanilla. Stir until chocolate melts. Add nuts; mix and pour into buttered 8x8 in. pan and chill in refrigerator for one or two hrs.

Mrs. Wilbur Koehn

Velvety Fudge

4 cups sugar
4 tbsp. corn syrup
⅓ cup cocoa
⅛ tsp. salt

1½ cups top milk or light cream
1 tsp. vanilla
1 cup walnuts
2 tbsp. butter

Mix together first five ingredients. Heat until sugars are melted; cover and cook five minutes. Uncover and finish cooking until syrup forms hard ball when dropped into cold water (250°). Remove from heat; add butter and vanilla. Let stand until partially cooled. Beat until creamy; add nuts. Pour into buttered pan and cut into squares.

Mrs. Don Nightengale

Candied Popcorn

½ cup light corn syrup
½ cup sugar
½ tsp. salt
¼ cup cooking oil
½ cup unpopped corn

Combine first three ingredients. Preheat electric skillet to 400°. When hot add oil and popcorn. Cover and let pop until all corn is popped. Add corn syrup mixture to popcorn, tossing lightly. Turn off heat; continue stirring.

Mrs. Leo Loetkeman, Enderby, B. C.

Caramel Popcorn Balls

8 qts. popped corn
3 cups sugar
1 cup white corn syrup
1 cup cold water
2 tsp. butter
2 tsp. soda
2 tsp. vanilla

Combine sugar, syrup and water in 3 qt. saucepan. Bring to a rapid boil, stirring until sugar is dissolved. Boil to med. crack stage (285°). Add butter and continue boiling until light brown. Quickly add vanilla and soda, stirring well. Pour over popped corn.

Mrs. Harvey Dyck, Atwater, Calif.

Popcorn Balls (1)

2 cups sugar
1 cup white corn syrup
1 cup cream
2 tsp. butter
½ tsp. vinegar
⅛ tsp. salt
⅓ tsp. soda

Cook to soft ball stage (240°). Remove from heat, add soda, stirring well. Food coloring or peanuts may be added. Pour over popcorn and mix.

Mrs. Lincoln Dirks, Greensburg, Kans.

Popcorn Balls (2)

4 qts. popped corn, sprinkle with salt. Melt 1 large pkg. marshmallows and ¼ lb. butter or oleo. Pour over popped corn and make balls. Moisten hands to keep from sticking. Wrap balls in wax paper.

Mrs. Henry Buller, Montezuma, Kans.

Popcorn Balls (3)

1¼ cups white sugar
1¼ cups brown sugar
½ cup light corn syrup
⅔ cup water

1 tbsp. butter or oleo
4 qts. popped corn
1¼ tsp. salt

Heat white sugar, brown sugar, syrup and water in saucepan stirring until sugar is dissolved. Add butter or oleo and continue cooking without stirring until temperature reaches 240°. or until mixture forms a soft ball when tested in cold water. Pour popcorn into large bowl and sprinkle with salt. Pour the hot syrup over the popcorn and mix thoroughly. Shape into small balls and wrap in waxed paper.

Mrs. Lincoln Ratzlaff, Johnson, Kans.

Cracker Jacks

3 qts. popped corn
½ cup peanuts
1 cup sugar
½ cup sorghum
½ cup water

¼ tsp. salt
¼ cup butter
1 tsp. vanilla
1 tbsp. vinegar

Boil sugar, water, sorghum, and salt to soft ball stage (238°). Add vanilla, vinegar, and butter; cook to hard ball stage (266°). Pour over popcorn and peanuts; mix together.

Joyleen Nightengale, Sublette, Kans.

Karmal Popcorn

Boil to soft crack stage (275°):
½ cup water
1 cup brown sugar

1 cup white sugar
1 cup dark syrup

Remove from heat and add:
1 tsp. soda
1 tsp. vanilla

1 tbsp. butter

Stir and pour over eight qts. popped corn which has been kept hot in slow oven. Stir until all popcorn is coated. If it hardens too fast, put back into oven to melt so popped corn can be evenly coated.

Mrs. Eli Unruh, Galva, Kans.

Peanut Popcorn Brittle

1½ cups sugar
½ cup water
½ cup dark corn syrup
½ tsp. salt

4 cups popped corn
1 cup raw peanuts
2 tbsp. butter
1 tsp. vanilla

Heat sugar, syrup, water, and salt together in cast iron skillet or heavy saucepan over low heat until sugar is dissolved. Cook over moderate heat to hard crack stage (300°). Spread popcorn and peanuts on a well greased cookie sheet. Heat in oven 10 min. at 350°. When syrup is ready, add butter and vanilla; quickly pour over popcorn and peanuts. Toss and spread out very thin. Let cool. Break into pieces. Makes 1¼ lbs. brittle.

Mrs. Earl Wiggers, Hesston, Kans.

Glazed Pecans

4 tbsp. cream
2 tbsp. water
½ cup white sugar

½ tsp. vanilla
2 cups pecans

Cook until mixture forms a syrup. Pour over pecans and stir until dry.

Mrs. Sam Jantz, Walnut Hill, Fla.

Roasted Pecans

Mix 4 cups pecans and ½ cup Wesson oil; drain. Bake at 200° for 2 hrs.; sprinkle with salt, continue baking for ½ hr.

Mrs. Sam Jantz, Walnut Hill, Fla.

My Favorite Taffy

2½ cups white sugar
1½ cups white corn syrup
1 tsp. Knox gelatine

½ cup sweet milk
1 tsp. flavoring
½ inch cut from narrow end of bar of paraffin

Soften gelatine in cup with 2 tsp. cold water. Set aside. Combine sugar, syrup and milk in sauce pan and bring to rolling boil. Add gelatine and wax. Continue boiling to very hard ball (265°). Pour into greased container and place in snow or ice-water to cool.

As the mixture begins to harden around the sides, fold it into the middle. Repeat this until it is cool enough to pull. Nail a hook in a cold place. Place candy on hook; pull into a rope, twisting it as you pull. Rehook and pull longer each time, up to 12 or 15 feet. Continue to pull until rope begins to break into threads. Remove from hook, coil on board dusted with powdered sugar. (Should be made in cold weather only.) Add fine crushed nuts to mixture before pulling for extra goodness.

Audra Jantz, Livingston, Calif.

English Toffee

1 cup chopped, roasted, un-blanched almonds
1 cup butter
1 cup sugar
⅓ cup brown sugar
2 tbsp. water
½ tsp. soda
3 sq. (3 oz.) semi-sweet choc. (or 3 to 5 Hershey bars)

Sprinkle one-half the almonds into a buttered 13"x9" pan. In a 3 qt. saucepan, melt butter; add sugar and water, mix well. Bring to boiling, stirring constantly. Continue to stir, cook to 300° or until hard crack stage when tested in cold water. Remove from heat; stir in soda, working fast. Pour and spread carefully over almonds in pan; let cool about 5 min. Grate or shave chocolate over top of toffee. (Heat from candy will melt chocolate.)

May Koehn, Winton, Calif.

Sugared Walnuts

1 cup brown sugar
¼ cup evaporated milk
1 tbsp. butter or margarine
⅛ tsp. salt
½ tsp. vanilla
2 heaping cups walnut halves

Combine sugar, cream, butter and salt. Cook until (254°) or when tested in cold water forms hard ball, cook about 5 min. Remove from heat, add vanilla and nuts. Stir until mixture becomes creamy. Place on waxed paper and cool.

Mrs. Norma Koehn, Livingston, Calif.

CHEESE AND EGGS

Cheese

Cheese Ball

½ lb. Old English Cheese,
  softened
5 small pkgs. Philadelphia
  cream cheese

1 lb. Blue Cheese
dash of salt
1 small onion, grated fine

Mix all ingredients thoroughly with mixer, place in refrigerator for 2 days. Remove and form into ball, roll in ½ cup chopped parsley and ½ cup chopped pecans. Return to refrigerator and let set for 2 days. (Use as spread on crackers or bread.)

Irene Nikkel, Inman, Kans.

Macaroni Casserole

2 cups macaroni (cooked)
1 cup soft bread crumbs
1 tbsp. chopped onion
1 cup grated cheese
1½ cups milk

2 eggs, well beaten
1 tbsp. chopped green pepper
1 tbsp. butter
salt and pepper to taste

Mix all together and put in casserole. Bake at 350° for 45 min.

Mrs. Franklin Wenger, Moundridge, Kans.

Soda Cheese

1 gal. sour milk
½ tsp soda
3 tbsp. butter

1 tsp. salt
1 cup cream
1 egg, beaten

Heat sour milk to 115°. Cut through both ways with knife. Pour into cloth bag and let stand overnight. When dry, crumble cheese and stir in soda and butter. Let stand 5 hrs. Place in double boiler and heat until it melts, add cream and stir until smooth. Add salt, egg, and butter coloring. Let come to a boil and pour into dish. Serve with homemade bread and butter. (This is served for dinner when the Amish have church).

Mrs. Daniel Martin, Mifflinburg, Pa.

Glumz Wareneki

3 cups cottage cheese
⅛ tsp. salt
Mix well and set aside
Mix:
1 cup milk
1 tsp. salt

3 egg yolks
⅛ tsp. pepper

3 egg whites
Enough flour to make a firm dough

Roll out thin and cut into squares. Fill with cottage cheese mixture and press together to form triangle. Place in boiling water and boil for 5 min. Serve with following sauce recipe and fried ham.

Sauce

1½ cups cream
⅛ tsp. salt
Boil until syrupy.

2 tbsp. sugar

Jake Toews, Swalwell, Alta.

Deluxe Macaroni and Cheese

2 cups broken macaroni
2 tbsp. butter
1 tbsp. flour
¼ tsp. dry mustard
1 tsp. salt

2 cups milk
2 cups grated American cheese
½ cup buttered crumbs
⅛ tsp. pepper

Cook macaroni in 2 qts. boiling, salted water until tender, about 10 min.; drain and pour into a buttered 1½ qt. casserole. Meanwhile, melt butter in saucepan over low heat. Blend in flour and heat until bubbly. Add seasonings and milk and cook, stirring constantly until sauce boils and thickens. Remove from heat and stir in grated cheese. Pour sauce over macaroni, stirring so that all macaroni is coated with sauce. Cover with buttered crumbs and bake in a moderate oven (350°) for 20 min. Serves 6.

Mrs. Marlin Jantz, Fredonia, Kans.

Macaroni and Cheese Casserole

In greased 1½ qt. baking dish mix 3½ cups cooked macaroni, 4 oz. can mushrooms chopped and ¼ cup finely cut pimento. Stir over low heat until cheese melts. Mix ¾ cup evaporated milk, 1¼ cups mild cheese, cubed, 3 tsp. chopped onion, 2 tsp. dry mustard, 1 tsp. salt, ¼ tsp. black pepper, and 1 tsp. worcestershire sauce. Pour over macaroni, top with cheese slices and one tomato sliced. Bake at 350° for 25 min.

Mrs. J. J. Esau, Winton, Calif.

Peroga, Vereniki, Cheese Pockets, or Cheese Dumplings

Dough:

2 cups flour
2 egg whites
2 tsp. salt

1 tbsp. shortening
½ cup water or milk

Filling:

2 cups dry homemade cottage cheese preferred, commercial
may also be used
2 egg yolks   salt and pepper to taste

Roll out dough to about ⅛" thickness, cut with large round cookie cutter, (3 or 4" in diameter), place a heaping tsp. of cheese filling on each circle and bring the opposite sides together and pinch the edges together well. Drop the peroga into boiling water and cook slowly for about 10 min., drain, brown lightly in butter. Serve hot or cold with sugar and cream or syrup.

Mrs. Alfred Boehs, Isabella, Okla.

Eggs

Baked Filled Eggs and Noodles

2 cups uncooked noodles
6 eggs, hard boiled
2 tbsp. mayonnaise
1 tsp. vinegar
¼ tsp. paprika
½ tsp. dry mustard
salt and pepper to taste

4 tbsp. butter
4 tbsp flour
1 tsp. salt
2 cups milk
1 cup cracker crumbs
2 tbsp. melted butter

Drop noodles into salted boiling water and cook until tender. Drain and rinse with cold water. Place in buttered casserole or six individual baking dishes. Cut eggs in half, remove and mash yolks, mix mayonnaise, vinegar, paprika, mustard, salt and pepper. Fill egg whites and place on top of noodles.

To make white sauce, melt butter, blend in flour and salt. Add milk and cook until thickened, stirring constantly. Pour sauce over eggs and noodles. Top with crumbs mixed with melted butter. Bake in moderate oven (350°) 20 min.

Mrs. LeRoy Wedel, Goltry, Okla.

Summer Relish

6 eggs
9 fresh onions
1 tsp. salt

3 tsp. butter, melted
¼ tsp. pepper

Boil eggs about 12 min., shell, and chop coarsely. Place in warm bowl; add butter, seasoning and onions cut fine. Serve with bread and butter.

Edith Litwiller, Middleton, Mich.

Tomato Rabbit

2 tbsp. fat
½ small onion, chopped
½ cup chopped celery
½ green pepper, chopped
1½ cups grated cheese

1½ tbsp. flour
1½ cups cooked tomatoes
½ tsp. salt
2 eggs, beaten
crackers

Cook onion, celery, and pepper in fat in skillet. Blend in flour. Add tomatoes and salt. Cook until thick, stirring often. Add small amount of hot mixture to eggs and blend to mixture. Fold in cheese. Serve on crackers or toast.

Wilma Martin, Kidron, Ohio

Baked Eggs

2 tbsp. bread crumbs
1 tbsp. cream

1 egg
Salt and pepper to taste

Cover bottom of individual baking dish with ½ the crumbs. Break egg on crumbs and add seasonings. Cover with remaining crumbs. Add cream or butter. Bake at 400° for 20 min. until white is set. Do not bake too hard.

Macaroni and Cheese (Creamed)

1 cup macaroni, uncooked	1 tsp. salt
1 cup diced American cheese	1 tbsp. butter
½ cup cream	

Cook macaroni in 1 qt. boiling, salted water until tender, about 10 min., drain. Stir in diced cheese, cream and butter.

Egg Noodles

6 egg yolks   1 tbsp. water, beat together

Flour to make a very stiff dough. Knead the dough until smooth. Divide into three parts. Roll out until very thin. Let dry 1 hr., then fold into fourths, roll and cut fine. Shake apart, let dry.

Mrs. Fannie Dyck, Hesston, Kans.

Omelet

4 eggs	⅛ tsp. pepper
¾ tsp. salt	½ tbsp. butter or oleo
¼ cup water	

Beat egg yolks until thick and lemon colored. Add seasonings. Beat egg whites until foamy. Add water and continue beating until stiff. Carefully fold into first mixture. Pour into hot frying pan containing butter or oleo. Cook over low fire until well puffed, slightly brown on bottom, and firm to the touch. Cook under a low broiler flame 2-3 minutes. After omelet is well puffed and slightly brown on the bottom, the cooking process may be completed in a moderate oven (375° F.) Crease omelet. Fold. Serve at once. If desired, ¼ cup finely chopped ham or grated cheese, or 2 tablespoons tart jelly, may be placed on ½ the omelet just before it is served. 4 servings.

Stuffed Eggs

6 hard cooked eggs	¾ tsp. salt
1 tsp. mustard	2 tbsp. mayonnaise dressing
1 tsp. vinegar	

Cut eggs in half lengthwise. Remove yolks. Mash. Add mustard, salt, vinegar, and mayonnaise. Mix thoroughly. Refill whites. Sprinkle with paprika.

COOKIES

Bars, Brownies, and Squares

(Golden) Apple Bars

⅔ cup shortening
2 cups brown sugar
2 eggs, beaten
1 tsp. vanilla
2 cups flour

2 tsp. baking powder
¼ tsp. salt
1 cup chopped raw apples
½ cup nutmeats

Mix together and spread in 13x9 in. pan and bake at 350° for 30 min. Cool and cut into bars.

Roberta Toews

Brown Honey Bars

1 egg
½ cup butter
½ cup sugar
½ cup honey
1 tsp. vanilla
1 cup flour

½ tsp. soda
½ tsp. baking powder
½ tsp. salt
1 cup oatmeal
1 cup coconut
⅓ cup nuts

Cream butter and sugar, add egg, honey and vanilla; beat until smooth. Sift dry ingredients together and add to creamed mixture. Mix until well blended. Stir in oatmeal, coconut and nuts. Bake in shallow pan in slow oven (325°) 25-30 min. or until brown. Ice with Butterscotch Icing.

Mrs. Denton Holdeman, Hesston, Kans.

Cheerios Squares

½ cup white sugar
½ cup corn syrup
⅓ cup butter
½ cup peanut butter

2 cups Cheerios
1 cup corn flakes
1 cup peanuts

Combine sugar, syrup and butter in sauce pan and bring to boiling; remove from heat; add peanut butter. Combine Cheerios, corn flakes and peanuts in mixing bowl. Pour boiled mixture over cereals and mix well. Pour into buttered pan; cool and cut into squares.

Leanna Friesen, St. Anne, Man.

Blarney Stones (1)

5 egg yolks
¾ cup sugar
¾ cup cake flour
5 stiff-beaten egg whites

2 tbsp. cold water
1 tsp. baking powder
½ tsp. salt
1 tsp. vanilla

Combine egg yolk and water, beat until egg yolks stand in peaks. Add sugar gradually; beat well. Sift together cake flour, baking powder, and salt, add to yolk mixture. Fold in vanilla and egg whites. Spread batter into wax-paper lined and greased 12"x8" pan. Bake at 350° for 25 min. Loosen sides and turn immediately onto towel. Cut into 12 to 16 squares. Ice on all sides and roll in salted peanuts, crushed fine with rolling pin.

Icing

1 lb. powdered sugar
2 sticks oleo, melted
1 egg, beaten

1 tsp. vanilla
1 lb. salted peanuts

Mix oleo and sugar, beating until smooth, add egg and vanilla; beat until of spreading consistency.

Mrs. Adin Holdeman, Hesston, Kans.

Blarney Stones (2)

3 eggs, separated
1 cup flour
¼ tsp. salt
½ tsp. vanilla

1 cup sugar
1⅓ tsp. baking powder
½ cup boiling water

Beat 2 yolks until lemon colored. Add sugar gradually, beat until mixture is creamy. Sift dry ingredients. Add alternately with boiling water. Add vanilla. Fold in stiffly beaten egg whites. Pour into ungreased cake pan. Bake 30 min. at 350°. Let cool, cut into 2 in. sq. then frost on all sides with frosting and roll in crushed salted peanuts.

Frosting:
½ cup butter
1 egg yolk

2¼ cups powdered sugar
1 tsp. vanilla
½ lb. salted peanuts

Cream, butter, yolk and sugar together, Add vanilla. Beat until smooth.

Mary Ann Wenger, Moundridge, Kans.

Coffee Date Squares

1½ cups flour
1¾ cups rolled oats
1 cup brown sugar

1 tsp. salt
1 tsp. soda
¾ cup margarine or lard

Filling:

2 cups dates
½ cup brown sugar

2 tsp. instant coffee
1 cup boiling water

Boil together till thickened.

Combine dry ingredients and add margarine. Mix until crumbly. Press ⅔ of mixture into 10x10 in. pan. Spread filling over top. Sprinkle remaining crumbs over top. Bake at 350° for 30 min. Cut into squares.

Mrs. Leo Loetkeman, Enderby, B. C.

Butter Tart Bars

1½ cups flour
½ cup brown sugar

⅔ cup butter

Mix and press into two 9"x9" pans. Bake at 350° for 12 min. Spread with topping and return to oven for 30 min. more. Cut into bars.

Topping

2 cup raisins
4 eggs
1 cup sugar
1 cup syrup

¼ tsp. salt
2 tsp. vanilla
½ cup flour

Blend eggs and sugar. Stir in syrup, salt and vanilla, flour and raisins.

Mrs. Leo Loetkeman, Enderby, B. C.

Congo Squares

2¾ cups flour
2½ tsp. baking powder
½ tsp. salt
⅔ cup shortening
   (melted or liquid)

2¼ cups brown sugar
3 eggs
1 cup chopped nuts
1 cup chocolate chips

Cream shortening and brown sugar. Add eggs one at a time, beating well after each addition. Add dry ingredients, nuts, and chocolate chips. Pour onto greased cookie sheet (10"x15"). Bake at 350° for 25-30 min. When cool cut into squares. Yield: 48 squares.

Mrs. John Wenger, Hesston, Kans.
Mrs. Lois Seiler, Archbold, Ohio

Brownies (for Diabetics)

½ cup butter or margarine
Nonnutritive sweetener equivalent to 1¼ cups sugar (if tablets
are used pulverize them to a fine powder)

2 eggs
½ tsp. vanilla
½ cup chopped walnuts

2 sq. unsweetened chocolate,
melted
¾ cup sifted flour
1 tsp. baking powder

Preheat oven to 350°. In a large bowl, cream butter or margarine
and nonnutritive sweetener until light and fluffy, add chocolate,
beat until smooth. Beat in eggs and vanilla, add flour, baking
powder, and walnuts. Beat well.

Spread butter in greased 8"x8"x2" pan. Bake 30 min. or until
surface of brownies is shiny. Cool in pan, cut into 16 pieces.
Serve cool.

Mrs. Robert L. Koehn, Montezuma, Kans.

Coconut Chews

¼ cup soft shortening
½ cup brown sugar, firmly
    packed
1 egg yolk

½ tsp. vanilla
1 cup sifted flour
1 tsp. baking powder
½ tsp. salt

Cream shortening, sugar, egg yolk, and vanilla, until fluffy. Sift
flour, baking powder and salt into creamed mixture. Mix until
crumbly. Press firmly into well greased and floured 9" pan.
Spread coconut topping evenly over crumb layer. Bake in preheated oven at 350° for 25 to 30 min. Remove from pan, cool
and cut into 1½" squares. Makes 3 doz.

Coconut Topping

Beat together until well mixed:

1 whole egg
1 egg white
1 cup brown sugar, firmly
    packed

1 tsp. vanilla
2 tbsp. flour
1 cup flaked coconut
½ cup chopped walnuts

Leona Nichols, Livingston, Calif.

Coconut Chocolate Meringue Bites

¾ cup butter
½ cup brown sugar
½ cup white sugar
3 eggs, separated
1 tsp. vanilla
2 cups flour
1 tsp. baking powder
¼ tsp. soda
¼ tsp. salt
1-6 oz. pkg. chocolate chips
1 cup coconut
¾ cup nuts
1 cup brown sugar

Cream butter, ½ cup brown sugar, white sugar, egg yolks and vanilla. Beat thoroughly. Blend dry ingredients, stir in. Spread dough in 9x13 in. pan. Sprinkle with chocolate chips, coconut and nuts. Beat egg whites, adding 1 cup brown sugar gradually, beating until stiff. Spread over nuts. Bake in 350° oven for 35 min. Yield: 40 bars.

Alice Schmidt, Newton, Kans.

Gold Rush Brownies

2 cups firmly packed gra-
ham cracker crumbs
1-6 oz, pkg. choc. chips
½ cup chopped nuts
1⅓ cups sweetened condensed
milk
½ cup coconut (optional)

Mix together cracker crumbs, choc. chips and nuts. Blend in milk. Pour into a 8x8x2 in. pan which has been greased and lined with waxed paper and greased again. Bake at 350° until golden brown, (about 40 min.) Remove from oven, let stand 10 min. Turn out of pan, remove waxed paper and cut into squares.

Roma Jantz, Hesston, Kans.

Fig Bars

½ cup sugar (brown or
white)
2 cups figs, ground
1½ cups water

Boil together and cool.
Mix the following:

2 cups brown sugar
2 eggs
5 cups flour
1 tsp. cream of tartar
1 cup butter
¼ cup milk
1 tsp. soda
1 tsp. vanilla

Roll out half the dough, cover with fig mixture. Place other half of rolled dough over top and bake in 350° oven 30 min. Cut into squares.

Leanna Friesen, Ste. Anne, Man.

Bran Apricot Squares

1½ cups dried apricots
1 cup water
½ cup butter

¼ cup sugar
½ cup flour
¾ cup bran

Simmer apricots in water for 10 min. Drain and chop. Let cool to use for topping. Cream butter and sugar, add flour and bran. Press into 9"x9" pan. Bake at 350° for 15 min.

Topping

2 eggs
1 cup brown sugar
½ tsp. vanilla

½ cup flour
½ tsp. salt
½ tsp. baking powder
½ cup walnuts, chopped

Beat egg until thick, add brown sugar and vanilla. Add flour, baking powder and salt. Stir in apricots and nuts. Pour over baked bran layer. Return to oven and bake at 350° for 20-30 min. Cool and cut into squares.

Nancy M. Esau

Date Apricot Bars

1 cup chopped dates
2 cups dried apricots, cooked drained and mashed

½ cup sugar
2 tbsp. apricot juice

Mix all ingredients in saucepan. Cook over low heat, stirring constantly until thickened. Remove from heat and cool.

Crumb Mixture

¾ cup soft shortening, part butter or oleo
1 cup brown sugar
1¾ cups flour

½ tsp. soda
1 tsp. salt
1½ cups rolled oats

Mix all ingredients thoroughly. Press one half of mixture into a greased and floured 9"x13" pan. Spread with cooled date-apricot filling; top with remaining crumb mixture, press lightly. Bake at 375° for 25 min. or until lightly browned. Cut into bars while warm and remove from pan. Yield: about 18 bars.

Mrs. Sam J. Koehn, Fairview, Okla.

Chocolate Chip Squares

1 cup sifted flour	2 eggs, well beaten
1 tsp. baking soda	6 oz. chocolate chips
1 cup brown sugar	½ cup brown sugar
¼ cup butter	½ cup walnuts
½ cup coconut	¼ cup melted butter
½ cup oatmeal	1 tbsp. flour

Sift 1 cup flour and baking soda onto wax paper. Mix 1 cup brown sugar and ¼ cup butter until crumbly. Stir in flour, coconut and oatmeal. Press firmly into 9 in. pan. Mix eggs, chips, ½ cup brown sugar, walnuts, ¼ cup melted butter, and 1 tbsp. flour. Pour over bottom layer. Bake 35 min. at 350°. Cool, cut into squares.

Mrs. Don Barkman, Steinbach, Man.

Fudge Brownies

2 eggs	⅓ cup melted margarine
1 cup sugar	½ cup cocoa
½ tsp. salt	¾ cup sifted flour
1 tsp. vanilla	1 cup chopped pecans

Beat eggs slightly. Add sugar, salt, vanilla, and melted margarine. Stir in cocoa, sifted flour and pecans. Pour into greased 8 or 9 in. sq. pan. Bake at 325° for 30 to 35 min. Cool. Cut in squares.

Mrs. Edward Koehn, Ulysses, Kans.
Mrs. Emerson Koehn, Cimarron, Kans.
Mrs. Howard Holdeman, Barton, Ga.

Graham Wafer Squares

Mix:
½ box graham wafers, crumbled	Boil together for 1 min.:
½ cup walnuts or coconut	¾ cup brown sugar
	¾ cup margarine
	2 eggs, beaten
	4 tbsp. cocoa

Mix with wafers:

Place in pan and frost with chocolate frosting. Store in refrigerator.

Mrs. Larry Toews, Langdon, S. Dak.

Fudge Squares

½ tsp. baking powder	1 cup sugar
¾ cup flour	½ cup butter melted together
3 eggs	with
1 cup broken black walnut meats	2 sq. unsweetened chocolate

Sift baking powder and flour together. Stir in slightly beaten eggs. Add sugar, butter, chocolate and nuts. Spread in a 9"x12" well greased pan. Bake in mod. oven (350°) for 20 min. Cool and cut into squares. Makes about 2 doz.

Frost if desired:

1 sq. chocolate	⅛ tsp. salt
1½ tbsp. butter	1 tsp. vanilla
2½ tbsp. milk	1 cup powdered sugar (maybe more)

Heat together first four ingredients; add powdered sugar and vanilla. Beat until smooth. Spread on cookies.

Mrs. Lorene Kuepfer, Harrison, Mich.

Hoosier Peanut Bars

2 cups flour-sifted	1½ cups brown sugar, firmly packed
2 tsp. baking powder	2 eggs, separated
1 tsp. soda	1 tsp. vanilla
½ tsp. salt	3 tbsp. cold water
½ cup shortening, creamed	1 cup chocolate chips
½ cup granulated sugar	

Sift first four ingredients, blend with creamed shortening, egg yolks, white sugar, ½ cup brown sugar and cold water. (This will be a stiff dough). Press into one large pan or two smaller pans. Sprinkle semi-sweet chocolate chips over dough, press gently. Beat egg whites until foamy, add vanilla and 1 cup brown sugar, gradually. Beat until stiff, spread over chocolate chips, top with walnuts or peanuts. Bake at 350° for 30 to 35 min. Makes about 24 bars.

La Verna Peaster, Winton, Calif.

Lemon Squares

1½ cups flour	½ cup oleo, melted
½ cup brown sugar	

Mix together and press into buttered 9"x13" pan. Bake at 275° for 10 min. or until light brown. Spread with topping.

Topping

2 eggs
1½ cups coconut
1 cup nuts
2 tbsp. flour

1 cup sugar
½ tsp. baking powder
¼ tsp .salt
½ tsp. lemon extract

Mix ingredients and spread over top of cake. Return to oven for 20 min. more at 350°.

Mrs. Raymond Ensz, Bancroft, S. Dak.

Grape-Nuts Butterscotch Bars

⅓ cup butter or oleo
½ cup Grape-Nuts
¾ cup light brown sugar, firmly packed
1 egg, well beaten
1 tsp. vanilla

¾ cup sifted flour
½ tsp. baking powder
⅛ tsp. soda
¼ tsp. salt
¾ cup coconut

Melt butter in saucepan. Add cereal and cook about 2 min. until it is softened. Remove from heat, stir in sugar, cool slightly. Add egg and vanilla, beat well. Measure sifted flour, add baking powder, soda, salt, and sift together. Add to cereal mixture. Stir in coconut. Spread in greased 8"x8" pan and press down evenly. Bake in moderate oven (350°) 20-25 min. Cool, cut into 20 bars.

Marble Squares

2¼ cups flour
1 tsp. soda
1 tsp. salt
1 cup shortening
2 eggs, beaten
¾ cup white sugar

¾ cup brown sugar, firmly packed
1 tsp. vanilla
½ tsp. water
1-6 oz. pkg. semi-sweet chocolate chips

Cream shortening and sugars, add eggs, vanilla and water. Sift together flour, soda and salt, add to creamed mixture; mix well. Spread dough into greased 13"x9"x2" pan. Sprinkle chocolate chips over top. Place in 375° oven for 1 min. Remove from oven and run knife through batter to marbelize. Return to oven and bake at 375° for 12 to 14 min. Cool; cut into 2" squares. Yield: 4 doz.

Marilyn Toews, Windom, Kans.

Matrimony Cake

2 cups flour
1 cup brown sugar
2 cups oatmeal
¾ cup melted shortening

1 tsp. salt
1 tsp. vanilla
1 tsp. soda dissolved in
1 tsp. hot water

Rub all ingredients together with hands.
Press ½ mixture into a 10" by 13" pan.

Filling

1 cup dates or raisins,
    chopped
1 cup brown sugar

1 cup water

Boil to a paste (about 20 min.) Pour filling over mixture in pan, put remaining dry mixture over top. Bake at 350° for 40 min.

Mrs. F. C. Fricke
Submitted by Mrs. George Friesen, Glenn, Calif.

Nut Bars

¾ cup flour
¼ tsp. salt
¼ tsp. soda

2 cups light brown sugar
2 eggs
1 cup walnuts, coarsely
    chopped

Sift together flour, salt, and soda, add sugar and eggs, blend with mixer at low speed. Then beat at high speed until fluffy. Add nuts. Bake in greased shallow 9"x9" pan at 350° for 30 min. Cool and cut into 32 bars.

Sophia and Susie Koehn, Montezuma, Kans.

Nut Squares

2 cups brown sugar
1 cup flour
2 cups nuts meats

2 eggs
1 tsp. vanilla

Beat eggs well. Add sugar, flour, vanilla, and nuts. Mix well. Spread into greased baking sheet, bake at 325° for 20 min..

Yvonne Schmidt, Winton, Calif.

Toffee or Dream Bars

½ cup brown sugar   1 cup flour, sifted
½ cup oleo

Grease very lightly a 12"x8" baking pan. Cream together the brown sugar and oleo. Stir in the flour and mix well. Press this mixture in the bottom of the baking pan, and about 1" up on the sides. Bake in a mod. oven 350° for 12 min. Cool and add this as directed below:

1 cup brown sugar, packed   2 eggs, well beaten
2 tbsp. flour   1 tsp. vanilla
½ tsp. baking powder   1 cup chopped nuts
1 cup coconut (optional)

Mix together the brown sugar, flour and baking powder. Add to the eggs and mix well. Add vanilla, nuts and coconut if desired. Spread over the cooled crust and return to the oven and bake 20 min. Cut into bars while warm. Remove from pan when cool.

Mrs. Alvin Giesbrecht, Davisboro, Ga.
Marlis Rose Holdeman, Halstead, Kans.
Toni Nightengale, Atwater, Calif.

Orange Saucepan Bars

½ cup butter or oleo   ½ tsp. baking soda
1 tsp. grated orange rind   1 egg
2 tbsp. orange juice   ½ cup chopped walnuts
½ cup sugar   ½ cup pitted dates, chopped
1 cup flour

Melt butter in saucepan; remove from heat. Add sugar, orange rind and juice, blend well. Stir in flour sifted with soda. Add egg and mix well. Add walnuts and dates, stir lightly to combine. Pour into greased 9"x9" pan. Bake at 350° for 25 min. or until done. Cool in pan; frost with Orange Frosting. Makes about 16 bars.

Orange Frosting

1 tbsp. butter or oleo   1 tbsp. plus 1 tsp. orange
1 cup powdered sugar   juice

Blend all ingredients and beat until smooth and creamy with mixer at med. speed.

Mrs. Dee Wayne Koehn, Livingston, Calif.

Orange Caramel Bars

1½ cups brown sugar
2 eggs
1⅓ cups flour

⅔ cup chopped pecans
⅔ cup cut up fresh orange slices with white skin left on

Beat sugar and eggs together. Stir in flour. Fold in orange pieces and pecans. Spread in greased jelly roll pan. Bake at 350° for 30 to 35 min. While warm spread with glaze.

Glaze:
⅔ cup powdered sugar
2 tbsp. cream

grated rind of orange

Violet Schmidt, Newton, Kans.

Orange Slice Bars

1 lb. orange slices,
    (or mixed candied fruit)
2 cups flour
⅛ tsp. salt
1 cup nuts

1 lb. light brown sugar
4 eggs, beaten
1 tsp. vanilla

Cut orange slices into flour. Mix and add remaining ingredients. Beat until well blended. Add nuts. Bake on buttered cookie sheet at 350° for 30 min. Cut into squares before completely cool.

Mrs. Leonard Boehs, Fairview, Okla.

Peanut Butter Brownies

6 eggs
3 cups brown sugar
1 cup white sugar
½ cup peanut butter
1 cup shortening or oleo

1 tsp. vanilla
4 cups unsifted flour
1½ tbsp. baking powder
1½ tsp. salt
½ cup chopped peanuts

Combine eggs, sugar, peanut butter, shortening, and vanilla, blend thoroughly. Add dry ingredients and mix only until smooth. Spread dough in two greased 15"x10" pans. Sprinkle with nuts. Bake in moderate oven (350°) 25 min. Cut into 80 bars.

Mrs. Pete Nickel, Hillsboro, Kans.

Raisin Mumbles

¾ cup butter
1 cup brown sugar
1¾ cups flour
½ tsp. salt
½ tsp. soda
1½ cups oatmeal

Blend butter and sugar. Add dry ingredients. Press half of mixture into pan. Mix:

2½ cups raisins
½ cup sugar
2 tbsp. cornstarch
¾ cup water
3 tbsp. lemon juice

Cook and cool. Pour filling into pan, and sprinkle remaining crumb mixture over top. Bake 400° for 20-30 min.

Mrs. Donald Seiler, Carson City, Mich.

Raisin Squares

1 cup raisins, cooked
1 cup sugar
1 cup sour cream
2 cups flour
2 eggs
1 tsp. soda
½ tsp. nutmeg
½ cup pineapple, crushed
(optional)

Mix ingredients together. Add cooked raisins. Spread on greased cookie sheet. Bake at 350° for 20 min. Ice while still warm with powdered sugar icing. (Prunes may be substituted for raisins)

Mrs. John W. Toews, Livingston, Calif.

Spicy Coffee Bars

¼ cup soft shortening
1 cup brown sugar
1 egg
½ cup hot coffee
1½ cups sifted flour
1 tsp. baking powder
¼ tsp. soda
1 tsp. salt
½ tsp. cinnamon
½ cup raisins
½ cup chopped nuts

Cream together shortening and brown sugar. Add eggs, mix well. Stir in hot coffee. Sift together and stir in dry ingredients. Blend in raisins and chopped nuts. Spread batter into a greased 9"x13" pan. Bake at 350° for 18-20 min. Frost while warm, with confectioners sugar icing. Makes about 2 doz. bars.

Mrs. Richard Jantz, Cleo Springs, Okla.

Drop Cookies

Applesauce Cookies with Cinnamon Frosting

½ cup margarine
1 cup brown sugar, firmly
  packed
1 egg, beaten
1 cup applesauce
2½ cups sifted flour
1 tsp. soda
1 tsp. cinnamon
½ tsp. nutmeg
¼ tsp. cloves
¼ tsp. salt
1 cup chopped raisins
½ cup chopped nuts

Cream margarine and sugar; add egg and applesauce. Sift dry ingredients together and combine with creamed mixture. (May use electric mixer.) Add raisins and nuts. Drop onto greased cookie sheet. Bake 12 to 15 min. at 375°. Makes 3 doz. cookies.

Cinnamon Frosting

1 cup powdered sugar
¼ tsp. cinnamon
1 tsp. soft margarine
1 tbsp. light cream
1 tsp. lemon flavoring
½ tsp. vanilla
few grains of salt

Beat until smooth and fluffy. Spread on applesauce cookies.

Mrs. Obed Koehn, Copeland, Kans.

(Chopped) Apple Cookies

½ cup butter
½ tsp. salt
½ tsp. cinnamon
2 cups flour
1 tsp. soda
¼ cup apple juice or milk if
  dough is too thick
1 cup chopped raw apples
1⅓ cups brown sugar
1 tsp. cloves
½ tsp. nutmeg
1 egg
1 cup chopped nuts
1 cup raisins

Cream butter, sugar, salt, spices and egg. Add sifted flour with soda. Stir in chopped apples, nuts, raisins, and juice.) Mix well. Drop from teaspoon onto greased cookie sheet. Bake at 350° for 10 min. Frost with powdered sugar icing.

Mrs. Ervin Nightengale, Scott City, Kans.

Brown Sugar Cookies (1)

2 cups brown sugar
1 cup shortening
1 cup milk
2 eggs
1 tsp. vanilla

3½ cups flour, sifted
1 tsp. soda
1 tsp. baking powder
1 tsp. cinnamon
1 cup nuts, raisins or chocolate chips

Cream shortening and sugar. Add eggs and vanilla. Sift together dry ingredients, add to creamed mixture alternately with milk. Blend in nuts, raisins, or choc. chips. Drop onto greased baking sheet. Bake at 350° 8-10 min.

Mrs. Elma Friesen, Archbold, Ohio

Brown Sugar Cookies (2)

Cream:
⅔ cup oleo
1½ cups brown sugar

Add:
2 eggs
1 tsp. vanilla

Stir in:
1 tbsp. vinegar with
1 cup evaporated milk
1 tsp. salt

1 tsp. soda
½ tsp. baking powder
3 cups flour

Drop on greased cookie sheet. Bake at 375°. Frost with:
Melt ¼ cup oleo, add ⅛ cup boiling water and 1 tsp. vanilla. Stir in enough powdered sugar to make right consistency. Sprinkle with nuts.

Wilma Martin, Dalton, Ohio

Brown Sugar Drop Cookies

1 cup white sugar
1 cup brown sugar
1 cup shortening
3 eggs
2 cups flour
1 tsp. baking powder
½ tsp. salt

¾ tsp. soda
2 tbsp. hot water
1 tsp. vanilla
2 cups rolled oats
2 cups cornflakes
1 cup shredded coconut
½ cup nut meats
1 cup raisins (optional)

Cream sugars and shortening until well blended, add slightly beaten eggs; continue beating. Sift dry ingredients except soda, add to creamed mixture. Dissolve soda in hot water and add to mixture. Add the rolled oats, cornflakes, coconut, nut meats and vanilla. Drop from teaspoon on greased baking sheet and bake at 375° for 12 min. Yield: about 9 doz. cookies.

Mrs. Rueben Schultz, Neodesha, Kans.
Eva Koehn, Galva, Kansas

Cereal Cookies

2 cups brown sugar
1 cup shortening
2 eggs
1 cup cereal flakes
2 cups rolled oats
2 cups flour
½ tsp. salt
1 tsp. baking soda
1 tsp. vanilla

Cream brown sugar, shortening and eggs. Add cereal flakes, flour, salt, soda and vanilla, mix well. Raisins, chocolate chips, nuts or cherries may be added if desired. Drop from teaspoon onto cookie sheet, press with fork. Bake 10 min. at 375°.

Mrs. Dave Reimer, Linden, Alberta

Butterscotch Coconut Drops

½ cup butter
½ cup brown sugar
1 tsp. vanilla
½ cup white sugar
2 eggs
2 cups flour
½ tsp. soda
½ tsp. salt
1 cup butterscotch or caramel chips
½ cup nuts
1½ cups coconut

Cream butter, sugars, vanilla and eggs together. Add flour, soda and salt. Add butterscotch chips. Chill. Drop by teaspoonsful into the coconut and roll. Form into balls. Place on greased cookie sheet. Top with nut half or maraschino cherry. Bake at 375° for 10 to 12 min.

Mrs. Roy Dyck, Hesston, Kans.

Butterscotch Cookies

1 cup shortening
2 cups brown sugar
3 eggs
3¼ cups sifted flour
½ tsp. soda
½ tsp. salt
1 tsp. vanilla
¾ cup coconut
1 cup butterscotch bits
3 tbsp. boiling water

Mix thoroughly the shortening, sugar, and eggs. Sift together flour, soda, and salt. Add vanilla, coconut, butterscotch bits and mix well. Add boiling water and stir until blended. Drop from teaspoon about 2" apart on lightly greased baking sheet. Bake at 375° until golden brown. Makes 5 doz.

Karen Gearig, Ithaca, Mich.

Butterscotch Nuggets

½ cup butter
½ cup brown sugar, firmly
  packed
¼ cup white sugar
1 egg
1 tsp. vanilla

1⅔ cups flour
1 tsp. salt
½ tsp. soda
1 cup coarsely chopped nuts

Cream butter, and sugars; add egg and vanilla, cream well. Sift flour, salt and soda. Add to creamed mixture. Add nuts, mix well. Drop 2 teaspoons of dough onto greased cookie sheet. Make depression in center of cookie before and during baking. Bake in mod. oven (375°) about 10 min. Cool. Fill center with chocolate frosting. Top with walnut halves. Makes 50 cookies.
Frosting: Melt ¼ cup butter or oleo and ½ pkg. (3 oz.) chocolate chips. Remove from heat. Add cream and confectioners sugar, beat until of spreading consistency.

Mrs. Marshall Harms, Atmore, Ala.

Luscious Carrot Cookies

¾ cup sugar
1 cup shortening
1 cup cooked, mashed carrots
1 egg

2 cups flour, sifted
2 tsp. baking powder
½ tsp. salt
1 tsp. vanilla

Cream sugar and shortening together; add carrots, vanilla, and egg; mix well. Sift dry ingredients together and add to creamed mixture. Drop from teaspoon onto lightly greased baking sheet. Bake at 350° for 15 min. Frost with orange flavored icing.

Icing

3 tbsp. butter, melted
2 tbsp. orange juice

⅛ tsp. salt
powdered sugar

Mix butter, juice, and salt. Add powdered sugar, beat until creamy and of spreading consistency.

Mrs. Richard Koehn, Halstead, Kans.
Mrs. Don Nightengale, Fairview, Okla.
Mrs. Abe Nichols, Ingalls, Kans.

Carrot Cookies

½ cup Mazola oil	½ tsp. salt
1 cup brown sugar	1½ tsp. baking powder
½ cup white sugar	2 cups flour
1 egg	¾ cup pecans
1 cup mashed cooked carrots	1 tsp. vanilla

Mix oil and sugar, add vanilla. Add carrots, flour, salt and baking powder. Drop from teaspoon onto greased baking sheet 2 to 3 in. apart. Bake at 375° 10 to 12 min.

Icing

1½ cups powdered sugar	1 tsp. softened butter
	powdered sugar

Cream softened butter and powdered sugar. Add juice and rind of 1 orange and beat until smooth.

Mrs. Emerson Litwiller, Middleton, Mich.

Chocolate Chips

1 cup shortening	1 tsp. salt
1 cup white sugar	¼ cup hot water
1 cup brown sugar	1 tsp. vanilla
2 eggs	1 cup chopped nuts
2½ cups sifted flour	1 6 oz. pkg. chocolate chips
1 tsp. soda	

Thoroughly cream the shortening and sugars. Add eggs and beat well. Sift together flour, soda and salt. Add to first mixture. Add water and vanilla, mix thoroughly. Stir in nuts and chocolate chips. Drop by spoon onto lightly greased cookie sheet. Bake at 375° for 10-12 min. Makes 5 doz. cookies. (For crunchy cookies place in plastic bags and freeze. They keep fresh for months.)

Verna Giesbrecht, Winton, Calif.

Chocolate, Chocolate Chip Cookies

2 6-oz. pkg. chocolate chips	3½ cups flour
1 cup shortening	1 tsp. soda
1 cup sugar	1 tsp. salt
2 eggs	½ cup water
½ cup chopped nuts	

Melt one pkg. chocolate chips. Blend shortening, sugar, eggs and melted chocolate chips. Stir in sifted dry ingredients alternately with water. Stir in nuts and one pkg. chocolate chips. Drop from teaspoon onto baking sheet. Bake 12 to 15 min. at 350°.
Delma Friesen, Conway, Kans.

Cinnamon Drop Cookies

½ cup butter
1 cup sugar
2 eggs
½ cup cream
1 tsp. vanilla
3 cups sifted flour
3 tsp. baking powder

Cream butter, and sugar; add eggs, and vanilla; beat well. Add sifted flour and baking powder alternately with milk. Chill dough. Mix sugar and cinnamon in a dish, drop dough of desired size into sugar mixture and roll into ball. Place on cookie sheet. Bake 10 to 12 min. in 375° oven.
Mrs. Ben L. Rempel

Crunchies

3 egg whites, stiffly beaten
1 cup sugar
1 cup nuts
1 tsp. vanilla
8 soda crackers, rolled fine

Fold mixture into beaten egg whites. Drop from teaspoon onto well greased baking sheet about 2 inches apart. Bake at 350°. Remove from pan at once and serve with whipped cream.
Mrs. John M. Jost, Hillsboro, Kans.

Coffee Break Cookies

2 cups flour
½ tsp. baking powder
1 tsp. soda
1 cup shortening
1 cup chocolate chips, coconut, nuts or raisins
½ tsp. salt
1 cup white sugar
1 cup brown sugar
2 eggs
2 cups oatmeal
1 tsp. vanilla

Sift together dry ingredients. Blend sugars and shortening. Add eggs and vanilla; beat well. Add flour mixture, oatmeal and nuts (or chips). If stiff enough press into small patties, or add a little milk and drop from teaspoon onto greased cookie sheets. Bake at 375° until light brown (for 10 min.)
Marlene Giesbrecht, Winton, Calif.

Chocolate Chip Cookies

2 cups light brown sugar
1 cup shortening
2 eggs, beaten
1 tsp. baking powder
1-12 oz. pkg. chocolate chips
1¼ tsp. soda dissolved in 3 tbsp. cold water
3 cups flour
¼ tsp .salt
1 tsp. vanilla

Cream shortening, sugar, eggs and vanilla. Add soda and water. Blend sifted dry ingredients. Add chocolate chips. Nut meats may be added, if desired. Drop from teaspoon onto baking sheet. Bake at 375° 8-10 min.

Mrs. Clifford Mastre, Grafton, N. Dak.

Chocolate Marshmallow Cookies

1¾ cup sifted cake flour
½ tsp. soda
½ tsp. salt
½ cup cocoa
½ cup shortening
1 cup sugar
½ cup milk
½ cup chopped pecans
1 tsp. vanilla
18 marshmallows, cut in half
36 pecan halves
1 egg

Sift flour, measure and sift again, with soda, salt and cocoa. Cream shortening. Add sugar gradually, blending thoroughly. Add egg, beat well. Add flour mixture and milk alternately, beating after each addition. Add chopped nuts and vanilla. Mix. Drop mixture from teaspoon about 2" apart onto well greased cookie sheet. Cookies will spread. Bake in mod. 350° oven for 8 min. Top with marshmallow half, cut side down. Return to oven and bake 2 min. until marshmallow softens. Cool, and frost with cocoa frosting.

Cocoa Frosting

2 cups sifted powdered sugar
5 tbsp. cocoa
4 tbsp. light cream
3 tbsp. melted butter
dash of salt
½ tsp. vanilla

Sift powdered sugar with cocoa and salt. Add melted butter, cream and vanilla. Beat until smooth and creamy. Spread on cookies. Top each cookie with a pecan half. Makes 3 doz.

Ruby Wesenburg, Ithaca, Mich.

Coconut Oatmeal Cookies

2 cups flour
2 tsp. baking powder
2 tsp. soda
1 tsp. salt
1 tsp. vanilla
1 cup shortening

1 cup brown sugar
1 cup white sugar
2 eggs
2 cups oatmeal
1 cup coconut

Sift flour, measure and sift again with baking powder and salt. Cream shortening and soda. Add sugar gradually and cream until fluffy. Add eggs, beat well. Add vanilla and dry ingredients, mix thoroughly. Add oatmeal and coconut. Shape dough into small balls. Bake at 350° for 12 to 15 min.

Mrs. Donald Hiebert, Yale, S. Dak.

Cream Cookies

3 cups light brown sugar
3 eggs
1½ cups oleo
2 cups heavy sweet or sour cream
1½ tsp. soda

¾ tsp. salt
1 tsp. vanilla
¾ tsp. cinnamon
1½ tsp. baking powder
7 or 7½ cups all purpose flour

Cream sugar and shortening. Add eggs and cream, beat well. Add dry ingredients. Chill. Drop or roll. Bake on greased cookie sheet at 375° for 10 to 12 min.

Mrs. Clarence Schneider, Ithaca, Mich.

Cream Ginger Cookies

1 cup brown sugar
1 cup sour cream or buttermilk
1 cup butter or lard
1 cup molasses

1 egg
2 tsp. ginger
3 tsp. soda
4 cups flour (more or less)

Cream butter and sugar, add egg and cream. Beat well. Add dry ingredients. Drop from tsp. onto cookie sheet. Bake at 375° for 10-12 min.

Mrs. Elmer Sommers, Minerva, Ohio

(Sour) Cream Drops

1 cup butter or shortening	2 tsp. baking powder
2 cups sugar	½ tsp. soda
3 eggs	1 tsp. salt
2 tsp. vanilla	1 tsp. nutmeg
1 cup sour cream	1½ cups broken nut meats
4 cups sifted flour	

Cream butter, add sugar gradually, creaming well; add eggs, one at a time, vanilla, and sour cream; beat well. Remove from mixer. Sift together dry ingredients. Blend into creamed mixture with a spoon. Add nuts. Drop from teaspoon onto greased cookie sheet, 2 in. apart. Butter bottom of a glass, dip into mixture of ¼ cup sugar and 1 tsp. cinnamon; use to flatten cookies. Bake at 350° for 15 min. Yield: 6 to 7 doz. cookies.

Mrs. Warren Johnson, Galva, Kans.

(Cookie Jar) Gingersnaps

2 cups sifted flour	¾ cup shortening
1 tbsp. ginger	1 cup sugar
2 tsp. baking soda	1 egg
1 tsp. cinnamon	¼ cup molasses
½ tsp. salt	

Measure flour, ginger, soda, cinnamon and salt into sifter. Cream shortening until soft, gradually add sugar and cream until mixture is fluffy. Beat in egg and molasses. Sift dry ingredients over creamed mixture; blend well. Form 1 tsp. of dough into small balls. Roll in granulated sugar; place on ungreased cookie sheets. Bake in mod. oven (350°) for 12 to 15 min. or until tops are slightly rounded, crackly and lightly browned. Cool and store in air tight container.

Mrs. Harold Wedel, Bonners Ferry, Ida.
Mrs. Harlin Gearig, Louisville, Ga.

(Soft) Ginger Drops

½ cup shortening	2 tsp. ginger
¾ cup sugar	1 tsp. cinnamon
1 egg	1 tsp. nutmeg
1¼ cups molasses	1 tsp. cloves
4½ cups flour	1 cup boiling water
2 tsp. soda	

Combine shortening, sugar, egg and molasses. Add sifted dry ingredients, then water. Drop on baking sheet. Bake at 400°.

Frosting

2 cups sifted powdered sugar   1 tsp. lemon extract
1 tbsp. soft butter   3 tbsp. milk

Catherine Sommers, Hartville, Ohio

Grass Root Dream Cookies

½ cup margarine
½ cup granulated sugar
½ cup brown sugar, firmly packed
1 egg
¾ tsp. vanilla
1 cup sifted flour
1 tsp. baking powder
¼ tsp. soda
¼ tsp. salt
½ cup rolled oats
1 cup cornflakes
½ cup coconut

Cream together margarine, brown sugar and white sugar. Add egg and vanilla, mix until smooth. Sift flour, baking powder, soda and salt together, add to creamed mixture. Stir in rolled oats, cornflakes and coconut. Drop from teaspoon onto lightly greased cookie sheet. Bake at 325° for 12 to 15 min. Makes 5 doz. crisp 2" cookies.

Mrs. Everett Wedel, Inman, Kans.

Hermit Cookies

1 cup shortening
2 cups brown sugar
2 eggs
3½ cups sifted flour
1 tsp. soda
1 tsp. cinnamon
½ tsp. nutmeg
¼ tsp. cloves
½ tsp. salt
2 tsp. instant coffee
¼ cup water
1½ cups raisins
1 cup chopped dates
1 cup chopped walnuts

Cream together shortening and sugar. Add eggs; beat well. Sift together soda, flour, spices, salt and instant coffee. Add alternately with water to creamed mixture. Stir in fruit and nuts. Drop from teaspoon onto lightly greased cookie sheet. Bake in mod. oven (375°) 12 to 14 min. Cool slightly, place on cooling rack. Makes about 72 cookies.

Mrs. Marshall Harms, Atmore, Ala.

Mincemeat Cookies

3¼ cups sifted flour
½ tsp. salt
1 tsp. soda
1-9 oz. pkg. condensed mincement

1 cup shortening
1½ cups sugar
3 eggs, well beaten

Sift together flour, salt and soda. Cream shortening; add sugar gradually. Cream together until fluffy. Add eggs, beat well until smooth. Add mincement, broken into small pieces, and flour, mix well. Drop from tsp. onto greased baking sheet. Bake at 400° for 12 min. Yield: about 4 doz.

Mrs. F. P. Schmidt, Chickasha, Okla.

(Oatmeal) Macaroons

½ cup white sugar
½ cup brown sugar
½ cup shortening, melted
½ tsp. salt
1 egg, beaten
½ cup coconut

1 tsp. vanilla
1 banana, mashed
½ tsp. soda
1 cup flour
2 cups oatmeal

Combine ingredients in order given. Mix well. Drop from teaspoon onto greased baking sheet; press with fork. Bake at 350° 12-15 min. Yield: 3 doz. cookies.

Mrs. Henry Penner, Wisc.

(Oatmeal) Macaroon Cookies

1 cup shortening
1 cup brown sugar
1 cup white sugar
1 tsp. vanilla
2 eggs

1⅓ cups flour
1 tsp. soda
½ tsp. salt
3 cups quick oatmeal
1 cup coconut

Combine shortening, sugar, vanilla and eggs; Beat well. Sift flour, soda and salt, add to creamed mixture. Stir in oatmeal and coconut. Drop from teaspoon onto greased cookie sheet. Bake in preheated oven, 350° for 12 to 15 min. (May be stored in refrigerator for several days).

Mrs. Arlin Yost, Sublette, Kans.

Macaroons

6 egg whites	6 cups cornflakes
3 cups sugar	1½ tsp. vanilla
3 cups coconut	1½ cups nutmeats

Beat egg whites until stiff and dry. Gradually fold in sugar. Add coconut, cornflakes, nutmeats and vanilla. Mix well. Drop from teaspoon onto well greased baking sheet and bake at 375° until golden brown. Yield: 6 doz. cookies.

Mrs. Newell Litwiller, Carson City, Mich.

Peanut Buck A Roons

1 cup shortening	½ tsp. salt
1 cup granulated sugar	1 tsp. baking powder
1 cup brown sugar	2 cups oatmeal
2 eggs	1 tsp. vanilla
2 cups flour, sifted	1 cup roasted salted peanuts
1 tsp. soda	

Cream shortening and sugars. Add eggs; mix well. Sift dry ingredients and add to greased mixture. Add vanilla. Fold in oatmeal and peanuts. Form into walnut sized balls, place on greased cookie sheet and press down. Bake at 375° for 10 min.

Mrs. John B. Koehn, Galva, Kans.

Oatmeal Applesauce Cookies

1½ cups sifted flour	1 cup sugar
1 tsp. baking powder	⅔ cup shortening
¼ tsp. soda	2 eggs
1 tsp. cinnamon	1 cup applesauce
⅛ tsp. salt	1½ cups quick oatmeal
¼ tsp. nutmeg	1 cup raisins

Sift dry ingredients. Add shortening, eggs and half of the applesauce, beat until creamy (about 2 min.). Fold in remaining applesauce, oatmeal and raisins. Drop from teaspoon onto greased baking sheet about 2" apart. Bake at 375° for 10 to 12 min.

Mrs. Marion Koehn

Oatmeal Cookies (1)

2 cups oleo
3 cups brown sugar
4 eggs
2 cups buttermilk or sour milk
4 cups rolled oats
2 cups raisins, chopped
5 cups flour

2 tsp. soda
2 tsp. cinnamon
2 tsp. baking powder
2 tsp. salt
2 tsp. vanilla
1-12 oz. pkg. choc. chips

Cream oleo and sugar. Add eggs and vanilla. Add buttermilk alternately with sifted dry ingredients. Add oatmeal, raisins and choc. chips. Drop from teaspoon onto baking sheet. Bake at 350° for 8-10 min.

Mrs. Clarence Schneider, Ithaca, Mich.

Oatmeal Cookies (2)

1 cup raisins
1 cup water
¾ cup shortening
1½ cups sugar
2 eggs
1 tsp. vanilla
2½ cups flour

½ tsp. baking powder
1 tsp. cinnamon
1 tsp. salt
1 tsp. soda
½ tsp. cloves
2 cups rolled oats
½ cup nuts, chopped

Simmer raisins in water over low heat for 20-30 min.; drain liquid into measuring cup, add water if necessary to make ½ cup. Cream shortening, sugar, eggs and vanilla, add raisin liquid. Sift flour, baking powder, soda, salt and spices, add to creamed mixture. Add oatmeal, nuts and raisins. Mix well. Drop from teaspoon onto greased baking sheet; let stand for half an hour. Bake at 375° for 8-10 min. Yield: about 6-7 doz. cookies.

Mrs. P. F. Barkman, Steinbach, Man.

Oatmeal Cookies (3)

1 cup shortening
1 cup white sugar
1 cup brown sugar
2 eggs, beaten
2 cups raisins, cooked

1 tsp. soda
2 cups flour, sifted
2 cups oatmeal
1 cup nut meats
1 tsp. vanilla

Cream shortening and sugars, add eggs, mix well. Cook raisins until 3 tbsp. juice remains, dissolve soda in the juice; add to creamed mixture. Add flour, oatmeal, nuts and vanilla. Mix until well blended. Drop from teaspoon onto greased cookie sheet and bake at 375° for 12 min.

Mrs. Henry Smith, Glenn, Calif.

Oatmeal Drop Cookies

½ cup shortening
1¼ cups sugar
2 eggs
⅓ cup molasses
1 tsp. soda
1 tsp. salt

1¾ cups sifted flour
1 tsp. cinnamon
2 cups rolled oats
½ cup chopped nuts
1 cup raisins

Thoroughly cream shortening, sugar, eggs and molasses. Sift together dry ingredients and add to shortening mixture. Stir in rolled oats, nuts and raisins. Drop from tsp. onto lightly greased baking sheet. Bake 10 min. at 400°.

Mrs. Paul E. Hiebert, Hillsboro, Kans.

(Soft) Molasses Cookies

4½ cups flour
2 tsp. baking soda
3 tsp. ginger
1 tsp. salt
1 cup butter or margarine

1 cup brown sugar
2 eggs
¾ cup molasses
¾ cup sour milk

Cream shortening and sugar. Add eggs and molasses, beat well. Mix soda with milk and add alternately with sifted dry ingredients. Drop onto greased cookie sheet and bake at 350° for 10-12 min.

Mrs. Dorothy Barkman, Steinbach, Man.

(Ground) Raisin Cookies

1 cup shortening
2 cups brown sugar
2 eggs
1 tsp. vanilla
1 cup ground raisins

2¼ cups flour
2 tsp. soda
1 tsp. salt
2 cups rolled oats
½ cup chopped nuts

Cream shortening and sugar. Add eggs, vanilla and ground raisins. Add dry ingredients, rolled oats and nuts. Bake as drop cookies at 375° for 10 min.

Mrs. Thos. M. Wiebe, Steinbach, Man.

Peanut Butter Tea Cakes

1 cup sugar
¼ cup peanut butter
¼ tsp. salt
½ tsp. vanilla
1¾ cups flour

1 stick butter
1 egg
2 tbsp. milk
2 tsp. baking powder

Cream butter, sugar, egg, peanut butter, milk and vanilla. Sift flour, salt, and baking powder. Add to creamed mixture. Chill for 30 min. Drop from teaspoon onto cookie sheet. Bake at 375° for 10 min.

Mrs. Joe Holdeman, Halstead, Kans.

Pride of Iowa Cookies

1 cup brown sugar
1 cup white sugar
1 cup shortening
2 eggs
2 cups flour
½ tsp. salt

1 tsp. soda
1 tsp. baking powder
1 tsp. vanilla
1 cup coconut
3 cups rolled oats
½ cup chopped nuts, or peanuts

Cream the sugars, shortening and eggs together. Add sifted dry ingredients; then vanilla. Stir in coconut, nuts and rolled oats. Drop from tsp. onto greased cookie sheet. Flatten with a fork. Bake at 375° for 8 min. Makes 5 doz.

Phyllis Jean Boeckner, Moundridge, Kans.

(Salted) Peanut Cookies

½ cup shortening
1¼ cups brown sugar
1 egg
1½ cups flour
¾ tsp. soda
¾ cup salted peanuts, crushed

½ tsp. baking powder
½ tsp. salt
¼ cup milk
1½ cups bran flakes, grapenut flakes or raisin bran

Cream shortening, add sugar gradually, creaming until light and fluffy. Add egg and beat well. Sift flour, soda, baking powder and salt. Add to creamed mixture, alternately with milk. Add cereal and peanuts. Mix well. Drop from teaspoon onto greased sheet. Bake at 375° 8 min. Yield: 4 doz. cookies.

Mrs. Wilmer Boehs, Walker, Mo.

Pineapple Cookies

2 cups brown sugar
2 cups white sugar
4 eggs, beaten
2 cups Mazola oil
2 cups crushed pineapple, drained

2 tsp. vanilla
4 tsp baking powder
1 tsp. salt
9 cups sifted flour
1 tsp. soda

Cream sugar and oil, add beaten eggs and mix thoroughly. Add pineapple and vanilla. Add dry ingredients, mix well. Drop from teaspoon onto lightly greased cookie sheet. Bake in preheated oven 375° for 10 min. (Good for freezing.)

Mrs. Emerson Litwiller, Middleton, Mich.

Spice Raisin Drops

1½ cups sifted flour
½ cup shortening
¾ cup sugar
1½ tsp. vinegar
2 tbsp. water
1 cup raisins

½ tsp. soda
½ tsp. salt
½ cinnamon
½ tsp. cloves
½ cup rich milk

Sift dry ingredients together. Cream shortening and sugar, beat until light and fluffy. Combine vinegar, water and milk, add alternately with dry ingredients. Mix until smooth. Add raisins. Drop from teaspoon onto greased baking sheet, bake at 375° about 10 to 12 min. or until golden brown.

Mrs. Vada Johnson, Galva, Kans.

(Soft) Sugar Cookies

2 cups dark brown sugar
1 cup shortening or Wesson oil
2 eggs
1 cup buttermilk

1 tsp. soda
4 cups flour
½ tsp. salt
1 cup chopped nuts
1 tbsp. dark molasses

Thoroughly mix sugar, shortening and eggs. Stir in buttermilk. Dredge nuts in ½ cup flour. Sift together remaining flour, salt, and soda. Stir into batter. Fold in nuts. Drop from a teaspoon onto greased cooky sheet. Bake at 400° for 10 min.

Mrs. Verle Seiler, Archbold, Ohio

Raisin Drop Cookies

1 cup seedless raisins
1 cup water
1¼ cups white sugar
1 cup dark brown sugar
1 cup shortening
1 tsp. vanilla
3 eggs, well beaten

4 cups flour
1 tsp. baking powder
1 tsp. soda
1 tsp. salt
1 tsp. cinnamon
¼ tsp. nutmeg
1 cup chopped nuts
(optional)

Add water to raisins and boil 5 min. Cool. Cream shortening, white and brown sugar. Add vanilla, eggs, raisins and their liquid. Add sifted dry ingredients, mix thoroughly. Add nuts, and drop from teaspoon onto greased baking sheet. Bake 12 to 15 min. at 350°. Makes about 6 doz.

Edith Litwiller, Middleton, Mich.
Mrs. David Ensz, Inman, Kans.
Mrs. Alvin Loewen, Linden, Alberta

Sugar Cookies (Drop)

1 cup shortening
2 cups sugar
2 eggs
1 tsp. vanilla
3½ cups flour

1 tsp. soda
2 tsp. baking powder
⅓ tsp. salt
1 cup sour milk or 1 cup
sweet milk plus 2 tbsp.
vinegar

Cream shortening and sugar. Add eggs one at a time, beating well after each addition. Add vanilla. Sift together flour, soda, baking powder and salt. Add to creamed mixture alternately with sour milk. Drop onto greased cookie sheet. Sprinkle with sugar. (Dough may be chilled overnight and rolled out on floured board). Bake at 425° for 10 min.

Mrs. Marvin Koehn, Copeland, Kans.
Mrs. Amandus Seiler, Mich.

Sugar Cookies

½ cup oleo
½ tsp. salt
½ tsp. grated lemon rind
½ tsp. nutmeg
1 cup sugar

2 eggs, well beaten
2 tbsp. milk
2 cups flour
1 tsp. baking powder
½ tsp. soda

Blend oleo, salt, grated rind and nutmeg. Add sugar gradually and cream well. Add eggs, and milk. Sift together flour, baking powder and soda. Add to creamed mixture, blend well. Drop from teaspoon onto cookie sheet and flatten with glass covered with damp cloth, dipped in sugar. Bake at 375° for 8 to 10 min. Yield 3½ doz.

Karen Schmidt, Hilmar, Calif.
Delma Friesen, Conway, Kans.

Holiday Cookies

Apple and Raisin Pinwheels

Syrup:

1 cup granulated sugar	1½ cups water
1 tbsp. lemon juice	

Combine sugar, lemon juice and water. Heat to boiling; let cool.

Dough:

1½ cups sifted flour	½ cup shortening
1 tsp. salt	½ cup rolled oats
3 tsp. baking powder	2 tbsp. melted butter or oleo
½ cup milk	

Sift together flour, salt and baking powder. Cut in shortening until mixture resembles coarse crumbs. Mix in rolled oats. Add milk; mixing lightly until dough is free from sides of bowl. (Add more milk if necessary). Roll out on lightly floured board to form a rectangle about 8x12 in. Brush with melted butter.

Filling:

½ cup brown sugar	1½ cups diced raw apples
1 tbsp. cinnamon	¾ cup raisins

Mix together brown sugar, cinnamon, apples and raisins. Sprinkle over dough. Roll as for jelly roll, sealing edges. Cut into 1½ in. slices. Place pinwheels cut side down in 8x12 in. pan. Cover with syrup. Bake in hot oven (400°) for 25 to 30 min. Serve warm, plain or with whipped cream. Makes 8 pinwheels.

Mrs. Erma Koop, Scio, Ore.

Bachelor Buttons

1 cup butter
1 cup light brown sugar
1 egg
1/8 tsp. salt

2 cups flour
1 tsp. soda
1 cup chopped black walnuts
   or pecans
1 cup coconut

Mix in order given. Roll into balls about 1" in diameter. Press centers with fork. Bake at 350° for 15 min. or until brown.

Mrs. Verle Peters, Atmore, Ala.

Cherry Winks

2¼ cups sifted flour
1 tsp. baking powder
½ tsp. soda
½ tsp. salt
¾ cup shortening
1 cup sugar

2 eggs
2 tsp. milk
1 tsp. vanilla
1 cup chopped nuts
1 cup chopped dates
⅓ cup maraschino cherries,
   chopped

Sift flour, baking powder, soda and salt. Thoroughly cream the shortening and sugar. Add eggs, milk and vanilla. Beat well. Blend in the sifted dry ingredients gradually; mix thoroughly. Add nuts, dates and maraschino cherries. Mix well. Drop by rounded teaspoon into 2½ cups crushed corn flakes or coconut. Toss lightly to coat; form into balls. Place on greased baking sheet. Top each cooky with ¼ maraschino cherry. Bake in mod. oven 375° for 12 to 15 min. Makes 5 doz. cookies.

Mrs. Jac. Toews, Linden, Alberta
Nelda Litwiller, Ithaca, Mich.

Cream Cheese Pastel Bonbons

2½ cups sifted confectioners
   sugar
few drops of green food
   coloring

1 pkg. (3 oz.) soft cream
   cheese
¼ tsp. vanilla
⅛ tsp. salt

Mix well. Refrigerate covered 1 hr. Shape in balls and roll in grated coconut.

Mrs. Herman Mininger, Harrison, Mich.

Date Cookies

1 cup shortening	4 cups flour
1 cup brown sugar	1 tsp. soda
1 cup white sugar	½ tsp. cinnamon
3 eggs	½ tsp. vanilla

Cream first four ingredients, add sifted dry ingredients, mix well. Place in refrigerator until chilled. Roll out with filling.

Filling:

1 lb. dates	½ cup butter or margarine
½ cup sugar	1 cup nuts, chopped

Cook until thick, adding water for right consistency. Cool, add nuts. Spread over rolled dough, roll as for jelly roll, chill. Slice, and bake at 350° for 20 min.

Mrs. Newlin Johnson, Goltry, Okla.
Mrs. Andy N. Troyer, Uniontown, O.

Date Logs

¾ cup sifted flour	1 cup sugar
1 tsp. baking powder	¼ tsp. salt
1 cup chopped pitted dates	3 eggs, well beaten
1 cup chopped walnuts	

Sift together dry ingredients. Stir in dates, walnuts and eggs. Pour into greased 9 in. sq. pan. Bake in slow oven (325°) 35 to 40 min. Cool and cut into 48 logs. Roll in confectioners sugar.

Mrs. Merle Yost, Huron, S. Dak.
Mrs. Mildred Koehn, Livingston, Calif.

Date Nut Fingers

¼ tsp. salt	1 tbsp. flour
3 egg whites	2 cups broken pecans
1½ cups powdered sugar	1 cup chopped dates
1 tsp. vanilla	

Add salt to egg whites; beat to stiff foam. Sift sugar and flour. Add to egg whites, one tbsp. at a time, continue beating until very stiff. Fold in nuts, dates and vanilla. Drop from tsp. onto ungreased cookie sheet covered with plain paper, shape in fingers. Bake in slow oven 300° for 30 min. Makes 24 fingers.

Maryellyn Koehn, Moundridge, Kans.

Cranberry Honey Nutballs

½ cup shortening
½ cup butter or margarine
1 cup light brown sugar
⅓ cup honey
3 eggs
1 tsp. vanilla
1 tsp. cinnamon

1¼ cups whole candied cranberries
1 cup chopped pecans
1 cup flaked coconut
4 cups sifted flour
1 tsp. soda
1 tsp. salt

Thoroughly cream together shortening, butter, sugar, honey and eggs. Stir in vanilla, cranberries, nuts and coconut. Add sifted dry ingredients and mix well. Chill dough thoroughly. Shape into 1" balls and roll in granulated sugar. Bake at 350° for 12 min. or until browned.

Mrs. Stanley Giesel, Burns, Kans.

Gum Drop Cookies

1 cup shortening
1 cup brown sugar
1 cup white sugar
2 cups flour
¼ tsp. salt
1 tsp. soda

1 tsp. baking powder
2 eggs, beaten
1 cup coconut
1 cup gum drops
2 cups oatmeal
1 tsp. vanilla

Cream shortening and sugar, blend beaten eggs, mix well. Add dry ingredients and vanilla. Add coconut, gum drops and oatmeal. Form into small balls, place on greased cookie sheet. Bake at 350° about 10 min.

Mrs. Glenn Peaster, Bonners Ferry, Ida.

New Year's Cookies

2 pkg. yeast
2 cups milk
½ cup butter
⅔ cup sugar
⅓ lb. raisins

2 eggs
½ lemon rind, grated
2 tsp. lemon juice
½ tsp. nutmeg
7 cups flour

Scald milk, cool to lukewarm. Add yeast; dissolve. Mix remaining ingredients; batter will be stiff, about as heavy cake batter. Let rise until double in bulk. Drop into hot fat with tbsp. Drain on absorbent paper. Roll in powdered sugar.

Mrs. Chester Unruh, McPherson, Kans.

Date Filled Cookies

½ cup shortening	3½ cups flour
2 cups brown sugar	½ tsp. salt
2 eggs, well beaten	1 tsp. soda
1 tsp. vanilla	1 tsp. cream of tartar

Thoroughly cream shortening, sugar, eggs and vanilla. Add sifted dry ingredients. Mix well. Form into a roll. Chill thoroughly (or overnight). Slice and arrange half the slices on cooky sheet. Place 1 tsp. date filling on each and top with remaining slices, pressing together slightly. Bake in mod. oven (350°) for 10 min.

Filling:
Combine 1 lb. dates, pitted and chopped, ½ cup brown sugar and ½ cup water. Cook until thick. Add ½ cup broken nut meats and cool.

Mrs. Herman Yost, Montezuma, Kans.
Mrs. Francis Peters, McDavid, Fla.

Oatmeal Date Filled Cookies

2 cups shortening	2 tsp. soda
2 cups brown sugar	½ tsp. salt
4 eggs	4 cups oatmeal
3½ cups flour	

Cream shortening, sugar and eggs. Sift flour, salt and soda. Add to creamed mixture. Add oatmeal. Drop from spoon and press gently. Bake at 350° 10 to 12 min. Spread filling between 2 baked cookies; press together.

Filling:

2 cups chopped dates	⅔ cup water
⅔ cup sugar	

Cook 6 min. Add 1 tbsp. butter and 1 tbsp. lemon juice.

Mrs. Sam Jantz, Atmore, Ala.
Mrs. Donald Seiler, Carson City, Mich.

Date Pinwheel Cookies

2½ cups dates, cut into small pieces
1 cup white sugar   1 cup water
Cook until thick, cool. Add 1 cup nut meats, chopped.

1 cup shortening	4 cups flour
2 cups brown sugar, firmly packed	½ tsp. salt
	½ tsp. soda
3 eggs, well beaten	

Mix and divide into two parts. Roll out to ¼ in. thickness.
Spread ½ of the date filling on each roll. Roll as for jelly roll. Let
cool. Slice ¼ in. thick. Bake at 375° for 10 to 12 min.

Mrs. Elmer J. Schmidt, Copeland, Kans.
Mrs. Ben Hiebert, Atmore, Ala.
Ila Koehn, Winton, Calif.

Peppernuts (1)

3 cups white sugar	1½ cups oleo
3 eggs	1 tsp. cardamon
1 tsp. mace	1 tsp. salt
1 tsp. nutmeg	1 tsp. cloves
1 tsp. cinnamon	1 tsp. ginger
1 tsp. allspice	1½ tsp. baking powder
1 tsp. anise	1½ tsp. soda
1 cup sour cream	10 cups flour (maybe more)
1 cup dark Karo syrup	

Mix all ingredients, add enough flour to make very stiff dough.
Knead until well blended and smooth. Let stand over night in a
cool place. Make into small long rolls and slice thin. Bake at
350°.

Adella Jantz, Hesston, Kans.

Peppernuts (2)

1 cup brown sugar	1½ tsp. soda
¾ cup butter or oleo	½ tsp. pepper
¾ cup shortening	⅛ tsp. allspice
½ cup sorghum	¼ tsp. cloves
½ cup white sugar	¼ tsp. nutmeg
1 cup honey	¼ tsp. cinnamon
6 cups flour	½ cup sour cream

Cream together brown sugar, butter and shortening. Stir in the sorghum, white sugar and honey. Sift together flour, soda, pepper and spices. Add to creamed mixture alternately with sour cream. Roll in flour, into long 1" rolls. Chill; cut into ½" pieces. Bake at 375° until brown.

Mrs. A. H. Koehn, Goltry, Okla.

Peppernuts (3)

1 egg
2 cups sugar
1 cup buttermilk
1¼ cups shortening
1 tbsp. anise seed
1 cup white syrup

1 tsp. soda
½ tsp. baking powder
⅔ tsp. cinnamon
2 cups chopped nuts
enough flour for stiff dough

Beat sugar, shortening and egg. Add syrup and buttermilk. Pour 2 tbsp. boiling water over anise seed and let set a while. Add to batter. Sift soda, baking powder and cinnamon into part of the flour; Add to mixture. Add nuts, and more flour. Roll out and cut into 1" sq. or use center part of doughnut cutter. Bake in mod. oven until light brown. Or roll dough in 1" rolls, wrap in wax paper and freeze.

Mrs. Noah Holdeman, Wrens, Ga.

Peppernuts (4)

1 cup shortening
1 cup sugar
2 eggs, well beaten
1 tsp. cinnamon
¼ tsp. allspice
¼ tsp. cloves
½ tsp. nutmeg

4 tbsp. anise seed or ½ tsp. anise oil
¼ cup light syrup
½ cup molasses
⅓ cup water
⅓ tsp. soda
6⅔ cups flour

Cream shortening and sugar thoroughly. Add beaten eggs, spices and anise seed or oil. Combine syrup, molasses, water and soda. Add to creamed mixture. Add sifted flour. Chill at least 4 hrs. or overnight. Mold into long rolls ½" in diameter. Cut into ⅓" pieces. Place cut side down on greased baking sheet. Bake in hot oven (400°) for 8 min.

Mrs. Robert Koehn, Montezuma, Kans.

Raisin Filled Cookies

1⅔ cups sugar	½ tsp. soda
⅔ cup shortening	2 tsp. baking powder
2 eggs	¼ tsp. lemon flavoring
3½ cups sifted flour	¾ tsp. vanilla
¾ tsp. salt	½ cup sour cream

Cream sugar, shortening and eggs together, add soda to above mixture. Sift flour, baking powder, and salt together. Add cream and flour alternately. Chill dough.

Filling:
2½ cups raisins cut up, soaked for half a day. Make a thickening of 2 tbsp. flour and ½ cup sugar. Stir into raisins and cook till thick. Add ¼ tsp. lemon juice. Cool. When ready to bake roll dough thin, put raisin filling between layers of cookie dough. Sprinkle with sugar and bake. (Cut with floured cooky cutter.)

Mrs. Jac H. Dyck, Hesston, Kans.

Roll Kuchen
(Cookies)

1 cup heavy cream	½ tsp. baking powder
2 eggs	1 tsp. salt
2 cups flour	

Sift flour, salt and baking powder into mixing bowl, make a well, add other ingredients. Mix well. Add a bit more flour if the dough is too soft to handle. Roll out on floured board; cut in strips, cut several slits in center. Roll out fairly thin; fry in deep, hot fat or Mazola oil.

Mrs. Jac. Toews, Linden, Alberta

Sandies

1 cup butter	1 tbsp. water
¼ cup powdered sugar	2 cups flour
2 tsp. vanilla	1 cup pecans, chopped

Cream butter and sugar, add vanilla and water. Add sifted flour and pecans. Mix well. Form into small rolls 1½ in. long. Bake on ungreased baking sheet in slow oven (300°) for 20 min. Roll in powdered sugar while hot. Yield: 3 doz.

Ruby Tuxhorn, Atwater, Calif.
Mrs. Dave R. Unruh, Montezuma, Kans.

Russian Rocks

1 cup white sugar	½ tsp. cinnamon
1 cup brown sugar	¼ tsp. nutmeg
1 cup butter	¼ tsp. allspice
3 eggs	1 cup currants
4 cups flour	1 cup walnuts
½ cup cream	1 cup dates
1 tsp. soda	1 cup coconut
¼ tsp. cloves	1 cup raisins

Grind currents, walnuts, dates, coconut and raisins. Cream butter and sugars. Add eggs and cream. Stir in ground mixture, and dry ingredients. Shape into balls the size of walnuts and roll in sugar. Bake at 350° about 10 min.

Mrs. Llewellyn J. Schmidt, Newton, Kans.

Russian Teacakes

1 cup butter	¼ tsp. salt
1 tsp. vanilla	¾ cup chopped nuts
2¼ cups sifted flour	½ cup sifted powdered sugar

Mix butter, sugar and vanilla thoroughly. Sift together flour and salt. Add to creamed mixture. Add nuts. Chill dough, and roll into 1" balls. Place on ungreased baking sheet, (cookies do not spread). Bake at 400° 10 to 12 min. or until set but not brown. While still warm roll in powdered sugar. Cool. Roll in powdered sugar again. Makes about 4 doz. cookies.

Mrs. Jake K. Goertzen Jr., Inman, Kans.
Mrs. Noah Koehn, Halstead, Kans.

Scotch Shortbread

1 cup butter, softened	2⅔ cups flour
⅔ cup brown sugar	

Cream butter and brown sugar thoroughly, blend in flour. Roll out one-fourth to one-third in. thick between two sheets of waxed paper. Cut into square or diamond shapes. Brush with egg yolk diluted with water. Bake at 300° until firm to the touch and very light brown.

Miss Glenda Penner, Ballico, Calif.

Snow Balls

1 cup butter	1 tbsp. vanilla
6 tbsp. powdered sugar	1 cup chopped nuts
2 cups sifted flour	

Cream butter and sugar. Add flour, vanilla and nuts. Chill 2 hrs. Roll in powdered sugar before and after baking. Bake on ungreased cooky sheet; at 275° for 30 min. then at 300° for 10 to 15 min.

Mrs. Jim Unruh, Scott City, Kans.

Whoopy Pies

4½ cups flour	1 cup cocoa
2 cups sugar	2 eggs
2 tsp. soda	2 tsp. vanilla
1 cup shortening	1 cup sour milk
1 cup water	

Mix and cool several hours. Drop onto baking sheet by spoonfuls. Bake in oven 375° for 10 to 15 min.

Filling

2 tbsp. flour	4 cups powdered sugar
2 egg whites	1 tsp. vanilla
1½ cups Crisco	

Mix with electric mixer. Put two cookies together with filling between.

Mrs. Daniel Martin, Mifflinburg, Pa.
Mrs. Daniel Kramer, Hartville, Ohio

Molded Cookies

(Ice Box) Sugar Cookies

1 lb. butter	1 tsp. vanilla
2 cups sugar	1 tsp. soda
3 eggs	1 tsp. salt
1 tbsp. molasses	5½ cups sifted flour

Cream butter and sugar. Add eggs and molasses, beat well. Add remaining ingredients. Chill 2 hrs. Roll into balls and flatten with a water glass pressed in sugar. Bake on greased cookie sheet at 375° for 10 to 12 min.

Mrs. Calvin Koehn, Montezuma, Kans.

Angel Crisps

½ cup brown sugar
½ cup white sugar
½ cup butter or oleo
1 egg
1 tsp. vanilla

2 cups flour
1 tsp. soda
1 tsp. cream of tartar
½ tsp. salt

Cream butter and sugars; add egg and vanilla. Sift dry ingredients and add to creamed mixture; mix well. Roll into small balls. Moisten half of ball in water and dip in sugar. Place on baking sheet sugar side up and dent cookie with finger tip. Bake at 375° for 12 min.

Mrs. Keith Toews, Wales, N. Dak.

Angel Food Cookies (1)

1 cup sugar
1 cup brown sugar
1½ cups shortening
12 egg yolks
2 tsp. vanilla

½ tsp. salt
1 tsp. soda
2 tsp. baking powder
3½ cups flour

Cream shortening and sugars, add egg yolks and vanilla. Sift together dry ingredients and add to creamed mixture. Mix well. Form into small balls and roll in sugar. Place on greased cookie sheet and flatten with meat tenderizer. Bake at 375° for 15 min.

Mrs. Dewey Smith, Montezuma, Kans.

Angel Food Cookies (2)

1 cup shortening
½ cup brown sugar
½ cup white sugar
1 egg, beaten
¼ tsp. salt

2 cups flour, sifted
1 tsp. soda
1 tsp. cream of tartar
1 cup coconut
1 tsp. banana or vanilla
  flavoring

Cream shortening and sugars, add egg. Sift flour, measure, sift with salt, soda, and cream of tartar. Add to first mixture, mix thoroughly. Add coconut and flavoring. Roll dough into small balls and dip in water, then roll in sugar. Place on greased and floured baking sheet. Bake at 375° for 15 min, or until brown. Yield: 4 doz. cookies.

Mrs. Daniel J. Schmidt, Montezuma, Kans.

Chocolate Icebox Cookies

2 cups sifted flour
¼ tsp. soda
½ tsp. salt
¾ cup shortening
1¾ cups sugar

2 tsp. vanilla
1 egg
2 sq. chocolate, melted (or 4 tbsp. cocoa)
1 tbsp. vinegar
¾ cup nuts

Sift together flour, baking soda and salt. Cream together shortening, sugar and vanilla. Beat in egg and chocolate, then vinegar. Blend in dry ingredients and nuts. Place in refrigerator and chill several hrs. Form into balls and roll in powdered sugar. Bake at 375° about 10 min. Yield: about 7 doz. cookies.

Mrs. Clarence Schmidt, Newton, Kansas

(Super Duper) Chocolate Cookies

½ cup shortening
4 sq. unsweetened chocolate
2 cups sugar
2 tsp. vanilla
4 eggs, unbeaten

2 cups flour
2 tsp. baking powder
⅛ tsp. salt
½ cup nuts, chopped
confectioners sugar

Melt shortening and chocolate; add sugar and vanilla; mix well. Add eggs, one at a time, beating well after each addition. Sift together flour, baking powder and salt. Add to chocolate mixture. Add nuts. Chill dough several hrs. Form into small balls; roll in confectioners sugar. Bake in 350° oven, 12 to 15 min.

Mrs. Lloyd Gearig, Louisville, Ga.

Maple Pecan Cookies

1 cup butter or oleo
3 cups brown sugar
2 eggs, well beaten
1 tsp. maple flavoring
4 cups flour

1 tsp. soda
½ tsp. salt
1 tsp. baking powder
1 cup pecans, chopped
2 cups coconut, chopped

Cream butter and sugar. Add maple flavoring and eggs. Sift together dry ingredients and add to mixture. Add coconut and pecans. Form into rolls, 2" in diameter. Roll in waxed paper and chill until firm. Slice ¼" thick and bake at 350° for 10 to 12 min. Makes 7 doz.

Mrs. Newell Eicher, Atmore, Ala.
Mrs. Richard Penner, Bonners Ferry, Ida.

Crunchy Nut Cookies

1 cup white sugar
1 cup brown sugar
½ cup soft shortening
2 eggs
1 tsp. vanilla

3 cups sifted flour
1 tsp. soda
½ tsp. salt
1 cup chopped nuts

Thoroughly mix sugars, shortening, eggs and vanilla. Sift together flour, soda and salt; add to creamed mixture. Add nuts. Shape 1 level tablespoon of dough into balls. Place on greased baking sheet, flatten with bottom of greased glass dipped in sugar. Bake at 350° for 8 to 10 min.

Mary Ann Friesen, Glenn, Calif.

Mexican Crinkles

¾ cup shortening
1 cup sugar
1 egg
¼ cup light corn syrup
2 (1 oz.) unsweetened
chocolate, melted

1¾ cups sifted flour
2 tsp. baking soda
¼ tsp. salt
1 tsp. cinnamon
¼ cup sugar

Cream together shortening, sugar, and egg. Stir in syrup and choc. Sift flour, soda, salt, and cinnamon into creamed mixture. Will make a stiff dough. Shape dough into balls the size of walnuts and roll in sugar. Place balls on ungreased baking sheet 3" apart. Bake at 350° for 15 min.

Mrs. Edwin Dyck, Bonner Ferry, Ida.

Oatmeal Cookies

3 cups quick oats
2 cups flour
½ tsp. soda
1 cup shortening, melted
2 eggs
½ tsp. salt

1 cup brown sugar
1½ cups white sugar
1 cup raisins
1 cup nut meats
1 tsp. vanilla

Cream shortening, sugars, eggs and vanilla. Add sifted dry ingredients, oatmeal, raisins and nuts. Mix well. Roll into balls and place on greased baking sheet. Bake at 350° 10-15 min.

Mrs. Willie Eck, Fairview, Okla.

Krispy Krunch Cookies

1 cup shortening
1 cup brown sugar
1 tsp. vanilla
1 tsp. soda
½ tsp. salt
2 cups rolled oats

1 cup white syrup
2 eggs
2 cups flour
1 tsp. baking powder
2 cups rice krispies
1 cup coconut

Cream shortening and sugar. Add eggs and vanilla. Mix until smooth. Add sifted dry ingredients and mix well. Add rolled oats, rice krispies and coconut. Roll into 1" balls. Place on greased cookie sheet and flatten with spatula dipped in milk. Bake at 350° for 11 min. (Chocolate chips may be used instead of coconut.)

Mrs. Robert Koehn, Montezuma, Kans.
Mrs. Marvin Schmidt, Hilmar, Calif.

Moab Crispies

2 cups flour
½ tsp. salt
¼ tsp. soda
¼ tsp. baking powder
2 tbsp. instant coffee
¾ cup shortening

½ cup light brown sugar
½ cup white sugar
1 egg
1½ tsp. vanilla
1 tbsp. milk

Sift together flour, salt, soda, baking powder and instant coffee. Cream shortening, white sugar and brown sugar until light and fluffy, add egg and vanilla beat well. Add milk, then gradually blend in flour mixture. Shape into 1" balls; place 2" apart on ungreased cookie sheets. Flatten to ⅛" thickness with bottom of designed glass. Bake 8 min. at 400° until edges are brown. (Do not overbake).

Mrs. Ruby Nightingale

Molasses Sugar Cookies
(Sometimes called Dusty Miller Cookies)

1½ cups shortening
2 cups sugar
½ cup molasses
2 eggs
2 tsp. baking soda

4 cups sifted all-purpose flour
1 tsp. cloves
½ tsp. ginger
2 tsp. cinnamon
1 tsp. salt

Place all ingredients into a large mixing bowl and mix well. Form into 1" balls. Roll in granulated or powdered sugar and place 2" apart on cookie sheet. Bake at 350° 8 to 10 min.

Mrs. Alvin Peaster, Winton, Calif.
Mrs. Viola Harms, Fla.
Mrs. Don Nightingale, Fairview, Okla.

Oatmeal Refrigerator Cookies

1 cup white sugar
1 cup brown sugar
1 cup shortening
2 eggs
1 tsp. vanilla

1½ cups flour, sifted
1 tsp. soda
1 tsp. salt
3 cups rolled oats

Cream shortening and sugars. Add eggs, beat until fluffy; add vanilla. Sift flour with soda and salt, stir into first mixture. Add rolled oats, blend well. Shape into rolls and store in refrigerator several hrs. or overnight. Slice and bake on greased cookie sheet at 400° 8-10 min.

Mrs. Arnold Unruh, Copeland, Kans.
Mrs. Robert Blosser, Halstead, Kans.

Orange Oatmeal Cookies

1 cup jellied orange slices, (candy)
1½ cups sifted flour
½ tsp. baking powder
½ tsp. soda
⅔ cup butter or margarine
⅔ cup white sugar

¼ tsp. salt
⅔ cup brown sugar
1 egg
1 tsp. vanilla
1½ cups quick oats
1 cup shredded coconut
⅔ cup nut meats (optional)

Reserve ½ cup flour; using floured scissors, cut orange slices into small pieces, add to reserved flour. Sift remaining flour, baking powder, soda and salt together. Cream shortening and sugars, add egg and vanilla. Stir in sifted dry ingredients, add coconut, oatmeal and floured orange slices. Mix well. Shape into balls using tbsp. of dough for each ball. Place on greased baking sheet and flatten slightly. Bake at 375° 10-12 min.

Mrs. Loren Becker, Tucumcari, New Mexico
Mrs. Frank Nichols, Fairview, Okla.
Mrs. Henry T. Ensz, Inman, Kans.

Peanut Blossoms

1 cup shortening
1 cup peanut butter
1 cup brown sugar
1 cup granulated sugar
2 eggs
3 cups flour

½ tsp. salt
2 tsp. soda
1 tsp. baking powder
1 tsp. vanilla
1 pkg. chocolate candy kisses

Cream shortening and peanut butter; add sugar and beat well. Add eggs and vanilla, beat until fluffy. Sift flour; measure add salt, soda and baking powder; sift again. Gradually add sifted dry ingredients to creamed mixture and mix thoroughly. Chill for several hours in refrigerator. Shape dough into balls 1" in diameter. Place balls 2 to 3" apart on greased baking sheet. Bake at 375° for 8 min. Remove from oven and press a chocolate kiss in the center of each cooky. Return to oven and bake for 4 min. more. Makes 7 doz.

Sharon Jantz, Winton, Calif.
Mrs. James Mlejneh, Rice Lake, Wis.

(Double) Peanut Cookies

1½ cups sifted flour
½ cup sugar
½ tsp. soda
¼ tsp. salt

½ cup shortening
½ cup creamy peanut butter
¼ cup light corn syrup

Sift together dry ingredients. Cut in shortening and peanut butter until mixture resembles coarse meal. Blend in corn syrup. Shape into 2" roll; chill. Slice slightly less than ¼" thick. Place half of slices on ungreased baking sheet; spread each with ½ tsp. peanut butter, cover with remaining slices; seal edges with fork. Bake in mod. oven (350°) 12 to 15 min. Cool slightly before removing from baking sheet.

Donella Holdeman, Hesston, Kans.

Pecan Roll Cookies

1 cup soft shortening
1 cup soft butter or oleo
3 cups powdered sugar
1 tbsp. vanilla

3 cups flour
3 cups cornflakes
2 cups chopped pecans

Beat together shortening, butter, sugar and vanilla until the consistency of thick whipped cream; add sifted flour and mix well. Stir in cornflakes. Divide dough into four equal portions; shape into rolls about 1½ in. Coat rolls with pecans; wrap each roll in waxed paper, refrigerate 12 hrs. Cut in ½ in. slices, place on ungreased cookie sheet. Bake at 350° about 15 min. **Yield:** 6 doz. cookies. (If dough is too soft to be shaped into rolls, chill before shaping as well as after).

Lydia Schmidt, Halstead, Kans.

Ranger Cookies

1 cup shortening
1 cup white sugar
1 cup brown sugar
2 eggs
1½ tsp. vanilla
½ cup water optional
2 cups white or whole wheat flour
1 tsp. soda
½ tsp. baking powder
½ tsp. salt
2 cups cornflakes or rice-krispies
2 cups rolled oats
1 cup coconut
¾ cup raisins (optional)

Cream shortening and sugars. Add eggs and vanilla. Stir in sifted dry ingredients alternately with water. Blend in cornflakes or rice krispies, oatmeal and coconut. Shape into balls the size of walnuts; place on cookie sheet and flatten. Bake at 350° 10-12 min. Yield: 50 cookies.

Mrs. Ben Giesbrecht, Glenn, Calif.
Mrs. Jonas Schmidt, Fairview, Okla.
Mrs. Dale Rhodes, Tampa, Kans.

(Tender Crisp) Sugar Cookies

½ cup butter
½ cup shortening
½ cup sugar
½ cup powdered sugar
1 egg
1½ tsp. vanilla
2¼ cups sifted flour
½ tsp. soda
½ tsp. cream of tartar
½ tsp. salt

Cream butter, shortening and sugars until light and fluffy. Add egg and vanilla, beat well. Sift dry ingredients; add to creamed mixture; mix thoroughly. Shape dough into 1" balls. Place on lightly greased cooky sheet. Dip bottom of glass in granulated sugar, press balls flat, redipping glass for each cookie. Bake at 375° for 10 to 12 min. or until lightly browned.

Florence Amoth

Roll Cookies

Amish Church Cookies

2½ cups white sugar
2½ cups brown sugar
3 cups shortening
enough flour to make suitable dough

3 cups sweet milk
3 tsp. soda
6 tsp. baking powder
3 tsp. vanilla or lemon flavoring

Cream sugars and shortening. Add sifted dry ingredients alternately with milk and flavoring. Roll out on floured board. Bake at 350° for 10 to 12 min.

Mrs. Melvin Beachy, Thomas, Okla.

Cream Cheese Cookies

1 cup shortening
3 oz. cream cheese
1 cup sugar

2 egg yolks
½ tsp. vanilla
2½ cups sifted flour

Cream shortening, add softened cream cheese, blend well. Add sugar, egg yolks, vanilla and flour, mix thoroughly, to thick mixture. Roll out dough on lightly floured board, cut in circles or as desired and bake at 350° for 10 to 15 min.

Mrs. Chester Koehn, Verden, Okla.

Sour Cream Cookies

4 cups brown sugar
2 cups sour cream
1 tsp. vanilla
4 tsp. baking powder

1½ cups butter or oleo
6 well beaten eggs
4 tsp. soda
7 cups flour, or enough to make soft dough

Cream sugar and shortening. Add eggs and cream. Beat well. **Add dry ingredients.** Place in refrigerator over night. Roll and bake at 400° for 10-12 min.

Mrs. Levi J. Plank

Crispy Cookie Coffee Cake

1 pkg. yeast
¼ cup warm water
4 cups sifted flour
1 tsp. salt
1 grated lemon rind
(optional)

1¼ cups sugar
1 cup oleo (2 sticks)
2 eggs, beaten
1 cup milk, scalded and
cooled to lukewarm
1 tbsp. cinnamon

Dissolve yeast in water in small bowl. In large bowl combine flour, salt, lemon rind, ¼ cup sugar, and cut in oleo with fork. Combine eggs, milk, dissolved yeast, and add to flour mixture. Combine lightly. Cover. Refrigerate over night. Divide dough in half. On a floured board roll each piece into 18"x12". Sprinkle with remaining cup sugar mixed with cinnamon. Roll up tightly beginning at the wide end. Cut each roll into 1 inch slices. Place cut side up on greased baking sheet. Flatten with palm of hand. Bake at 400° about 12 min. Makes 3 doz.

Mrs. Ben Holdeman, Harrison, Mich.

Sour Milk Cookies (Old Fashioned)

2 cups sugar
1 cup oleo
2 eggs
1 cup sour milk or buttermilk
1 tsp. soda

1 tsp. baking powder
1 tsp. salt
1 tbsp. vanilla
5 cups flour (to make a soft
dough)

Cream sugar, oleo and eggs. Add remaining ingredients and mix well. Roll out and cut. Place on cookie sheets and sprinkle with sugar; press a raisin in the center of each cookie. Bake in mod. oven (350°) for 10 to 12 min.

Mrs. Lorene Kuepfer, Harrison, Mich.

Unbaked Cookies

Peanut Butter Squares

½ cup white syrup   ½ cup sugar

Bring mixture to boiling point to dissolve sugar. Add ⅔ cup peanut butter and stir. Add 5 cups rice krispies. Cut into squares.

Mrs. Floyd Yost, Moundridge, Kans.

Candy Haystacks

Combine: 50 graham crackers, rolled fine

½ cup pecans
2 tbsp. margarine   1½ cups coconut

Boil together 1 min.:

¼ cup brown sugar   ½ cup milk
1 tsp. vanilla   1 cup sugar

Add: 1 tsp. vanilla

Stir syrup mixtures into crumb mixture and form into cone shapes or balls. Chill or freeze.

No Bake Chocolate Oatmeal Cookies

2 cups sugar   3 cups uncooked 3 min. oats
4 tbsp. cocoa   ½ cup walnuts or
½ cup milk or cream   ½ cup peanut butter
½ cup margarine

Combine sugar, cocoa, milk and margarine. Bring to boiling and boil for 1 min. Remove from heat and stir in oats and nuts. Drop from teaspoon onto waxed paper.

Verda Wedel, Meade, Kans.
Wilma Martin, Dalton, Ohio
Mrs. Gilbert Koehn, Burns, Kans.

Unbaked Chocolate Cookies

2 cups sugar   3 cups oatmeal
⅓ cup cocoa   1 cup coconut
½ cup butter or oleo   ½ cup nuts, chopped
½ cup milk   1 tsp. vanilla

Mix first four ingredients in saucepan and boil for three min. Remove from heat; add vanilla. Mix oatmeal, coconut and nuts. Pour the milk mixture over the dry ingredients and mix thoroughly. Drop from teaspoon onto waxed paper. Yield: 3½ doz. cookies.

Velma Jantz, Horton, Mo.

Unbaked Chocolate Oatmeal Cookies

2 cups white sugar
½ cup milk
½ cup crunchy peanut butter
3 cups quick oats
¼ cup cocoa
½ cup oleo
1 tsp. vanilla

Mix sugar, cocoa, milk and oleo in saucepan. Boil one min. Remove from heat; stir in peanut butter, vanilla and oatmeal. Drop from teaspoon on waxed paper; let stand until hardened.

Mrs. Duane Johnson, Atwater, Calif.
Mrs. Monroe Holdeman, Harrison, Mich.

Unbaked Cookies

1 cup sugar
1 cup syrup
12 oz. crunchy peanut butter
4 cups rice krispies
1 pkg. chocolate chips
1 pkg. butterscotch chips

Melt the sugar and syrup until dissolved. Fold in peanut butter and rice krispies. Spread into 8"x12" pan. Melt and blend together the chocolate chips and butterscotch chips and spread over top. Cut in squares.

Mrs. Eugene Wedel, Copeland, Kans.

Graham Cracker Bars

Cover bottom of 9x13 inch pan with whole graham crackers. Boil together for 2 minutes the following:

1 egg slightly beaten
1 cup sugar
1 stick oleo

Remove from heat and add;

1½ cup graham cracker crumbs
1 tsp. vanilla
1½ cup coconut

Spread over whole graham crackers in the pan. Top with whole graham crackers, press firmly. When cool cut into 1x2 inch bars.

Haystacks

1 6 oz. pkg. butterscotch morsels
1 3 oz. can Chow Mein noodles
2 tsp. salad oil
2 cups miniature marshmallows

In double boiler over hot (not boiling) water, melt butterscotch morsels.

Stir in salad oil. In large bowl, mix chow mein noodles and marshmallows; pour on butterscotch and mix thoroughly with fork.

Drop mixture by heaping teaspoonfuls. (If mixture thickens, place over hot water a few minutes.) Chill until set.

No Bake Cookies

Mix in saucepan:

2 cups sugar
⅔ cup milk

Boil for three min. Remove from heat; add 1 tsp. vanilla and 6 tbsp. peanut butter. Then mix in ¼ lb. soda crackers, crumbled. Stir until completely mixed. Drop from teaspoon on waxed paper. Cool.

DESSERTS AND TOPPINGS

Baked Puddings and Desserts

Baked Apples

Prepare apples and cut in half. Place in a loaf pan, 9x13".

2 cups sugar	2 tbsp. flour
1 tsp. cinnamon	little milk
1 cup cream	

Mix together and pour over the apples. Bake in preheated oven at 350° for 30 min. then reduce heat to 300° and bake until done.

Mrs. Roy Dyck, Hesston, Kans.

Apple Crisp (1)

4 cups sliced apples	1 tsp. cinnamon
½ cup water	1 cup sugar
¾ cup flour	½ cup butter or oleo

Mix together apples, cinnamon and water. Pour into an 8" buttered baking dish. Mix together flour, sugar and butter until crumbly. Press over top of apples. Bake at 375° for 30 min. Top with whipped cream.

Mrs. Martha Nichols, Neodesha, Kans.
Mrs. Donald Schmidt, Fredonia, Kans.

Apple Crisp (2)

Arrange 2 cups raw apples, pared and diced, in an 8"x8" baking pan. Sprinkle as desired with cinnamon. Mix:

1 cup flour	1 cup sugar
1 unbeaten egg	½ tsp. salt
1 tsp. baking powder	

Stir with a spoon into coarse crumbs. Sprinkle over apples and pour over all ⅓ cup melted butter. Bake 30 min. at 350°. Serve with a dip of ice cream.

Irene Eicher, Ithaca, Mich.
Mrs. Freeman Schmidt, Fairview, Okla.

Golden Brown Apple Dumplings

2 cups sugar	2 cups flour
2 cups water	1 tsp. salt
1/4 tsp. cinnamon	2 tsp. baking powder
1/4 tsp. nutmeg	3/4 cup shortening
1/4 cup butter	1/2 cup milk
6 apples	

Sauce: Combine sugar, water, cinnamon and nutmeg. Cook 5 min. Add butter. Pare and core apples. Sift flour, salt and baking powder. Cut in shortening. Add milk, stir just until flour is moistened. Roll 1/4 inch thick. Cut six 5 inch squares. Place 1 apple on each square. Sprinkle with sugar and spices. Fold corners, pinch edges. Place 1 inch apart in greased pan. Pour sauce over dumplings. Bake at 375° 35 min. Serve hot with cream. Serves 6.

Mrs. Emery Yost, Halstead, Kans.

Apple Dumplings

Prepare 1 recipe of baking powder biscuit dough:

6 apples pared and cored	1/4 tsp. salt
2 tbsp. melted butter or magarine	1/4 tsp. nutmeg
	2 tbsp. lemon juice
1/2 cup sugar	1 tsp. cinnamon

Syrup

Combine:

1 cup white sugar	2 cups water
1/2 cup brown sugar	2 tbsp. tapioca

Let apples soak in water a few min. then boil for 5 min. Roll the biscuit dough to 1/8 in. thickness. Cut into 6 squares. Place an apple in each square. Fill centers of apples with a mixture of butter, lemon juice and spices. Pinch corners of squares together over each apple. Place in greased baking dish. Pour syrup over the dumplings and bake at 450° for 10 min. then reduce temperature to 350° and continue baking for 35 to 40 min. or until apples are tender Baste occasionally with syrup mixture during baking. Serves 6.

Mrs. Herman P. Koehn, Chickasha, Okla.

Apple Goodies

10 med. apples	½ cup oatmeal
1 cup sugar	½ cup brown sugar
1 tbsp. flour	¼ cup butter or oleo
⅔ tsp. cinnamon	½ cup flour
⅛ tsp. salt	⅛ tsp. soda
⅓ cup water	⅛ tsp. baking powder

Peel apples, slice thin and place in 9"x9" baking pan. Blend sugar, one tbsp. flour, cinnamon and salt, mix with apples. Add water. Combine oatmeal, brown sugar, butter, one-half cup flour, soda, and baking powder, mix until crumbly. Sprinkle over apples and pat firm. Bake one hour at 175°.

Mrs. Gary Koehn, Halstead, Kans.
Mrs. Menno Koehn, Halstead, Kans.
Anna S. Hibner, Mich.
Mrs. Marlin Wedel, Galva, Kans.

Apple Pudding

1 cup white sugar	¼ tsp. salt
½ cup butter	1 tsp. cinnamon
1 egg	1 tsp. nutmeg
1 cup raisins	1 tsp. soda
1 cup chopped nuts	2 cups peeled, chopped apples
1 cup sifted flour	

Cream butter and sugar, add egg; beat well. Add apples, raisins and nuts, then flour sifted with salt, soda and spices. Bake in oiled 9"x12" pan at 350° for 40 min. Serve with whipped cream.

Mrs. Raymond Ratzlaff

Bread Pudding (Old Fashioned)

5 slices buttered bread	1 cup raisins
4 cups milk	4 eggs
¾ cup sugar	1½ tsp. vanilla
1 tsp. nutmeg	½ tsp. salt

Cut bread into 1½ in. squares into large bowl. Beat eggs, add sugar, milk, raisins and remaining ingredients. Mix with bread cubes. Pour into a 2 qt. greased baking dish. Cover. Bake 1 hr. and 15 min. at 350°.

Mrs. Leonard Peaster, Winton, Calif.

Mock Apple Strudel

2 cups flour	1 cup milk
1 tsp. salt	4 apples
4 tsp. baking powder	¼ cup raisins
¼ cup butter	¼ cup sugar
1 egg, beaten	

Sift flour, salt and baking powder and blend in butter. Add beaten egg and milk. Place dough in 9"x9" baking pan. Peel and slice apples and press in dough. Sprinkle with raisins and sugar and bake about 30 min. at 350° or until nearly done. Then pour over the creamed custard mixture and bake 30 min. longer.

Creamed Custard

2 tbsp. butter	1 egg, beaten
3 tbsp. sugar	½ cup milk

Frank H. Burns, Hesston, Kans.

Apple Turnover

4 cups apples	1 tbsp. water
⅔ cup sugar (brown pre-	1 cup sour cream
ferred)	¼ tsp. salt
1 tbsp. butter	1 tsp. soda
½ tsp. cinnamon	1 cup flour

Place apples in 9" pie pan. Sprinkle sugar, butter, cinnamon, and water over apples Make a batter of sour cream, salt, soda, and flour. Spread over apples. Bake in 350° oven until apples are tender and top is brown. Turn upside down on serving plate. Serve hot with cream and sugar.

Mrs. Bessie Mastre, Galva, Kans.

Apricot Krisp

1 qt. sweetened apricots

Heat and thicken. Pour into greased baking dish, cover with mixture of:

1 cup sugar	⅛ tsp. salt
1 cup flour	¾ tsp. baking powder
1 egg	

Mix all together until crumbly. Bake at 350° until topping is golden brown. Serve with vanilla sauce:

¼ cup sugar	2 cups rich milk
1 tbsp. corn starch	⅛ tsp. salt
½ tsp. vanilla	

Stir while cooking until slightly thickened.

Mrs. Dale Haynes, Ithaca, Mich.

Baked Chocolate Float

1 cup sugar	1 cup flour
1½ cups water	½ tsp. salt
12 marshmallows	1 tsp. baking powder
2 tbsp. butter	3 tbsp. cocoa
1 tsp. vanilla	½ cup milk
	½ cup chopped nuts

Cook ½ cup sugar and water 5 min. Pour into casserole. Top with marshmallows. Cream butter, ½ cup sugar and vanilla. Add flour, salt, baking powder and cocoa, alternately with milk. Add nuts. Drop from spoon over marshmallows. Cover. Bake in moderate (350°) oven for 45 min.

Velma Dyck, Hesston, Kans.

Brown Pudding or Hot Fudge Pudding

1 cup sifted flour	½ cup milk
2 tsp. baking powder	2 tbsp. melted butter
½ tsp. salt	½ cup nuts
¾ cup sugar	1 sq. melted choc. or 2 tbsp. cocoa

Sift flour, baking powder, salt, sugar and cocoa together into bowl. Stir in milk and butter. Blend in nuts. Spread in 9x9 in. pan. Sprinkle batter with ½ cup sugar and ½ cup brown sugar and 4 tbsp. cocoa. Pour 1 cup cold water over top. Bake at 350° for 40 min. (During baking cake rises and choc. sauce settles to bottom). Serve with ice cream.

Mrs. Jake K. Goertzen Jr., Inman, Kans.
Mrs. Jake H. Loewen, Glenn, Calif.

Blueberry Dessert

20 graham crackers
½ cup sugar

½ cup butter or oleo

Blend and press into 13"x9" pan.

2 eggs
1 large pkg. cream cheese

1 cup sugar
1 tsp. vanilla
1 can blueberry pie filling

Cream together eggs, sugar, cream cheese and vanilla. Spread on top of cracker crust and bake 350° for 20 min. Cool. Heat one can blueberry pie filling, add 1 tbsp. lemon juice, cool. Then spread on cheese and refrigerate.

Carolyn Wenger, Newton, Kans.

Brown Sugar Pudding

1 cup sugar
2 cups flour
2 tsp. baking powder

¼ tsp. salt
1 cup milk
1 tsp. vanilla

Syrup

1½ cups brown sugar
1⅓ cups water

2 tbsp. butter

Combine brown sugar, water and butter; cook 5 min. until syrupy. Sift sugar, flour, baking powder and salt together. Add vanilla to milk and pour all into dry ingredients. Beat until thoroughly mixed. Pour syrup into buttered baking dish. Drop dough by spoonsful over hot syrup. Bake at 350° for 45 min. Makes 6 servings.

Cherry Crunch (1)

1 cup flour
1 cup brown sugar
⅛ tsp. salt

1 cup oatmeal
½ cup soft butter
3 cups cherries

Mix all but fruit till crumbly. Put ½ of the mixture in a greased pan. Pour thickened or ready mix fruit over crumbs. Spread remainder of crumb mixture over top of fruit. Bake 30 min. at 350°. Serve with ice cream or whipped cream. (Blueberry, apple or other fruits may be used.)

Mrs. Kenneth Nightengale, Copeland, Kans.

Cherry Pudding (1)

Heat to boiling point:
1 cup sugar   1 can sour cherries

Mix:
1 cup sugar   2 tsp. butter
1 cup flour   ½ cup milk
1 tsp. baking powder

Sift dry ingredients together. Cut in butter, add milk, beat and pour over hot cherry mixture in a deep baking dish. Bake at 375° about 35 min.

Mrs. Dale Schmidt, Plains, Kans.

Cherry Pudding (2)

2 tbsp. butter   1 tsp. baking powder
1 cup sugar   1 cup cherries
½ cup milk   ¾ cup sugar
1 cup flour   ¼ cup warm water

Cream butter and sugar, add milk and flour with baking powder added. Pour into greased baking dish. Add sugar to cherries; heat until sugar is dissolved; add water. Pour cherries over batter at 350° for 40 min.

Mrs. Vernie Smith, Goltry, Okla.

Cherry Pudding (3)

1 cup sugar   2 tbsp. butter
1 cup milk   ⅛ tsp. salt
2 cups flour   2 tsp. baking powder

Blend and pour into well buttered pan.
2 cups cherries   1 tbsp. butter
1 cup sugar   1 cup cherry juice

Mix and pour over top of batter. Bake at 350°. Serve with whipped cream. Serves 12.

Eva Koehn, Galva, Kans.

Cherry Crunch (2)

40 graham crackers, rolled fine   ¾ cup sugar
1 tsp. cinnamon   1½ sticks margarine

Melt butter, mix in sugar, cracker crumbs and cinnamon. Press ¾ of crumbs into bottom and sides of a buttered 2 qt. pan.

1 qt. cherries   5 tbsp. cornstarch
1½ cups sugar

Cook until clear and thick, stirring constantly. Pour over crumbs in pan. Beat 5 egg whites until stiff, add ¼ cup sugar. Spread over cherries and top with remaining crumbs. Bake until brown at 350° for 30 min. Cut in squares. Serve plain or with whipped cream.

Mrs. Delbert Hiebert, Middleton, Mich.
Delma Friesen, Conway, Kans.

Crispy Cherry Crumble

¼ cup sifted flour   1 cup sugar
¾ cup cherry juice   1 No. 2 can sour cherries,
¼ tsp. red food coloring   drained
1½ cups flour   1 tsp. salt
½ teaspoon soda   1 cup brown sugar
1 cup oatmeal   ½ cup shortening

Mix ¼ cup flour and sugar thoroughly, add cherry juice and coloring; cook until mixture thickens, stirring constantly. Add cherries; cool. Sift 1½ cups flour, salt and soda. Add brown sugar and oatmeal. Cut in shortening until particles are size of small peas. Press half the mixture into ungreased 13"x9" pan. Spread with cherry filling. Sprinkle with remaining oatmeal mixture, pressing gently. Bake at 350° for 30 min. Serve with whipped cream.

Mrs. Donald Giesbrecht, Glenn, Calif.

Cherry Pineapple Crisp

1 cup canned, crushed pineapple   ¼ tsp. soda
2½ cups canned pitted cherries   1 cup sugar
3 tbsp. quick cooking tapioca   1 cup sifted flour
1 tbsp. lemon juice   1 cup quick cooking oats
(optional)   ⅔ cup brown sugar
                                      ½ cup melted butter or oleo

Filling: Cook first 5 ingredients until clear, stirring constantly; cool. For Crumb Crust: Sift flour and soda. Mix in oats, brown sugar and butter. Place one-half of the oats mixture in 9" sq. pan. Pour filling over crumbs. Top with remaining oats mixture. Bake in hot oven (400°) for 25 min. Serve warm or cold with whipped cream, ice cream or milk.

Mrs. Rodney Koehn

Cocktail or Mystery Dessert

1¼ cups unsifted all-purpose   1 cup sugar
   flour   ½ tsp. salt
1 tsp. soda

Beat in 1 egg, add 2 cups fruit cocktail and mix all together. Put in ungreased 9"x14" pan.
Topping: Mix ¾ cup brown sugar and ½ cup nut meats.
Sprinkle on top. Bake at 325° for 40 to 50 min. Serve plain or with whipped cream, ice cream or hard sauce.

Mrs. Aaron Boeckner, Moundridge, Kans.
Leanna Friesen, Ste. Anne, Man.

(Quick) Cherry Dessert

1 can cherry pie filling   1 box white cake mix
¼ lb. oleo

Spread dry cake mix over top of cherry filling. Slice oleo thin and lay on top of dry cake mix. Bake at 275-300° for 20-30 min. Serve warm with ice cream.

Mrs. Maynard Peters, Wrens, Ga.

(Bohemian Fruit) Cobbler

Use cherries, prunes or rhubarb—4 cups in 8"x9" pan. Sprinkle generously with sugar and cinnamon.
Topping:

1⅓ cups Bisquick   1 tsp. vanilla
¾ cup sugar   1 egg
3 tbsp. shortening   ¾ cup milk

Mix ¼ cup milk with all the ingredients. Beat well. Stir in remaining milk and beat well until smooth. Pour over fruit. Sprinkle with sugar and cinnamon. Bake at 350° for 45 min.

Lambert Janda, Atwater, Calif.

(Quick) Cobbler

1 cup sugar   1 cup milk
1 cup flour   ⅛ tsp. salt
2 tsp. baking powder

Melt 1 stick oleo in cake pan. Pour batter over melted oleo. Do not stir. Pour sweetened fruit and juice over batter. Bake 40 min. at 375°.

Mrs. Rodney Koehn

Cracker Pudding

Cook together:

2 cups broken crackers   1 cup coconut
4 cups milk   2 egg yolks
1 cup sugar   ½ cup raisins (optional)

Beat egg whites and spread over pudding in 9"x9" pan. Bake until golden brown at 325° for approximately 20 min.

Myrtle Blosser, Pettisville, Ohio

Crumb Pudding

1 cup flour   1½ tbsp. butter
½ cup sugar

Mix and reserve ¼ cup for crumbs. Add 1 tsp. baking powder and ½ cup milk to make a thick batter. Pour into pie plate and sprinkle crumbs over top. Bake at (375°) for 25 min. Serve with sauce.

Sauce

Heat 2 cups milk and cream. Make batter of ½ cup sugar, 3 tbsp. cornstarch, and 1 tsp. vanilla. Add to milk, boil until thickened.

Mrs. Anna Wenger, Moundridge, Kans.

Date Pudding (1)

1½ cups chopped dates   1 egg
1 tsp. soda   ½ tsp. salt
1 cup hot water   1 cup flour
1 cup sugar   ½ cup nuts
1 tbsp. butter

Add hot water and soda to dates, let set. Mix remaining ingredients; add dates. Pour into 7½"x12" pan; bake at 350° for 30 min. or until done. Serve warm with whipped cream.

Mrs. Ben Hiebert, Atmore, Ala.

Date Pudding (2)
(Amish)

1 cup boiling water
1 cup chopped dates
1 cup sugar
1 tsp. soda

1 tbsp. butter
1 egg
1 cup flour
½ cup nuts

Pour boiling water over dates, add sugar, soda and butter; cool; mash with potato masher; Add egg, flour and nuts, mix well. Bake at 350° for 45 min. or until set; cool. Crumble; serve with layers of whipped cream and bananas.

Mrs. Jacob Hochstetler, Apple Creek, Ohio
Mrs. Ura Yoder, Louisville, Ga.

Date Nut Pudding

1 cup sugar
1 cup chopped dates
1 cup chopped walnuts
1 cup sifted flour

2 tsp. baking powder
¼ tsp. salt
¼ cup milk

Mix and pour into greased pan.

1 cup brown sugar
2 tbsp. butter

2 cups boiling water

Mix and pour boiling hot over mixture in pan. Bake in moderate oven (350°) for 45 min.

Mrs. Eugene Unruh, Copeland, Kans.

Lemon Chiffon Pudding

Cream:
5 tbsp. flour
1 cup sugar
3 tbsp. butter

Add:
2 egg yolks, beaten
¼ cup lemon juice
1 cup milk
½ tsp. salt

Fold in 2 egg whites, stiffly beaten. Bake in an 8 in. casserole, or individual custard cups set in a pan of warm water. Bake 35 min. at 360-375°. (Will form a cake top with layer of custard below.) Serves 4-6.

Eva Koehn, Galva, Kans.

Mocha Dessert

¾ cup sugar
2 tbsp. cocoa
1¼ cups milk
1 tsp. instant coffee

1 envelope unflavored
  gelatine
¼ cup water
1 cup cream, whipped
½ cup nuts, (optional)

Combine sugar, cocoa and milk, cook over low heat; add coffee. Dissolve gelatine in water and add to cooked mixture. Cool; fold in whipped cream and nuts; chill. (May be used as a pie filling or with following crumb mixture recipe).

Crumb Mixture

1 cup flour
½ cup shortening

¼ cup sugar

Mix, and bake as pie crust. Cool and crumble. Place ½ of mixture into bowl; add cooked mixture and sprinkle remaining crumb mixture over top.

Mrs. Wilbur Boeckner, Moundridge, Kans.

Orange Pudding

4 or 5 sweet oranges, peeled
1 cup sugar
1 tbsp. cornstarch, dissolved in a little cold milk.

1 pt. milk
3 eggs, separated

Slice oranges and cover with sugar. Bring milk to boiling, add cornstarch, and egg yolks. Stir constantly while cooking. Add oranges. Beat egg whites until stiff, add 1 tbsp. sugar. Spread over pudding, and bake at 325° for 20 minutes. Serve warm or cold.

Mrs. Eli Johnson, Rich Hill, Mo.

Ozark Pudding

1½ cups sugar
1½ cups flour
3 tsp. baking powder
¼ tsp. salt

2 chopped apples
1 cup chopped nuts
2 eggs, beaten
2 tsp. vanilla

Combine sugar, flour, baking powder and salt. Add nuts and apples. Add beaten eggs and mix well. Bake in greased baking dish at 350° for 35 min. Serve with whipped cream.

Joetta Koehn, Hesston, Kans.

Poor Man's Pudding

In a 9"x9" baking pan mix 2 cups water, 2 cups brown sugar place on burner, bring to a boil and simmer while making batter.

Cream:

½ cup sugar	1 tbsp. butter
½ cup milk	½ cup raisins
1 tsp. nutmeg	**2 tsp. baking powder**

Add 1 cup flour and mix to stiff batter. Drop spoonsful of dough into boiling syrup in pan. Bake immediately in 350° oven until brown on top.

Mrs. Henry Schneider, Hesston, Kans.

Quick Raisin Pudding

1 cup flour	2 tsp. sugar
2 tsp. baking powder	3 tbsp. shortening
⅛ tsp. salt	1 cup raisins
½ cup milk	

Sift together flour, baking powder, and salt into mixing bowl; add sugar. Cut in shortening, mix until well blended. Add raisins, gradually add milk; stirring lightly with fork. Mix only until blended. Turn batter into 1½ qt. greased baking dish. Mix sauce and pour over batter. Bake in preheated oven at 375° for 30-35 min. Serve warm. Yield: 6 servings.

Sauce:

1 cup brown sugar	2 cups boiling water
1 tbsp. butter	

Mrs. Ben L. Remple, Morris, Man.

Raisin Pudding

1 cup flour	2 tsp. baking powder
1 cup sugar	1 cup raisins
¼ tsp. salt	½ cup milk

Sauce:

1 cup brown sugar	1 tbsp. butter
	2 cups boiling water

Mix first group of ingredients; pour into pan. Pour sauce over top and bake at 350° for 35-40 min.

Pauline Bender

Rhubarb Crunch

1 cup sifted flour	½ cup butter, melted
¾ cup oatmeal	1 tsp. cinnamon
1 cup brown sugar, firmly packed	4 cups rhubarb, diced

Mix all ingredients (except rhubarb) until crumbly and press one half of mixture into a greased 9" baking pan. Pour rhubarb over crumbly mixture in pan. Combine and cook until thick and clear:

1 cup sugar	1 cup water
2 tbsp. corn starch	1 tsp. vanilla

Pour over rhubarb and top with remaining crumbly mixture. Bake at 350° for 1 hr.

Anna Hibner, Ithaca, Mich.

Baked Rhubarb Dessert

Cut enough fresh rhubarb into chunks to fill a large loaf pan ½ full. Mix 2 cups sugar and 3 tbsp. min. tapioca together; sprinkle over rhubarb. Sprinkle 1 box white Jiffy cake mix or ½ larger box cake mix over top, just as it comes from the box. Dot with butter and bake 30 min. at 350°.

Mrs. Clarence Schneider, Ithaca, Mich.

Rice Pudding

Cook:

1 cup rice

Mix:

1 qt. milk	1½ cups raisins
4 eggs, beaten	1 tbsp. butter
1½ cups sugar	

Pour into greased baking dish. Sprinkle over top with cinnamon. Bake at 325° for 30 min. or until done.

Sauce for Rice Pudding

3 tbsp. cornstarch	1 tbsp. butter
1 cup sugar	2½ cups water

Boil, add ½ tsp. vanilla, ¼ tsp. nutmeg and ¼ tsp. cinnamon.

Mrs. Andrew Koehn, Goltry, Okla.

Rhubarb Rosettes

1 cup sifted flour	¼ cup butter or oleo
1½ tsp. baking powder	⅓ cup milk
1 tbsp. sugar	2 cups rhubarb cut in ½"
¼ tsp. salt	pieces
	¾ cup sugar

Prepare 8"x8" pan by measuring 2 tbsp. of melted oleo. Sift together into mixing bowl the flour, baking powder, 1 tbsp. of sugar and the salt. Cut or blend in the margarine or butter with a fork or pastry blender until the mixture resembles cornmeal. Add milk. Stir until flour is well moistened and dough holds together in a ball. Turn onto lightly floured board and knead lightly. Roll out to a long sheet (a scant ½" thick and about 12" long). Mix ¾ cup sugar and rhubarb. Spread evenly over dough. Dot with oleo. Roll up like cinnamon rolls. Seal the edge. With a sharp knife cut across the roll to make 9 slices about 1½" thick. Place rolls, cut side down into prepared pan. Bake in a mod. oven (400°) for 30 min. Place rosettes in a dessert dish and spoon sauce from the bottom of the pan. Serve warm.

Mrs. Monroe Holdeman, Harrison, Mich.

Steamed Puddings

(New England) Plum Pudding

Sift together:

1¾ cups sifted flour	1 tsp. salt
½ tsp. soda	1 tsp. cinnamon

Mix and add:

½ cup chopped seedless raisins	½ cup finely cut citron

Mix and blend into mixture:

½ cup sour milk or sweet milk	½ cup molasses

Pour into a well greased 1 qt. mold. Steam. Serve piping hot with Fluffy Hard Sauce.

Fluffy Hard Sauce

1 beaten egg white	2 tsp. vanilla

Cream until soft ½ cup butter. Blend in gradually 1½ cups sifted confectioners sugar.

Darlene Smith, Goltry, Okla.

Suet Pudding

(Mothers favorite)

1 cup chopped suet	2 heaping tsps. baking
1 cup sugar	powder
1¼ cups milk	1 tsp. salt
1 cup raisins	4 cups flour
	2 tsp. vanilla

Combine ingredients and fill 2 fruit juice cans; set in boiling water and cover. Steam for 1¾ to 2 hrs.

Sauce:

1 egg	¼ cup butter or margarine
1 cup sugar	½ tsp. lemon flavoring

Combine ingredients, add water to desired consistency. Season to taste. Heat slightly. (Over heating will cause it to curdle.)

Mrs. Aaron Boeckner, Moundridge, Kans.

Refrigerator Puddings

Apricot Delight

2 cans apricots, mashed	2 cups sugar
1 pkg. orange jello	3 tbsp. tapioca
2 cups water	

Drain juice from apricots: add water, jello and tapioca to juice. Bring to boiling, add sugar and apricots. Cool.

Mrs. Ivan Schneider, Perrinton, Mich.
Mrs. Dorvin Holdeman, Stapelton, Ga.

(Jellied) Applesauce Dessert

2 pkg. cherry jello	1-12 oz. bottle 7-up
1 cup boiling water	1 cup cream
2½ cups sweetened applesauce	¼ cup sugar

Dissolve jello in boiling water. Add applesauce and 7-up. Stir gently. Pour into 13"x9" pan. Chill until set, then cut into ½" squares. Whip cream, add sugar and whip until sugar is dissolved. Fold jello squares into cream.

Mrs. Myron Koehn, Fairview, Okla.

Angel Custard Dessert

3 eggs, separated   ¾ cup sugar
1 rounded tbsp. flour   1½ cups milk

Mix flour and sugar, add to egg yolks and milk; mix well. Boil until slightly thickened. Dissolve 1 envelope Knox Gelatine in ¼ cup cold water; add to hot custard. Add ½ tsp. vanilla. Fold in 3 well beaten egg whites. Break Angel Food Cake into pieces; alternate cake with custard and 1 pt. sweetened fresh strawberries in bowl until all is used. Chill; serve with whipped cream. Sprinkle with nuts.

Mrs. Eli Unruh, Galva, Kans.

Angel Food Delight

2 pkgs. Cherry Jello   1 qt. vanilla Ice Cream
2 cups boiling water   1 med. can Crushed Pine-
1 Angel Food Cake   apple (drained)

Dissolve jello in hot water. Add ice cream; stir until dissolved. Add drained pineapple. For variations use bananas or fruit cocktail as desired.

Place cake, broken in bite sized pieces, into bottom of pyrex pan, approximately 9x13x2 in. Then pour mixture over cake and refrigerate.

Myrtle Giesbrecht, Winton, Calif.

Broken Glass Torte

Three pkgs. of jello, each a different color. Dissolve each pkg. separately in 1½ cups boiling water; chill until firm in shallow pans. Soften 1 envelope plain gelatine in ¼ cup cold water. Dissolve in 1 cup heated pineapple juice. When cool and thick add 2 cups cream, whipped, to which ½ cup sugar and 1 tsp. vanilla have been added. Cut jello into small cubes and add to cream mixture reserving ½ cup of each color; Mix until crumbly; 2 cups crushed graham cracker crumbs, ½ cup soft butter or oleo, ½ cup sugar. Reserve ½ cup crumbs for top. Put crumbs in dish; Add cream mixture; spoon remaining jello over top. Sprinkle with remaining graham crumbs.

Mrs. Lois Seiler, Archbold, Ohio

Chocolate Pudding

3 cups milk	2 tbsps. cocoa
1 cup sugar	2 eggs
6 tbsp. flour	1 tsp. vanilla

Scald milk. Mix dry ingredients; add eggs and small amount of milk, stir until free from lumps. Pour into the hot milk and stir constantly until thickened. Remove from heat; add vanilla. (Use a skillet to prevent scorching.)

Mrs. Raymond Ratzlaff

Cottage Cheese Cake

Graham cracker crust:

1½ pkgs. graham crackers, crushed	⅓ cup brown sugar
⅓ cup melted butter or oleo	

Bake for about 10 min. at 350° Cool.

1 pt. cottage cheese	2 boxes instant lemon pudding mix

Beat cottage cheese and pudding mix until it begins to thicken. Pour into pans or dish which has been lined with ½ of the crumbs. Sprinkle remaining crumbs over top. Chill in refrigerator.

Mrs. Melvin Jantz, Ballico, Calif.

Date Loaf

1 lb. dates, chopped	1 lb. graham crackers, rolled fine
1 lb. miniature marsh-mallows	2 cups sweet cream
1 lb. nuts, chopped	

Combine dates, marshmallows, nuts, and cream, mix well. Spread ½ cup graham crackers into loaf pan, and firmly press above mixture over crumbs, then sprinkle ½ cup cracker crumbs over top. Let set over night.

Mrs. Don Nightengale, Fairview, Okla.

Fruit Cocktail Treat

For a fast chilled fruit dessert, dissolve 1-3 oz. pkg. of gelatin in 1 cup of boiling water. Add 1 pint of ice cream, stir until melted and mixture is slightly thickened. Add drained 1 lb. 1 oz. can of fruit cocktail and chill until firm.

Mrs. Aaron Becker, Rich Hill, Mo.

Graham Cracker Dessert

1 lb. marshmallows
1 cup milk
1 can crushed pineapple
1 cup cream, whipped
20 graham crackers

Melt marshmallows in milk, cool. Crush graham crackers, place ⅔ of crackers into bowl. Mix pineapple with marshmallow mixture, and whipped cream. Pour into bowl, add remaining crumbs over top.

Mrs. Frank F. Haynes, Middleton, Mich.

Graham Cracker Fluff

2 egg yolks
½ cup sugar
¾ cup milk
1 pkg. gelatine
½ cup cold water
2 egg whites
1 cup whipping cream
3 tbsp. melted butter
3 tbsp. sugar
12 graham crackers
1 tsp. vanilla

Beat egg yolks and add sugar and milk. Cook in double boiler until slightly thickened. Soak gelatine in cold water. Pour hot mixture over softened gelatine and stir until smooth. Chill until slightly thickened. Add stiffly beaten egg whites, vanilla and whipped cream to chilled mixture. Combine melted butter, cracker crumbs and sugar; mix until crumbly. Spread half the crumbs in the bottom of serving dish. Add pudding mixture and sprinkle remaining crumbs over top. Chill in refrigerator until set. Makes 6-8 servings.

Mrs. Eli Nightengale, Cimarron, Kans.
Mrs. Lydia Nichols
Mrs. Phillip Unruh, Burns, Kans.

Marshmallow Dessert (1)

Heat ⅔ cup milk to boiling point. Add 1½ sq. grated baking chocolate; and 30 marshmallows, let melt; cool. Whip 1 cup cream, add to first mixture. Crush 13 graham crackers and mix with 1 tbsp. melted butter. Line a 12" by 8" pan with one half of crumbs. Pour in creamed mixture and spread remaining crumbs over top. Place in refrigerator to set. Cut in squares. Serve plain or with whipped cream and a maraschino cherry.

Miss Anna M. Toews, Wales, N. Dak.

Marshmallow Dessert (2)

1 cup powdered sugar
½ cup butter or margarine
1 can Hershey's syrup

3 eggs, separated
25 marshmallows, cut up
20 graham crackers

Cream butter and powdered sugar, add egg yolks, beating after each addition. Add hershey's syrup and marshmallows cut fine. Beat egg whites and fold in. Crush graham crackers and also some finely chopped nuts. Put half on bottom of pan. Add mixture and rest of crumbs on top. Chill for several hrs. Serve with whipped cream.

Mrs. Peter P. Toews, Clayton, Wisc.

Graham Wafer Slice

1 cup brown sugar
1 egg
½ cup butter

½ tsp. vanilla
½ tsp. salt

Bring to a boil. Add 1 cup coconut and 1 cup graham cracker crumbs. Line a 9"x9" cake pan with whole graham wafers. Pour boiled mixture over crumbs. Add another layer of whole graham wafers.

Topping

8 tbsp. brown sugar
4 tsp. butter
3 tsp. cream

¼ tsp. salt
½ tsp. vanilla

Boil for 3 min. Beat until it is thickened and spread over graham crackers.

Mrs. Gladwin Barkman, Steinbach, Man.

Honey Lemon Dessert

1 pkg. lemon gelatin
1¼ cups boiling water
⅓ cup honey
1 tsp. grated lemon peel
⅛ tsp. salt

3 tbsp. lemon juice
1 cup heavy cream, whipped or 1-13 oz. can evaporated milk—chilled
1 cup vanilla wafer crumbs, or graham cracker crumbs

Dissolve gelatin in water; add honey, lemon peel, juice and salt. Chill until partially set; beat until fluffy and thickened. Fold in whipped cream. Spread ½ the crumbs in bottom of a 10x6 in. baking dish; spoon gelatin mixture over crumbs and sprinkle remaining crumbs. Chill until firm.

Eva Schultz, Neodesha, Kans.
Mrs. Harold Wedel, Bonners Ferry, Ida.

Jello Dessert (1)

1 pkg. raspberry jello
1 cup hot water
1 large can condensed milk
1 8-oz. pkg. Philadelphia
    cream cheese
1 cup sugar
1 tsp. vanilla
30 graham crackers
¼ lb. oleo, softened
2 tbsp. powdered sugar

Dissolve jello in hot water; cool. After it has thickened, beat well. Beat milk until thick. Combine softened cream cheese, sugar and vanilla with jello and whipped milk. Beat well. Roll graham crackers into fine crumbs; mix in oleo and powdered sugar. Put ½ of graham cracker mixture into bowl. Add jello mixture, and sprinkle remaining cracker crumbs over top. Chill.

Mrs. Jacob J. C. Unruh, Greensburg, Kans.

Jello Dessert (2)

1 pkg. orange jello
1 pkg. lime jello
1 pkg. dark jello
1 pkg. strawberry jello
20 graham crackers
1 pkg. pineapple jello
1 cup cream, whipped
1 tsp. vanilla
½ cup sugar

Dissolve the first four jellos in separate dishes with 1½ cups water each. Let set over night. The following morning dissolve pineapple jello with 2 cups of pineapple juice. Cool until it begins to set; add whipped cream. Dice the other four jellos and add to pineapple jello. Crush graham crackers and line bottom of large pan. Pour jello mix over crackers and add crackers over top. Let set over night. Cut into squares. Serves 16.

Mrs. Gerald Davis, Glenn, Calif.

Jello Cheese Dessert

30 graham crackers, crushed   ¼ lb. softened butter

Blend. Line casserole with crumbs, reserving 1 cup for topping.

Filling:

1 pkg. lemon jello
½ cup sugar

1-8 oz. pkg. cream cheese
1 large (4 oz.) pkg. dream whip, whipped

Dissolve jello in 1 cup boiling water. Cool until it begins to congeal. Combine sugar and cheese, add to jello, beat until smooth. Beat dream whip according to directions on box. Add to jello mixture and mix well. Pour over crumbs in dish and sprinkle top with remaining crumbs. (Nut meats may be added if desired.) For variation use lime or orange jello.

Mrs. Robert Williams

Jello Delight

¼ lb. butter   ½ lb. graham cracker crumbs

Combine butter and crumbs and press into a buttered 8x12" pan. Bake at 400° until slightly browned.

1 envelope plain gelatin
¼ cup boiling water
1 small can pineapple
1 pint cream, whipped

2 doz. marshmallows, cut up
1 cup nuts
½ cup sugar
1 tsp. vanilla

Dissolve gelatin in boiling water. Cool. Combine remaining ingredients and spread over crumb crust. Place in refrigerator. Dissolve 2 boxes of (desired) Jello and let set until thick enough to drop from spoon. Spread over whipped cream mixture. Set in refrigerator over night. Cut in squares.

Lorene Becker

Just for Fun

2 cups milk
1 lb. marshmallows
1 cup whipping cream
1 tsp. vanilla

1 no. 2 can pineapple tidbits, drained
½ cup nuts, chopped
2 cups graham cracker crumbs

Bring milk to boiling in double boiler. Add marshmallows, stir until melted, let cool. Whip cream add vanilla and fold into marshmallow mixture. Add pineapple and nutmeats. Sprinkle one half the cracker crumbs into oblong dish. Pour in mixture, top with remaining crumbs. Chill overnight. Serve topped with whipped cream and a cherry.

Elaine Schultz, Neodesha, Kans.

Lemon Ice Box Dessert

1 large can evaporated milk
⅔ cup lemon juice
1¼ cups sugar
5 eggs, separated
2 tbsp. grated lemon peel
20 graham crackers

Pour milk into ice cube trays and chill until crystals form. Mix egg yolks, sugar, lemon juice and peel. Beat egg whites until stiff. Fold into yolk mixture. Beat chilled milk until stiff and carefully fold into egg mixture. Pour into 9"x13" cake pan, lined with graham cracker crumbs. Chill.

Mrs. Arthur Sundberg, Hoople, N. Dak.

Chocolate Marshmallow Roll

Melt 3 sq. chocolate with 2 tbsp. butter. Add following ingredients:

1 cup powdered sugar
1 beaten egg
1 cup chopped walnuts
1 tsp. vanilla
½ tsp. salt
1 pkg. colored marshmallows

Mix well and form into 3 rolls. (Grease hands with butter) Roll in coconut or crushed graham crackers. Wrap in aluminum foil and freeze. Slice just before serving. Keeps indefinitely in freezer.

Mrs. Lorne Toews

Paradise Pudding

½ box cherry jello
1 box lemon jello
4 tbsp. sugar
1 cup crushed pineapple
1 cup whipping cream

Let cherry jello set until firm. Chill lemon jello until slightly thickened. Whip lemon jello until light and foamy. Mix in pineapple. Whip cream and add sugar. Fold into lemon jello mixture. Beat cherry jello with a fork and add last. Add bananas if desired.

Mrs. Wilbur Boeckner, Moundridge, Kans.

Pineapple Bavarian Cream

1 envelope Knox Gelatine
½ cup sugar
⅛ tsp. salt
2 eggs, separated
1¼ cups milk
½ tsp. vanilla
1 cup heavy cream, whipped
1 cup pineaple, drained
⅓ cup nuts, chopped

Mix gelatine, sugar, and salt in top of double boiler. Beat egg yolks and milk together. Add to gelatine mixture. Cook over boiling water 5 min. Remove from heat and add vanilla. Chill. Beat egg whites until stiff; add ¼ cup sugar. Fold into gelatine mixture. Fold in pineapple and whipped cream. Sprinkle with nuts, and chill.

Donnella Unruh, Galva, Kans.

Pineapple Coconut Delight

1⅔ cups crushed pineapple
1 envelope Knox Gelatine
¼ tsp. vanilla
½ cup instant nonfat dry milk and ½ cup ice water or (1 cup whipping cream)
½ cup coconut
2 tbsp. lemon juice
¼ cup sugar

Drain syrup from pineapple; add water to make 1 cup liquid. Sprinkle gelatine into syrup-water mixture to soften. Place over low heat and stir until gelatine is dissolved. Remove from heat; add pineapple and vanilla. Chill until partially set, (to resemble unbeaten egg whites). Beat cream until soft peaks form. Add lemon juice. Continue beating until firm peaks form. Gradually add sugar, fold gelatine mixture and coconut into whipped cream. Spoon into dessert dishes and chill. Makes 6-8 servings. (May be used as a pie filling or as a cake frosting.)

Mrs. Erma Koop, Scio, Ore.

Glorified Rice

1 cup cooked, cold rice
1½ cups crushed pineapple, drained
½ cup sugar
1 cup whipping cream, whipped
½ tsp. vanilla
8 marshmallows, diced

Mix all ingredients, chill thoroughly before serving. Makes 6 to 8 servings. (May add nuts, diced apples or sliced bananas).

Mrs. Henry Wiens, Hesston, Kans.

Marshmallow Strawberry Delight

24 graham crackers
5 tbsp. melted butter
1 cup milk
1 cup chopped marshmallows
1 cup whipping cream
½ cup chopped nuts
1½ cups strawberries, drained

Crush graham crackers, add melted butter. Press ½ of crumbs into bottom of buttered dish. Scald milk add chopped marshmallows. Stir for 2 min. and set aside to cool. Add crushed fruit, nuts, and whipped cream. Cover with remaining crumbs and chill for 12 hrs. in refrigerator. (Crushed pineapple may be used in place of strawberries.) Makes 6 servings.

Mrs. Allen Holdeman, Hesston, Kans.

Strawberry Dessert

2 pkgs. Dream Whip
1 large pkg. cream cheese
1 box strawberry jello
1½ cups water
1 can strawberry pie filling
12 graham crackers, crumbled
3 tbsp. sugar
3 tbsp. butter

Mix together cracker crumbs, sugar and butter; line bottom and sides of pan. Prepare Dream Whip according to directions; fold in cream cheese which has been softened with a little milk. Pour over crumbs and chill until firm. Dissolve jello in hot water. Cool until partially congealed; add pie filling and spread over cheese mixture.

Mrs. Galen Nichols, Greensburg, Kans.

Strawberry Swirl

1 cup graham cracker
  crumbs
1 tsp. sugar
¼ cup melted butter
2 cups fresh sliced strawberries
1 cup boiling water
1 (3 oz.) pkg. strawberry
  jello
½ lb. marshmallows
½ cup milk
1 cup whipping cream

Mix cracker crumbs and butter, press mixture into 9x2 in. dish; chill. Sprinkle sugar over berries and let stand for ½ hr. Dissolve jello in boiling water, add juice from strawberries. Chill until partially set. Melt marshmallows in milk and cool. Fold in whipped cream. Add berries to jello and swirl in marshmallow mixture to achieve a marbled effect. Pour into crust and chill until set.

Mrs. DeWayne Schafer, Newton, Kans.

Ice Creams and Desserts

Caramel Custard Ice Cream

2 cups brown sugar, firmly packed
4 cups milk
1 cup flour
2 cups white sugar
3 eggs, well beaten

Melt brown sugar over low heat until thoroughly caramelized, stirring constantly. Scald milk, add flour, sugar and eggs. Mix thoroughly. Cook until thickened. Add hot caramelized sugar to hot milk mixture, a little at a time, beating vigorously. Mix until well blended. Cool thoroughly.

Combine:
¼ tsp. salt
4 cups milk
4 cups whipping cream
1 tbsp. vanilla
1 cup chopped pecans

Pour both mixtures into one gallon size ice cream freezer, blending well. Freeze until of mushy consistency. Add nuts and freeze until hard.

Marlene Haynes, Wisc.

Dairy Queen Ice Cream

Soak 2 envelopes Knox Gelatine in ½ cup cold water. Heat, (do not boil), 5 cups milk. Remove from heat. Add gelatine, 2 cups white sugar, 2 tsp. vanilla, and 1 tsp. salt. Cool. Add 3 cups cream. Place in refrigerator and chill 5 to 6 hrs. before freezing. Flavors may be varied. Makes one gallon.

Mrs. Atlee J. Miller, Alliance, Ohio

Chocolate Ice Cream Bars

1 pkg. chocolate pudding
⅓ cup sugar
3 cups milk
1 cup cream

Combine pudding and sugar in saucepan, add milk gradually. Bring to boiling and cook for one min. stirring constantly. Remove from heat, cool, stir in cream. Pour into molds or wax paper lined freezing tray and freeze. Sticks may be inserted when mixture is partly frozen.

Mrs. Rueben Buller, Halstead, Kans.

Homemade Ice Cream

(For ½ gal.)

1 cup sugar	2 Junket tablets
3 eggs	dash of salt
1 pt. cream	milk
⅛ cup water	2 tsp. vanilla

Beat eggs until light. Stir in salt, vanilla, and cream. Warm milk to lukewarm, (test on wrist). Add to cream mixture. Add Junket tablets which have been dissolved in water. Pour into can and fill within 1" of top. Freeze.

Mrs. Verda Wedel, Meade, Kans.

Homemade Vanilla Ice Cream

Beat: 2 eggs, add ½ cup sugar and 2 cups milk. Bring to boiling, stirring constantly. Let cool. Add: 2 cups cream, whipped, 2 pkgs. Junket freezing mix, dash of salt, 1 tsp. vanilla, ½ cup sugar, 5 cups milk. Pour into ice cream freezer and freeze. Makes one gal.

Eva Koehn, Galva, Kans.

French Vanilla Ice Cream

Set refrigerator control for fast freezing. Blend in a saucepan:

½ cup sugar	1 cup milk
¼ tsp. salt	3 egg yolks, beaten

Cook over medium heat stirring constantly until mixture comes to boil. Cool. Then add:

1 tbsp. vanilla	½ tsp. lemon flavoring

Pour into refrigerator tray. Freeze until mixture is mushy and partly frozen (½ to 1 hr.) Whip until stiff:

1 cup whipping cream,
  whipped

Empty partially frozen mixture into chilled bowl, beat until smooth. Fold in whipped cream. Pour into two refrigerator trays and freeze until firm, stirring frequently and thoroughly during first hour of freezing. Freezing time will be 3 to 4 hrs. Makes 6 to 8 servings (1 qt.).

Marlys Penner, Mifflinburg, Pa.

Freezer Ice Cream

(1½ Gallon)

9 eggs
3 cups sugar
1 qt. cream

2 tsp. vanilla
1 tsp. salt

Beat eggs well, gradually add sugar and beat until very thick. Add cream, vanilla and salt. Pour into freezer and fill with milk.

Mrs. Henry T. Ensz, Inman, Kans.

Vanilla Wafer Ice Cream Dessert

2 qts. ice cream, softened
1 pt. frozen strawberries, thawed

1 pkg. (13 oz.) vanilla wafers
3 tbsp. brown sugar
3 tbsp. melted butter

Crush vanilla wafers, add butter and brown sugar. Mix well. Place one half of crumb mixture in 10" square pan. Add softened ice cream; spread evenly top with berries. Spread remaining crumb mixture over top. Freeze until firm. Cut in squares.

Mrs. Warren Johnson, Galva, Kans.

Topping for Ice Cream

1 qt. strawberries
2 tsp. vinegar

1 qt. sugar

Boil strawberries and vinegar for 3 min. Add sugar and boil 5 min. more. Let stand overnight. Pour while cold into jars and seal.

Mrs. Lena Mayeske, Fredonia, Kans.

Butterscotch Sauce

1½ cups brown sugar
⅔ cup light corn syrup
⅓ cup water
¼ cup oleo

⅛ tsp. salt
⅔ cup evaporated milk
½ tsp. vanilla

Combine first four ingredients in saucepan. Cook to soft ball stage; stirring frequently. Remove from heat; cool 15 min. Add milk gradually, stirring, add salt and vanilla; mix well. Store in refrigerator in covered jar. Serve on ice cream or other desserts.

Mrs. Myron Koehn, Fairview, Okla.

Chocolate Ice Cream Topping

¼ cup butter
2-1 oz. sq. unsweetened
  chocolate
1½ cups sugar

¼ tsp. salt
¾ cup milk
¾ cup cream

Melt butter, add chocolate and melt. Add sugar slowly, then milk and cream; bring to boiling. Serve warm.

Gladine Schneider, Moundridge, Kans.

Rainbow Snowball Cake

1 qt. strawberry ice cream
1 qt. orange sherbert
1 pt. heavy cream, whipped

1 qt. lime sherbert
2 qts. vanilla ice cream

Chill 10 in. angel food cake pan with removable section. Using small scoop shape balls of strawberry ice cream, orange and lime sherbert, place balls on cookie sheet. Chill in freezer until firm. Soften vanilla ice cream: whip until fluffy as whipped cream. Arrange layer of colored balls in pan. Add whipped ice cream to fill spaces. Repeat until pan is filled. Freeze several hours. Remove from pan. 16 to 18 servings.

Wilda Yost, Ulysses, Kans.

Miscellaneous Desserts

Prune Mousse

(Some of Mother's cooking)

1 qt. whey
4 tbsp. flour
1 cup raisins
1 cup heavy cream

½ cup sugar
1 cup prunes
½ tsp. cinnamon

For thickening combine flour, sugar and cream. Cook raisins and prunes until done. Heat whey to boiling. Stir in thickening. Add prunes and raisins, cook a few min.
(Buttermilk may be used instead of whey. Whey makes a smooth finished product while buttermilk is grainy.)

Mrs. Noah Koehn, Halstead, Kans.
Submitted by Mrs. Adam J. Schmidt, Montezuma, Kans.

Prune Gish

(Pluma Moas)

Boil prunes and raisins until well done. Add desired amount of sugar and several dashes of cinnamon while cooking. When prunes are well done, crush slightly so juice oozes out. Prepare a thickening of ⅓ cup flour and enough sweet or sour cream to make smooth paste; add to 1 qt. buttermilk. Pour mixture into boiling fruit, stirring constantly until it reaches boiling. (Our old fashioned Pluma Moas mother used to make).

Mrs. Fred B. Nightengale, Fairview, Okla.

Prune and Raisin Mousse

2 cups pasteurized cultured buttermilk	2 tbsp. flour
¾ cup raisins	½ cup sweet cream
½ cup prunes	2 cups water or enough so fruit will be covered when
⅔ cup sugar	done

Cook raisins and prunes until tender. Make thickening of flour and a little water. Add cinnamon and cream; add to fruit, stirring constantly. Bring to boiling; add sugar. Let cool. Add buttermilk. (For smooth texture, do not cook the buttermilk.)

Mrs. Daniel J. Schmidt, Montezuma, Kans.

Chocolate Ice Cream Roll

Beat until stiff 6 egg whites and ½ tsp. cream of tartar. Beat in ½ cup sugar gradually.
Beat 6 egg yolks until thick and lemon colored.
Beat in ½ cup sugar and sift:

4 tsp. flour	¼ tsp. salt
4 tsp. cocoa	1 tsp. vanilla

Carefully fold into the egg white mixture. Put in 15x10½" pan lined with wax paper. Bake just until surface springs back when touched with finger. Immediately turn upside down on towel sprinkled with confectioners sugar. Remove paper and roll up. Cool. After it is cool, unroll and spread with ice cream and roll again. Frost. Freeze until ready to serve.

Chocolate Icing

1½ cups confectioners sugar   ¼ tsp. salt
1 large egg   ¼ cup shortening
1½ sq. chocolate, melted

Beat together until fluffy.

Mrs. Stanley Sundberg, Grafton, N. Dak.

Cream Puffs

Heat to rolling boil in sauce pan:
1 cup water   ½ cup butter

Stir in all at once 1 cup flour. Stir vigorously over low heat until mixture leaves the pan and forms into a ball, about 1 min. Remove from heat. Beat in thoroughly, 4 eggs, one at a time. Beat mixture until smooth and velvety. Drop from spoon into ungreased baking sheet. Bake until dry in mod. hot oven (400°) 45 to 50 min. Allow to cool slowly. Cut top from cream puff and dip in powdered sugar. Fill with cream filling. Replace top.

Mrs. D. G. Boeckner, Moundridge, Kans.

Chocolate Roll

6 tbsp. flour   4 egg whites
½ tsp. baking powder   ¾ cup sugar
¼ tsp. salt   4 egg yolks
6 tbsp. cocoa   1 tsp. vanilla

Sift together flour, baking powder, salt, and cocoa. Beat egg whites until stiff add sugar, beaten egg yolks and vanilla. Sift dry ingredients into egg and sugar mixture. Blend thoroughly. Line 9"x12" pan with waxed paper, pour batter into pan. Bake at 400° for 15 min. Remove from pan and turn onto damp cloth sprinkled with powdered sugar. Trim hard edges and spread with whipped cream or a filling as soon as removed from oven.

Filling:
1 egg white   3 tbsp. cold water
1 cup sugar   1 tsp. cream of tartar
1 cup coconut

Mix together and cook in double boiler over rapidly boiling water, beat mixture with rotary beater until stiff, remove from heat and add shredded coconut.

Mrs. Arnold Koehn, Newton, Kans.

Chocolate Whipped Cream Roll

¼ cup sifted cake flour	3 eggs, separated
¼ cup cocoa	½ tsp. vanilla
½ tsp. baking powder	1 cup powdered sugar
¼ tsp. salt	

Sift flour, cocoa, baking powder and salt three times. Beat egg whites until foamy; gradually add ½ cup powdered sugar and continue beating until mixture stands in peaks. Beat vanilla and egg yolks together until light colored and very thick. Gradually add remaining ½ cup powdered sugar; beat until well blended. Fold egg yolk mixture into egg white mixture, thoroughly but carefully. Then fold in sifted dry ingredients a small amount at a time. Grease bottom only, of a shallow pan, 15"x10½"; line with waxed paper. Grease paper. Spread batter evenly; bake in mod. hot oven (375°) 12 to 15 min. As soon as cake is taken from oven, invert on cloth sprinkled with powdered sugar; trim off edges and roll as for jelly roll. Wrap cloth around roll and allow to cool. Unroll carefully; spread with sweetened whipped cream and reroll. Slice in ¾" slices.

Mrs. Marvin D. Koehn

Coconut Crunch Torte

1 cup graham cracker crumbs	4 egg whites
½ cup coconut	¼ tsp. salt
½ cup chopped nuts	1 cup sugar

Combine crackers, coconut and nuts. Beat egg whites with salt and vanilla until frothy. Gradually add sugar and continue beating until egg whites form stiff peaks. Fold in cracker mixture and pour into well greased shallow baking dish about 9" sq. Bake at 350° for 25 min. Cool, cut in wedges and top with ice cream.

Wilma Martin, Dalton, Ohio

Ice Cream Roll

4 egg whites	1 cup powdered sugar
4 egg yolks	⅛ tsp. salt
¼ cup flour	1½ tsp. vanilla
3 tbsp. cocoa	

Beat yolks until thick. Combine salt, sugar, cocoa and flour; sift and add to yolks. Beat until smooth. Fold in stiffly beaten egg whites. Pour into greased pan. Bake at 350° for 20 min. After baked, place on towel, sprinkle with powdered sugar and roll. When cool, unroll, fill with ice cream and put in deep freeze.

Mrs. Henry Dirks, Montezuma, Kans.

Jelly Roll

5 eggs	1 tsp. vanilla
1 cup sugar	2 cups flour
1/3 tsp. salt	1/2 cup sweet cream
4 tsp. baking powder	

To the well-beaten eggs, add salt, cream and sifted dry ingredients. Pour into well-buttered shallow baking pan. Bake about 20 min. at 350°. Turn on damp cloth. Spread with jelly or whipped cream and roll. Wrap towel around roll until ready to serve. Sprinkle with powdered sugar.

Mrs. Elma Wiggers, Hesston, Kans.

Ice Cream

(For 1 gal.)

2½ cups sugar	2 tbsp. vanilla
5 eggs	1 quart cream
1 pkg. Junket ice cream mix	

Beat eggs well. Gradually add sugar and beat till thick. Add ice cream mix and beat. Add cream and vanilla. Fill with milk. Freeze.

Peach Sherbet

2 cups finely chopped peaches	1½ cups cream
1/3 cup sugar	1/2 tsp. vanilla
1 cup water	1/4 tsp. salt

Select ripe fine flavored peaches. Chop fruit fine. Add sugar and water to pulp. Add cream, vanilla and salt. Chill for one half hour. Freeze as usual.

Wheat Chex Dessert

½ cup brown sugar   4 tbsp. oleo
½ cup white sugar   4 tbsp. cream

Put in saucepan and bring to a boil.

Pour over one box Wheat Chex which have been crushed, mix well and pat part of mixture in a buttered 9x13 pyrex dish. Put one half gallon ice cream (softened) over mixture and rest of Chex mixture on top. Place in freezer. To serve cut in squares.

Peach Delicious

3 eggs   ¼ tsp. baking powder
1 cup sugar   ½ cup nuts, chopped
14 soda crackers, crushed 1 tsp. vanilla
1 cup cream whipped, sweetened
Sliced peaches, sweetened (fresh or canned)

Beat egg whites stiff; add sugar gradually. Mix remaining ingredients and add to egg white mixture. Put into a buttered 8"x8" inch pyrex dish and bake 30 min. or until golden brown. Cool. Top with peaches and whipped cream. Place in refrigerator and chill for at least 6 hours. Cut in squares.

Strawberry Dessert Cake

Mix 1 large pkg. white cake mix as directed on pkg. Bake in 9x13 inch pan. While cake is baking mix 2 pkgs. (3 oz. size) strawberry gelatin with 2 cups boiling water. Let stand at room temperature. When cake is done, immediately punch full of holes with a fork. Pour gelatin over cake very slowly. Reserve ½ cup of gelatin to use in the topping. Put cake in refrigerator and let set until cold. Whip 2 pkgs. Dream Whip as directed on pkg. or use cream. Add 1 box (10 oz.) pkg. of thawed frozen strawberries, and the ½ cup gelatin to the topping. Spread over chilled cake. Return to refrigerator and let set two to three hours before serving. Makes 12 to 15 servings.

FROSTINGS

Frostings

Browned Butter Icing

½ cup butter
½ cup cream
6 cups sifted powdered sugar

1 tsp. vanilla
¼ tsp. salt

Brown butter over low heat, stirring constantly. Pour into mixing bowl, add sugar alternately with cream, beating until smooth and fluffy. Add vanilla and salt. Spread between layers, top and sides. Garnish with slivered almonds or other nut meats.

Mrs. Ivan Schmidt, Fredonia, Kans.
Mrs. Harvey Yost, Greensburg, Kans.

Butterscotch Icing

5 tbsp. butter
1 cup brown sugar

¼ cup milk

Melt butter in saucepan; add sugar and bring to boiling, add milk and boil slowly for 3 min. Cool; add powdered sugar; mix to spreading consistency.

Mrs. Denton Holdeman, Hesston, Kans.

Caramel Butter Icing

⅓ cup butter or oleo, melted
1 cup brown sugar, firmly packed
2½ cups confectioners sugar

¼ cup milk
½ tsp. vanilla
Dash of salt

Combine melted butter and brown sugar. Sift and add confectioners sugar alternately with the milk. Beat until smooth. If frosting is too thick to spread easily beat in ½ tsp. milk at a time. Add vanilla.

Butter Icing

1 cup milk
5 tbsp. flour
1 cup sugar

1 cup butter
1 tsp. vanilla

Mix flour to milk and boil until thickened. Cool. Combine sugar, butter and vanilla, beat with mixer until creamed. Remove from mixer, fold in milk-flour mixture and beat by hand. Cut each layer of cake in two with a thread. Fill and frost.

Mrs. Levi Koehn, Barron, Wisc.

Beat and Eat Frosting

(Substitute for 7 min. frosting)

1 egg white
¾ cup sugar
¼ tsp. cream of tartar
1 tsp. vanilla
¼ cup boiling water

Combine unbeaten egg white, sugar, cream of tartar and vanilla in small deep bowl. Mix well. Add boiling water and beat until mixture stands in peaks—about 4 to 5 min. Spread on cake.

Mrs. Jesse Giesbrecht, Glenn, Calif.
Mrs. Ervey Unruh, Montezuma, Kans.

Carrot Cake Icing

1 lb. confectioners sugar
½ stick margarine, melted
1 8-oz. pkg. cream cheese
2 tsp. vanilla
1 cup nuts, chopped

Mix all ingredients, except nuts, and beat until smooth. Ice cake, sprinkle with nuts.

Mrs. Vernon Peters

Brown Sugar Meringue

(For Cakes)

2 egg whites
Dash of salt
1 cup brown sugar, firmly packed
Chocolate chips or nuts

Beat egg whites and salt until foamy. Add brown sugar, two tbsp. at a time, beating after each addition until sugar is blended. Continue beating until meringue will stand in peaks. Swirl meringue over cake, covering completely. Add nuts or choc. chips if desired. Place in oven at 375° and bake 15 min. or until meringue is lightly browned.

Mrs. Marshall Harms, Atmore, Ala.

Cheese Fondant Icing

2 pkgs. Philadelphia cream
cheese
1 egg yolk
3 cups powdered sugar

1 tsp. vanilla
½ tsp. salt

Cream the cheese, add beaten egg yolk, powdered sugar, vanilla, and salt.

Mrs. Adam J. Schmidt, Montezuma, Kans.

Chocolate Cream Cheese Icing

1-3 oz. pkg. cream cheese
3 tbsp. milk
⅛ tsp. salt

3 cups powdered sugar
2 sq. chocolate, melted

Soften cream cheese by adding 1 tbsp. milk at a time, add sugar gradually. Blend in chocolate and salt. Beat well.

Mrs. Dewey Wedel

Chocolate Frosting

1 cup sugar
½ cup sweet cream
6 large marshmallows

½ cup chocolate chips
1 tsp. vanilla
1 tbsp. oleo

Boil sugar, cream and marshmallows three minutes. Add chocolate chips, vanilla and oleo. Stir and beat until chocolate chips melt. If plain frosting is desired omit chocolate chips but boil 1 min. longer.

Mrs. Ervin Nightengale, Scott City, Kans.

Chocolate Fudge Icing

⅔ cup milk
4 tbsp. cocoa
2 cups sugar

1 tsp. corn syrup
Dash of salt
2 tbsp. butter

Place milk and cocoa over low heat, stir until mixture is smooth. Stir in sugar, corn syrup, and salt. Cook gently, stirring occasionally, to soft ball stage. Remove from heat and add butter. Cool without stirring until lukewarm.

Mrs. Robert D. Smith, DeRidder, La.

Cocoa Fudge Frosting

1 cup sugar
1 tbsp. cornstarch
1 tbsp. butter
3 tbsp. cocoa

Dash of salt
1/4 cup milk
1 tsp. vanilla

Combine all ingredients. Boil 1 min. Remove from heat and add vanilla. Let cool, beat until of spreading consistency.

Mrs. Joe Holdeman, Halstead, Kans.

Coconut-Pecan Frosting

1 cup evaporated milk
1 cup sugar
3 egg yolks

1/4 lb. oleo
1 tsp. vanilla

Combine in saucepan, cook and stir over med. heat until mixture thickens. Remove from heat.

Add:
1 1/3 cups coconut   1 cup chopped pecans
Beat until cool and thick enough to spread.

Cream Filling for Doughnuts

Prepare your favorite doughnut recipe. When cutting the doughnut do not cut out the hole in the center. When it fries it becomes hollow inside. Punch a little hole on the top and fill doughnut with a cream pudding.

Cream Pudding

3/4 cup sugar
3 tbsp. cornstarch
1/4 tsp. salt
2 eggs

2 cups milk
1 tbsp. butter
1 tsp. vanilla

Combine sugar, salt, cornstarch. Add 1 1/2 cups of the milk. Cook until thickened. Beat egg yolks add to the other 1/2 cup milk. Add egg mixture to custard and cook 2 min. more. Add butter and vanilla. Cool. If doughnut isn't very hollow then pull out a little from the inside. After the pudding is inside of the doughnut put chocolate frosting on top of it.

Mrs. A. Gene Koehn

Creamy Chocolate Icing

2 cups sugar
¼ cup white syrup
½ cup milk
½ cup shortening

2 sq. unsweetened chocolate (2 oz.)
¼ tsp. salt
1 tsp. vanilla

Stir over slow heat until chocolate and shortening are melted, stirring constantly, bring rapidly to full boil. Boil 220°, or one min. Remove from heat, beat gently until lukewarm. Add vanilla.

Mrs. Ben Dyck, Atmore, Ala.

Cup Cake Filling

½ cup condensed milk
3 tbsp. flour
¾ cup confectioners sugar or

½ cup granulated sugar
½ cup shortening
1 tsp. vanilla

Mix milk and flour to smooth paste and bring to boil until thick. Add remaining ingredients; beat until thick and fluffy. Cut a round hole in top of cup cake and remove some of the cake. Fill with filling and replace top of cupcake. Cover with frosting.

Mrs. Daniel Kramer, Hartville, Ohio

Family Frosting

1 cup sugar
3 tbsp. flour
1 cup rich milk
3 tbsp. butter or oleo

1 tsp. vanilla
1 cup coconut
½ cup nuts

Mix sugar, flour, milk and butter in saucepan. Cook until thickened. Remove from heat. Add vanilla, coconut and nuts. Beat until of spreading consistency. (For two-layer cake).

Donella Holdeman, Hesston, Kans.

Fluffy Marshmallow Icing

1 cup sugar
⅓ cup water
¼ tsp. cream of tartar

2 egg whites
8 soft marshmallows, quartered
1 tsp. vanilla

Combine sugar, water, cream of tartar in saucepan. Boil rapidly until syrup spins a thread. (242°). Beat egg whites until stiff enough to hold a peak. As soon as syrup reaches 242° stir in the marshmallows, allow to dissolve. Pour hot syrup slowly in a thin stream into egg whites, beating constantly. Add vanilla. Beat until of spreading consistency.

Marlene Giesbrecht, Winton, Calif.

Fudge Frosting

⅓ cup milk
¼ cup butter
2 cups powdered sugar, sifted

1 cup semi-sweet choc. chips
1 tsp. vanilla

Combine milk and butter, bring to boiling, stirring constantly. Remove from heat; add choc. chips and vanilla. Stir until smooth. Gradually add powdered sugar. Beat until of spreading consistency. (May be used either for cake or cookies).

Mrs. Perry Johnson, Galva, Kans.

Marshmallow Icing

1⅓ cup sugar
½ cup cold water
1 tbsp. corn syrup

1 egg white
6 large marshmallows
1 tsp. vanilla

Cook sugar, water and syrup until mixture forms a medium ball stage when tested in cold water. Beat egg white stiff, add cut marshmallows. Pour syrup into egg and marshmallow mixture slowly, beating constantly. Add vanilla and continue beating until right spreading consistency.

Mrs. Archie Decker, Lafontaine, Kans.

Fluffy Frosting

1 cup powdered sugar
½ cup butter
1 tsp. vanilla

3 tbsp. cold water
3 tbsp. boiling water

Cream butter until fluffy. Add sugar, ¼ cup at a time. Add cold water 1 tbsp. at a time, beating thoroughly. Add vanilla, and hot water in the same way as the cold water. Spread on cake.

Sadie Frank, Copeland, Kans.

Fluffy Mocha Frosting

⅔ cup sugar
½ cup white corn syrup
2 egg whites
3 tbsp. strong coffee

⅛ tsp. cream of tartar
⅛ tsp. salt
1 tsp. vanilla

Combine in double boiler over rapidly boiling water. Beat with rotary beater until mixture stands in peaks. Remove from heat. Blend in vanilla and continue beating until of spreading consistency.

Mamie Schmidt

Frosting

2 egg yolks
⅔ cup cream evap. milk
⅔ cup sugar

⅓ cup oleo
1 tsp. vanilla
1 cup coconut
½ cup nuts

Combine first four ingredients. Cook and stir over med. heat until thick—about 8-10 min. Add coconut, nuts and vanilla. Beat until of spreading consistency.

Mrs. Helen Schmidt, Livingston, Calif.

Icing

⅔ cup milk or cream
1½ cup sugar

1 tsp. vanilla
Dash of salt

Cook to soft ball stage. Beat thoroughly while cooling and add vanilla.

Mrs. John N. Penner, Mifflinburg, Pa.

Lemon Butter Cream Frosting

¼ cup soft butter or margarine
1 tsp. grated lemon peel

2 cups sifted confectioners sugar
2 tbsp. lemon juice

Cream butter, add lemon peel. Add sugar and lemon juice alternately, creaming well after each addition, until of spreading consistency.

Mrs. Dan P. Koehn, Montezuma, Kans.

Mixer Icing

1 cup sugar
2 unbeaten egg whites
1 tsp. vanilla

½ tsp. cream of tartar
¼ tsp salt
3 tbsp. water

Place above ingredients in top of double boiler. When water is boiling rapidly in lower part of double boiler remove from heat and place top of boiler in it. Beat icing 5 min. with electric mixer at high speed.

Mrs. Vernard Unruh, Halstead, Kans.

One Minute Fudge Icing

1 cup sugar
4 tbsp. cocoa
¼ cup milk

¼ cup margarine
1 tsp. vanilla

Mix sugar and cocoa, add milk and margarine, bring to a boil over low heat. Boil one min. Remove from heat, add vanilla and let cool. Then, beat until right consistency to spread.

Mrs. Leroy Koehn, Halstead, Kans.

Quick Chocolate Frosting

½ cup cocoa
1 cup sugar
⅓ cup milk

¼ cup shortening
¼ tsp. salt
1 tsp. vanilla

Bring mixture to full boil. Cook 1½ or two min. Beat until spreading consistency.

Mrs. Harry Wenger, Hesston, Kans.

Seafoam Frosting

2 unbeaten egg whites
1½ cups brown sugar
⅓ cup cold water

2 tsp. corn syrup
Dash of salt
1 tsp. vanilla

Place all ingredients in top of double boiler (not over heat); beat 1 min. with electric mixer at high speed. Place over boiling water; cook and beat until stiff peaks form, about 7 min. Remove from heat. Add vanilla; beat until of spreading consistency, about 2 min. Fold in 1 tbsp. chocolate chips. Frost cake, dot with choc. chips.

Mrs. Lyle Litwiller, Perrinton, Mich.
Mrs. Marshall Harms, Atmore, Ala.

Speedy Caramel Frosting

½ cup butter or margarine   ¼ cup milk
1 cup brown sugar, firmly   2½ cups sifted powdered sugar
  packed   ½ tsp. vanilla
¼ tsp. salt

Melt butter, blend in brown sugar and salt. Cook over low heat 2 min., stirring constantly. Add milk; continue stirring until mixture comes to a boil. Remove from heat. Blend in powdered sugar gradually, add vanilla and mix well. Thin with small amount of cream if necessary. Add nuts if desired.

Mrs. Marshall Harms, Atmore, Ala.

Vanilla Frosting

¼ cup shortening   3 cups confectioners sugar,
½ tsp. salt   sifted
1½ tsp. vanilla   ¼ cup milk

Combine shortening, salt, vanilla and add ¼ of the sugar. Add milk and remaining sugar alternately, mix until smooth and of spreading consistency.

Mrs. Herman Goertzen, Buhler, Kans.

White Fudge Frosting

3 cups sugar   3 tbsp. butter
1 cup rich milk or cream 1½ tsp. vanilla
4 tbsp. white corn syrup ½ cup cream

Combine in saucepan: sugar, milk, corn syrup, and butter. Cook without stirring to a hard ball stage, keeping covered the first three min. Remove from heat. Let stand until it starts to harden then add vanilla and cream. Beat until desired thickness.

Joy Holdeman

Coconut Icing

2 cups powdered sugar   4 tbsp. butter or oleo
3 cups coconut   1 cup milk

Mix well and boil until thick, about 6 min.

Mrs. Oscar Unruh, Fairview, Okla.

JAMS AND PRESERVES

Jams and Preserves

Grape Lade

Heat 1 qt. grapes, 3 tbsp. water and 2 lbs. sugar. Take all ingredients and bring to a boil, stirring continually until boiling. Boil for 15 min. stirring occasionally. Put through ricer, pressing as much pulp through as possible. Stir and put in glasses. Pour wax over lade or freeze.   Marie Buskirk, Middleton, Mich.

Orange and Peach Marmalade

12 large peaches, peeled   3 large oranges, unpeeled
5 oz. jar maraschino cherries

Grind fruits through coarse grinder. Measure; add equal amount of sugar. Boil 15 to 20 min. or until thickened. Pour into jars and seal.

Mrs. Lloyd Koehn, Lehigh, Kans.

Rhubarb Preserves

5 cups rhubarb, cut up   4 cups sugar
1 pkg. red Jello

Cook and stir constantly for 12 min. Remove from heat. Add Jello. Pour into jars and pour paraffin over top.

Edna Mininger, Pettisville, Ohio

Strawberry Jam (1)

Combine 1 qt. strawberries and 3½ cups sugar. Let set until it forms its own juice, then boil for 6 min.; add 1 more cup sugar and cook 4 min. longer. Let set overnight. Stir and pour into jelly jars. May be used as ice cream topping.

Mrs. Elton Wenger, Hesston, Kans.

Strawberry Jam (2)

Pour hot water over 1 qt. strawberries, drain. Add 1 cup sugar and boil for 5 min. Add another cup of sugar and boil for 5 min. more. Add 1 cup more sugar and boil 5 min. Let set for 3 or 4 days. Pour into jars and seal.

MEATS, SAUCES, AND DRESSINGS

Beef

Barbecue Roast Beef

1 roast—size and kind you prefer.

Sauce:

1 cup catsup	1 cup water
½ cup minced onion	1 tbsp. brown sugar
2 tsp. worcestershire sauce	

Salt, pepper, and flour roast. Brown in skillet and roast covered in oven until tender (or prepare roast your favorite way). Combine ingredients for sauce and simmer a few min. Remove bone and fat from roast and cut in pieces. Pour sauce over meat and bake in 325° oven 1-1½ hrs. This is an excellent way to fix left over roast.   Mrs. Glade Schmidt, Goltry, Okla.

Breaded Steak

6 servings of steak, trimmed, and pounded

Add together:

very fine cracker crumbs	¼ cup milk
1 egg (beaten)	salt

Dip steak into egg mixture, then in cracker crumbs and brown on both sides, arrange in shallow baking dish, cover, and bake 1 hr. or until tender.   Mrs. Ben Hiebert, Atmore, Ala.

Beef Stew

2 lb. round steak, cubed	2 tsp. vinegar
⅓ cup fat	⅓ cup catsup
2 tbsp. flour	3 cups carrots
3 cups water	4 cups diced potatoes
1 tbsp. salt	1 onion, sliced

Saute' round steak cubes in the fat. Stir in flour, add water, salt, vinegar, catsup and simmer 30 min. Add the carrots and simmer 15 min. longer, then add the diced potatoes and onion and simmer at least 1 hr. or until done.

Mrs. Jay Diller, Walnut Hill, Fla.

Old Time Beef Stew

It's the browning long and slow that gives the rich color and flavor men like.

2 lbs. beef chuck	1 clove garlic
2 tbsp. fat	4 cups boiling water
1 onion	1 tbsp. lemon juice
1 tbsp. salt	1 tsp. worcestershire sauce
1 tsp. sugar	$\frac{1}{2}$ tsp. paprika
$\frac{1}{2}$ tsp. pepper	1 bay leaf
$\frac{1}{8}$ tsp. allspice	

Cut chuck into 1½" cubes and brown on all sides in hot fat for about 20 min. Slice onion and clove of garlic (which is put on a toothpick so you can retrieve it). Add boiling water, salt, lemon juice and spices. Cover and simmer for 2 hrs. Stir occasionally to prevent sticking. When meat is nearly done add 6 carrots cut in quarters, 1 lb. small white onions and a few potatoes, diced. Simmer stew for 30 min. longer till all is tender. Remove garlic and bay leaf. Gravy Making:
Mix ¼ cup flour and ½ cup cold water to make batter. Remove from heat and push meat and vegetables to one side of pan. Stir in batter. Cook and stir until gravy thickens. Cook for a few min.

Mrs. David (Verbie) Koehn, Livington, Calif.

Pot Roast 'N Noodles

3 lbs. pot roast	1½ cups water
Heavy duty aluminum foil	1 pkg. (8 oz.) noodles
2 tsp. salt	2 tsp. poppy seed (optional)
¼ tsp. pepper	Parsley

Place meat on double thickness, heavy duty foil in shallow baking pan, allowing enough foil to include noodles later. Brown meat on both sides under broiler. Sprinkle with 1 tsp. salt, pepper as desired. Wrap meat tightly in foil, sealing edges with double fold. Bake in slow oven 325° for 1½ to 2 hrs. Open foil, saving all meat liquid. Add water, place noodles in broth. Sprinkle with poppy seed and 1 tsp. salt. Seal foil, bake about 1 hr longer or until noodles are done. Serves 6.

Mrs. Arthur R. Koehn, Walker, Mo.

Salisbury Steak

Mix 2 lbs, ground beef with 2 cups finely rolled cracker crumbs (about 1 pkg.) and 2 eggs.   Add ½ cup catsup or tomato juice or canned tomatoes.

2 tbsp. grated onions   ½ tsp. pepper
2 tsp. salt   2 tbsp. chopped parsley
1 tsp. worcestershire sauce   ½ tsp. marjoram
½ tsp. nutmeg

When well mixed mold the mixture into 8 large patties or smaller if desired.   They will be of good size and fairly thick.   Place in shallow baking dish and bake in a mod. oven 325° for 40 to 50 min. or until done and brown.   Make gravy from drippings in pan.   If desired make a sauce of:

1 can condensed cream of   ½ tsp. garlic salt
   Mushroom soup   1 cup milk
2 tbsp. butter

Mix, heat and pour over patties and bake.   This not only seasons the patties but keeps them moist.

Mrs. Everett Wedel, Inman, Kans.

Sunday Dinner Steak Bake

2-3 round steaks   1 large onion
1 can tomato soup   salt and pepper
1 can cream of mushroom   1 tbsp. Kitchen Bouquet
   soup
1 can water

Flour and brown steak in frying pan, season as desired.   Add 1 cup water to pan drippings and add to soups in saucepan. (If you wish to make gravy save pan drippings instead of adding to sauce.) Heat sauce.   In large roaster layer one layer of meat, spread with chopped onion and part of sauce.   Continue making layers until your ingredients are used, ending with sauce.   Bake in oven, 300° for 2 hrs.

Leona Nichols, Livingston, Calif.

Aunt Kate's Beef and Gravy

Slice and fry 1 or 2 onions in skillet, put them in a kettle. Next brown the meat (bite size pieces of beef) in the skillet. Season to taste. When nice and brown place meat pieces in the kettle. Sprinkle in 2 or more tbsp. of flour (you may need to add more shortening) and brown, when nice and brown add warm water and cook a few min, for the gravy. Pour gravy on meat and onion and cook on a slow burner, stirring often to keep from sticking. Cook for 3 hrs. this keeps well in a refrigerator, and can be made several days before needed.

Edith Litwiller, Middleton, Mich.

Spicy Pot Roast

1-4 lb. roast	1 tbsp. salt
2 cups vinegar	1 tbsp. sugar
4 cups water	¼ cup butter
12 cloves	2 bay leaves

Mix spices, vinegar, water, salt and sugar. Pour over roast and marinate in refrigerator over night. Drain meat and save juice. Dredge meat with flour and brown in butter. Add ½ marinate. Cover and simmer about 2½ hrs. or until tender. Turn meat once. Add more marinate if necessary.

Mrs. Paul Toews, St. Mary, Ont.

Swiss Steak (1)

1½ to 3 lbs, round steak (about 1 in. to 1½ in. thick)	2 tbsp. fat
	1½ tsp. salt
⅓ cup flour	⅛ tsp. pepper
1 large onion peeled and sliced	2 cans tomato sauce

Fry onions in fat till brown. Take out onions and flour meat, and fry in fat till brown. Put onions back on top of meat. Add salt, pepper and tomato sauce, and a little water if needed. Turn down heat and simmer till done. If desired thicken drippings to make gravy.

Mrs. Gerald Davis, Glenn, Calif.

Swiss Steak (2)

Round or chuck steak, 1½ or 2 in. thick.

Mix:

½ cup flour   ½ tsp. pepper
2 tsp. salt

Pound into steak. Brown steak in a little fat in deep skillet. Brown one side, turn over. While other side browns, mix 1 can tomato soup, ½ onion, ¼ green pepper, chopped, 1 soup can water. Pour over steak. Cook in moderate oven (325°) 2 to 2½ hrs.

Mrs. Franklin Wenger, Moundridge, Kans.

Swiss Steak and Vegetables

3½ lb. round steak   1½ cans condensed tomato
½ cup flour   soup
1½ tsp. salt   1 can water
¼ cup fat   6 carrots, quartered
2 cups sliced onions   1 pkg. frozen peas

Early in day, cut round steak in 8 pieces, mix flour with salt and pepper, pound into steak. Brown in deep fat on both sides. Add onion and brown a bit. Add soup and water, cover and let simmer until meat is tender . Whole allspice may be added while simmering. To serve, heat meat mixture to simmering point, in meantime preboil carrots until almost done. Then add to meat, pour peas on top and simmer until peas are done.

Mrs. Robert Boehs, Helena, Okla.

Zesty Roast

Beef roast   Mustard
Worcestershire sauce   Salt and pepper

Rub meat with salt and pepper and worcestershire sauce. Then with hands rub well with mustard. Bake at 350° basting with worcestershire sauce. After roast has well browned (be sure all mustard is browned) add a little water to keep from burning, then baste with drippings. Remove roast 20 min. before serving and add desired water to pan and thicken with cornstarch mixed with a little cold water.

Mrs. Olin Schmidt, DeRidder, La.

Whole Meal Casserole

1 lb. ground round steak	1 large can tomatoes
1 large onion, sliced	1 can (no. 303) peas
1 lb. cooked spaghetti	1 can ripe olives
1 can (no. 303) whole corn	½ lb. American cheese

Brown onions and meat in oil in frying pan. If desired, add one garlic and ½ bell pepper, sliced. Mix in spaghetti and rest of the ingredients. Add salt and pepper to taste. Blend thoroughly with fork and put in large baking dish. Grate or cut cheese in small pieces. Add salt and pepper to taste. Blend thoroughly small pieces. Sprinkle over top of mixture. Bake in 350° oven 30 to 45 min. or until cheese is melted and is bubbly. Makes about 8 servings.   Mrs. Harry Koehn, Livingston, Calif.

Hamburger Dishes

American Casserole

1 lb. ground beef	1 medium onion, diced
1 can stewed tomatoes or	1 can corn
tomato soup	4 tbsp. cornmeal
¾ cup raisins	1 tsp. salt
¼ tsp. chili powder	

Fry ground beef with onion until slightly brown. Add remaining ingredients and bake in greased casserole for 45 to 50 min. in 325° oven.   Mary Ann Friesen, Glenn, Calif.

Baked Beef and Rice

1 lb. ground beef	½ tsp. pepper
1 cup rice	1 tsp. paprika
1 small onion, chopped	2 cups tomato juice
2 tbsp. lard or drippings	1½ cups boiling water
1 tsp. salt	½ cup grated cheese

Cook beef, rice, and onion in drippings until lightly browned. Season. Add tomato juice and boiling water. Place in 1½ qt. casserole, cover, and bake at 300°, 1 hr. Uncover, sprinkle with cheese and continue baking about 10 minutes. 6 servings.

Delma Friesen, Conway, Kans.

Beef-In-A-Skillet

1 lb. ground beef

1 egg

¼ cup milk

¼ cup fine crumbs

1½ tbsp. finely chopped onion

2 tbsp. flour

1 10½ oz. can tomato soup

¾ cup milk

1½ cups cooked assorted vegetables

½ tsp. salt

Combine first six ingredients. Form small meat balls, roll in flour and brown in grease. When brown, arrange meat balls around the edge of skillet. Gradually add soup and milk which has been mixed together into center of skillet. Place vegetables over soup and add salt. Cover and simmer.

Mrs. Jake Wohlgemuth, Landmark, Man.

Corn Bread Meat Pie

Combine in a skillet:

1 lb. ground beef   1 large onion, chopped

Brown well and add:

1 can (8 oz.) tomato sauce   1¾ cups water

1 tsp. salt   ¾ tsp. black pepper

1 tbsp. chili powder   1 can (12 oz.) whole kernel

½ cup chopped green pepper   corn

Mix well and let simmer 15 min. Turn into greased casserole. Top with corn bread. Bake in a 350° oven for 20 min.

Corn Bread Topping

Sift together:

¾ cup corn meal   1 tbsp. sugar

1 tbsp. flour   1½ tsp. baking powder

Add:

1 egg, well beaten   ½ cup milk

1 tbsp. melted grease

Turn onto beef mixture. Do not worry if this topping sinks during baking it will rise and cook crispy.

Mrs. David B. Holdeman, DeRidder, La.

Baked Peppers

4 large green peppers	½ cup crushed soda crackers
½ lb. sausage or hamburger	½ tsp. salt
1 cup canned or fresh corn (or lima beans)	⅛ tsp. pepper

Cut peppers in half lengthwise. Remove seeds and veins parboil for 5 min. and allow to cool.

Brown meat slightly, add corn or (lima beans) and seasonings. Fill pepperhalves and top with cracker crumbs. Arrange in greased baking dish. Bake at 375° for 25 min. Serves 6 to 8.

Mrs. Clifford Koehn, Winton, Calif.

Beef Stroganoff

4 tbsp. flour	4 tbsp. butter
1 lb. beef sirloin cut into ¼ in. wide strips	2 tbsp. cooking sherry
½ cup chopped onions	½ tsp. salt
1 tbsp. tomato paste	1 cup thinly sliced mushrooms
1¼ cups beef stock or 1 can beef broth	1 clove garlic, minced
	1 cup sour dairy cream

Combine 1 tbsp. flour and salt, dredge meat in mixture. Heat skillet and add 2 tbsp. butter, let melt add sirloin strips and brown quickly on all sides. Add mushroom slices, onions, and garlic, cook 3 to 4 min. or until onion is tender. Remove meat and mushrooms from skillet. Add 2 tbsp. butter to pan drippings, let melt, blend in 3 tbsp. flour, and tomato paste. Slowly add cold meat stock. Cook, stirring constantly until mixture thickens. Return meat and mushrooms to skillet. Add sour cream and sherry. Simmer.

Adella Jantz, Hesston, Kans.

Company Casserole

8 oz. pkg. med. noodles	8 oz. pkg. cream cheese
1 lb. ground beef	½ cup green onions chopped
3 tbsp. butter or oleo	1 tbsp. green peppers, chopped (optional)
2 (8 oz.) cans tomato sauce	2 tbsp. melted butter
1 cup cottage cheese	1 cup cream, sour or sweet

Cook noodles and drain. Brown meat in 3 tbsp. butter, stir in tomato sauce. Combine cottage cheese, cream cheese and cream. (Beat with electric mixer.) Combine all ingredients with noodles. Put into 2 qt. casserole or baking dish. Pour 2 tbsp. melted butter over top and bake in 350° oven for 30 min.

Mrs. Delton Nikkel, Marquette, Kans.

Elizabeth's Goulash

2 lbs. hamburger
1 box Kraft dinner
1 can Campbells tomato soup
  or juice

salt and pepper to taste
½ tsp. chili powder
¼ tsp. enchilada powder
1 med. onion

Brown onion and hamburger in large skillet. Cook macaroni in salt water until tender, add to hamburger mixture. Add tomato soup or juice, chili, enchilada powder, salt, pepper and grated cheese. Mix well. Let simmer for about 30 min. Add water if too thick.

Mrs. Clarence J. Boehs, Goltry, Okla.

Evening Main Meal

1 tbsp. butter
1 cup celery

¼ cup chopped onion
1 cup tomato juice

Brown onion in butter. Add juice and celery. Cook 15 min. Add salt and pepper.

1 lb. hamburger, brown, add above mixture and boil slowly till done about 15 min. Cook ½ cup rice, put in casserole. Put meat mixture on top. Then ½ cup grated cheese and melt under broiler.

Mrs. Clarence Schmidt, Newton, Kans.

Fried Rice

1 cup rice
1 lb. ground beef
1 tsp. salt

½ tsp. pepper
¼ cup catsup
1 small onion, diced

Cook rice until done. Fry ground beef, salt, pepper, catsup and onion until done, add drained rice. Simmer.

Mrs. Gerald Davis, Glenn, Calif.

Ground Beef Oriental

2 onions, finely chopped
1 cup sliced celery
3 tbsp. butter
½ cup rice, uncooked
1 lb. ground beef
1 can cream of mushroom soup

1 can cream of chicken soup
1½ cup water
¼ cup soy sauce
¼ tsp. pepper
1 can (1 lb.) bean sprouts
chinese noodles

Brown onion and celery in butter, remove from pan. Brown rice and ground beef, put aside. In buttered 2 qt. casserole combine soups, water, soy sauce and pepper, salt to taste. Add browned onion, celery, ground beef and rice, stir in bean sprouts lightly. Bake covered in mod. oven 350° for 30 min. Uncover and bake 30 min. longer, serve with warm crunchy chinese noodles, makes 6 to 8 servings.

Mrs. Harry Koehn, Livingston, Calif.

Hamburger Potato Dish

2 lbs. hamburger
1 onion
1 can mushroom soup

1 can water
6 med. potatoes, peeled and cubed
salt and pepper to taste

Brown hamburger and onion and add soup and water, potatoes and seasoning. Bake in casserole or cook in skillet, stirring occasionally.

Mrs. Clarence Schneider, Ithaca, Mich.

Hamburger-Sauerkraut

1 lb. hamburger
1 medium onion
2 cups sauerkraut

½ cup rice
1 tsp. salt
2 cups water

Fry onion and meat till brown. Add rice, water and salt. Simmer till rice is done. Add sauerkraut and cook some more. Add more water if necessary.

Mrs. Percy Fast, Bancroft, S. Dak.

Ground Beef Pinwheels

3 cups Bisquick   Milk
1½ tsp. Tabasco sauce, divided   1½ lb. ground beef, fried
1 cup corn flakes   2 tsp. salt
1 med. onion, (chopped)   1 tbsp. minced parsley

Follow directions on pkg. for rolled biscuits but add ½ tsp. tabaso to the milk. Roll into rectangle about 10x15". Sprinkle remaining tabasco over ground beef, add rest of ingredients. Mix well. Spread evenly over dough roll as for jelly roll. Cut into 12 slices ¾" thick, place in buttered shallow baking pan. Bake in 375° oven until brown, about 30 min.

Mushroom Sauce: Combine
1 can mushroom soup   ½ cup milk
1 beef boullion cube   ¼ tsp. tabasco sauce
Heat, stirring until hot.

Mrs. Abe P. Toews, Wales, N. Dak.

Hamburger Sauerkraut Casserole

1 qt. sauerkraut   ½ cup rice, uncooked
1½ lb. hamburger-seasoned   1 pt. tomato juice
    with salt and onion

Put in layers between sauerkraut. Bake one hour or until rice is done.

Johanna Toews, Hilmar, Calif.

Hamburger and Spaghetti

½ lb. hamburger   ¼ lb. cheese
¼ small onion, cut fine   ½ tbsp. butter
1 cup tomato   ½ to ¾ cup spaghetti,
    salt and pepper to taste   uncooked

Brown onion, add hamburger and brown lightly. Then add tomatoes simmer together 30 min. after that add grated cheese and butter. Let simmer 5 min. longer. Last add cooked spaghetti. Also can be finished in oven after onion and hamburger are browned. Then add cooked spaghetti and all other ingredients and bake in oven one hr. at 350°

Mrs. Marion Jantz, Horton, Mo.

Hamburger Cheese Casserole

1 8 oz. pkg. macaroni
½ lb. hamburger
½ tsp. salt

1 can cream celery soup
½ can cheddar cheese soup

Boil macaroni in salted water until done, drain and add 2 tbsp. cooking oil and mix to keep macaroni from sticking. Meantime brown hamburger over medium heat add ½ tsp. salt.   Add browned hamburger to cooked and drained macaroni. Add cream of celery soup, cheddar cheese soup with enough milk to bring to proper consistency.   Mix thoroughly, pour into buttered casserole, top with crushed potato chips or 1 cup buttered bran flakes and bake. 30 min. at 350°

Mrs. Ivan Eicher, Ithaca, Mich.

Hamburger Casserole

1 lb. ground beef
¼ cup uncooked rice
1 egg
  salt and pepper to taste

1 small head cabbage
¾ cup water
2 tbsp. butter
  tomato juice

Cut the cabbage leaves loose at stem and steam for 10 min. in part of the water.   Mix the beef, rice, egg, salt and pepper. Of this take about one tbsp. and wrap in cabbage leaf; place side by side in roaster over this, pour the water used in steaming the cabbage, also the remaining water together with the melted butter.   Cook in moderate oven (350°) 1½ hr.   Pour over enough tomato juice to cover and cook ½ hr. more.   Serves eight.

Mrs. Stanley Penner, Rich Hill, Mo.

Hamburger Noodle Casserole

1 lb. hamburger
1 chopped onion
¼ lb. noodles

1 10½ oz. can of cream of
  chicken soup
1½ tsp. salt

Fry hamburger and onion until slightly brown. Cook noodles in salt water until tender. Add browned meat and noodles. Season. Pour into greased casserole and bake at 350° for 35 to 40 minutes.   Serve 6-8.

Mrs. Kenneth Holdeman, Halstead, Kans.

Hamburger-Corn Pone Pie

1½ lb. hamburger
1 tbsp. shortening
1 cup beans cooked
(or pork and beans)
1 tsp. salt

½ cup catsup
2 cups tomatoes
½ cup chopped onion
3 tsps. chili powder

Brown meat and onion in shortening. Add seasoning and tomatoes. Cover and simmer over low heat until meat is well cooked. Add cooked beans and heat mixture thoroughly. Pour hot mixture into the baking pans. Top with corn bread batter. Spreading carefully with a wet knife. Bake 425° for 20 min. until done.

Mrs. Albert Friesen, Inman, Kans.

Hamburger Rice Stew

Brown in:
1 tbsp. fat in hot skillet   2 lbs. ground beef

Add, cover and simmer 30 min.
3 cups diced celery
2 onions, diced
juice drained from two cans
bean sprouts (1 lb. cans)

1½ tsp. salt
1½ cups leftover beef gravy
1 tsp. soy sauce
½ cup uncooked rice

Add and heat:
2 cans bean sprouts   Dash of pepper

Leftover cubed roast may be used in place of ground beef. Serve with tea and a jello salad. Serves 10.

Mrs. Dick Loewen, Glenn, Calif.

Hamburger-En Casserole

1 large onion, minced
2 tbsp. fat
1 lb. ground beef
½ lb. cooked green beans
1 10-oz. can tomato soup

5 med. size potatoes
(cooked)
½ cup warm milk
1 beaten egg
1 tsp. salt
½ tsp. pepper

Brown onion and meat in fat. Add beans and soup. Mix thoroughly. Pour in greased baking dish. Mash potatoes and add milk, egg, and seasoning. Put on top of meat mixture. Bake 350° for 30 min. (Left over mashed potatoes may be used.)

Mrs. Edward Friesen, Almena, Wisc.

Hamburger Pie

(Very good for a quick meal)

2 lbs. ground beef
1 large onion, chopped
1 tsp. salt
1 can water

⅛ tsp. pepper
1 can green beans or Mexican style corn
1 can tomato sauce

Lightly brown meat. Add seasonings, beans or (corn) and tomato sauce and water. Bring all to a boil. Pour into flat loaf pan 13"x9". Top with one or two cans of refrigerator biscuits. Bake at 425° for 10 min. then sprinkle with grated cheese, and bake 5 to 10 min. more. Serves 6 to 8.

Mrs. LeRoy Smith, DeRidder, La.

Hamburger "Luscious"

1 lb. hamburger
1 stalk chopped celery
2 cups fine dried noodles
⅛ tsp. pepper

½ lb. American cheese, sliced
1 (No. 2 can) tomatoes
1 tsp. salt

Brown meat slightly in a skillet, season with salt, pepper, and onion. Arrange the remaining ingredients in layers as listed, over browned meat. Sprinkle salt and pepper over noodles. Cover, bring to a boil on high heat; then reduce to simmer and cook for 30 minutes. Occasionally remove cover and press noodles into the liquid.

Mrs. Melvin Dirks

Hot Hamburger Dish

1 lb. hamburger, browned
4 medium sized potatoes

1 can cream of vegetable soup
1 can water

Season to taste, bake in casserole 1 hr. or until potatoes are done.

Mrs. Curt Ensz, Cimarron, Kans.

Hamburger, Corn Casserole (1)

1 lb. hamburger
1 small onion, diced

1 can corn
1 can tomato soup, undiluted

Fry hamburger and onion until browned. Add corn and tomato soup. Bake at 350° for 30 min.

Mrs. Willard Holdeman, Hesston, Kans.

Hamburger, Corn Casserole (2)

Peel and dice into casserole 2 or 3 med. sized potatoes, add ½ cup milk and butter the size of a walnut. Salt and pepper to taste. Bake in oven at 350° until nearly done.
Fry 1 lb. hamburger in skillet until done. Add small amount of onion if desired and 1 tsp. salt.
Put hamburger over the potatoes in casserole, then add 1 can of creamed corn over top of hamburger. The corn may be thinned with a little milk if necessary.
Return to oven and bake 20 to 30 minutes more. Grated cheese or catsup may be added if desired. Serve hot.

Mrs. Albert Nichols, Winton, Calif.

Hurry Up Spanish Rice

¼ cup fat	1¾ cups hot water
¾ cup sliced onions	2-8 oz. cans tomato sauce
⅓ cup green peppers	1½ tsp. salt
1⅓ cups cooked rice	⅛ tsp. pepper
½ lb. ground beef	1 tsp. prepared mustard

Melt fat in skillet, add onions, peppers, rice and ground beef. Cook and stir until all are lightly browned, add water, tomato sauce and seasonings, stir well, bring to a boil quickly, cover tight and simmer 10 min. Makes 4 servings.

Mrs. John Unruh, Ithaca, Mich.

Italian Spaghetti (1)

1 med. onion, chopped	3 lbs. hamburger
2 slices bacon, chopped	

Make meat balls, fry in bacon. Saute onion and green pepper.
Add:

4 cans tomato paste	garlic salt or buds to taste
2 qts. canned tomatoes	2 tbsp. sugar
3 bay leaves	1 to 1½ tsp. salt
	red hot pepper to taste

Put all together and simmer for 2 hrs. or more. Cook spaghetti in salt water, drain, and serve with sauce on top. Garnish with Italian Grated Parmesan Cheese. Garlic and red peppers makes it mild or hot, so fix to suit your own family.

Betty Haynes

Italian Spaghetti (2)

1 lb. spaghetti, boiled in
salted water
2 tbsp. olive oil
1 lb. hamburger
1 green pepper, chopped
2 garlic cloves, chopped
2 onions, chopped

1 tsp. parsley
salt and pepper to taste
2 cans hot sauce or tomato
sauce
1 can tomato paste
1 oz. dried mushroom with
bay leaf

Mix hamburger, green pepper, garlic, onions, parsley, salt and pepper; fry in olive oil for 20 min. Add: hot or tomato sauce, tomato paste, mushroom and spaghetti. Blend well and continue simmering for 2 hrs. or more.

Mrs. Roy Toews, Scio, Ore.

Italian Spaghetti and Meat

1½ lb. ground beef
1 tbsp. chopped onion

½ sweet pepper, chopped

Fry the above until beef loses red color and then add:

8 oz. Italian style spaghetti
1 pt. tomato juice

1-8 oz. can tomato sauce
1 tbsp. brown sugar

Salt and pepper to season. Simmer until done.

Mrs. David Ensz, Inman, Kans.

Lasagne (1)

2 cans mushroom soup
1 lb. ground beef
1 lb. longhorn cheese
1 clove garlic, minced
1 pkg. lasagna noodles

4 hard boiled eggs, sliced
¼ cup grated parmesan
cheese
1 small onion, diced
2 tbsp. olive oil
salt and pepper to taste

Brown onions and garlic in olive oil. Add ground beef and brown. Add soup, salt and pepper and simmer 15 min. Cook lasagna noodles as directed. Arrange a layer of cooked lasagna in buttered baking dish, a layer of sliced cheese and eggs, a layer of meat, and mushroom sauce, sprinkle with grated cheese. Repeat until all ingredients are used. Top with sauce and grated cheese. Bake at 375° for 20 min. Serves 6.

Verna Giesbrecht, Winton, Calif.

Lasagne (2)

1 lb. ground beef
2 cloves garlic, chopped fine
2 tbsp. salad oil
1-18 oz. can tomato sauce
1 no. 2 can tomatoes, drain and save juice

1-8 oz. pkg. Lasagne noodles
1½ tsp. salt
½ tsp. pepper
½ tsp. oregano
½ lb. Mozzarella cheese

¾ lb. Ricotta cheese(cottage cheese may be substituted)
½ cup grated Parmesan cheese

Brown ground beef and garlic in salad oil.   Add tomatoes, tomato sauce, salt, pepper, and spices.   Cover and simmer for 15 min., until slightly thickened.   Cook noodles in boiling, salted water until tender.   Drain and rinse.   Fill casserole with alternate layers of noodles, cheeses, meat, tomatoes, tomato sauce, and grated Parmesan cheese.   Top with layer of tomato sauce and Parmesan cheese.   Bake at 375° 15-20 min.

Erlene Holdeman, Hesston, Kans.

Mashed Potato Casserole

1 lb. hamburger
2 tbsp. shortening
1 can tomato soup (or 2 cups tomatoes)
1 can green beans

¼ tsp. pepper
¾ cup mild cheese, grated
2 cups mashed potatoes
½ cup finely chopped onion, (optional)

Brown hamburger and onion in shortening.   Add tomatoes, green beans and seasoning.   Pour into greased 2 quart casserole.   Fold cheese into potatoes.   Arrange over top of casserole and bake in 350° about 30 to 40 minutes.   Makes 6 to 8 servings.

Mrs. Anna Jantz, Hesston, Kans.

One Dish Meal

1 lb. hamburger
salt to taste

2 eggs
1 cup milk

Beat eggs and milk.   Add bread to soak up eggs and milk.   Add to hamburger, mix. Put in the middle of small roaster or casserole, then add 6 potatoes cut in quarters.   Add 6 or 8 carrots.   Mix 1 can mushroom soup with ½ cup milk.   Pour over the above mixture and bake until done.   In 375° oven for about an hour.

Mabel Hostettler, Jeromesville, Ohio

Meat Gloupseah (Russian Dish)

1 large cabbage head or 2 small ones. Cut out the core and put head in very hot water to which ¼ cup vinegar has been added. Separate leaves after they are wilted and they will roll up easier.

1 lb. hamburger	2 eggs—well beaten
1 cup cooked rice	1½ tsp. salt
½ cup crushed corn flakes	1 tbsp. prepared mustard
½ cup onions—chopped	pepper and paprika to taste

Mix all together, then put 1 big tbsp. in a cabbage leaf and roll up and fasten with toothpicks. Put the rolls close together in a frying pan with ¼ cup fat in it and quickly brown on all sides. Then put in a baking dish and pour 3 or 4 cans of tomato sauce over the rolls. Cover and bake for 2 hrs. in 350°. Then pour 1 cup cream over this to make a gravy. (The more cream the better). Bake ½ hr. longer. Serve on platter swimming in gravy.

Mrs. P. E. Penner Jr., Ballico, Calif.

Pressure-Pan Hamburger

1½ cups diced onion	2½ cups canned tomatoes
1 lb. hamburger	1½ tsp. salt
2 tbsp. fat	⅛ tsp. pepper
1 pkg. (10 oz.) frozen peas	1 cup diced carrots
2 cups uncooked macaroni	

Brown onion and hamburger in fat in pressure pan. Add remaining ingredients. Cook under pressure for 10 min. Serves 6.

Quick Skillet Supper

1 lb. ground beef	½ cup sour cream
1 cup chopped onion	2 tsp. salt
1 tbsp. fat	⅛ tsp. celery salt
3 cups noodles, uncooked	2 tsp. Worcestershire sauce
3 cups tomato juice	½ cup water

Cook beef and onion in hot fat. Place uncooked noodles over top of meat mixture. Combine remaining ingredients and blend well. Pour over noodles, taking care to moisten noodles well. Do not stir; bring to boiling. Turn heat low: cover and simmer for 30 min. or until noodles are tender.

Mrs. D. G. Boeckner, Moundridge, Kans.

Poor Man's Steak

3 lbs. hamburger
1 cup cracker crumbs
1 cup cold water
salt and pepper to taste

Mix well and press into cookie sheet and chill long enough to set. Cut in squares, roll in flour, fry on both sides in a small amount of grease to golden brown. (Not too much). Place in baking dish. Pour over 1 can of mushroom soup undiluted. Put in oven.

Mrs. Heber Good, Dalton, Ohio
Vesta Koehn, Wauseon, Ohio

Quick Supper Casserole

Butter casserole. Pare and slice 3 medium potatoes and arrange in casserole, add salt and pepper. Pare 3 medium carrots. Slice into casserole, add salt and pepper. Sprinkle ½ cup uncooked rice over carrots. Brown ¾ lb. hamburger. Season. Spread over rice. Slice 1 raw onion over meat. Pour 2 cups tomatoes over all. Put buttered bread crumbs on top. Bake uncovered at 350° for 1 hr. Makes 6 servings. (May add green beans or peas if you like.)

Mrs. Ronnie Jantz, Winton, Calif.

Russian Beruchas

1 med. size cabbage, chopped
1 med. onion, chopped
1 lb. hamburger
½ tsp. salt

Mix cabbage, onion and hamburger, cook until done. Prepare your favorite bread dough, let rise double in bulk, and roll out to ¾ in. thickness. Cut into about 4 in. squares. Place a tbsp. of mixture on each square and pinch edges together. Let rise 20 min. Bake at 400° until brown.

Mrs. George Mayeske, Fredonia, Kans.

Ravioli

1 onion, chopped
1 green pepper
1 clove garlic—optional
1 lb. hamburger
1 can corn
1 can tomato soup or juice
1 small pkg. spaghetti (cooked)
2 tsp. Worcestershire sauce
¼ tsp. chili powder
½ lb. grated cheese

Fry onion and meat, add other ingredients. Pour into greased baking dish. Sprinkle top with cheese. Bake at 350° for 45 min.

Mrs. Marshall Harms, Walnut Hill, Fla.

Russian Cabbage Rolls

¾ cup uncooked rice
3 pt. water
2½ tsp. salt
1 lb. ground beef
¾ cup chopped onion
1 tsp. salt

½ tsp. pepper
6 large cabbage leaves
1 can tomato soup
½ cup sour cream
2 tbsp. grated cheese

Cook rice in boiling water (salted, 1 tsp. salt) in a tightly covered pan 15 min. Combine meat, onions, seasonings and cooked rice. Blanch cabbage leaves in small amount of boiling water in covered pan two or three minutes. Divide meat mixture into six portions. Wrap in cabbage leaves and secure with toothpick. Place cabbage rolls in covered casserole. Combine soup and cream and pour over rolls. Sprinkle cheese on top and bake 1½ hours in preheated 375° oven.

Mrs. Menno Koehn, Halstead, Kans.

Russian Kraut

1 lb. hamburger
1 lb. sausage

Fry just enough to get grease out, then drain.

4 onions (optional)
3 green peppers (optional)
1 no. 2½ can kraut

1 no. 2½ can tomato juice
¼ cup sour cream (optional)

Bake or simmer with lid for one hour.

Mrs. Anna Jantz, Hesston, Kans.

Sarah's Hamburger Stew

1 lb. ground beef
¼ cup diced onion
2 tbsp. butter
1 tsp. salt
⅛ tsp. pepper
½ cup water

½ pkg. 10 oz. frozen cut
    green beans or 1 can yellow beans
1 cup diced potatoes
1 cup diced carrots
1 cup thinly sliced celery

Brown meat and onion in butter in heavy skillet. Add remaining ingredients. Cover and simmer for 30 to 40 min., until vegetables are tender. Makes 6 servings.

Mrs. John Nichols, Montezuma, Kans.

Spanish Rice (1)

1 lb. ground beef
½ med. onion, minced
¼ sweet green pepper,
  minced
1 tsp. chili powder
1 tsp. salt

pepper to taste
1 can tomato sauce
2 cans water
1¼ cups long grain rice,
  cooked

Brown meat with onions and pepper in large skillet. Add seasonings, sauce, water and cooked rice. Mix well and simmer about 10 min. Stir once or twice. If not moist enough add a little more water. Serve with green peas and fruit salad.

Mrs. Paul Smith, DeRidder, La.

Spanish Rice (2)

1 cup water
1 cup rice
1 small onion
1 tsp. chili powder

1½ cups tomato juice, gravy
  or broth
1 cup fried hamburger,
  roast or chicken
1 tsp. salt

Brown rice in just enough grease to coat. When golden brown add 1 cup water, and 1½ cups tomato juice, gravy or broth, chili powder, salt, and meat. When mixture starts to boil lower heat, cover and cook 20 min. or until moisture disappears. Rice should be light and fluffy. Serve hot.

Leola Willard, Mexico

Spanish Rice Supreme

1 lb. hamburger
1 tbsp. butter or margarine
2 cups sliced potatoes
½ cup chopped onion
1 cup sliced carrots
¼ cup chopped green pepper

½ cup chopped celery
½ cup white rice
2 cups tomatoes
1 tsp. salt
¼ tsp. pepper

Brown hamburger in fat, crumbling with fork. Place in 2 quart baking dish and cover with a layer of each of the vegetables in the order given. Add seasonings and hot water to cover. Bake in covered dish in slow oven (325°) about two hours. Add more water if needed.

Mrs. Franklin Nichols, Greensburg, Kans.

Stuffed Cabbage Rolls

1 lb. ground beef	2-8 oz. cans tomato sauce
¼ cup chopped onions	½ sauce can of water
2 tbsp. shortening	1 tbsp. Worcestershire
1 tsp. salt	sauce
¼ tsp. pepper	1 head cabbage
½ cup rolled oats	½ cup grated sharp cheese

Heat oven to 350°. Brown beef and onion in shortening. Drain and put into bowl. Add salt, pepper, and oats. Mix well. Combine tomato sauce, water, and Worcestershire sauce into the sauce and add ½ cup to meat. Mix well. Separate 8 cabbage leaves, wash and drop into boiling salted water and cook 3 min. Drain. Fill each leaf with meat mixture, roll up and secure with tooth-picks. Place rolls in baking dish or pan. Pour remaining sauce over cabbage rolls. Bake for 45 to 50 min. Baste occasionally with tomato sauce. Sprinkle grated cheese over rolls 10 min. before end of baking time.

Mrs. Vernon Giesbrecht, Cimarron, Kans.

Six Layer Dinner

Grease deep baking dish. Slice real thin two potatoes, salt, sprinkle ⅓ cup rice over. Crumble 1½ lb. hamburger on top of rice, 1 tsp. salt and ⅛ tsp. pepper, 1 diced onion on top of meat, grate 2 or 3 carrots. Put on top 1 can whole tomatoes and 1½ tsp. sugar. Dot with butter. Bake at 350° for 2½ hr.

Mrs. Leonard Peaster, Winton, Calif.

Supper Spaghetti

3 cups boiled spaghetti	½ cup fat or oil
1 lb. ground beef	1 cup diced celery
¼ lb. ground chicken or	2 tsp. salt
calves' liver	2 tsp. chili powder
3 cups stewed tomatoes or	¼ cup chopped parsley
juice	½ cup shredded yellow
1 cup diced carrots	cheese

Simmer the meat with the vegetable and fat or oil for 1 hr. or until vegetables are tender. Add salt and chili powder. Stir in 2 tbsp. of parsley. Serve on spaghetti and garnish top with re-maining parsley and shredded cheese.

Mrs. Glen Peaster, Bonners Ferry, Ida.

Savory Noodle Goulash

Cook until browned in 1 tbsp. hot fat:

¾ lb. ground pork, beef, and veal (or ¾ lb. pork or beef alone)

Add and cook 10 min.

2 small onions, minced   2 cups diced celery

Gently mix in. . .

drained hot boiled noodles (5 to 6 oz. uncooked)
2 cups cooked tomatoes   ¾ cup shredded cheese
1 tsp. salt   ⅛ tsp. pepper

Simmer 30 mins. or place in buttered 2 qt. casserole and bake at 350° for 45 min. Serve hot.

Mrs. Duane Johnson, Atwater, Calif.

Supper Casserole

1½ lbs. ground beef
1 cup diced celery
1 can mushroom soup, un-diluted (may substitute cream of chicken soup)

1 cup chopped onion
1 can tomato soup, undiluted
1 large can Chow mein noodles

Brown meat and onions in skillet. Cook celery in salt water 10 min., drain. Add soups and celery to meat and onions. Then add one half can of noodles. Mix well and put mixture into buttered casserole. Spread remaining noodles over top and bake at 350° for 30 min.

Vada Johnson, Galva, Kans.

Vegetable Meat Pie

1½ lbs. boiling beef
2 tsp. salt
4 cups water
6 med. potatoes, diced

2 carrots, diced
1 med. onion
2 tbsp. cornstarch or flour
your favorite biscuit recipe

Cut beef into 1 in. cubes. Add 4 cups water, and salt. Cook 1½ hrs. or until meat is almost tender—add potatoes, carrots, and onion. Cover and cook another 30 min. Blend cornstarch with water, add to above mixture, stir until thickened. Pour into oblong pyrex dish and place biscuits on top (bake remaining biscuits separate). Bake at 400° for 20 min.

Mrs. Dave R. Unruh, Montezuma, Kans.

Seven Layer Casserole

1 lb. ground beef
(more if desired)
½ green or Bell pepper
1 cup cooked sweet corn

¾ cup min. or uncooked rice
2 cans (8 oz.) tomato sauce
½ med. or small onion
1 cup green peas

Preheat oven to 350°. Place rice in bottom of casserole or baking dish. (even out on bottom) Next place your corn, then peas. Pour 1 can tomato sauce evenly over peas, then add the can full of water over the same. Dice up onions and peppers finely, place your seasoned meat over those layers and pour 1 can of tomato sauce and 1 can of water over all. Place in oven for 1 hr. with a lid covering, then remove lid and continue to bake for 30 min. Serve hot.

Mrs. Clinton Holdeman, Burrton, Kans.

Stuffed Pepper Deluxe

1 lb. ground beef
⅓ cup chopped onion
2 tbsp. fat
1¾ cups sliced tomatoes
1 cup cooked rice
2 tsp. salt

1 tsp. sugar
2 tbsp. flour
⅛ tsp. pepper
¼ cup buttered crumbs
¼ cup grated cheese
8 green peppers

Brown beef and onions in fat. Add tomatoes, rice, salt, pepper, sugar and flour. Bring mixture to boiling. Cover and simmer 15 min. stirring occasionally. Wash peppers, cut off tops and remove seeds. Drop in boiling water for one min. Drain and stuff with meat mixture and sprinkle top with buttered crumbs mixed with grated cheese. Bake at 375° for 30 min. Serves 8.

Mrs. Delbert Hiebert, Middleton, Mich.

Kima (from India)

1 lb. ground beef
½ cup finely chopped onion
1 tsp. salt
½ tsp. cumin
½ tsp. ginger
1 med. potato, cubed (about 1⅓ cup)

¼ tsp. turmeric
1 bay leaf
2 med. tomatoes, diced
1 10 oz. pkg. frozen peas
½ cup water or more

Fry meat and onions until brown. Stir in seasonings, potatoes and tomatoes. Add frozen peas and water. Cover. Cook over low heat about 20 to 25 min. or until potatoes are done. Kima should be moist, but not soupy. Serve with steamed rice.

Meat Balls and Meat Loaf

Beef and Rice Meat Balls

2 lbs. ground beef
1 cup rice
6 tbsp. chopped onion
2 tsp. salt
2 cups water
½ tsp. pepper
½ tsp. poultry seasoning
6 tbsp. fat
4 cans tomato sauce

Mix all ingredients but fat, tomato sauce and water. Form into small balls. Brown lightly in fat. Drain off excess fat. Add tomato sauce and water. Cover and simmer 45 to 50 min. or until rice is tender. Makes about 2 dozen balls. May be baked in oven also.

Mrs. Wilbur L. Koehn, Cimarron, Kans.

Meat Balls

1 lb. hamburger
3 slices bread soaked in milk
1 cup rice (swelled)
1 tsp. sage

Form into balls, and simmer in 1 qt. of tomatoes for 1 hr.

Mrs. A. L. Yost, Moundridge, Kans.

Meat Balls With Mushroom Soup

2½ lb. hamburger
¼ cup chopped onion
1⅓ cups cracker crumbs
3 eggs
2 cans mushroom soup
2½ tsp. salt
½ tsp. pepper
½ cup catsup
½ cup cream

Mix all ingredients and shape into small balls. Brown meat balls in skillet and put into casserole. Add mushroom soup to drippings in skillet (drain grease from skillet, leaving 1 or 2 tbsp). Add enough milk to make a thin gravy, stir until heated. (Gravy thickens as it bakes). Pour over meatballs. Cover and bake at 325° for 1¼ hrs. Serves 12 to 14.

Twila Jantz, Winton, Calif.

Meat Balls A La Russe

1¼ lbs. ground sirloin or   4 slices crustless bread
   hamburger   1 cup milk
1 beaten egg   salt and pepper

Shape in small balls and broil or fry.

Sauce:

   ½ clove garlic   1 small onion
   ½ green pepper   1 small can mushrooms

Fry slowly in just a little oil—do not brown. Add the following liquids after you have added enough flour to thicken.

   1 can consomme and liquid from mushrooms (or mushroom soup)
   1 tbsp. catsup
   a few drops of Worcestershire Sauce
   1 tbsp. mayonnaise

Mix mayonnaise with a little consomme before adding. Pour over balls and serve immediately. Serve with fluffy boiled rice.

Mrs. Marlin Jantz, Fredonia, Kans.

Porcupine Meat Balls

Mix together and form into balls:

   1 lb. ground beef   ½ cup uncooked rice
   ¼ cup minced onion   salt and pepper to taste

Place into greased casserole with tight fitting cover. Combine in pan 1 can cream of celery soup and ½ cup water. Pour over meat balls. Cover and bake at 350° for 1¼ hrs. 4 to 6 servings.

Roberta Toews

Swedish Meat Balls

1¼ lbs. ground beef   ½ cup milk
¼ lb. ground pork   1 tsp. salt
¾ cup bread crumbs   ⅛ tsp. pepper
1 tsp. minced parsley   1 tsp. worcestershire sauce
minced onion, (optional)   ¼ tsp. barbecue sauce
                        1 egg

Mix and shape into small balls. Brown in hot fat in skillet. Remove meat balls and stir into skillet 2 tbsp. flour, 1 tsp. paprika, ½ tsp. salt, ⅛ tsp. pepper. Add 2 cups milk and ½ cup cream. Return meatballs to gravy and simmer 20 min.

Mrs. Percy Toews, Barron, Wisc.

Tasty Glorified Meat Balls

1½ lbs. hamburger
4 slices white bread

1 cup milk
1 egg, beaten
salt and pepper

Mix thoroughly, form into balls and fry. Serve with following sauce: Fry 1 small onion, ½ clove garlic, ½ green pepper chopped, in oleo. When onion mixture is well cooked add enough flour to thicken the following liquid. Beat 1 tbsp. of mayonnaise into 1 can of consomme soup, adding a little at a time to keep smooth, add a few drops of worcestershire sauce, 1 tbsp. of catsup, salt and pepper. Combine this mixture slowly with onion and flour in pan, stirring all the while, until the sauce is of proper consistency. Pour over meat balls. Serve with mashed potatoes.

Mrs. Monroe Toews, Scio, Ore.

Mrs. John Jantz Jr., Atwater, Calif.

Best Meat Loaf

¾ cup dry bread crumbs
½ cup milk
1½ lbs. ground beef
½ lb. ground pork
2 beaten eggs
½ cup chopped onion

¼ cup chopped green pepper
1½ tsp. salt
¼ tsp. pepper
¾ tsp. sage
chili sauce

Soak crumbs in milk; add remaining ingredients except chili sauce; mix well. Pack into 8½x4½x2½ in. loaf pan to shape. Invert on shallow baking pan. Score loaf diagonally with handle of wooden spoon. Bake in moderate oven (350°) 1 hr. Fill scored marks on top with chili sauce; bake 15 min. longer. Makes 6 to 8 servings.

Mrs. F. P. Schmidt, Chickasha, Okla.

Meat Loaf (1)

1½ lbs. ground beef
¾ cup oatmeal
2 eggs, beaten
1 cup tomato juice

¼ cup chopped onion
2 tsp. salt
⅛ tsp. pepper

Combine all ingredients thoroughly and pack firmly into a loaf pan. Bake in a moderate oven 350° for one hr.

Mrs. Walter E. Koehn, Moundridge, Kans.

Meat Loaf (2)

2 lbs. hamburger meat
1 small onion
3 cups corn flakes
salt and pepper to taste

3 eggs
½ cup catsup
1 cup tomato juice

Mix and bake 325° for 1½ hr.

Mrs. Tobe H. Koehn, Montezuma, Kans.

Meat Loaf (3)

¾ cup bread crumbs
1 cup milk
⅛ tsp. pepper
½ tsp. sage
1 lb. ground beef
1 lb. pork sausage
¼ tsp. dry mustard
2 tbsp. chopped celery

2 beaten eggs
¼ cup ground onion
1 tsp. salt
¼ tsp. poultry seasoning
1 tbsp. Worchestershire
sauce
3 tsp. brown sugar
¼ cup catsup
1 tsp. prepared mustard

Soak bread crumbs in milk, add all ingredients except last three. Mix well: form in loaf and place in pan. Mix sugar, catsup and prepared mustard together and spread over loaf. Bake 1 hr. at 350°.

Mrs. Lincoln Jantz, Haviland, Kans.

Meat Loaf (4)

3 lbs. ground beef
4 eggs
2 cups cracker crumbs
1 cup sweet milk

1 tbsp. chopped onion
2½ tsp. salt
½ tsp. pepper
1 tsp. sage, to taste

Form in loaf and bake at 350° for 1¾ hr.

Mrs. Frank Wenger, Moundridge, Kans.

Cheese Meat Loaf

2½ lbs. ground beef
1 cup chopped cheese
3 tbsp. chopped green pepper
⅔ cup chopped onion
2½ cups dry bread crumbs
2½ cups tomato puree

1 tbsp. salt
½ small bay leaf, crushed
¼ tsp. thyme
⅛ tsp. garlic salt
3 eggs, beaten

Mix all ingredients thoroughly. Place in a loaf pan. Bake at 350° for 1 hr. Note: This meat loaf may be frozen unbaked. To freeze, wrap unbaked meat loaf in aluminum foil, or you may put in metal containers. Then wrap in foil, seal and freeze. When ready to use bake frozen uncooked meat loaf in a mod. oven (350°) uncovered for about 1½ to 2 hrs. Serves 12 to 15.

Mrs. John L. Buller, Montezuma, Kans.

Delicious Meat Loaf

½ lb. beef ground
½ lb. veal ground
½ lb. pork ground
2 cups bread crumbs
1 egg
1 can tomato soup
½ cup milk
4 tbsp. chopped onion

¾ tsp. pepper
2 tsp. salt
¼ tsp. paprika
2 tbsp flour
3 tsp. prepared mustard
⅓ tsp. sage
1 tsp. parsley

Mix meat with seasonings, add bread crumbs, egg, soup, milk and flour, etc. Form loaf in greased pan. Bake at 350° for 1 hr.

Mrs. Leanna Friesen, Ste. Anne, Manitoba

Dutch Meat Loaf

1½ lbs. ground beef
1 med. onion, chopped
½ can tomato sauce or paste
½ cup bread crumbs

1 egg
salt and pepper to taste
sweet green pepper
(optional)

Mix all ingredients thoroughly. Bake for 10 min. at 425° then add Sauce:

½ cup tomato sauce or paste
½ cup water
2 tbsp. brown sugar

2 tbsp. mustard
1 tbsp. vinegar

Continue baking at 325° for 1½ hr., or until done.

Mrs. Marion Koehn
Mrs. William Haynes, Almena, Wisc.

Meat Loaf Piquant

⅔ cup dry bread crumbs	¼ cup chopped onion
1 cup milk	1 tsp. salt
1½ lbs. ground beef	½ tsp. sage
2 beaten eggs	⅛ tsp. pepper

Soak bread crumbs in milk, add meat, eggs, onion and seasonings; mix well. Place in loaf pan and cover with Piquant Sauce:

Combine:

6 tbsp. brown sugar	½ tsp. nutmeg
½ cup catsup	2 tsp. dry mustard

Bake in moderate oven (350°) 45-50 min.

Mrs. Harold Wedel, Bonners Ferry, Ida.

Chicken

Baked Chicken

1 chicken ½ cup oleo or butter, melted
crushed potato chips or bread crumbs

salt and pepper for seasoning

Cut up chicken, melt oleo, first dip chicken in melted oleo and then roll in the crumbs. 1 tbsp. of Parmesan cheese and 1 tbsp. of garlic salt may be added to crumbs if desired. Put on cookie sheet and bake 1 hr. Temp. 350°.

Mrs. Earl Schmidt, Ingalls, Kans.

Bohemian Breaded Fried Chicken

3 lb. fryer cut in pieces

Dredge each piece in flour. Then dip in condensed milk, and roll in fine bread crumbs, patting on well. Brown on both sides, add ½ cup water, bake at 325° 45-60 min. Remove cover the last 10 min. to crisp crust.

Lambert Janda, Winton, Calif.

A Busy Day Russian Meal

1 fat baking hen, cut into serving pieces, salt, pepper and roll in flour. Put into large roaster and cover. Bake at 350° until almost tender. It is important not to let meat get dry or too brown. Add 1 cup of water at the beginning, add more if necessary. When meat is almost tender, Add:

    6 potatoes, cut in half
    3 med. sweet potatoes, cut in half
    6 apples, cut in half and cored
    Bake 45 min.

Make a cake batter of the following ingredients and pour over meat, potatoes, and apples.

    1 cup cream   1 cup flour
    1 cup sugar   1 tsp. salt
    1 egg   1 tsp. baking powder
    1 tsp. vanilla

Bake ½ hr. longer. Serve while hot directly from roaster.

Mrs. Clayton Wenger, Moundridge, Kans.

Baked Chicken and Dressing

Cut 1 chicken as for frying. Season with salt and pepper. Heat ½ cup cooking oil or shortening in roaster. Roll chicken in flour. Place in roaster and cover. Bake at 400° until about one half done. Remove chicken from roaster, pile dressing into roaster, place chicken over dressing. Continue baking uncovered until browned. About 1 hr. (If browned too fast cover chicken with aluminum foil and lower oven temperature to 350°). Dressing:

    3 eggs   2 cups milk
    4 tbsp. sugar   1 cup cream
    ½ small onion, chopped   2 cups bread crumbs
    2 cups cooked macaroni or 1 cup raisins
      spaghetti   salt and pepper to taste

Beat eggs and sugar until blended, add remaining ingredients in order given. Toss until well mixed.

Mrs. Bert Schmidt, Goltry, Okla.

Baked Chicken and Noodles

4 pieces chicken
3 cups water with salt, pepper and bay leaf
Lipton (2 pkgs.) Chicken and Noodle Soup mix
1 large package med. size Noodles
½ cup cream or top milk
1 tbsp. flour
1 can Cream of Mushroom Soup
2 cups buttered bread crumbs

Cook chicken until tender in water with salt, pepper, and bay leaf. Take meat and bay leaf out. Cook noodles in Liptons Chicken and Noodle soup mix (following directions) and add the chicken broth. Break chicken meat into noodles and put in a casserole or long baking dish. Heat cream, flour, dash salt and pepper until thick. Pour over noodles. Then pour Cream of Mushroom Soup over noodles, and buttered bread crumbs on top and bake at 350° for 1 hr. or until thick and brown.

Mrs. Orval Johnson, Walnut Hill, Fla.

Chicken and Rice (1)

3 cups cooked rice=1 cup raw
1 pkg. dried onion soup mix
2 cut up fryers (salted)
½ cup condensed milk
4 tsp. oleomargarine

Put cooked rice in bottom of long baking dish, and sprinkle ½ of the onion soup over it. Arrange chicken pieces on rice and pour milk over it. Sprinkle the rest of the onion soup on top of chicken and dot with margarine. Bake at 350° for 1¼ to 1½ hr.

Della Rose, Winton, Calif.

Chicken and Rice (2)

2 tbsp. fat
1 stewing chicken
6 cups water
2 bay leaves
1 tbsp. salt
½ tsp. pepper
3 med. onions, halved
6 med. carrots, halved
1 cup whole corn
1 cup uncooked rice

Melt fat in large soup kettle or roasting pan. Add chicken pieces to fat. Brown on all sides. Slowly add 4 cups of the water. Add bay leaves, salt, and pepper. Cover and simmer for 2 hrs. or until chicken is very tender. About 40 min. before chicken is done add onions and carrots. Cover, and continue cooking for 15 min. then stir in corn, rice, and remaining 2 cups of water. Be certain all rice is covered with liquid. Cover and cook until rice is tender. This dish is also good with the vegetables left out.

Mrs. John Nightengale, Copeland, Kans.

Chicken Casserole

1 large hen cooked and removed from bone
1½ cups diced celery, cooked
1½ cups diced cheese
1 small onion
1 tsp. salt
⅛ tsp. pepper
4 cups chicken broth
4 cups crackers
2 eggs, beaten
1 can mushroom soup

Arrange chicken, crackers, cheese, and celery in layers. Combine eggs, broth and mushroom soup and pour over chicken-cracker mixture. Bake at 350° for 1 hr.

Mrs. Ben Becker, Rich Hill, Mo.

Hawaiian Turkey or Chicken Casserole

2 tbsp. butter
½ cup sliced onions
1 (No. 2) can pineapple tidbits
1¼ cups turkey (or chicken) broth
2 tbsp. cornstarch
1½ tsp. salt
½ cup chopped green pepper (may be omitted)
3 cups (½ in. cubes) toasted bread cubes
1½ cups cooked chopped turkey (or chicken)
¼ cup slivered almonds

Melt butter in a 10-inch skillet and simmer onions until they are transparent. Drain pineapple tidbits and add turkey broth to pineapple liquid to make 2 cups. Dissolve cornstarch and salt in liquid. Add liquid and green pepper to onions in skillet. Cook until sauce thickens, stirring constantly. Arrange layers of bread cubes, turkey, pineapple and almonds in a greased 1½-quart casserole and cover with half of the sauce. Repeat layers ending with bread cubes and pour other half of sauce over the top. Bake in a mod. oven (350°) for 30 minutes.

Mrs. Clara Friesen, Ithaca, Mich.

Creamy Chicken

1—2½ lb. fryer cut up   ½ tsp. salt
⅓ cup shortening   4 carrots, cut in thin strips
1 can cream of chicken soup   12 small onions
⅔ cup milk   1—10 oz. pkg. frozen peas
½ tsp. dried tarragon

Brown chicken pieces in fat in large skillet. Remove chicken pieces to casserole. To make gravy blend chicken soup with the milk into skillet stirring to scrape bottom of skillet. Add vegetables and the chicken in a 2 qt. casserole. Cover with soup mixture from skillet. Cover and bake at 350° for 1 hr. Add a green salad and bread to serve.

Andree Friesen, Winton, Calif.

Huntington Chicken

1 good sized chicken cooked and cut fine
4 cups broth thickened with ½ cup flour
2 cups macaroni boiled in salted water and drained
½ cup cream   ½ lb. cream cheese or
4 to 6 hard boiled eggs   Velveeta
    sliced

Mix all ingredients together and put in baking dish. Spread bread crumbs or crushed potato chips on top and bake 20 to 30 minutes.

Mrs. Wilford Holdeman, Halstead, Kans.

Never Fail Chicken Pie

1 chicken, well cooked and diced

Place in large casserole or pan. Pour over the following filling which has been well cooked together:

2 tbsp. butter   5 tbsp. flour; well mixed
Add:
5 cups chicken broth   1 cup milk

Place in 375° oven, 1 hr. Twenty minutes before serving cover top with small biscuits and bake until biscuits are nicely browned.

Mrs. Junior Smith, Fairview, Okla.

Oven Crusty Chicken

1—2½-3 lb. frying chicken   4 cups Rice Krispies
  cut in pieces   1 tsp. salt
½-⅔ cup butter or mar-   ¼ tsp. pepper
  garine melted

Wash chicken pieces and dry thoroughly. Crush rice krispies slightly. Combine melted butter with salt and pepper. Dip chicken pieces in seasoned butter, then roll in rice krispies crumbs until well coated. Place skin side up in shallow baking pan lined with aluminum foil; do not crowd pieces. Bake in mod. oven 350° about 1 hr. or until tender. Do not cover pan or turn chicken while baking.

Mrs. Archie Decker, Fredonia, Kans.

Scalloped Chicken

1 stewing hen   1 bunch parsley
2 carrots   3 tsp. salt
1 onion   1 bay leaf
3 stalks celery

Cook chicken and vegetables until done and drain. Pick meat from bones and dice. For gravy combine 6 tbsp. flour, 6 tbsp. fat, and the broth. If the bird is not fat enough use 1 stick oleo, salt and pepper to taste, 1 tsp. sage, 1 onion diced fine, 2 qts. bread cubes. Put meat and bread in casserole and add the gravy. Bake 40 min. at 375° or until set.

Mrs. George K. Martens, Inman, Kans.

Southern Chicken Gumbo

1 roasting chicken   salt
½ cup flour   pepper
3-4 tbsp. fat   7 or 8 bay leaves
¼ cup chopped onion   hot pepper (optional)
¼ cup chopped celery   1 tbsp. gumbo file

Brown the chicken. Brown the flour until very brown, adding the chopped onions and celery. Place the chicken and flour into a large pot, add salt and pepper to taste, bay leaves, hot pepper and enough water to cover well. Cook until chicken is very tender. Add the gumbo file just before serving. Serve with rice and saltine crackers.

Mable Smith, DeRidder, La.

Oven Barbecue Chicken

1-3 lb. fryer	½ cup milk
1 egg	¼ cup butter

Melt the ¼ cup butter in baking pan. Beat egg and add milk and dip the chicken in this mixture. Then roll in flour to which salt and pepper has been added. Place chicken skin side down in melted butter. Bake at 400° for 30 min. Turn chicken, cover with barbecue sauce. Bake for 30 min. more, or until tender. Baste with more sauce as needed. Barbecue Sauce: Saute 1 onion, finely chopped in ¼ cup butter. Add

¼ cup vinegar	¼ cup lemon juice
1 cup water	2 tsp. chili powder
1 tsp. mustard	1 tsp. salt
1 cup tomato catsup	¼ cup brown sugar
¼ cup worcestershire sauce	

Simmer for ½ hr.

Mrs. Leo Classen, DeRidder, La.

Texas Barbeque Chicken

3 lbs. chicken, frying size	¼ tbsp. red pepper
2 tbsp. worcestershire sauce	2 tbsp. sugar
	3 tbsp. catsup
2 tbsp. vinegar	1 tsp. chili powder
4 tbsp. water	1 tsp. dry mustard
2 tbsp. oleo	1 tsp. paprika

Mix sauce thoroughly, salt and pepper chicken, dip each piece in barbecue sauce, and place in baking dish, pour the rest of the sauce on, and cover very tightly. Bake 15 min. at 500°. Lower temperature to 350°. Bake for 1 hr. and 15 min. more. Do not open oven till time is up.

Elizabeth Frank, Copeland, Kans.

Poultry Dressing

Any-Day Dressing

Brown one medium onion chopped fine in 4 tbsp. bacon drippings. Add 8 to 10 slices of bread (cubed) 1½ tsp. salt, ¼ tsp. pepper, 1 tsp. sage and ½ cup chopped celery. Add 1 can chicken rice soup, ½ can of water and mix well. Pour mixture into well greased baking dish and bake at 325° for about one hr. This amount will serve four.

Mrs. John Nightengale, Copeland, Kans.

Poultry Stuffing

1 loaf home made bread sliced and toasted. Break into pieces
1 medium onion, diced
3 medium apples, peeled and diced (optional)
¾ cup raisins
3 eggs, beaten
¼ cup sugar
  salt and pepper to taste
1 tsp. sage, if desired
3 cups milk or enough to moisten

Mix all together. If desired grind onions and raisins with giblets.

Place fowl in covered roaster and roast 3 or 4 hrs. at 300° until about half done and covered. Remove giblets to grind and add to dressing also the broth that has formed around the fowl. Fill inside the fowl with dressing and remaining around the fowl. Reduce heat to 200° roast 2 or 3 hrs. longer.

Mrs. Herby Wenger, Newton, Kans.
Mrs. Elton Wenger, Hesston, Kans.

Turkey Dressing

½ lb. sausage
1 small can oysters
1 can mushroom soup
3 medium onions, diced

1 cup diced celery
bread (enough to fill a small roaster)
sage to taste
salt and pepper

Broth of turkey, enough to moisten the dressing good, let stand over night. The next day put some more broth on till it is quite juicy. Bake one hr. or more till done.

Mrs. Pete J. Unruh

Sage Dressing

12 cups lightly toasted bread, cubed (preferably home baked
  bread)

½ cup butter or oleo	½ cup chopped celery
giblets from one fowl	2 qts. milk
¼ cup chopped onion	4 eggs, beaten slightly
3 tbsp. sage	2 cups hot water

Melt butter in heavy skillet, add chopped giblets and fry slightly.
Add onion and celery, fry until tender. Add bread cubes, milk,
eggs and sage; mix and heat thoroughly. Stuff fowl which has
been salted inside and out. Place remaining dressing in a cloth
bag and place beside fowl in roaster. Add hot water and bake
slowly at 325° for 3 hrs. or until done. (Drain liquid from fowl
and use for gravy.)

Mrs. Archie Holdeman, Hesston, Kans.

Fish

Baked Tuna Dish

2 cups cooked rice	2 beaten eggs
1½ cups grated cheese	1½ cups milk
1 can tuna	

Bake in buttered casserole at (350°) for 45 min. or until set and
lightly browned.

Sauce

1 tbsp. butter	1 cup grated cheese
1 tbsp. flour	1 can mushroom soup
1½ cups milk	

Combine and bring to boiling. Pour over tuna.

Florence Amoth, Bonners Ferry, Idaho

Baked Noodles and Tuna With Mushrooms

⅓ lb. noodles	1 cup canned Tuna
1½ qts. boiling water	10½ oz. can mushroom soup
1½ tsp. salt	½ cup buttered crumbs

Cook noodles in salt water until tender and drain. Flake the tuna with a fork. Mix with noodles and soup. Turn into a greased baking dish. Sprinkle with crumbs and bake at (350°) for 40 min. Serves 6.

Mrs. Robert Holdeman, Dalton, Ohio

Spaghetti and Tuna Casserole

2 cans spaghetti and tomato   1 can Cream of Chicken or
  sauce with cheese   Mushroom Soup
1 can Tuna (9½ oz. size)

Alternate spaghetti and Tuna in buttered casserole. Put undiluted can of soup over top, and cut through with knife several times to mix soup. Bake in (350°) oven for 25 min. Crushed potato chips or grated cheese may be sprinkled over top if desired. Serves six.

Mrs. John H. Schmidt, Goltry, Okla.

Tuna Casserole (1)

Cook 1 pkg. broken noodles in water. Drain and mix with 1 can Cream of Mushroom or Cream of Chicken soup.

1 cup milk   1 cup grated cheese
1-7 oz. can Tuna   ⅓ cup onion, chopped

Pour into greased 1½ qt. baking dish. Top with cracker crumbs or crushed potato chips and if desired, paprika and more grated cheese. Bake in (425°) oven 15 min. until bubbly hot.

Mrs. Le Roy Wedel, Goltry, Okla.

Tuna Casserole (2)

Cook in salted water until almost tender 1-6 oz. pkg. (2 cups) noodles. Arrange a border of noodles in greased 8 in. sq. baking dish. Arrange in center of noodles 1-7 oz. can flaked tuna. Sprinkle ¼ cup finely chopped onion and 2 hard boiled eggs chopped over tuna.

Combine:
1-10½ oz. can condensed mushroom soup
1 tsp. Worcestershire sauce   ⅛ tsp. pepper
½ tsp. salt

Pour sauce over tuna, sprinkle with ¼ cup grated American Cheese. Bake at 350° about 30 min. Serves 4 to 6.

Mrs. Valeda Koehn, Winton, Calif.

Tuna-Celery Bake

1-6 oz. pkg. egg noodles
1-10½ oz. can condensed
  celery soup
½ cup milk
1-7 oz. can tuna, flaked
1 tsp. minced onion
1 cup buttered bread crumbs
½ cup grated American
  Cheese

Cook noodles in boiling salted water until tender. Drain. Combine soup and milk. Alternate layers of noodles, tuna, and minced onion in greased casserole. Pour soup mixture over combination. Top with buttered bread crumbs and grated cheese. Bake at 350° for 20 min.

Mrs. Pete D. Schmidt, Copeland, Kans.

Tuna Noodle Casserole (1)

1 med. size pkg. noodles
3½ tbsp. butter
3 tbsp. flour
2 to 2½ cups milk
½ cup grated cheese
salt
pepper
7 oz. can tuna

Cook noodles until tender. Drain and put in baking dish. Add tuna and mix slightly. Use remainder of ingredients to make a white sauce. Melt butter, then mix in flour. Add milk, cheese (optional), and seasonings. Stir until sauce thickens. Pour over noodles and tuna. Bake in oven at 350° for 30 to 40 min.

Mrs. Harold Koehn, Montezuma, Kans.

Tuna Noodle Casserole (2)

2 tbsp. minced onion
½ of small green pepper
  (optional)
1 stalk celery
3 cups cooked noodles
1 can cream of mushroom
  soup
1 can Tuna Fish (chunk
  style)
½ cup milk

Cut the onion, pepper and celery fine and fry in oil or margarine till partially tender. Mix with noodles, Mushroom soup, milk and Tuna. Put in buttered casserole and bake in oven for 30 min. at (350°).

Alma Dyck, Livingston, Calif.

Salmon-Macaroni Dish

1-8 oz. pkg. macaroni	1 lb. can salmon
¼ cup catsup	1 cup peas
1½ cups milk	2 tbsp. flour
2 tbsp. butter	¼ cup bread crumbs

Cook macaroni in salt water until tender. Make sauce of butter, flour, and milk. Cook until thick, add catsup. Add flaked salmon and peas to sauce. Drain macaroni and rinse. Add to salmon and mix well, place in baking dish. Sprinkle with crumbs and dot with butter. Bake in mod. oven (350°) until slightly brown, about 30 min.

Margaret Ensz, Inman, Kans.

Tuna and Chips

14½ oz. pkg. potato chips	1 cup wide egg noodles
1 No. ½ can tuna	2 tsp. pimento (optional)
1 can condensed cream of mushroom soup	

Cook noodles until done. Drain. Fold in tuna, including oil. Add pimento and mushroom soup. Crush potato chips for bottom and top. Place chips in bottom of shallow 1½ qt. casserole. Pour tuna mixture over and cover with remaining chips. Heat thoroughly in 350° oven. Serves 6. Make this in 20 min.

Mrs. Warren Koehn, Scott City, Kans.

Tuna, Macaroni and Mushroom Soup Casserole
(An excellent emergency dish)

1¼ cups macaroni	⅔ cup milk
1 can condensed mushroom soup	1 (7 oz.) can flaked tuna

Cook macaroni until tender, drain. Combine soup and milk in a pan, bring to boil, than add flaked tuna, which has been separated with a fork. (Be careful not to mince it as that isn't nearly as good.) Add cooked macaroni. Pour mixture in greased casserole. Cover top with buttered cracker crumbs. Bake in hot oven till heated through and top is brown.

Mrs. Jake Smith, Fairview, Okla.

Tuna Sauce on Toast

2 cups milk
4 tbsp. flour
¼ cup water

4 tbsp. oleo or butter
1½ tsp. salt
1 can Tuna

Combine all ingredients and cook slowly for 5 min. or until it gets thick. Serve on buttered toast.

Mrs. Orval Johnson, Walnut Hill, Fla.

Tuna Potato Cakes

1½ cups mashed potatoes
1-7 oz. can tuna, drained and
  flaked
1 slightly beaten egg

2 tbsp. finely chopped onion
1 tbsp. butter
¼ tsp. salt
1 dash pepper

Combine all ingredients, mix well and form into 8 small patties. Brown in hot fat about 5 min. per side. Makes 4 servings. A good way to use left over potatoes.

Mrs. Abe H. Koehn, Cimarron, Kans.

Pork

Baked Ham Loaf

4½ lbs. ground meat (½ ham and ½ lean pork)
9 eggs (slightly beaten)   3½ cups cracker crumbs
1 qt. milk   salt, pepper, parsley

Mix well. Put in uncovered baking dish and place in shallow pan of water in a slow oven (about 300°). Bake an hour or longer.

Syrup: Boil together:

2 cups brown sugar   ¾ cup vinegar
                          3 tbsp. dry mustard

Pour this syrup over meat when ready for oven.
Mustard sauce to serve with above.

1 cup white sugar   3 tsp. dry mustard
1 tsp. corn starch   ⅛ tsp. salt
2 tsp. turmeric   1 beaten egg
                          1 cup vinegar

Cook in double boiler until thick.

Mrs. Henry Amoth, Bonners Ferry, Idaho

Barbecued Frankfurters

¼ cup chopped onions	2 tbsp. brown sugar
1 cup catsup	3 tbsp. Worcestershire sauce
½ cup water	2 tbsp. vinegar
½ cup chopped celery	1 tbsp. mustard
(optional)	½ tsp. salt
¼ cup lemon juice	dash of cayenne
	1½ lbs. wieners

Cook onions in hot fat till tender. Combine remaining ingredients, except wieners. Add to onions. Cover and simmer 20 min. Prick wieners, add to sauce. Cover and simmer 15 min. more.

Mrs. Tobe Koehn, Burns, Kans.
Mrs. Chester Johnson, DeRidder, La.

Boiled Potpie (1)

Cover 1 lb. of cut up pork with 1 qt. water, add 1 tsp. salt and stew until almost tender. Then add 1 potato, quartered, parsley and pepper to taste. Prepare dough sqs. for potpie and drop into boiling broth, one by one, covering whole top of stew. When half the sqs. have been added, stir before adding the rest. Cover tightly and continue boiling for 20 min. Makes 6 to 8 servings.

Potpie Dough Squares

Combine 1 egg, ⅓ cup milk, ⅓ tsp. salt, and enough flour to roll.

Miss Lena Steiner, Hesston, Kans.

Boiled Potpie (2)

Cover a cut-up 3 lb. stewing chicken with 2 qts. of water, add 2 tsp. of salt and stew until tender. Then add 4 potatoes, quartered, 1 diced onion, 1 tbsp. minced parsley and black pepper to taste. Prepare dough squares for potpie (see following recipe) and drop in boiling broth, one by one, covering whole top of stew. When half the squares are added, stir before adding rest. Cover tightly and continue boiling for 20 min. Serves 6 to 8.

Potpie Dough Squares

Combine 2 cups sifted flour with 1 tsp. baking powder and ½ tsp. salt. Cut in 2 tbsp. lard, as for pastry. Add ⅓ cup water to one beaten egg and mix flour. Roll out thin on floured board. Cut in 2 in. squares with knife.

Virginia Dirks, Livingston, Calif.

Delicious Ham Loaf

1 lb. smoked ham	1 tbsp. parsley
1 lb. fresh pork	1 tbsp. celery
1 cup bread crumbs	1 cup milk
2 eggs	1/3 tsp. paprika
1 tbsp. onion	

Grind ham and pork. (no fat on meat.) Mix ham, pork, bread crumbs, eggs, onion, parsley, celery, milk, and paprika, like meat loaf. Put in a shallow pan. Bake 1½ hr. mod. oven. Baste after first 45 min. and every 15 min. following.

Basting

⅔ cup brown sugar	⅓ cup vinegar
1 tsp. cinnamon	½ cup water
¼ tsp. dry mustard	Boil for 2 min.

Mrs. Leon Koehn, Johnson, Kans.

Franks and Cheese Casserole

1½ cups evaporated milk	½ tsp. salt
2 cups grated cheese	4 cups cooked noodles
2 cups sliced frankfurters	

Simmer milk and salt over low heat to just below boiling point. Add cheese and stir until cheese melts. Pour over cooked noodles and wieners, in a buttered 2 quart casserole. Bake in preheated 350° oven 30 minutes. Yield: 6 to 8 servings.

Mrs. Eldon Smith, Burns, Kans.

Fried Ham and Onion Gravy With Noodles

6 slices ham	½ cup sour cream
3 onions	2 cups uncooked noodles

Fry slices of ham until brown. Remove ham from pan and add sliced onions to ham drippings when onions are browned. Add sour cream. Let come to a boil and pour over hot cooked noodles.

Ham Dinner

Put 5 or 6 servings of thick sliced cured ham on bottom of small roaster. Bring to boiling point: 1 qt. milk, ⅓ cup sugar, ½ cup raisins, ⅛ tsp. salt. Add 1 small loaf bread (preferably homemade) to make a real juicy dressing. Pour over ham and bake 2 hrs. in 350° oven. Add water or milk if dressing gets dry. An hour before the ham is done, add potatoes around the roast. When meat dressing and potatoes are done, make your favorite cole slaw or tossed green salad. With a light dessert you have a complete meal.

Mrs. Elmer Unruh, Rich Hill, Mo.

Ham Loaf (1)

1 lb. ham (cured), ground
1 lb. fresh pork, ground
1 lb. beef, ground
    salt and pepper

2 cups cracker crumbs or cornflakes
½ cup milk
3 eggs

Baste with:

1½ cups brown sugar
½ cup water

½ cup vinegar
¼ tsp. mustard

Bake for one hour at 375°, basting frequently.

Delores Dirks, Copeland, Kans.

Ham Loaf (2)

1 lb. pork, ground
1 lb. beef, ground
1 lb. ham, ground
3 eggs
1 cup milk
1½ tsp. dry mustard

4 tbsp grated onion
1½ cups bread crumbs
½ cup catsup
    salt to taste
1 tsp. pepper

Bake in loaf at 375° for 1½ hrs. Baste every ten minutes with sauce made of:

1 cup brown sugar
4 tbsp. vinegar

4 tbsp. water

Carol Holdeman, Hesston, Kans.

Pork Head Cheese

Cook the head, liver and heart. When done cut into pieces and grind with coarse plate of grinder. (Add onions if desired.) Add salt and pepper to suit taste. Bake in a slow oven (250°).

Mrs. Adam J. Schmidt, Montezuma, Kans.

Pork Chops With Spaghetti

6 pork chops
3 cups cooked spaghetti
1 chopped onion
½ cup grated cheese

1 can tomato soup
1 tsp. salt
⅛ tsp. pepper

Brown the chops well in hot shortening. Remove pork chops and cook the onion until tender. Add spaghetti and seasoning. Pour tomato soup with equal amount of water over spaghetti. Place chops over the top. Cover closely and let simmer about 1 hour. Before serving sprinkle cheese over the top.

Mrs. Juanita Toews, Barron, Wisc.

Quick Fix Wieners

Cut 6 to 8 wieners, into halves or quarters and place in sauce pan. Add 1 can tomato sauce, ½ cup water, and 2 tbsp. chopped onions. Cover with tight fitting lid. Steam about 15 to 20 min. or until wieners swell. Add thickening to tomato sauce to make a gravy. Serve with mashed potatoes.

Mrs. Donald Schmidt, Fredonia, Kans.

Raisin Sauce for Ham

½ cup brown sugar
1 tsp. mustard
1 tbsp. flour
2 tbsp. vinegar

2 tbsp. lemon juice
¼ tsp. lemon rind grated
1½ cups water
⅓ cup raisins

Mix brown sugar, mustard, flour, add vinegar, lemon juice, rind, water and raisins cook over low heat until thick. Stir constantly. Serve with ham.

Nina Holdeman, Hesston, Kans.

Sauerkraut and Spareribs

1½ lbs. pork chops, spareribs
   or pork steaks
1 qt. sauerkraut

1 tbsp. brown or white sugar
prunes and raisins
(optional)

Place pork in pan and fry out the fat, then pour fat off and add sauerkraut, sugar and fruit. Bake about 1 hr. at 350°.

Mrs. Norma Koehn, Livingston, Calif.

Sausage Supper

1 lb. Sausage Links	1½ tsp. salt
5 medium potatoes, sliced	¼ tsp. pepper
2 large onions, sliced thin	1-10½ oz. can cream of
3 tbsp. chopped green pepper	tomato soup

Brown sausages, remove from skillet. Pour off excess fat, add potatoes and brown. Place sliced onions over potatoes, and sprinkle green pepper over top. Season with salt and pepper. Arrange sausages over vegetables and pour soup over the top. Cook on low simmer until potatoes are done.

Mrs. Alpha Unruh, Cimarron, Kans.

Sauerkraut Spareribs and Potatoes

1 can Kraut	⅛ tsp. pepper
2 lbs. spareribs	1 tbsp. brown sugar
1 tbsp. fat	(optional)
1 tsp. salt	5 or 6 medium sized potatoes
⅔ cup water	(whole)

Brown spareribs in hot fat in pressure cooker. Add salt and pepper. Put kraut in bottom of pan and sprinkle with brown sugar if desired. Place ribs and potatoes over kraut. Add water and cover pan. Cook 20 min. at 10 lbs. pressure. Allow pressure to go down normally.

Mrs. John Schmidt, Neodesha, Kans.

Sweet and Sour Spareribs

2 lbs. spareribs

Cut up spareribs and bake at 400° for one hr. Make sauce and pour over ribs and bake for two hrs. longer.

Sauce

1 clove garlic (optional)	½ cup sugar
4 tbsp. flour	4 tbsps. soya sauce
½ tsp. dry mustard	2 cups water
1 tsp. salt	½ cup vinegar

Serve with hot rice.

Mrs. Leonard G. Barkman, Steinbach, Man.

Savory Pork Chops

6 loin or shoulder pork chops	2 tbsp. lemon juice
¼ tsp. salt	2 beef bouillon cubes
⅛ tsp. pepper	2 cups water
1 large onion, sliced	¼ cup chopped parsley
1 carrot, cut in half	2 tbsp. flour
	1 cup evaporated milk

Cut a little fat from pork chops; heat in skillet, then brown meat in it (about 10 min.) Pour off excess fat. (or use a little other shortening or oil). Sprinkle chops with salt and pepper. Add onion, carrot, lemon juice and bouillon cubes, dissolved in ½ cup water. Bring to a boil; cover. Reduce heat to low. Simmer 40 min., less time if chops are thinner. Add a little water if needed. Remove chops to warm platter. Sprinkle with parsley. Mash onion and carrot with a fork. Add flour; blend thoroughly. Add evaporated milk and 1½ cups water. Bring to a boil, stirring constantly. Makes 6 servings.

Mrs. John Wiens, Atwater, Calif.

Veal Pie

2½ lbs. stewing veal	3 whole cloves
water to cover	2 tsp. salt
3 bay leaves	1½ cups diced, raw potatoes
1 onion, sliced	2 onions, chopped
2 peppercorns	1 cup diced celery
	1 cup sliced, raw carrots

Add water and seasonings to meat; cover and simmer until veal is tender. Cool. Remove meat. Add vegetables to liquid; cook until tender. Thicken with flour and water to make a paste. Pour into casserole with veal and top with Carrot-Parsley Biscuits.

Carrot-Parsley Biscuits

2 cups flour	¼ cup shortening
3 tsp. baking powder	¼ cup grated carrots
½ tsp. salt	2 tbsp. chopped parsley
	¾ cup milk

Sift together flour, baking powder, and salt. Cut in shortening. Add carrots, parsley and milk; mix lightly. Roll out and cut with doughnut cutter. Arrange on casserole of veal pie and bake in hot oven (450°) 15 to 20 minutes. Serves 8.

Mrs. Vernard Unruh, Halstead, Kans.

Chop Suey and Chow Mein

American Chop Suey (1)

1 lb. gound beef	¼ cup soy sauce
¾ cup uncooked rice	1 can mushroom soup
1½ cups chopped celery	2 cans water
2 small onions, chopped	1 can bean sprouts

Put uncooked rice in bottom of casserole. Brown meat but do not season. Add chopped celery, onion, mushroom soup, soy sauce, and water. Pour over rice and bake at 350° for 1 hour. Do not stir. Just before serving heat 1 can bean sprouts. Drain off liquid and spread bean sprouts over casserole. Serve hot.

Mrs. Clyde Jantz, Winton, Calif.

American Chop Suey (2)

1 small can tomato soup	½ box spaghetti
1 small can chili con carne	1 onion
1 lb. hamburger	Salt and pepper

Fry hamburger and onion until brown. Boil spaghetti until done and drain. Mix meat, tomato soup, chili con carne and spaghetti together. Bake in moderate oven (350°) for 30-40 minutes.

Mrs. Menno Wedel, Goltry, Okla.

Cabbage Chop Suey

2 tbsp. butter	1 cup diced celery
1 tbsp. meat fryings	1 green pepper, minced
4 cups shredded cabbage	1 med. onion, chopped

Melt shortening in skillet. Add vegetables, salt and pepper. Cover with tight lid and steam until tender, stirring once in a while.

Chop Suey (1)

(The real Chinese way.)

1 bunch green onions (also a
little of the tops)
3 tbsps. soy sauce
1½ cups water
1 can bean sprouts
(optional)
¼ tsp. garlic
Salt and pepper

1 lb. ground beef
½ chicken cut in small
pieces
4 pork chops or steaks
3 carrots
3 cups cabbage
2 cups celery

Form beef into small balls. Brown beef balls, chicken and pork chops or steak in a little shortening. Cut up vegetables into ½ inch pieces. Combine vegetables and water; cook until done. Add the meat and seasonings and simmer for 15 minutes or until done. Cornstarch may be added for slight thickness. Add bean sprouts with meat if desired. This recipe is delicious and was given to me by a Chinese lady from Indonesia. This Chop Suey is good over home-made noodles or Chow Mein noodles.

Mrs. Cornelius Toews, Garden City, Kans.

Chop Suey (2)

½ bunch celery
1 large onion
3 tbsp. sugar
1 tsp. salt
1 can mushrooms in brown
gravy
3 cans (Chum King) bean
sprouts

1 lb. pkg. rice
2 lbs. fatty hamburger or
1 lb. hamburger and 1 lb.
ground pork
3 cans (qt. size) chop suey
noodles
5 tbsp. cornstarch

Fry meat to brown. Cook celery in salt water until done. Combine in large kettle: meat, celery and onion. Simmer 30 minutes with water added. Add bean sprouts and mushrooms. Mix cornstarch and sugar with water and stir into boiling mixture, simmering another 30 minutes. Cook rice in a large kettle of boiling water with a little salt over low fire. Do not stir for 30 minutes. Drain and serve with the first mixture and chop suey noodles. Serves 16.

Donnella Unruh, Galva, Kans.

Chow Mein (1)

1 lb. lean pork
2 tbsp. lard
3 cups chopped cabbage
1 cup celery
1 chopped green pepper
1 cup onion

1 cup water
1 can bean sprouts
1 tbsp. soya sauce
1 tsp. salt
2 tbsp. cornstarch
Chow Mein noodles

Cut meat in small cubes; fry in lard until brown. Cook chopped cabbage, celery, pepper, and onion in 1 cup water 10 minutes. Add meat, bean sprouts, soya sauce, and salt; cook 5 minutes longer. Mix cornstarch with small amount of water; stir until thickened. Serve hot over noodles and season with soya sauce.

Mrs. Lincoln Jantz, Haviland, Kans.

Chow Mein (2)

Heat in skillet:

2 tbsp. cooking oil
¼ tsp. salt
¼ tsp. pepper

2 cups sliced celery
Onion

Cook until tender.

Add:

2 cans bean sprouts, drained
4 oz. can water chestnuts (drained and sliced)
1 can sliced, drained mushrooms, if desired

1¾ cups broth
2 cups cooked, sliced chicken, beef, pork, turkey or tuna

Heat to boiling; thicken with 2 tbsp. cornstarch mixed in 4 tbsp. soy sauce. Simmer. Serve over fried noodles. This is better if made ahead, allowed to cool and reheated to serve.

Nancy M. Esau

Pork Chow Mein

Cook 2 sliced onions and 2 cups sliced celery in 1 tbsp. vegetable oil for 5 minutes. Add 2 cups each, diced, cooked pork and water, 3 tbsp. soy sauce, 1 tbsp. molasses; simmer 15 minutes. Add 1 can (19 oz.) bean sprouts, drained. Heat; then stir in 3 tbsp. cornstarch blended with a little cold water. Cook until thickened. Serve on Chow Mein noodles.

Mrs. Clarence Wadel, Fredonia, Kans.

Chicken Chow Mein

4 tbsp. vegetable oil
2 cups thin onion strips
2½ cups diced celery
1 tsp. salt
2 tsp. sugar
1½ cups clear chicken stock

1 can (1 lb.) bean sprouts
3 tbsp. cornstarch
3 tbsp. soy sauce
2 cups diced cooked chicken
1 or 2 cans Chow Mein
noodles

Heat oil over 12 inch skillet over low heat. Mix in onions and celery; sprinkle with salt and sugar. Add chicken stock. Cover and boil gently about 10 minutes. Drain bean sprouts. Mix Cornstarch and soy sauce until smooth with ¼ cup of the bean liquid. Add to skillet; cook and stir until thickened. Add drained bean sprouts and chicken; mix and reheat. Serve with Chow Mein noodles. Makes 4 large or 6 medium servings.

Mrs. Dayton Unruh, Lehigh, Kans.

Enchiladas, Tacos, and Tortillas

Easy Enchilada Casserole

1 doz. corn tortillas (broken)
1 8-oz. can cream of mushroom soup
2 lbs. uncooked hamburger
1 large can enchilada sauce
1 med. onion (chopped)

½ can pitted olives
1 cup shredded cheese
Pepper
1 tbsp. each, oregano, salt,
cumin; garlic powder if desired

Mix all ingredients and put into a large casserole. Bake at 350° for 1 hour.

Romona Nightengale, Livingston, Calif.

Enchiladas (1)

Fry in skillet ½ lb. hamburger, scrambled. Add salt, pepper and chili powder; sprinkle 1 heaping tbsp. flour over hamburger. Add enough water to make a nice gravy. Spread on hot tortillas; top with chopped onions, diced cheese, lettuce and sliced tomatoes.

Mrs. Susie Nichols, Isabella, Okla.

Enchiladas (2)

1½ lb. hamburger   Salt and pepper
1 med. onion

Fry until done. Make gravy of the following:
¾ stick margarine
½ cup flour

Add:

1 cup tomato juice   8 tsp. chili powder
4 to 5 cups water   ½ lb. grated cheese
   Salt and pepper   12 tortillas

Heat tortillas in gravy. Place a layer in baking dish; sprinkle with meat and grated cheese. Alternate layers of tortillas, meat and cheese until all is used. Bake 1½ hrs. at 250°.

Mrs. Pete F. Nickel, Hillsboro, Kans.

Enchilada Pie Casserole

1 med. size pkg. corn chips   1 No. 2 can chili with beans
1 large onion, chopped   1½ cups grated longhorn
                                  cheese

Place ½ pkg. corn chips, ½ of chopped onion, ½ can chili, and ¾ cups cheese in buttered casserole. Repeat with the other half of the ingredients. Bake at 325° for 15-30 minutes or until bubbly.

Mrs. Richard Koehn, Halstead, Kans.

Enchilada Meat and Bean Filling

Brown ½ onion (size of an egg), and 1 lb. hamburger. Add 1 tsp. salt and ¼ tsp. pepper. Put into a mixing bowl and add 1 No. 303 can pork and beans, and ½ tsp. chili powder. Put lard or oil into same pan; drop tortillas in to heat one at a time. Put several tbsp. meat and bean mixture on each tortilla. Bring sides together with a toothpick. Put close together in a 8x12 inch baking pan. Mix 2 tbsp. flour with 1½ cups tomato juice and pour around tortillas. Bake at 350° for 35 to 45 minutes. If desired cheese slices may be added a few minutes before serving.

Mrs. Eli Unruh, Galva, Kans.

Hot Tacos

1½ lbs. hamburger
3 chile peppers and pepper juice
¼ bottle taco sauce
¼ bottle chile ketchup
¼ tsp. chile powder
Onion, if desired

Fry together for 20 minutes or more. Mix lettuce, cheese and tomato. Place hamburger mixture on warmed or fried tortilla; top with lettuce, cheese and tomato.

Mrs. Evelyn Schmidt, Winton, Calif.

Tortillas

1½ cups whole wheat flour
1 tsp. baking powder
¼ tsp. salt
½ cup white flour
3 tbsp. lard
½ cup water

Mix and knead well. Roll out without flour as thin as possible, about 5 inches across. Heat on both sides until they start to brown on a pancake grill. Put into plastic bag or wrap in a cloth to keep them from getting too hard. Makes 15.

Mrs. Eli Unruh, Galva, Kans.

Pizzas

Individual Pizzas

1 can refrigerator biscuits
1 lb. hamburger
1 8-oz. can tomato sauce
½ cup chopped onion
1 or 2 cloves garlic
Tabasco sauce, oregano, salt and pepper to taste
Grated sharp, or Mozzerella cheese

Brown hamburger; add onion and cook 5 min. longer. Add tomato sauce, garlic, and spices to taste. Spread mixture on rolled-out biscuits. Sprinkle with cheese. Bake 10 min. at 425°.

Mrs. Norman Schmidt, Goltry, Okla.

American Pizza (1)

Crust:

1 pkg. yeast	3½ cups flour
1 cup warm water	1 tbsp. melted shortening
2 tsp. sugar	1½ tsp. salt

Soften yeast in warm water. Add sugar; beat in 1½ cups flour. Mix in shortening and salt. Stir in remaining flour. Knead until smooth and elastic. Place in greased mixing bowl. Cover and let rise about one hour. Punch down and place in refrigerator until cold. Cut dough into two parts and roll out into a 10 in. circle. (Larger circle if you want a thinner crust.) Place on greased cookie sheets. Brush with salad oil.

Filling:

1½ lbs. smoked sausage or hamburger	¼ cup minced onion 2-3 oz. cans sliced mushrooms
2 cans tomato paste	
½ tsp. ground sweet basil	3⅓ cups grated American or cheddar cheese
½ tsp. ground oregano	
¼ tsp. salt	⅔ cup grated Parmesan cheese
⅛ tsp. pepper	

Brown meat. Combine tomato paste, basil, oregano, salt, pepper, and onion. Spread each dough circle with ¼ of mixture. Cover with meat and mushrooms. Sprinkle with cheese. Top with remaining sauce and sprinkle with Parmesan cheese. Bake at 425° for 20 min. Serve hot!

Mrs. Monroe Toews, Scio, Ore.

American Pizza (2)

2 lbs. hamburger	1½ tbsp. chili powder
1 small onion, chopped	1 tsp. oregano (optional)
1½ tsp. salt	1 tsp. sweet basil (optional)
Pepper to taste	½ lb. grated mild cheese
1⅓ cups tomato paste	⅔ cup catsup (optional)

Pie or biscuit dough using 2½ cups flour. Spread dough in a large greased pan. Add meat mixture with seasonings and onion added. Add tomato paste. Sprinkle with cheese. Bake at 400° for 20 min. Remove from oven; add more grated cheese. Return to oven until cheese is melted.

Mrs. Ben Giesbrecht, Glenn, Calif.
Carolyn Kay Friesen, Inman. Kans.

Pizza (1)

1 pkg. yeast
1¼ cups warm water
2 tbsp. vegetable oil

4 cups flour
1 tsp. salt

Dissolve yeast in water; stir in oil. Sift flour and salt together and add to oil and water mixture. Knead until smooth. Shape into ball and grease bowl and dough with oil. Let rise 10 to 25 min. Form dough into 4 balls and line four 9 or 10 in. pans with dough. Brush dough with oil and fill. Top with sliced or shredded Mozzarella or other cheese.

Filling

1 6-oz. can tomato paste
½ cup hot water

½ tsp. oregano
1 tsp. salt
⅛ tsp. black pepper

If desired put hamburger or other meat with filling before topping with cheese. Bake at 450° for 15 min.

Mrs. Roger Barkman, Steinbach, Man.

Pizza (2)

3½ cups flour
1 tsp. sugar
1½ tsp. salt

1 cup warm water
1 pkg. dry yeast
2 tbsp. olive oil

Dissolve yeast in warm water, add sugar, salt, oil, 2 cups flour and beat. Add 1½ cups flour and knead until smooth. Cover and let rise in a warm place until double. Punch down and put into 2—13"x9"x2" pans or if a thin pizza dough is desired, put in 3 cookie sheets.

Pizza Topping

2-6 oz. pkgs. Mozzarella
  Cheese
2-6 oz. cans tomato paste
1 cup water
2 tsp. salt

⅛ tsp. pepper
2 tsp. crushed Oregano
1 tsp. olive oil
2 tsp. Parmesan Cheese

Place Mozzarella Cheese on dough. Combine rest of ingredients. Spread on dough and sprinkle with Parmesan Cheese. Sausage, wieners, bologna, fried hamburger, or sliced canned mushrooms may be spread on top. Bake at 450° for 25 min.

Mrs. Jesse Jantz Jr., Halstead, Kans.

Pizza (3)

½ pkg. dry yeast
1 cup scalded milk
1 tbsp. shortening
1¾ cups sifted flour

2 tbsp. warm water
1 tbsp. sugar
1 tsp. salt

Soften yeast in warm water. To milk add sugar, shortening, and salt. Cool to lukewarm and add softened yeast. Gradually stir in flour for soft dough. Turn out on lightly floured board and knead a few times. Place in greased bowl; turn to grease entire surface. Cover and let rise in a warm place until doubled in bulk. about 1 hr. While dough is raising prepare topping as follows:

½ lb. hamburger
¼ lb. smoked sausage
1 med. onion, chopped
1 green or red pepper, chopped
1 can tomato paste
1 cup water

1 cup sliced small mushrooms or
1 can undiluted mushroom soup
½ tsp. cayenne pepper
½ tsp. Italian seasoning
1 cup grated Parmesan cheese
2 tbsp. chives, chopped

Saute hamburger, sausage and chopped onion together; then drain off all fat. Add chopped pepper, tomato paste, water, mushrooms, cayenne pepper, and seasoning. Bring to a boil; turn heat very low and simmer until quite thick, stirring occasionally. When dough is ready, turn onto lightly floured board and roll as for pie crust, about ¼ in. thick, in a circle to fit pizza pan or other large pan about 12 in. in diameter. Grease pan lightly; fit dough into pan and pinch to edge. Let rise about 15 to 20 min. Bake about 10 min. in 400° oven. Remove from oven and spread topping over the crust. Sprinkle grated cheese and chopped chives on top. Return to oven and bake 5 min. more at 350°.

Make a large batch of this and freeze the bread and topping separately. When ready to serve, heat the bread; spread on topping and cheese and return to oven for five min. Serve hot.

Mrs. Archie Holdeman, Hesston, Kans.

Pizza (4)

Pizza Dough

2 cups flour   ⅔ cup milk
1 tbsp. baking powder   ⅓ cup salad oil
1 tsp. salt

Sift flour, baking powder and salt into bowl; add milk to oil and pour all at once into dry ingredients. Stir with a fork until mixture rounds up into a ball. Knead about 10 times without flour. Roll the dough between sheets of waxed paper to fit a 14 in. pizza pan or two 15½x12 in. cookie sheets or two 10 in. pie pans.

Pizza Sauce

1 lb. hamburger   1 tsp. oregano
1-6 oz. can tomato paste   ½ tsp. black pepper
¼ cup water   1½ cups shredded Mozzarella
¼ tsp. salt   cheese

Combine tomato paste, water, oregano, salt and pepper. Mix to a smooth paste. Spread dough with ½ of the cheese. Cover with sauce and sprinkle with hamburger and remaining cheese. Bake in 425° oven 15 or 20 min. Remove from oven; cut into wedges and serve.

Roma Jantz, Hesston, Kans.

Pizza Burgers

Measure into bowl ¾ cup warm water; sprinkle 1 pkg. dry yeast on water. Stir until dissolved. Add 2½ cups biscuit mix and beat vigorously. Knead until smooth. Divide into 8 pieces and roll each into a 4 in. circle. Place on ungreased baking sheet and press to make edges of circles slightly thick. Set aside in warm place to rise.

Mix together:

¾ cup chopped onion   1½ lbs. ground cooked beef
1 clove garlic, chopped   ½ cup chopped green pepper
2 cups tomato sauce   Salt and pepper to taste

Heat together and spread on dough. Sprinkle with 1 tsp. oregano. Bake in hot oven (425°) for 10 min. Top with 2 cups grated American cheese. Return to oven 5 to 10 min. until crust is brown and filling bubbly. Serve immediately.

Mrs. Elmer Boehs, Isabella, Okla.

Tamales

American Tamale Pie

2½ cups boiling water
¾ cup cornmeal

1 tsp. salt
½ cup ready-to-eat bran (optional)

Add cornmeal to boiling, salted water. Cook until thick; add bran if desired. Cover and set aside.

1 lb. ground beef
3 tbsp. shortening
2½ cups canned tomatoes
¼ cup dry, grated cheese

½ cup chopped green pepper
⅛ tsp. pepper
1½ tsp. salt
1 tbsp. chili powder

Melt shortening; add meat and cook until brown, stirring to break the meat into pieces. Add green pepper, tomatoes and seasonings. Simmer about 15 min. Arrange alternately in layers in casserole with cornmeal mixture. Sprinkle with grated cheese and bake at 400° about 15 minutes. Serves six.

Mrs. Harvey Dyck, Atwater, Calif.

Hot Tamale Pie

2 cups ground meat
1½ cups gravy or meatstock
1 tbsp. chili powder
Salt

1 small clove garlic (minced)
1 qt. cooked, very thick cornmeal mush

Mix meat with gravy or meatstock; add chili powder, salt and garlic. Line baking dish sides with mush. Pour in meat mixture and pat more mush over top. Bake 20 or 30 min. in hot (400°) oven.

Mrs. Fanny Holdeman, Hesston, Kans.

Hot Tamales

Boil meat until tender (preferably chicken; de-bone and chop)

1 onion, cut fine	½ tsp. red pepper
½ cup fresh corn	½ tsp. salt
3 diced tomatoes	½ cup cornmeal

Combine meat, onion, fresh corn, tomatoes, red pepper and salt. Stir in a small amount of broth; mix in cornmeal. Wash and boil fresh corn husks for 20 minutes. Use three husks for each tamale; tie at both ends. Brown them in skillet and using some of the broth, simmer for 20 minutes.

Mrs. A. G. Hiebert, Hillsboro, Kans.

Tamale Casserole

1 lb. hamburger	2¼ cups tomatoes
3 tbsp. fat	1-12 oz. can vacuum pack
1 med. onion	corn
1 tsp. salt	1 tbsp. chili powder
	¼ cup cornmeal

Fry hamburger and onion in fat until brown. Add tomatoes, corn, chili powder, salt and cornmeal. Cook 5 min. Top with the following:

½ cup cornmeal	3 tbsp. oil or melted
½ cup flour	shortening
1¼ tsp. baking powder	½ tsp. salt
1 beaten egg	½ cup milk

Sift flour, cornmeal and baking powder. Mix and add the rest of the ingredients. Arrange olives on top if desired. Bake 25 to 30 min. in 425° oven.

Alma Dyck, Livingston, Calif.

Texas Tamale Pie

Chili Base

1 lb. ground beef	1½ tbsp. chili powder
⅓ cup chopped onion	1 tsp. oregano
1 can (1 lb.) kidney beans	2 tbsp. flour
1 can (1 lb. 4 oz.) tomatoes	1 tbsp. water

Topping

½ cup sifted flour	1 egg
½ cup yellow cornmeal	⅓ cup milk
¼ tsp. salt	2 tbsp. soft shortening
2 tsp. baking powder	½ cup chopped green
2 tbsp. sugar	pepper (optional)

Heat oven to 425° degrees.

For the base, brown ground beef and onion in small amount of fat in large frying pan. Add kidney beans, tomatoes, chili powder, salt and oregano. Combine flour and water; stir slowly into meat mixture. Cook over med. heat until mixture thickens slightly. Transfer to a 2 qt. casserole. For the topping, sift together flour, cornmeal, salt, baking powder and sugar into a bowl. Add egg, milk and shortening. Beat with rotary beater until smooth, about one minute. **Do not over beat.** Stir in green pepper. Drop topping by spoonfuls onto chili base. Bake in preheated oven for 15 to 20 min. Serves six.

Mrs. Archie Holdeman, Hesston, Kans.

Sauces for Meats

Barbecue Sauce for Fried Chicken

1 lb. onion finely chopped	1 qt. water
⅔ cup fat or pan drippings	½ cup brown sugar
1½ cups cider vinegar	¼ cup prepared mustard
1½ cup sweet pickle juice	2 tsp. Worcestershire sauce
1 qt. catsup	1 tsp. chili powder
1¼ cups sweet pickles, finely chopped	1 tsp. salt

Method; Brown onion in fat combine remaining ingredients, simmer 30 min. Have partly fried chicken pieces ready in pan. Pour sauce over chicken and bake at 350° 30 min. or until chicken is tender. Sauce may be prepared ahead and stored in refrigerator. Yield: 1 gal. for 50 servings.

Mrs. Jacob N. Yost, Durham, Kans.

Barbecue Sauce (1)

(for spareribs, wieners, etc.)

Brown:
  ½ cup chopped onion
  1 tsp. butter

Add 2 heaping tbsp. brown sugar, 1 tsp. mustard, ⅛ tsp. pepper, 1 tbsp. vinegar and ½ cup catsup. Cook 2 min. (Add the above when meat is half done.)

Mrs. Ervin Nightengale, Scott City, Kans.

Barbecue Sauce (2)

½ cup catsup
1 tbsp. brown sugar or
  honey
1 tbsp. soy sauce or
  Worcestershire sauce
1 tbsp. vinegar

1 tsp. chili powder
1 tsp. liquid smoke
¼ tsp. dry mustard
½ tsp. onion salt
½ tsp. garlic salt

Brown chicken which has been rolled in flour then place in baking dish and pour the above mixture over chicken and bake slow at (300°) for 2 hr. You may use this sauce on wieners or spareribs but brown them first.

Thelma Mae Koehn, Moundridge, Kans.

Barbecue Sauce (3)

1 bottle catsup (12 oz.)
2 tbsp. brown sugar
1 tsp. mustard
1 tsp. horseradish
1 tsp. liquid smoke
2 tbsp. vinegar

½ tsp. Worcestershire
  Sauce
2 dashes Tabasco Sauce
  several shakes of garlic
  salt

Brush on meat (pork, beef, or chicken) for grilling or broiling.

Mrs. Herman Mininger, Harrison, Mich.

PASTRIES

Pastry

Easy Rolled Flaky Pie Crust

4 cups unsifted flour	1 tbsp. vinegar
1 tsp. baking powder	1½ tsp. salt
1½ cups shortening	1 egg
	½ cup water

Sift flour, baking powder, and salt together. Cut in shortening. Add vinegar, egg and cold water.

Mrs. Allen Wiebe, Almena, Wisc.
Mrs. Levi Plank, Ohio

Egg Yolk Pie Crust

5 cups sifted flour	½ tsp. baking powder
4 tsp. sugar	1½ cups shortening
½ tsp. salt	2 egg yolks
	cold water

Combine dry ingredients. Cut in shortening. Place egg yolk in measuring cup, stir with fork until smooth, add enough water to make scant cupful, sprinkle over dry ingredients. Toss with fork to make a soft dough. Roll out. Makes about 3 double pie crusts.

Martha Hiebert, Middleton, Mich.

Pie Crust (1)

1 cup shortening	1 tbsp. vinegar
3 cups flour	1 egg
½ tsp. salt	7 tbsp. cold water

Mix flour, shortening and salt until fine. Beat egg, add vinegar and water; add to dry ingredients and mix. Makes 5 single crusts.

Mrs. Albert Unruh, Montezuma, Kans.

Pie Crust (2)

1½ cups flour	½ tsp. salt
	½ cup lard or shortening

Cut shortening into flour until well mixed. Add water to moisten mixture, approximately ⅓ cup. Divide into two portions for a double crust pie.

Pie Crust (3)

3 cups flour
1¼ cups shortening
1 tsp. salt
1 egg
5½ tbsp. water
1 tsp. vinegar

Mix flour, shortening, and salt until crumbly. Beat egg, water, and vinegar together. Make a well in the flour mixture, add the liquid. Makes 4 one-crust pie shells.

Stir and Roll Pie Crust

2 cups sifted flour
½ cup Wesson oil
1½ tsp. salt
¼ cup cold milk

Mix and divide into two portions. Place one portion between two pieces of waxed paper 12 in. square to roll. Lightly dampen table top to prevent slipping of bottom waxed paper before rolling. Peel top paper and place paper side up in pie pan. Roll top crust same way and cut slits in top.

Meringue and Pie Topping

Meringue

½ cup cold water
2 tbsp. sugar
1 tbsp. cornstarch

Combine and cook until thickened, set aside to cool. Beat 3 egg whites until stiff; add cooked mixture and beat until blended. Spread on pie and brown. (For 1 pie)

Mrs. Herman P. Koehn, Chickasha, Okla.

Perfect Meringue

Mix 1 tbsp. cornstarch with 1½ tsp. water; Stir into ½ cup boiling water. Cook until thick and clear. Beat 3 egg whites until stiff. Add 3 tbsp. sugar and ⅛ tsp. salt. Add cooked cornstarch and continue beating until mixture stands in peaks. Spread on pie and brown in 375° oven. (This makes a tender meringue which will stand up and won't weep).

Mrs. Lloyd Koehn, Lehigh, Kans.

Pie Topping

½ cup brown sugar, firmly   1 cup flour
    packed
½ cup butter

Blend until crumbly. Use as pie topping in place of top crust.
Bake as usual.

Mrs. Marshall Harms, Walnut Hill, Fla.

Pastry Shell Pies

Angel Food Pie

1½ tbsp. cornstarch   3 egg whites
¾ cup sugar   3 tbsp. sugar
1½ cups boiling water   1½ tsp. vanilla
⅜ tsp. salt   ½ cup cream

Mix cornstarch and sugar in saucepan. Add boiling water, stirring constantly, and cook until clear and thick. Beat egg whites
and salt until stiff. Add sugar and vanilla, beating until egg
whites are creamy. Pour hot cornstarch slowly over egg whites,
beating continually. Cool slightly and pour into baked pie shell.
Spread with whipped cream and sprinkle with grated chocolate
or nut meats. (Fills two pie shells).

Mrs. David Decker, Scott City, Kans.

Butterscotch Pie (1)

¼ cup cornstarch   2 cups milk
½ cup brown sugar   2 eggs
½ cup white sugar   ¼ tsp. salt
¼ cup butter   1 tsp. vanilla

Melt ¼ cup of brown and ¼ cup of white sugar with the ¼ cup
of butter to slightly carmelize. Add 1½ cups milk, this will get
hard but will melt as the milk gets hot. Now add ½ cup milk
to ¼ cup cornstarch. Beat egg yolks, add to milk and cornstarch. Add all to the hot milk, stirring all the time till it is
thick. Add 1 tsp. vanilla, and ¼ tsp. salt.

Meringue

2 egg whites
¼ tsp. salt

⅛ tsp. cream of tartar

Beat until stiff adding ⅓ cup sugar and continue beating. Brown in oven at 350° or 400° till nice and brown.

Mrs. Ezra Inninger, Middleton, Mich.

Butterscotch Pie (2)

2 eggs (separated)
¼ cup water
1 tbsp. light corn syrup
1 cup brown sugar, firmly packed
¼ cup butter

½ cup granulated sugar
3 tbsp. flour
2 cups milk
3 tbsp. cornstarch
¼ tsp. salt

For butterscotch mixture, combine water, syrup, brown sugar and butter. Cook to hard boil stage (250°). Let set to use later in recipe. Scald milk, add gradually to remaining dry ingredients. Boil over low heat, stirring constantly, until smooth. Add hot butterscotch mixture, beat until well blended. Slowly add beaten egg yolks, cook 1 min. more. Pour into 9" baked pie shell. Spread with meringue or whipped cream.

Mrs. Fred J. Bortz, Bellaire, Kans.

Cherry-O-Cream Cheese Pie

1-9" graham cracker pie shell
1-8 oz. pkg. cream cheese, softened
⅓ cup lemon juice

1-15 oz. can sweetened condensed milk
1 tsp. vanilla
1-1 lb.-6 oz. can of prepared cherry pie filling

Whip cream cheese until fluffy. Gradually add sweetened condensed milk; continue to beat until well blended. Add lemon juice and vanilla, blend well. Pour into baked pie shell. Chill 2 or 3 hrs. Garnish top of pie with cherry pie filling.

Mrs. Lyle Holdeman, Clarksdale, Miss.

Cherry Cream Pie

1⅓ cups sweetened condensed milk
1 tsp. vanilla
⅓ cup lemon juice
½ cup whipping cream, whipped
½ tsp. almond extract

Combine milk, lemon juice and flavorings. Stir until mixture thickens. Fold in whipped cream and spoon into shell. Top with cherry glaze.

Cherry Glaze

2 cups or 1 lb. can pitted sour cherries, drained
⅔ cup cherry juice
1 tbsp. cornstarch
¼ cup sugar
2-3 drops red food coloring if desired

Set aside drained cherries. Blend juice with sugar and cornstarch, cook over low heat, stirring constantly until mixture thickens and is clear. Add cherries. Spread over cream filling.

Margaret Loewen, Glenn, Calif.

Cream Pie (1)

¾ cup sugar
⅓ cup flour
⅛ tsp. salt
2 eggs, well beaten
2 cups milk, scalded
½ tsp. vanilla
2 tbsp. butter

Combine butter, sugar, salt, flour, and eggs. Add milk slowly, stirring constantly. Cook over hot water until thick and smooth. Add flavoring. Pour into baked pastry shell. Cool. Serve with whipped cream or top with meringue. Brown meringue in slow oven (325°).

Variation for the above recipe:
Chocolate Pie—2 sq. of semi-sweet chocolate, melted
Coconut Pie—¾ cup flaked coconut
Cherry Cream Pie—1 cup sour cherries, drained
Banana Pie—2 bananas, sliced
Caramel Cream Pie—Caramelize ½ cup sugar in heavy skillet. Dissolve with ½ cup water and boil until syrup is reduced to ½ cup. Reduce the amount of milk in the above recipe to 1¾ cup.   Mrs. Emery Yost, Halstead, Kans.

Cream Pie (2)

Crumb enough bread to fill unbaked 9" pie shell even full.

½ cup sugar   2 cups milk
1 tsp. vanilla

Mix sugar, milk and vanilla. Pour over bread crumbs. Bake at 400° for 40 min. until very lightly browned.

Mrs. F. W. Holdeman, Hesston, Kans.

Chocolate Layer Pie

2 eggs   1 tbsp. butter
2 cups milk   ¾ tsp. vanilla
¾ cup sugar   1-8" baked pie shell
⅓ cup flour   ½ cup chocolate bits
¼ tsp. salt   ¼ cup chopped pecans

Mix egg yolks and ¼ cup milk in double boiler top. Thoroughly mix ½ cup sugar, flour and salt. Add to egg yolk mixture and blend. Add remaining milk and mix well. Cook over boiling water, stirring constantly until thickened, about 6 or 7 min. Cover and cook 15 min. longer, stirring occasionally. Remove from boiling water. Stir in butter and vanilla. Pour into baked pie shell. Sprinkle chocolate and pecans over filling. Beat egg whites until foamy, add remaining ¼ cup sugar, 1 tbsp. at a time. Continue beating until stiff peaks form. Spread over pie filling. Bake at 475° until lightly browned.

Delores Dirks, Copeland, Kans.

Vanilla Cream Pie

¾ cup sugar   3 slightly beaten egg yolks
⅓ cup all-purpose flour or 3   2 tbsp. butter or margarine
    tbsp. cornstarch   1 tsp. vanilla
¼ tsp. salt   2 cups milk

Mix all dry ingredients. Add egg yolks and enough milk to make a paste. Add remaining milk. Bring to boiling, stirring constantly. Cook 2 min. Add butter and vanilla. Cool to room temperature. Pour into baked pastry shell.

Mrs. Robert D. Smith, De Ridder, La.

Date Cream Pie

1 cup dates, cut up	1 tbsp. flour
1 cup cream	2 egg yolks
¾ cup sugar	

Stew dates in water until tender. Drain, add cream, mix sugar, and flour together. Add to cream mixture. Cook five min. Add the egg yolks and cook until filling thickens. Add vanilla. Pour into baked pie shell and top with meringue or whipped cream.

Mrs. Fred Mininger, Barron, Wisc.

Jello Ice Cream Strawberry Pie

1 pkg. strawberry jello	1¼ cups hot water and straw-
1 pt. vanilla ice cream	berry juice
	strawberries

Dissolve jello in hot liquid, thoroughly blend in ice cream; set in refrigerator until partially congealed. Add fresh, sliced or thawed and drained, frozen strawberries. Mix and spoon into 1-9" baked pie shell. Spread with dream whip and garnish with strawberry halves.

Mrs. Lincoln C. Koehn, Moundridge, Kans.

Jello Ice Cream Pie

1 pkg. gelatin, any flavor	1 cup drained, sweetened,
1¼ cups boiling water	sliced strawberries
1 pt. vanilla ice cream	1-8" graham cracker crumb
	pie crust

Dissolve gelatin in boiling water. Stir in ice cream until melted. Chill until very thick. Fold in strawberries. Pour into crust. Chill until firm, garnish with berries.

Clara Koehn, Winton, Calif.

Lemon Cream Pie

1 qt. milk	2 cups sugar
3 tbsp. cornstarch	dash of salt
4 eggs, separated	1 tsp. butter or oleo
½ tsp. vanilla	1 tsp. lemon extract

Pour milk into saucepan and heat. Dissolve cornstarch in ¾ cup of the milk. Beat egg yolks slightly and mix with milk and cornstarch. Bring milk in saucepan to boiling, add cornstarch mixture, sugar and salt. Stir constantly until thickened. Remove from heat; add butter, and lemon extract. Cool slightly and pour into baked pie crusts. Spread with meringue.

Mrs. Orval Johnson, Walnut Hill, Fla.

Lemon Pie

Juice of ½ lemon
¾ cup cold water
2 egg yolks, beaten

1 cup sugar
1 pkg. lemon jello pie filling
1¾ cups boiling water

Add lemon juice to cold water. Mix sugar and jello pie filling, add one-half of cold water mixture. Add egg yolks and remaining cold water. Add boiling water, boil and stir until thickened and clear. Pour into 9" baked pie shell. Top with meringue.

Mrs. Noah Holdeman, Wrens, Ga.

Orange Pie

¾ cup sugar
⅓ cup flour
¼ tsp. salt
1¼ cups milk

3 egg yolks
2 tbsp. lemon juice
1 tbsp. grated orange rind
½ cup orange juice

Mix sugar, flour, salt and milk. Boil over hot water 20 min. Add beaten egg yolks. Boil five min. more. Add juices and rind. Pour into baked pie shell. Cool. Spread with meringue, and brown lightly.

Gladys Schmidt, Winton, Calif.

Peanut Butter Pie

2 cups milk, scalded
2 tbsp. peanut butter
⅛ tsp. salt
2 egg yolks

1 tsp. vanilla
½ cup sugar
2 tbsp. flour
¼ cup cream

Mix egg yolks with cream. Add sugar, flour, salt, peanut butter, and vanilla. Stir into hot milk until thickened. Pour into baked pie shell. Spread with meringue.

Mrs. Fred Koehn, Montezuma, Kans.

Pineapple Angel Food Pie

2 cups crushed pineapple
1 cup pineapple juice
3 tbsp. cornstarch
1½ cups sugar
¼ tsp. salt
¾ cup cold water
4 egg yolks

Cook together all ingredients. Remove from heat, cool 15 min. and add beaten egg whites. Pour into 2 baked pie shells. Top with whipped cream.

Mrs. Abe Troyer, Apple Creek, Ohio

Sour Cream Pineapple Pie

3 egg yolks, well beaten
1 cup sugar
1 cup pineapple and juice
1 cup sour cream
3 tbsp. flour

Mix all ingredients well. Cook in double boiler until thickened. Cool. Pour into baked, 9 in. pie shell. Spread with meringue.

Mrs. Willard Dirks, Greensburg, Kans.
Mrs. Le Roy Smith, De Ridder, La.

Wild Plum Pie

1 pkg. peach flavored
   gelatin
1 cup boiling water
2 cups whipping cream
¾ cup sugar
1 cup sand hill plum pulp

Dissolve gelatin in boiling water. Cool until partially firm. Whip cream; add sugar and fold into gelatin together with plum pulp. Pour into baked pie shell or graham cracker crust. Chill. Garnish with whipped cream and slivered almonds.

Mrs. John Unruh, Greensburg, Kans.

Raisin Cream Pie

1 cup raisins
½ cup sugar
1 cup water
1 tbsp. flour
2 egg yolks, beaten
1 tsp. vanilla
1 cup cream or milk
⅛ tsp. salt

Cook raisins, water and sugar until syrupy. Mix remaining ingredients and add to raisin mixture. Boil until thickened. Pour into baked pie shell. Spread with meringue.

Elda Schmidt, Winton, Calif.

French Raisin Pie

1 cup raisins
½ cup white sugar
1 cup sour cream or
1 cup canned milk with 1
   tsp. vinegar

1 tsp. soda
2 egg yolks
⅛ tsp. salt
½ tsp. cinnamon

Mix all ingredients and cook about 20 min., stirring constantly.
Pour into baked pie shell. Spread with meringue.

Mrs. Earvey Ensz, Almena, Wisc.

Heavenly Pumpkin Pie

1 tbsp. unflavored gelatine
1¼ cups cooked, mashed
    pumpkin
¾ cup milk
1 cup sugar
1 tsp. pumpkin pie spice

¼ cup cold water
2 eggs
½ tsp salt
1 pkg. Dream Whip
½ tsp. vanilla

Soften gelatine in water. Cook pumpkin, milk, egg yolks, ½
cup sugar, salt, and spice over boiling water 10 min. stirring
constantly. Stir in gelatine. Chill until thick. Prepare Dream
Whip as directed on package. Beat egg whites until stiff, add
remaining sugar gradually. Fold pumpkin, vanilla, 1 cup Dream
Whip into egg whites. Pour into pie shell; chill. Top with
Dream Whip.

Marian Barkman, Steinbach, Man.

Pumpkin Ice Cream Pie

¼ cup honey or brown
   sugar
¾ cup canned or cooked,
   mashed pumpkin
½ tsp. cinnamon
¼ tsp. salt

¼ tsp. ginger
Dash of nutmeg
Dash of Cloves
1 qt. vanilla ice cream
⅓ cup broken pecans, if
   desired

Combine honey, pumpkin, spices and salt. Bring just to boiling
stirring constantly, cool. Beat in softened ice cream and nuts.
Spread into baked shell. Freeze until firm. Trim with whipped
cream and pecan halves.

Mrs. Paul Toews, St. Marys, Ont.

Rhubarb Cream Pie

Melt 2 tbsp. butter, add 2 cups diced fresh or frozen rhubarb and 1 cup sugar. Cook slowly until tender. (A few drops of red food coloring may be added).

Combine:

3 egg yolks	¼ cup sugar
2 tbsp. cornstarch	¼ cup light cream
⅛ tsp. salt	

Add to rhubarb and cook until thick. Cool and pour into baked pie shell. Top with meringue and bake until brown.

Mrs. Carl Litwiller, Ithaca, Mich.

Glazed Strawberry Pie

½ cup water	A few drops red food
¾ cup light corn syrup	coloring
2 tbsp. cornstarch	1 qt. fresh strawberries,
2 tbsp. water	drained
¼ tsp. almond extract	9" pie shell, baked

Heat water and syrup to boiling. Mix cornstarch and water to a paste. Add to syrup and water. Cook, stirring constantly, until thickened. Add coloring. Cool. Stir in extract. Slice berries and arrange in pastry shell. (For variety, use fresh or frozen, drained peaches and a few drops yellow food coloring.) Pour into pie shell. Chill, and serve with whipped cream or topping below.

Topping for Pie

Boil until it strings: ⅓ cup sugar ¼ cup water
Beat 1 egg white with ⅛ tsp. cream of tartar. Add boiled syrup and ½ tsp. vanilla. Beat till stiff.

Rebecca Holdeman, Hesston, Kans.

Strawberry Pie

1 qt. fresh strawberries (firm and ripe)
1 cup sugar (less if frozen strawberries are used)
2 tbsp. cornstarch   1 cup whipped cream

Mash 1 pt. of fresh or use 1 pt. of frozen berries. Place over fire with sugar and cornstarch. Cook 10 min. Let cool. Place remaining fresh berries in baked pie shell. Spoon cooked mixture over top of berries. Top with whipped cream.

Mrs. Earl Wiggers, Hesston, Kans.

Walnut or Pecan Pie

2 eggs
¾ cup brown sugar
¼ cup white sugar
⅛ tsp. salt

3 tbsp. flour
2 cups milk or 1 cup cream
  and 1 cup water
1 cup nuts

Combine flour, sugar, and milk.' Bring to boiling point until thickened. Add egg yolks. Pour over 1 cup nuts into baked pie shell. Top with meringue.

Mrs. Ben Becker, Rich Hill, Mo.

Chiffon Pies

Peanut Crust Chocolate Chiffon Pie

1 cup sifted flour
⅓ cup shortening

½ tsp salt
⅓ cup salted peanuts
  (crushed)

Cut shortening into flour until particles are the size of peas. Add crushed peanuts. Sprinkle 3-4 tbsp. cold water over mixture, moistening enough to hold together. Roll out on floured board and put into a 9 in. pie pan. Prick with fork and bake in 425° oven 12 to 15 min.

Chocolate Chiffon Filling

1 envelope Knox gelatine
¼ cup cold milk
¾ cup sugar
¼ tsp. cinnamon
¾ cup milk

2 sq. Chocolate or 4 tbsp.
  cocoa
2 egg yolks
¼ tsp. salt
½ tsp. vanilla

Soften gelatine in ¼ cup cold milk. Melt chocolate in top of double boiler over hot water. Add sugar, egg yolks, cinnamon and salt. Blend in ¾ cup milk gradually. Cook until mixture thickens and will coat a spoon, stirring constantly. Remove from heat. Add vanilla and softened gelatine; stir until dissolved. Chill until mixture begins to thicken. Beat 2 egg whites until stiff, add 2 tbsp. sugar. Whip ¾ cup heavy cream until stiff. Fold into chocolate mixture which has been beaten with a rotary beater. Pour into cooled pie shell. Chill 2-3 hours. Before serving top with whipped cream and crushed peanuts.

Mrs. Jay Diller, Walnut Hill, Fla.

Coconut Pumpkin Chiffon Pie

1 envelope unflavored Knox Gelatine softened in
¼ cup cold water
1¼ cups cooked, mashed pumpkin
¾ cup evaporated milk
½ cup water
2 egg yolks slightly beaten
¼ tsp. ginger
½ cup brown sugar, firmly packed
½ tsp. salt
½ tsp. nutmeg
½ tsp. cinnamon

Combine all ingredients except gelatine. Cook in double boiler 10 min. stirring constantly. Stir in softened gelatine until thoroughly dissolved. Chill until slightly thickened. Beat 2 egg whites until foamy, add ¼ cup brown sugar and continue beating until stiff. Fold into pumpkin mixture. Add 1 tsp. vanilla and ¾ cup toasted coconut. Pour into a 9 in. baked pie shell. Chill until firm. Top with ⅓ cup sweetened whipped cream. Decorate with ¼ cup coconut toasted.

To toast coconut: Spread coconut thinly in shallow pan. Toast in moderate oven (350°) about 10 min. stirring often until delicately browned.

Mrs. Erma Koop, Scio, Ore.

Pumpkin Chiffon Pie

2 envelopes unflavored gelatine
½ cup water
2½ cups mashed pumpkin
3 eggs, separated
2 cups sugar
1 tsp. salt
½ tsp. ginger
1½ cups milk
½ tsp. nutmeg
1 tsp. cinnamon
½ tsp. allspice (optional)
1 tsp. vanilla

Combine pumpkin, egg yolks, 1 cup sugar, salt, milk and spices. Boil together; add gelatine softened in water. Cool. Beat egg whites until foamy; gradually add 1 cup sugar beating until stiff. Add vanilla. Fold into pumpkin mixture. Pour in 2 baked pie shells.

Mrs. David Ensz, Inman, Kans.

Strawberry Chiffon Pie

1 pt. fresh strawberries, cut in halves and ½ cup sugar. Let stand in refrigerator 1 hr. Drain; combine berry juice and enough water to make 1 cup juice. Bring to boiling. Dissolve

1 pkg. strawberry flavor gelatin in juice. Beat 3 egg yolks until light. Pour hot gelatin slowly into egg yolks, stirring constantly. Add ¼ tsp. salt. Cool. Add berries. Chill, stirring often until thickened. Beat 3 egg whites until stiff; add ¼ cup sugar. Fold into gelatin mixture. Spoon into 9" baked pie shell. Chill 2 or 3 hrs. Spread with whipped cream. (Red raspberries may be substituted in place of strawberries).

Mrs. Martha Hiebert, Middleton, Mich.

One-Crust Pies

Apple Pecan Pie

1 egg	½ cup (golden) syrup
⅔ cup sugar	3 tbsp. flour
¼ cup water	1 cup pecans
2 tbsp. melted butter	2 apples, sliced

Put apples into an unbaked pie shell. Mix the above ingredients and pour over apples. Bake in moderate oven at (375°) for 45 min.

Jannette Unruh, Galva, Kans.

Grated Apple Pie

2 eggs	5 small apples, grated
½ cup sugar	1 cup cream
1 rounded tbsp. flour	dash of cinnamon
2 tbsp. butter	

Mix together all ingredients. Pour into unbaked pie shell. Bake at 350° 40 to 45 min.

Bob Andy Pie

2 cups brown sugar	3 egg yolks
1 tsp. cinnamon	2 cups milk
½ tsp. allspice	3 egg whites
4 tbsp. flour	

Mix all but egg whites. Add beaten egg whites and stir well to blend spices. Pour in 2 unbaked pie crusts. Bake at 350° until knife inserted comes out clean.

Mrs. Carl Litwiller, Ithaca, Mich.

Butter Nut Pie

7/8 cup sugar	1½ cups chopped dates
2 tbsp. flour	½ tsp. vanilla
1 tbsp. butter	7 tbsp. light cream
2 eggs, separated	½ cup chopped nuts

Combine sugar and flour, add butter, beaten egg yolks, dates, vanilla, cream and nuts. Mix well and fold in stiffly beaten egg whites. Pour into 1-8" unbaked pie shell and bake at 400° 10 min., then at 350° 40 min. or until filling is set.

Mrs. Menno Koehn, Halstead, Kans.

Picnic Baked Chocolate Pie

3 large eggs	⅛ tsp. salt
¾ cup sugar	2 cups rich milk
2 tsp. cornstarch	⅓ cup flaked coconut
¼ cup cocoa	⅓ cup chopped pecans
1 tsp. vanilla	(optional)

Mix together all ingredients. Pour into deep 10" unbaked pastry pie. Bake at 325° for 40 to 45 min. or until almost set. Do not overbake. Remove from oven while still a little soft in center.

Mrs. Kenneth Jantz, Livingston, Calif.

Old Fashioned Cream Pie

1 cup sugar	1 tbsp. melted butter
3 tbsp. flour	1 tsp. vanilla
1½ cups thick cream	¼ tsp. salt

Mix all ingredients; pour into unbaked pie shell. Sprinkle top with cinnamon. Bake at 350° for 1 hr. or until set.

Mrs. Donald Seiler, Ithaca, Mich.

Sour Cream Pie

1 cup sour cream	1 cup sugar
½ cup seedless raisins	½ tsp. cinnamon
(optional)	3 eggs
¼ tsp. cloves	

Mix and pour into unbaked pie shell. Spread with meringue.

Mrs. William P. Koehn, Montezuma, Kans.

Swiss Cream Pie

Mix together:

½ cup brown sugar   2 heaping tbsp. flour
½ cup white sugar   ⅛ tsp. salt

Add 2 cups cream and mix well. Add 1 tsp. vanilla, mix and pour into unbaked crust and bake at 425° for 10 min. then 325° until set.

Mrs. Willard Holdeman, Hesston, Kans.

Coconut Syrup Pie

2 eggs, beaten   2 tbsp. butter or margarine
¾ cup white syrup   1 tsp. lemon juice
½ tsp. salt   1½ cups coconut
½ cup sugar

Mix all ingredients together, adding coconut last. Pour into unbaked 9" pie shell. Bake at 400° for 15 min. then at 350° for 30-35 min. (Filling should appear slightly less set in center then at outer edge).

Mrs. Robert Koehn, Montezuma, Kans.

Cottage Cheese Pie

1 cup homemade cottage   2 egg yolks, beaten
     cheese   1 tbsp. melted butter
⅔ cup sugar   ¼ tsp. vanilla
⅔ cup milk   ⅛ tsp. salt

Mix together ingredients in order given. Pour into unbaked pie shell. Bake at 350° for 30 min. or until done. Cool slightly. Spread with meringue and brown. Serve warm.

Mrs. Marion Jantz, Rich Hill, Mo.

Crumb Pie

2 cups flour   ⅛ tsp. salt
½ cup lard or butter   ½ cup sugar

Work flour, salt and shortening into crumbs as for pie shell. Add sugar and toss lightly to blend. Spread lightly into unbaked 9" pie shell. Bake at 350° oven for 30 to 40 min.

Mrs. F. W. Holdeman, Hesston, Kans.

Coconut Custard Pie

3 eggs, separated
1½ cups sugar
¼ cup milk
1½ cups shredded coconut
¼ tsp. salt
2 tbsp. butter
1 tsp. lemon juice

Add salt to egg yolks and beat until thick and lemon colored. Add sugar, ½ cup at a time, beating after each addition. Add milk, butter and lemon juice. Fold in stiffly beaten egg whites and coconut. Pour into unbaked pie shell and bake 50 min. at 375°, or until mixture doesn't adhere to knife.

Nelda Litwiller, Ithaca, Mich.

Custard Pie

2½ cups milk
½ cup sugar
1 tsp. vanilla
¼ tsp. salt
½ tsp. almond extract
(optional)
4 eggs
1-9 in. pie shell

Scald milk; add sugar, flavorings, and salt. Mix together. Stir slowly into beaten eggs. Pour into unbaked pie shell. Sprinkle with nutmeg. Bake in hot oven (400°) 20 to 25 min.

Mrs. Weldon Wenger, Hesston, Kans.

Fruit Pie

2 cups fresh fruit
1 cup sugar
¾ cup cream and milk
2 tbsp. flour

Pour fruit into unbaked pie shell. Sprinkle flour over fruit, then sugar. Pour cream and milk over sugar, sprinkle with cinnamon. Bake at 400° for 10 min., reduce heat to 350° for 45 min.

Mrs. Jac. H. Dyck, Hesston, Kans.

Lemon Sponge Pie

1 cup sugar
1 tbsp. flour
1 cup milk
⅛ tsp. salt
2 egg yolks
juice & rind of 1 lemon
butter the size of walnut

Mix all ingredients, then fold in beaten egg whites. Pour into unbaked pie shell and bake in slow oven (350°.)

Mrs. Howard Miller, Ithaca, Mich.

Milk Pie

Mix together:

½ cup sugar	3 tbsp. flour
¼ tsp. salt	2 cups milk

Mix the dry ingredients together and pour into an unbaked pie crust and add the milk. Bake at 350° for 1 hr. Chill thoroughly.

Mrs. Francis Peters, McDavid, Fla.

Oatmeal Pie (1)

Mix together

1 cup sugar	½ cup milk
¾ cup dark syrup	2 eggs, beaten
¾ cup oatmeal	2 tbsp. soft butter
½ cup coconut	⅛ tsp. salt

Pour into unbaked pie shell. Bake at 350° until done.

Mrs. Jesse Nichols, Isabella, Okla.

Oatmeal Pie (2)

3 eggs, well beaten	2 tbsp. butter
⅔ cup white sugar	⅔ cup coconut
1 cup brown sugar	1 tsp. vanilla
⅔ cup quick cooking oats	

Blend all ingredients and pour into unbaked pie shell. Bake at 350° for 30 to 35 min. (Similar to a pecan pie but not as rich).

Mrs. Archie Schmidt, Greensburg, Kans.

Deluxe Pecan Pie

3 eggs, beaten	1 tsp. vanilla
1 cup dark corn syrup	1 cup sugar
⅛ tsp. salt	2 tbsp. melted butter or
1 cup pecans	margarine

Mix in order given. Pour into unbaked pastry shell, bake in hot oven (400°) for 15 min. Reduce heat to moderate (350°) and bake 30 to 35 min. longer or until a knife inserted in center of filling comes out clean.

Mrs. Robert Koehn, Montezuma, Kans.
Mrs. Norman Wenger, Moundridge, Kans.

Pecan Pie (1)

3 eggs, well beaten
½ cup sugar
½ cup light corn syrup
½ cup waffle syrup
1 tsp. vanilla

2 tbsp. melted oleo
½ cup oatmeal
½ cup coconut
½ cup broken pecans

Mix all ingredients together and pour into unbaked pastry shell. Bake at 350° for one hour or until done.

Mrs. Milton Unruh, Greensburg, Kans.

Pecan Pie (2)

3 egg whites, stiffly beaten
¼ tsp. baking powder
1 cup pecans, chopped

1 cup sugar
11 graham crackers, crushed

Add baking powder to beaten egg whites. Add sugar. Stir until sugar dissolves. Add cracker crumbs and nuts. Mix well. Pour into an unbaked pie shell. Bake 30 min. at 350°.

Mrs. Aaron Becker, Rich Hill, Mo.

Pecan Pie (3)

3 eggs
1 cup corn syrup
1 cup pecans

¾ cup sugar
1 tbsp. butter
2 tbsp. flour

Beat eggs, add syrup, nuts, cream together sugar, butter, and flour, combine mixtures, mixing well. Pour into unbaked pie shell. Bake at 450° for 10 min. then at 350° until knife comes out clean when tested.

Mrs. Evelyn Schmidt, Winton, Calif.

Pecan Pie (4)

3 eggs, well beaten
½ cup sugar
½ cup light corn syrup
½ cup dark corn syrup

¼ tsp. salt
1 tsp. vanilla
1 cup pecans
¼ cup melted butter

Combine eggs, sugar, and corn syrups. Mix well. Add butter, salt, vanilla, and nut meats. Pour into unbaked pie shell. Bake at 350° to 375° for 30 min, or until set.

Mrs. Jake Smith, Walnut Hill, Fla.

Pumpkin Pie

2 cups pumpkin
2 cups sugar
2 cups milk

4 eggs
1 tsp. nutmeg
2 tsp. cinnamon

Mix and put into 2 unbaked pie shells. Bake at 425° for 5 min. then at 350° for 30 or 40 min.

Mrs. Franklin Smith, Hesston, Kans.

Sour Cream Raisin Pie

1 cup raisins
⅓ cup water
1 cup sugar
1 tbsp. flour
1 tsp. cinnamon

½ tsp. allspice
½ tsp. salt
1 egg
1 cup sour cream
1 tbsp. vinegar

Combine raisins and water in saucepan. Bring to boiling; simmer for 5 min. or until water is absorbed. Remove from heat. Combine sugar, flour, spices, and salt; add to raisins. Add beaten egg, sour cream and vinegar. Bring to boiling, cook for 1 min., stirring constantly. Pour into unbaked pie shell. Adjust top crust. Bake in moderate (375°) oven until brown.

Mrs. Harlan Nightengale, Fairview, Okla.

Raisin Cream Pie

1 cup raisins
⅔ cup sugar
¾ cup water
¼ tsp. salt

½ cup cream or milk
2 egg yolks
1 tbsp. cornstarch

Cook raisins with sugar, water, and salt until done. Mix egg yolks, cornstarch, and cream or milk, pour into raisins. Cook until thickened. Pour into baked pie shell. Top with meringue and brown.

Mrs. Newell Mininger, Harrison, Mich.

Grandma's Pumpkin Pie

4 eggs, beaten
2 cups milk
1 tsp. cinnamon
3 cups pumpkin

1 scant tbsp. flour
½ tsp. nutmeg
2 tsp. vanilla
½ tsp. salt
2 cups sugar

Mix in order given. Pour into 2 unbaked pie shells. Bake until set, 425° for 10 min. then 350° for 30 min.

Mrs. Lee Koehn, Winton, Calif.

Rhubarb Cream Pie

2 cups rhubarb, chopped
1 cup sugar
1 tbsp. flour

2 egg yolks
¼ tsp. salt
½ cup cream
½ cup water

Pour rhubarb into unbaked pie shell. Mix remaining ingredients and pour over rhubarb. Bake at 350° for 45 min. Top with meringue. Return to oven and brown lightly.

Eva Koehn, Galva, Kans.

Rhubarb Pie

2 cups rhubarb
1 cup sugar
⅔ cup milk

1 heaping tbsp. flour
2 egg yolks

Cut rhubarb into unbaked pie shell. Mix sugar, flour, egg yolks, and milk. Pour over rhubarb. Bake at 350° until set. Use egg whites for meringue. Cover with meringue and brown.

Mrs. Newell Mininger, Harrison, Mich.

Sweet Potato Pie

3 cups moist, mashed sweet potatoes (using cooking water for moistening)
1 cup brown sugar
2 tbsp. white sugar
½ stick butter
⅛ tsp. cloves

1 tsp. vanilla
⅛ tsp. salt
⅛ tsp. cinnamon

Pour into pie shell, bake at 325° for 45 min. Serve warm with a dip of vanilla ice cream.

Denise Jantz, Livingston, Calif.

Two-Crust Pies

Apple-Raisin Pie

¾ cup sugar
2 tbsp. flour
¼ tsp. salt
½ cup water

1 cup raisins
3 or 4 tart apples
1 tsp. cinnamon
1 tsp. lemon juice

Blend sugar, flour and salt. Stir in water. Cook until mixture thickens, about 5 min. Add lemon juice and cinnamon. Pare apples and slice thin; add together with raisins to sugar mixture. Line 9" pie plate with pastry. Add filling mixture. Adjust top crust. Bake in hot oven (450°) for 10 min., then at 375° for 35 min.

Mrs. Donald Seiler, Carson City, Mich.

Green Tomato Mincemeat

1 pk. green tomatoes
  ground
½ pk. apples
2 large cups ground suet
  Juice and grated rind of 2
  lemons
4 lbs. sugar
½ lb. citron

2 lbs. raisins
1 pt. boiled cider
1 tbsp. each ground cloves
  and allspice
1 tsp. nutmeg
2 tbsp. salt
1 tbsp. cinnamon

Cover tomatoes with cold water, cook 30 min. Drain. Melt suet in a pan and mix all ingredients and cook in suet until thick. Bring to a full boil and seal in jars. For pies.

Mrs. A. R. Holdeman, submitted
by Mrs. Ora Manny

Fig Pie

2 cups stewed dry figs,
  diced
2 tbsp. lemon juice

⅔ cup sugar
1 tbsp. flour

Mix and pour into unbaked pie shell. Adjust top crust. Bake at 350° for 1 hr.

Mrs. Elias Mininger, Winton, Calif.

Cherry Pie (1)

2 tbsp. cornstarch	¾ cup cherry juice
¾ cup sugar	2 cups drained cherries
¼ tsp. salt	½ tsp. vanilla

Blend all ingredients and boil, stirring constantly until thick and clear. Bake in double crust at 425° for 10 min., then at 350° for 40 min.

Esther Schmidt, Fairview, Okla.

Cherry Pie (2)

Combine and bring to boiling:

¾ cup juice	2 tbsp. corn syrup

Mix 2 tbsp. cornstarch with ¼ cup of juice and add to first mixture, boil until clear. Add ¾ cup sugar, pour cherries (or youngberries) into lined pie shell and pour cooked mixture over top. Dot with butter. Cover with top crust.

Mrs. Harry Wenger, Hesston, Kans.

Mincemeat Pie

1 cup beef, ground	½ tsp. allspice
2 cups apples, sliced	½ tsp. cloves
1 cup raisins	1 cup vinegar or
¾ cup sugar	(½ cup sweet pickles
½ tsp. salt	juice and ½ cup vinegar)

Boil beef, apples, and raisins. Mix with other ingredients. Bake in double pastry at 375° for 30 min.

Mrs. Harvey Yost, Greensburg, Kans.

Raisin Pie

1 cup brown sugar	¼ tsp. salt
2½ tbsp. flour	1 tsp. butter
1 cup cold water	1 tsp. vanilla
1 cup raisins	

Mix ingredients, cook until mixture thickens. Bake in double crusts at 425° until brown.

Mrs. Frank Barkman, Steinbach, Man.

Ritz Cracker Pie

2 cups hot water
1½ cups sugar
2 tsp. cream of tartar

cinnamon
butter
20 Ritz crackers

Combine hot water, sugar and cream of tartar. Bring to boiling. Add crackers and boil for 2 min. Stir and submerge crackers so all will be cooked. Pour into unbaked pie shell, sprinkle with cinnamon and dot with butter. Adjust top crust. Bake at 450° for 10 min., then at 350° for 25 min.

Mrs. Monroe Holdeman, Harrison, Mich.

Tarts

Apple Roll-Ups

2 cups flour
2½ tsp. baking powder
⅔ cup shortening

1 tsp. salt
½ cup milk

Mix pastry lightly. Roll out a little thicker than for pie. Spread with softened butter; sprinkle with ½ cup brown sugar and 1 tsp. cinnamon. Wash, core and dice 6 med. apples and spread over pastry. Roll up as a jelly roll and cut into 8 slices. Set on end in a greased baking dish.

Syrup

1½ cups brown sugar
¼ tsp. nutmeg

1½ cups water

Combine and boil for a few min. Pour syrup over roll-ups and bake at 375° for 35 min. Serve hot or cold with milk.

Donella Holdeman, Hesston, Kans.

Raisin Tarts

Line muffin tins with pie pastry. Make a filling of 1 egg, beaten.

1 cup brown sugar
1 cup raisins
2 tbsp. milk

1 tbsp. butter
½ cup coconut

Cream butter and brown sugar; add remaining ingredients and spoon into unbaked pastry. Bake in 450° oven, 15 min.

Mrs. Daniel Martin, Mifflinburg, Pa.

Tarts

2 eggs
1 cup sugar
2 tbsp. honey

1 tsp. vanilla
butter

Mix all ingredients except butter. Prepare favorite pastry recipe, line cup cake pans with pastry. Pour tart mixture into individual cups and place small dab of butter on each tart. Bake at 375° for 25 min.

Mrs. Amandus Seiler, Carson City, Mich.

Crumbly Crust Pies

Graham Cracker Cream Pie

2 cups milk
2 tbsp. cornstarch
½ cup sugar

3 egg yolks, beaten
1 tsp. vanilla

Scald milk, add cornstarch, sugar, egg yolks and vanilla. Boil until thickened. Pour filling into baked crumb crust. Spread with meringue and sprinkle remaining crumbs over top and brown lightly.

Crust

20 graham crackers
½ cup sugar

½ cup butter

Roll graham crackers with rolling pin. Add sugar and butter. Mix until crumbly. Press into pie pan, reserving ½ cup of crumb mixture for top of pie. Bake at 400° for 8 min. Makes 1 large crust.

Mrs. Monroe Holdeman, Harrison, Mich.

Fruit Festival Pie

2 envelopes Knox
   Unflavored Gelatine
½ cup sugar
⅛ tsp. salt
1½ cups water
1 tsp. almond flavoring
   (optional)

1-6 oz. can frozen, plain or
   pink lemonade or limeade
   concentrate
1 cup cold evaporated milk
1-9" corn flake crumb pie
   crust

Thoroughly mix gelatine, sugar and salt in saucepan. Add water and cook over low heat, stirring constantly until gelatine is dissolved. Remove from heat; stir in undiluted concentrate and flavoring. Chill until consistency of unbeaten egg whites. Chill evaporated milk in ice cube tray until ice crystals form around edge; whip until stiff. Fold into gelatine mixture. Spread lightly into crumb crust. Arrange a ring of fruit on outside edge of filling next to crust. Chill until firm.

Crumb Crust

Combine 1 cup crumbs, (corn flakes or graham crackers), 2 tbsp. sugar, ⅓ cup melted butter or margarine. Mix well. Press evenly and firmly into 9" pie pan. Chill.

Mrs. Adrian Goossen, Rich Hill, Mo.

No Crust Pies

Easy Apple Pie

¾ cup sugar 1 tsp. baking powder
½ cup flour ¼ tsp. salt

Mix ingredients together.

2 small eggs, well beaten 1 cup chopped apples
½ cup nuts

Add to first mixture. Place in well greased 9" pie pan. Bake ½ hr at 350°. Serve with whipped cream or ice cream.

Mrs. Ivan Jantz, Montezuma, Kans.

Mystery Pie

20 soda crackers, crushed 1 tsp. vanilla
 fine 1 tsp. baking powder
1 cup chopped pecans 3 egg whites, stiffly beaten
1 cup sugar

Mix together and spread in well greased pie pan. Bake at 350° about 30 min. Cool thoroughly. Spread with whipped cream.

Mrs. LeRoy Wedel, Goltry, Okla.

English Apple Pie

1 egg	1/4 tsp. salt
3/4 cup sugar	1/2 tsp. vanilla
1/2 cup flour	1/2 cup chopped nuts
1 tsp. baking powder	1 cup peeled, chopped apple

Beat egg well, add sugar and vanilla. Sift dry ingredients and add to egg-sugar mixture. Add apple and nut meats. Spread in well buttered pie plate. Bake at 350° for 25 to 30 min. Serve with sauce; whipped cream or ice cream. (Quick and easy to make. Pie forms its own crunchy crust).

Mrs. Willis Koehn, Almena, Wisc.

Crustless Custard Pie

4 eggs	1 tsp. vanilla
1/2 cup sugar	Nutmeg
2 cups milk	4 level tbsp. flour

Beat eggs with sugar until light and fluffy; add flour, milk and vanilla. Pour into lightly greased pie pan; sprinkle with nutmeg. Bake one hour at 350 degrees, or until knife inserted in center comes out clean. During the baking, the flour settles to the bottom and forms a very light crust, which enables this to be cut and served as pie.

No Crust Pie

3 eggs	1/2 cup honey
1/2 tsp. ginger	1/2 tsp. salt
1/2 tsp. cinnamon	1 3/4 cups pumpkin
1/2 tsp. nutmeg	1 cup evaporated milk

Beat eggs slightly. Add honey, spices, salt and pumpkin. Add undiluted evaporated milk. Butter a deep 9 inch pie pan. Bake in slow oven (325 degrees) one hr. or until knife blade comes out clean. Cool thoroughly before cutting. Serve in pie-shaped wedges topped with honey sweetened whipped cream.

PICKLES AND RELISHES

Pickles

Aristocratic Pickles

1 gallon sliced cucumbers

Soak in salt brine (strong enough to float an egg.) for 7 days, stir daily. Drain and rinse well. Boil in water with 1 tbsp. alum for 10 min. Drain and boil in water with 2 tbsps, ground mustard 10 min. Drain and rinse well. Mix the following and add pickles.

1 qt. vinegar   3 tbsp. celery seed
3 lbs. sugar

Boil until transparent. Pack in jars and seal.

Elaine Holdeman, Hesston, Kans.

Bread and Butter Pickles (1)

1 tsp. turmeric powder   Mixed spices, ¼ tsp. for
1 cup vinegar   each qt.
1¼ cups sugar   1 cup water

Slice cucumbers and soak in mild salt water overnight. The following morning drain pickles and pack into jars. Mix solution and pour while cold over pickles. Add sliced onion if desired. Place in hot water bath. Bring to a boil and turn off heat. Sterilize for 15 min.

Mrs. John M. Dyck, Hesston, Kans.

Bread and Butter Pickles (2)

Cut cucumbers into thin slices. For 1 qt. cucumbers add 6 small onions, peeled and sliced. Sprinkle with salt and let stand 1 hr. Drain and add the following:

1 cup vinegar   ½ tsp. cinnamon
1½ cups sugar   2 sweet peppers, chopped
1 tsp. celery seed   1 tsp. turmeric powder

Boil 20 min. Pack in jars and seal.

Mrs. Martha Barkman, Ewart, Man.

Chunk Pickles

Brine: 1 pt. salt   1 gal. boiling water

Wash 5 lbs. cucumbers, cover with brine, let stand 1 week. Drain; soak in clear water for 3 days changing water each day. On the 4th day cut pickles into chunks, cover with 1 oz. alum to 5 pts. water. Simmer 2 hrs. Dip into weak vinegar solution and bring to boiling. Pack into jars; cover with boiling syrup and seal.

8 cups sugar   1 stick cinnamon
1 qt. vinegar   1 tsp. celery seed
Bring to boiling.

Mrs. Rex. Schmidt, Hydro, Okla.

Dill Pickles

Pack cucumbers in jars, add a bunch of dill, horse radish leaves, and 2 or 3 cloves of garlic in each jar. Mix a brine of 1 gal. cold water, 1½ cups vinegar, 1 cup salt; fill jars and seal. Place jars in canner and pour cold water over them. Heat very slowly, do not boil. Leave jars in water bath from 3 to 4 hrs. (until cucumbers turn from green to pale color). If water gets too hot, turn off heat, let cucumbers stand in hot water for remaining period of time. Remove from hot water and let cool. Place in cold water. (Best results for sealing when cooled faster).

Eva Koehn, Galva, Kans.

Half and Half Pickles

Select med. sized pickles. Mix ¾ cup pickling salt to 1 gal. of water. Pour over pickles and add a bunch of dill. Let stand 4 days and drain. Split pickles and wash. Mix hot water with 1 tsp. alum. Pour over pickles and let stand 1 to 2 hrs. drain. Mix the following solution.

2 cups sugar   1 tsp. whole cloves
2 cups vinegar   1 tsp. allspice
2 cups water

Bring to a boil. Pack pickles in jars and pour hot mixture over pickles and seal.

Mrs. Marvin O. Koehn, Montezuma, Kans.

Canadian Dills

Prepare small cucumbers, wash and pack in jars; add dill, garlic, cherry and horse radish leaves. Combine 6 cups water, 2 cups vinegar, ½ cup salt, ½ cup sugar. Pour boiling hot over pickles and seal.

Mrs. Adam J. Schmidt, Montezuma, Kans.

Cucumber Dill Pickles

12 cups water
1 cup salt
1 tsp. dry mustard seed

4 cups vinegar
1 cup sugar

Mix all ingredients, bring to boiling point. Fill jars with cucumbers, bunch of dill and clove of garlic. Pour hot solution over pickles and seal. Place jars with pickles in hot water and let stand until cool to seal jars.

Mrs. Henry B. Koehn, Montezuma, Kans.

Heinz Pickles

Wash 1 peck small cucumbers and split (to prevent shriveling). Place in a large crock jar and cover with salt water (2 cups salt to 1 gal. water). Let stand one week. Drain and cover with boiling alum water (1 tbsp. alum to 1 gal boiling water). Let stand 24 hrs. Drain. Cover with clear boiling water; let stand another 24 hrs. Drain and cover with the following mixture.

2½ qts. vinegar
1 stick cinnamon
1 tsp. whole cloves

6 cups sugar
1 tbsp. celery seed

Let boil and pour over pickles, let stand three days. Drain solution, add 1 cup sugar, reheat and pour onto pickles, let stand three days. Repeat until three cups sugar have been added. Pack pickles into jars, heat vinegar solution, pour over pickles and seal. (Will also keep without sealing).

Mrs. Monroe Holdeman, Harrison, Mich.

Icicle Pickles

Cut peeled cucumbers in quarters lengthwise. Soak cucumbers and peeled onions in ice water for 2 hrs. (1 small onion per qt.) Remove and pack in jars that have a bunch of dill in bottom and cut up onion on top. Cover with solution that has been heated to boiling point, seal. Hot water bath just until cucumbers change color.

Brine per qt.:

1 cup sugar	½ cup vinegar
1 cup hot water	1 tbsp. salt

Mrs. Curt Ensz, Cimarron, Kans.

Lime Sweet Pickles

7 lbs. cucumbers, dill size, cut into ¼ in. thick slices
1 gal. cold water   1 cup hydrated lime

Mix water and lime, pour over cucumbers and let sit for 24 hrs. stirring several times a day. Drain and wash 3 or 4 times with cold water. Cover with ice water for 3 hrs. Drain. Mix the following pickling solution.

2 qts. vinegar	1½ tbsp. salt
9 cups sugar	2 tsp. pickling spices
2 tsp. celery seed	

Bring to boiling. Pour while hot over cucumbers, let stand over night. The following morning simmer pickles until juice is clear. Pack in jars and seal.

Myrtle Giesbrecht, Winton, Calif.

Peach Pickles

1 qt. vinegar	8 cups sugar
1 tsp. whole allspice	½ tsp. whole cloves
1 large stick cinnamon, broken	7 lbs. whole peaches, peeled

Bring sugar, vinegar and spices to a boil in large kettle with a tight cover. During cooking period carefully lift peaches from bottom of kettle allowing top peaches to drop into hot syrup. Cook until peaches are heated through, but not soft. Pack peaches loosely into sterilized jars, filling ⅔ full. Pour boiling syrup over peaches and seal.

Mrs. Sam J. Koehn, Fairview, Okla.

Pickles

12 cups water	1 tbsp. mixed spices or
4 cups vinegar	mustard seed
1 cup salt	1 cup sugar

Mix ingredients and bring to a boil. Fill jars with small cucumbers. Add bunch of dill, garlic and a small piece of red pepper over top of cucumbers. Pour boiling hot solution over pickles. Heat in water bath just enough to seal. (Do not boil as boiling makes them soft.)

Mrs. Marlyn Ensz, Rich Hill, Mo.

Quick Spiced Peaches

1 (no. 2½) can cling	2-3" sticks cinnamon
peach halves	½ tsp. whole cloves
¾ cup sugar	½ tsp. whole allspice
½ cup vinegar	

Drain peaches. To syrup from peaches, add sugar, vinegar and spices. Boil 5 min. Add peaches and simmer 5 min more. Allow fruit to remain in pickling syrup several hrs. (If peaches are to stand overnight, remove spices, as they will darken the fruit. One fourth water may be used if vinegar is strong.

Mrs. Pete D. Schmidt, Copeland, Kans.

Sliced Cucumber Pickles

2 qts. sliced cucumbers	2 tsp. salt

Let stand 3 hrs., then drain. Mix the following ingredients:

2 tsp. mixed pickling spices	2 cups sugar
2 cups vinegar	cucumbers

Boil for 3 min. Put in jars and seal.

Clara Schneider, Moundridge, Kans.

Sweet Dill Pickles

Wash medium sized cucumbers and pack in sterilized jars. Bring the following solution to a boil and pour over cucumbers. Seal.

2 cups water	½ cup sugar
½ cup vinegar	1 tbsp. salt
mixed spices, if desired	large stalk of dill for each jar

Mrs. Eli Johnson, Rich Hill, Mo.

Sour Sweet Slices

10 med. sized cucumbers   2 tbsp. mixed pickling
    boiling water   spices
8 cups sugar   5 tsp. pickling salt
                             4 cups vinegar

Cover whole cucumbers with boiling water,let stand. Repeat this procedure every day for 3 days. On fourth day, slice cucumbers. Combine sugar, spices, salt and vinegar, bring to a boil, pour over sliced pickles. Let stand 2 days. Drain liquid; bring to a boil, pack pickles in jars. Pour hot solution over pickles and seal. Makes 6 half pts.

Mrs. Eugene Unruh, Copeland, Kans.
Mrs. Frank Haynes, Middleton, Mich.

Sweet Chunk Pickles

4 qts. cucumbers   8 cups sugar
4 cups vinegar   2 tbsp. mixed pickling spices

Wash cucumbers, cut in slices or chunks, cover with brine prepared by dissolving 1 cup salt in 1 gal. water. Let stand 24 hrs. Prepare syrup by boiling together vinegar, 2 cups sugar and spices tied in cloth for 5 min. Pour hot syrup over pickles. On three succesive days drain off syrup add 2 cups sugar and reheat to boiling and pour over pickles; let stand 24 hrs. On the 4th day drain syrup, heat to boiling. Pack cucumbers into hot jars and pour hot syrup over cucumbers and seal.

Mrs. Paul Koehn, Halstead, Kans.

Watermelon Pickles (1)

Cut red part of melon into cubes or chunks, salt to taste. Let sit 2 hrs. Drain. Simmer in 2 cups sugar, 3 cups white vinegar, 2 tbsp. mixed pickling spices, tied in cloth, for 5 min. or until it reaches boiling. Pack into sterilized jars, and seal.

Mrs. Claude Unruh, Durham, Kans.

Watermelon Pickles (2)

Pare the green off one large melon. Cut into small shapes about an inch square; cook until tender in 1 gal. of water, 1 tbsp. salt, 1 tsp. alum. Drain and place in stone jar or crock. To 1 qt. vinegar add 3 qts. sugar, 1 stick cinnamon, 1 tsp. whole cloves. Heat mixture and boil 3 min., pour over pickles. Repeat process for 9 successive days, drain syrup, bring to boiling and pour over pickles each day. On last day bring all to boiling; pack into jars and seal.

Mrs. Franklin Nichols, Greensburg, Kans.

Piccalilli, Relishes and Catsup

Catsup

30 lbs. tomatoes (put through a sieve)	2 tsp. cinnamon
1 cup salt	3 tsp. paprika
3½ cups vinegar	1 tsp. pepper
8 cups sugar	4 onions, ground fine

Add salt, sugar and vinegar near end of cooking time so as not to darken catsup. Boil tomato juice and onions rapidly in open kettle to thicken quickly. (Several hrs.) Stir frequently when it begins to thicken to avoid scorching. Pour into hot jars. Seal. Makes about 10 pts.

Mrs. Robert Holdeman, Dalton, Ohio

Garden Relish
(for hot dogs)

4 large onions	10 green peppers
1 head cabbage	10 red peppers (or carrots for color)
20 green tomatoes	12 large cucumbers

Grind all vegetables, add ½ cup salt and let stand overnight. Rinse with cold water and drain. Combine the following solution.

6 cups sugar
4 cups vinegar
1 tbsp. celery seed
1½ tsp. turmeric
2 tbsp. mustard seed

Heat to boiling. Add vegetables and simmer 3 min. Pack in jars and seal.   Mrs. Andy Powell, Hesston, Kans.

Piccalilli (1)

1 qt. chopped green tomatoes
2 large mild onions, chopped
2 med. sweet red peppers, chopped
2 cups brown sugar firmly packed
2 med. green peppers, chopped
½ cup salt
3 cups vinegar
1 small head cabbage
2 tbsp. mixed pickle spices

Combine the vegetables; mix with salt. Let stand overnight, rinse vegetables. Drain and press in a cloth to remove all liquid possible. Combine vinegar and sugar. Tie spices loosely in a thin cloth. Add to vinegar mixture, bring to a boil. Add vegetables and simmer about 30 min. Remove spices. Pack into hot sterilized jars. Seal.

Mrs. Llewellyn J. Schmidt, Newton, Kans.

Piccalilli (2)

6 green peppers
½ gal. green tomatoes
6 red peppers
1½ pt. vinegar
7 small onions
1½ tsp. salt
1 head cabbage
2 cups sugar

Grind all ingredients, boil until juice becomes slightly thickened. Pack into jars and seal.

Mrs. Jacob N. Yost, Durham, Kans.

Tomato Relish

5 cups ripe tomatoes, peeled
4 cups coarsely chopped onions
3 cups chopped celery
2 cups sugar
2 green peppers, chopped
1 tsp. salt
1½ cups vinegar

Combine all ingredients and boil slowly for 2 hrs. pack into sterilized jars and seal.

Mrs. Waldon Barkman, Steinbach, Man.

Grandmother Mininger's Piccalilli

3 qts. corn
2 qts. cabbage
1 pt. mangos
1½ qts. lima beans

3 qts. small cucumber or larger cucumbers, cut into chunks
1 qt. string beans

Cook corn, lima beans and string beans until done, add remaining ingredients and cook ten min. more.

Add:

2 cups sugar
1 pt. water

3 tbsp. salt
3 tbsp. celery seed
1½ pts. vinegar

Simmer until well flavored

Edna Mininger, Pettisville, Ohio

Green Tomato Relish

1 peck green tomatoes   ¾ cup salt

Grind and pour boiling water and salt over tomatoes and let stand 1 hour. Drain.

6 green peppers
6 red peppers
15 large onions
2 tbsp. mustard seed

3 tbsp. celery seed
2 pt. vinegar
6 cups sugar

Grind all ingredients, add spices, vinegar, and sugar. Cook until done (about 30 min.) Pack in jars and seal.

Mrs. Herby Wenger, Newton, Kans.

Hot Dog Relish

5 cups ground cucumbers
3 cups ground onions
3 cups chopped celery
2 sweet red or green ground peppers
1 qt. white vinegar

¾ cup salt
1½ qts. water
3 cups sugar
2 tsp. mustard seed
2 tbsp. celery seed

Combine cucumbers, onions, celery, and peppers. Add salt and water. Let stand overnight and drain. Heat vinegar and sugar, mustard and celery seed. Heat to boiling. Cook slowly 10 minutes. Seal in hot sterilized jars. It makes five pints.

Mrs. Henry Schneider, Hesston, Kans.

Indian Relish

2 lbs. sugar
3 qts. green tomatoes
1 qt. onions
1 pt. vinegar
6 peppers

3 tbsp. mustard seed
2 tbsp. celery seed
1 tbsp. turmeric powder
½ cup salt

Wash tomatoes, onions, and peppers, cut into quarters; measure. Chop through coarse grinder; strain. Combine in large kettle and bring to boiling. Pack in pt. jars and seal. Makes 7 pts.

Emma Helms, Ithaca, Mich.
Mrs. Emerson Litwiller, Middleton, Mich.

Sweet Pepper Jelly

6 large mangoes, red or
    green
1 cup vinegar

1½ cups sugar
salt to taste

Grind the peppers through coarse food chopper, add salt. Let stand 3 hrs., then rinse in cold water and let drain 1 hr. Add remaining ingredients and cook until thick (about 15 min.) Pack in jars or bottles and seal. Makes about 1 pt. (Serve on meat or use in mayonnaise dressing.)

Mrs. Monroe Holdeman, Harrison, Mich.

Uncooked Tomato Relish

1 pk. ripe tomatoes
1 pt. chopped celery
1 pt. chopped onions
3 cups sugar
2 tsp. cinnamon
2 tsp. pepper

1 cup salt
½ cup celery seed
3 red peppers, chopped
3 pts. vinegar
2 tsp. cloves
2 tsp. ground mace

Wash tomatoes and chop fine. (Discard celery leaves; remove seeds from peppers). Drain chopped tomatoes of all juice and put them in a stone crock. Add remaining ingredients to tomatoes and mix thoroughly. Cover and place in a cool dry place.

Dill Pickles

Brine—
  18 cups water
  ⅔ cup salt
  3 or 4 cloves of garlic

  2 cups vinegar
  1 or 2 bay leaves
  alum the size of a walnut
  dill

Pack cucumbers in jars. Heat brine and pour over cucumbers. Seal.

Cucumber Relish

  1 gal. cucumbers, sliced
  8 small onions, sliced

  2 red and green sweet peppers, chopped

Place chipped ice over vegetables and let stand 4 hrs. and drain.

Heat to boiling point:
  ½ cup salt
  5 cups sugar
  5 cups vinegar

  2 tbsp. mustard seed
  1 tsp. celery seed

Strain out spices. Add the drained vegetables. Heat to boiling, pack in jars and seal.

Sweet Cucumber Pickles (Superb)

  16 lbs. cucumbers (½ bu.)
  10 lbs. sugar
      salt water to float an egg
  1 gal . vinegar

  1 box pickle spice (1¼ oz. size)
  ½ box alum (2¼ oz . size)

Soak whole cucumbers in brine water and cover. Let stand for 14 days. Remove from water and slice, then soak overnight in alum water. Rinse cucumbers and cover with vinegar and let set for 6 hrs. Drain off vinegar (throw away). Place cucumbers, sugar, and spices in a stone jar by layers. Cover and let set; in a few days syrup will have formed to cover cucumbers. Keeps indefinitely. May be put in pt. jars later if desired.

SALADS AND DRESSINGS

Fruit Salads

Ambrosia Salad

1 can mandarin oranges	½ pkg. miniature
1 can crushed pineapple	marshmallows
1 jar maraschino cherries	½ cup coconut
	1 carton sour cream

Mix fruit and coconut together. For dressing mix marshmallows and sour cream together; pour over fruit. Mix lightly and serve.

Virginia Dirks, Livingston, Calif.

Apple Salad

8 apples (Golden delicious	½ cup raisins
or Grimes golden	½ cup chopped celery
preferred)	½ cup chopped head lettuce
1 banana	½ cup nuts
1 orange	

Dice apples. Add other ingredients. Make a cooked dressing as follows:

1 cup water	¼ tsp. salt
1 tsp. lemon juice	¾ cup sugar
1 tbsp. cornstarch	

Cook together until thickened. Add ¼ cup cream, 1 tsp. vanilla. Pour over the apples.

Mrs. Heber Good, Dalton, Ohio

Banana Salad

Boil together until thickened:

2 eggs	½ cup pineapple or orange
2 tbsp. flour or cornstarch	and lemon juice

Refrigerate until ready to use. Then add:

1 cup whipped cream	1 cup marshmallows
2 tbsp. sugar	½ cup crushed pineapple
¼ cup nuts	2 bananas

Mrs. Orval Mastre, Galva, Kans.
Mrs. Raymond Withers, Copeland, Kans.
Mrs. Manford Nichols, Sublette, Kans.

Bride's Salad

Combine:

2 egg yolks   ½ cup milk

Cook slowly until spoon films over. Cool. Add juice of ½ lemon. Fold in 1 cup cream, whipped.

Drain and combine:

1 can Royal Anne cherries and 1 can pineapple chunks. Add 2 cups miniature marshmallows. Top with whipped cream mixture. Stir gently. Cover, and let set in refrigerator overnight.

Nelda Litwiller, Ithaca, Mich.

Coconut Fruit Bowl Salad

2½ cups pineapple tidbits, drained

⅓ cup mandarin oranges drained

1 cup Thompson seedless grapes

1 cup miniature marshmallows

2 cups dairy sour cream

¼ tsp. salt

⅓ cup flaked coconut

Combine fruits, marshmallows and coconut, mix well. Chill overnight. Serves 8.

Mrs. Herman P. Koehn, Chichasha, Okla.

Cottage Cheese Salad

1 qt. cottage cheese

1 can pineapple, drained

1 cup cream, whipped

1 lb. marshmallows (cut)

½ cup sugar

2 tbsp. mayonnaise

½ tsp. salt

Mix all together. Serve on shredded lettuce. Can be made the day before serving.

Fruit Salad

2 bananas, sliced

1 can fruit cocktail

2-3 oranges, cut up

2 apples, sliced

¾ cup coconut

1 cup miniature marshmallows

Place in bowl and top with whipped cream

Diane Holdeman, Hesston, Kans.

Frozen Fruit Salad

1 can pineapple tidbits
1 large jar maraschino
  cherries, cut into fourths

1 small pkg. miniature
  marshmallows

Mix the above ingredients and place in refrigerator for 2 hrs.
Add:

3 or 4 bananas, sliced

1 cup chopped nuts

For dressing use:

3 tbsp. sugar
1 well beaten, egg

1 tbsp. flour
Juice from pineapple and
  cherries

Cook until thick, stirring constantly. Add 1 tbsp. lemon juice,
cool. Add dressing to the fruit salad. Fold in 1 cup cream,
whipped. Freeze.

Mrs. Gary Unruh

Green Grape Salad

1 can crushed pineapple
2 lbs. seedless white grapes
1 cup nuts
1 small pkg. marshmallows

2 tbsp. butter
2 tbsp. flour
1½ cups milk

Melt butter, add flour and milk. When cooked add marshmallows. Whip when cooled and pour over grapes, nuts, and
drained pineapple. Cool.

Priscilla Schmidt, Neodesha, Kans.

Hawaiian Marshmallow Salad

1 cup heavy cream
¼ cup sugar
16 marshmallows, cut in ¼

1 cup cooked rice, cold
1 cup crushed pineapple,
  drained
⅓ cup chopped nuts

Whip cream and sugar until stiff. Fold in remaining ingredients; chill. Serves six.

Mrs. Vernon Peters, McDavid, Fla.

Picnic Salad

20 marshmallows (large) cut up with scissors dipped in flour
1/4 lb. process cheese, diced   1 No. 2 can pineapple
                                     chunks

Combine and cook:
  3 tbsp. sugar   2 tbsp. flour
  1 egg   1/8 tsp. salt

Juice drained from can of pineapple (if this is too thick add
water or lemon juice). This will be like a pudding. Pour over
marshmallow, cheese, and pineapple and stir while it is still hot.
Place in refrigerator to set.

Mrs. Fred P. Koehn, Montezuma, Kans.
Mrs. Jerry Koehn, Fairview, Okla.
Mrs. Walter Yost

Pineapple Salad

1 large can of pineapple   10 marshmallows, cut in
  chunks   quarters
1 can mandarin oranges   1 cup broken nut meats
1 cup seedless grapes

Drain pineapples, pour juice in double boiler and add:
  2 eggs, beaten   2 tbsp. flour
  1/2 cup sugar   1/2 tsp. salt

Cook until thick. Cool; add 1 cup of cream, whipped, fruit, nuts
and marshmallows. Let set 6 hrs. or overnight.

Mrs. Wm. Seiler, Carson City, Mich.

Salad

1 large can pineapple   1 cup nuts
2 oranges   10 marshmallows

Drain pineapples, pour juice into double boiler and add:
  2 eggs, beaten   2 tbsp. flour
  1/2 cup sugar   1/4 tsp. salt

Cook until thick. Cool; add 1 cup whipped cream, fruit, marshmallows and nuts. May be frozen.

Mrs. Vernon Giesbrecht, Cimarron, Kans.

Twenty-four Hour Salad

2 cups pineapple tid-bits	1 cup whipping cream
2 cups Royal Ann cherries	3 egg yolks
or fruit cocktail (drained)	2 tbsp. sugar
2 oranges cut in pieces	2 tbsp. vinegar
2 cups miniature	2 tbsp. pineapple juice
marshmallows	1 tbsp. butter
	⅛ tsp. salt

In top of double boiler, beat egg yolks slightly. Add sugar, salt, vinegar, butter, and pineapple juice. Cook until thick, cool. Fold in whipped cream, fruits and marshmallows. Decorate with fresh fruit. Cover and chill for 24 hours.

Verna Koehn, Winton, Calif.
Mrs. Edward A. Penner, Livingston, Calif.

Vegetable Salads

Bean Salad

1 can yellow wax beans	1 can kidney beans
1 can green beans	½ green pepper
½ med. onion	

Drain all beans and chop pepper and onion. Pour dressing over vegetables and let stand in refrigerator for 24 hrs.

Dressing

½ cup sugar	½ cup salad oil
½ cup white vinegar	1 tsp. salt
	½ tsp. pepper

Cover and stir occasionally. Drain liquid before serving.

Mrs. D. G. Boeckner, Moundridge, Kans.

Cheese Salad

To chopped head lettuce add diced cheese, marshmallows and pineapple. Combine pineapple juice, 2 tsp. sugar, 1 beaten egg, ½ tsp. salt and 2 tbsp. flour. Cook until thickened. Cool; pour over lettuce mixture; mix lightly.

Nora Friesen, Winton, Calif.

Cucumber Salad

1 box lime jello
¾ cup boiling water

2 tbsp. lemon juice

Dissolve jello in boiling water. Add lemon juice. Let congeal. Add:

1 cup mayonnaise
1 grated cucumber

1 small carton cottage
cheese
1 small onion, grated

Mix. Sprinkle with salt over top.

Green Top Salad

2 pkgs. orange jello
1 pkg. miniature
marshmallows
½ pt. whipping cream

2 cans crushed pineapple
1 pkg. lime jello
½ cup mayonnaise
2 pkg. cream cheese

Dissolve orange Jello in 3 cups boiling water. Add marshmallows and stir until melted. Cool. Add pineapple, put into refrigerator to thicken. Cream mayonnaise and cheese, mix with cream which has been whipped and combine with jello. Pour into mold and refrigerate until firm. Dissolve lime jello in 2 cups boiling water. Cool until thick and pour over first mixture. Chill until firm. Cut into squares and serve on lettuce.

Mrs. Andrew Koehn, Goltry, Okla.

Macaroni Salad

1 cup cooked, cold macaroni
2 hard boiled eggs, chopped
½ cup olives

1 cup chopped celery
½ cup chopped green peppers
1 cup diced cheese

Mix all ingredients. Pour ½ cup salad dressing over mixture and blend well.

Mrs. Sam Jantz, Walnut Hill, Fla.

Pea Salad

1 can peas
1 bunch green onions
⅛ tsp. paprika

Cheddar cheese
mayonaise
½ jar pimento

Drain peas, chop onions, adding some of the green tops. Add to peas. Cover and chill. When ready to serve add diced pimento and cheese and toss lightly with mayonnaise. Sprinkle with paprika.

Mrs. Olin Schmidt, DeRidder, La.

Potato Salad

7 med. sized, cooked potatoes	½ cup cream
3 hard boiled eggs	1 tbsp. vinegar
1 med. sized onion	⅓ cup salad dressing
1 med. sized dill pickle	1½ tsp. prepared mustard
	salt and pepper to taste

Slice potatoes thin; add diced eggs, chopped pickles and onions. Mix well. Mix cream, vinegar, salad dressing, mustard, salt and pepper; stir into potato mixture.

Mrs. Perry Johnson, Galva, Kans.

Protein Salad Bowl
(A meal in itself with crackers)

1 med. head lettuce	6 dill pickles, quartered
4 eggs—hard boiled	½ cup walnuts or other nuts
4 tomatoes—peeled	1 small onion cut in rings
4 thick slices of cheese (American, Swiss, or Blue)	2 6½-oz. cans tuna; other meats may be substituted such as summer sausage, or ham

Tear lettuce into large chunks and place in salad bowl. Quarter or dice eggs and tomatoes. Cut cheese into bite size chunks. Add pickles, walnuts, onion rings and top with tuna or other meat. Toss with favorite dressing or serve plain. Serve chilled with assorted crackers. Serves four.

Mrs. Adam J. Schmidt, Montezuma, Kans.

Quick Tossed Carrot Salad

Peel and core 1½ red or yellow delicious apples, shred on small shredder), add ½ cup crushed pineapple immediately and stir, to keep apples from turning dark. Peel and shred 3 large carrots, add to apples with a dash each of pepper and salt, 3 tbsp. sugar, 2 tbsp. sweet cream, and ½ cup pecans (chopped). Mix well and serve. May be refrigerated for 30 min.

Mrs. Bert Schmidt, Goltry, Okla.

Tossed Fresh Vegetable Salad

lettuce	radishes (small red)
celery	Green peppers
tomatoes	carrots
cucumbers	onion (fresh or otherwise) small amount

Cut, dice or slice vegetables into a bowl. Season with a dash of salt. Add "Wish-Bone Dressing" and toss gently just before serving.

Gelatin Salads

Beauty Salad

(Half recipe makes nice size salad)

2 pkg. lemon jello	1 cup cream, whipped
1 No. 2 can crushed pineapples	2 pkg. raspberry or cherry jello
1 small pkg. cream cheese	½ cup salad dressing
20 marshmallows, cut up	

Dissolve lemon jello as directed. Let cool until syrupy, but not set. Combine pineapple, cream cheese, marshmallows, whipped cream and salad dressing and add to cooled jello. Pour into long dish and place in refrigerator until set. Dissolve raspberry jello according to directions on pkg., chill until syrupy. Pour carefully over lemon mixture. Chill until set.

Mrs. Obed Johnson, Halstead, Kans.

Bing Cherry Salad (1)

1 pt. canned Bing cherries	1 pkg. black cherry or raspberry jello
1 pt. crushed pineapple	1 cup Pepsi

Mix jello as directed on pkg. add juice of cherries and pineapple in place of water. Heat juices to boiling. When jello is dissolved, add Pepsi; stir well. Add pineapple and cherries. Let set until firm.

Mrs. Harvey Yost, Greensburg, Kans.

Bing Cherry Salad (2)

Combine 1 pkg. cherry jello, 1 cup boiling water and 1 pkg. cream cheese. Beat until dissolved. Add 1 cup sweet cherry juice. Let set until partially jelled; fold in 1 cup pitted, sweet cherries and ½ cup nuts.

Mrs. Don Nightengale

Cherry Coke Salad

1-No. 303 can Bing Cherries
1-4 oz. can crushed pine-
    apple
1-6 oz. pkg. cherry gelatin
2-6½ oz. bottles Cocoa
    Cola

Drain juice from fruit; add water if necessary to make 2 cups. Heat juice to boiling, add gelatin, stir until dissolved. Cool, add cola and fruit. Pour into 1½ qt. mold. Chill until set. Serve with dressing made of the following:

Dressing

1 egg, beaten
1 tbsp. flour
1 cup pineapple juice
½ cup sugar

Cook until thick. Cool till completely cold. Whip about 1 cup cream and add to dressing.

Mrs. Everett Wedel, Conway, Kans.

Cherry Grape Salad

1 pkg. unflavored gelatin
¼ cup maraschino cherry
    juice
1 small can crushed pine-
    apple
¼ cup sugar
2 tbsp. lemon juice
1 small jar maraschino
    cherries, diced
1 cup seeded, dark grape
    halves
1 cup cream, whipped
1 tbsp. mayonnaise
½ cup nutmeats

Soften gelatin in cherry juice. Heat pineapple to boiling and add gelatin. Stir until gelatin dissolves and add ¼ cup water. Stir in sugar and lemon juice. Chill until partially thickened. Fold in cherries and grapes. Cool until nearly set; add mayonnaise to whipped cream, beat until well blended; fold into jello; add nuts. Chill until firm. Serves 8.

Mrs. Marshall Harms, Walnut Hill, Fla.

Cottage Cheese Apricot Salad

1 pkg. lemon gelatin
¾ cup boiling water
¾ cup apricot liquid from 16 oz. can apricot halves
1 cup whipping cream
1½ cups creamed cottage cheese
½ cup chopped nuts
½ cup chopped maraschino cherries

Dissolve gelatin in water. Add apricot juice and chill until partially set. Fold in chopped apricots, cottage cheese, whipped cream, nuts and cherries. Chill until firm.

Mrs. Franklin Nichols, Greensburg, Kans.

Cottage Cheese Salad (1)

1 box lime gelatin
1 box lemon gelatin
1 cup boiling water
1—303 can crushed pineapple
1½ cups cottage cheese
1 cup sweet cream, whipped
⅓ cup sugar

Dissolve gelatin in water and add pineapples. Let chill, add cottage cheese. Chill until it begins to set, then add whipped cream to which ⅓ cup sugar has been added.

Joetta Koehn, Hesston, Kans.

Cottage Cheese Salad (2)

1 box lemon jello
1 cup cottage cheese
½ cup sugar
1½ cups hot water
1 cup drained crushed pineapple
½ pt. cream

Dissolve jello in hot water. Cool until it starts to congeal. Whip jello. Mix rest of ingredients and add to jello. Whip cream and fold into jello. Chill until firm.

Mrs. Levi J. Plank

Cranberry Salad (1)

Grind 1 lb. cranberries. Add 1½ cups sugar. Let stand for several hrs. Add 1 lb. Tokay grapes, 1 small pkg. of marshmallows and 1 cup whipped cream. Chopped nuts may be added if desired.

Mrs. Vada Johnson, Galva, Kans.

Cranberry Salad (2)

Dissolve 1 box raspberry jello and 1¼ cups boiling water. Set aside. Grind 1 cup cranberries add 1 cup sugar and bring to boiling. Cool and add to jello when slightly thickened. Add 1 cup crushed pineapple and 1 cup chopped nuts. Pour into mold or pan and chill.

Mrs. Jacob Hochstetler, Apple Creek, Ohio

Cranberry Salad (3)

2 pkg. cherry jello
3 cups boiling water
½ lb. uncooked cranberries
4 apples, unpeeled
½ cup nutmeats
2 cups sugar
2 cups seeded red or green grapes

Dissolve jello in water and set aside to cool. Chop apples and cranberries with med. blade of food chopper. Add sugar, nuts and grapes. Mix together with jello. Chill in refrigerator until set.

Mrs. Gerald Wenger, Hesston, Kans.

Cranberry Salad (4)

2 cups cranberries
2 cups apples
1 cup pineapple
1 pkg. strawberry jello
½ cup hot water
20 marshmallows, cut in quarters
2½ cups sugar

Grind cranberries, apples, and pineapple. Dissolve jello in hot water, add marshmallows and sugar. Add cranberry mixture, mix well. Place in refrigerator to set.

Mrs. Merle Koehn, Ulysses, Kans.

Cranberry Salad (5)

1 lb. ground cranberries
2 cups sugar
½ lb. marshmallows
2 apples, diced or
1 lb. grape halves
1 cup pineapple cubes
½ cup chopped nuts
1 pt. whipping cream

Add sugar to cranberries; let set for 2 hrs. Add diced marshmallows, apples or grapes, pineapple and nuts. Chill overnight. Fold in whipped cream.

Mrs. Adin Holdeman, Hesston, Kans
Mrs. Eva Koehn, Halstead, Kans.

Blueberry Salad

2 boxes black raspberry
jello
1 pkg. Dream Whip (about
2 cups)

1 No. 2 can blueberries
1 small can crushed
pineapple

Dissolve jello in 2 cups boiling water (use juice from berries and pineapple.) Take out ¾ cup jello and cool until it congeals. Add to this the whipped, dream whip. To the rest of the cooled jello, add blueberries, drain pineapple, and nuts (if desired). Pour into flat glass pan. Let set until it congeals, then cover with whipped mixture. Refrigerate until firm, cut into squares.

Mrs. Arlin Yost, Sublette, Kans.
Mrs. Oliver H. Unruh, Hesston, Kans.

Candied Cranberries

4 cups (1 lb.) firm cran-
berries

3 cups sugar
2 cups hot water

Wash and drain berries. Slit each berry several times with the sharp point of a paring knife. Mix together, sugar and water; bring to a full boil. Cool. Stir in berries and place over heat. Without stirring, let syrup rise slowly just to boiling. Remove from heat, shake gently to mix berries and syrup. Cover and let stand over night. Berries will absorb some of the syrup. (To keep berries whole, shake mixture instead of stirring.) Drain syrup from berries. Bring syrup to a full boil. Reduce to med. heat and cook 20 min. Cool. Add berries and heat mixture; Cook slowly 5 min. Cover and let stand over night. Again heat mixture and cook slowly 5 min. Cover and let stand over night. The following day warm mixture just enough to pour easily. Thoroughly drain syrup from berries. Spread berries on a platter to dry for 48 hrs. at room temperature. Store in tightly covered container and refrigerate until used. (Also may be frozen). The berries may be used for fruit cakes, the syrup may be served on waffles or pancakes.

Mrs. Stanley Geisel, Burns, Kans.

Cranberry Marshmallow Salad

24 marshmallows
¾ cup cream, whipped
½ cup sugar
1 cup ground cranberries

1—9 oz. can crushed pineapple
½ cup nuts

Combine whipped cream and marshmallows; let stand 2 hrs. Add sugar to cranberries, let stand 2 hrs. also. Combine whipped cream and cranberries; add drained pineapple. Place in refrigerator for 6 hrs. or overnight. Add nuts.

Edna Haynes
Mrs. Donald Seiler
Mrs. Ezra Unruh, Copeland, Kans.
Mrs. Ira Redger, Canton, Kans.

Cranberry Salad, Set

3 pkgs. strawberry jello
3 cups boiling water
3 cups ice cubes
1 can crushed pineapple, drained

2 large apples, diced
1 can (whole berry) cranberry sauce
½ cup chopped nuts

Dissolve jello in boiling water and add ice cubes. Stir until partially set and remove any unmelted ice. Add fruits and nuts. Refrigerate until firm.

Viola Harms, Atmore, Ala.

Crystal Salad

1 pkg. lemon gelatin
1¼ cups hot water
½ cup pineapple juice
½ cup cream, whipped
½ cup diced apples

½ cup salad dressing
½ cup pineapple
½ cup celery, diced
8 marshmallows, cut fine

Dissolve gelatin in water; add juice, fruits, celery and marshmallows. Let set until partially firm. Add salad dressing to whipped cream; fold into gelatin mixture. Chill.

Mrs. Maynard Litwiller, Ithaca, Mich.

Cranberry Nut Salad

Combine 2 cups cranberries and ¾ cup water; cook until skins burst. Add 1½ cups sugar; cook 3 min. longer. Combine 1 pkg. lemon jello and ½ cup boiling water; stir until gelatin dissolves. Combine cranberries and gelatin. Chill until partially congealed. Add 1 cup diced celery and ½ cup chopped nuts. Chill. Serve with whipped cream dressing.

Mrs. Richard Litwiller

Frosted Orange and Apricot Salad

3 pkgs. orange jello
3 cups boiling water
3 cups ice cubes.

1 can pineapple chunks, drained
1 can apricots, drained
3 large bananas, sliced

Dissolve jello in boiling water, add ice cubes. Stir until partially set and remove unmelted ice. Add canned fruits and bananas. Place in refrigerator until firm.

Custard

½ cup sugar
3 tbsp. flour

1 egg, beaten
1 cup fruit juice

Mix and cook until thickened. Remove from heat and add 2 tbsp. butter. Cool. Spread over jello and refrigerate until firm. (If desired add 1 cup whipped cream folded into custard. Sprinkle with grated cheese and nuts.)

Mrs. Viola Harms, Atmore, Ala
Roberta Toews

Lime Souffle Salad

1 pkg. vanilla pudding mix
  (or any vanilla pudding
½ cup diced American cheese

1 pkg. lime gelatin
1 cup crushed pineapple
  drained

Prepare pudding according to directions. Let cool. Prepare gelatin using only 1¾ cups water, part of which is juice drained from pineapple. Chill. When gelatin is firm, whip. Continue whipping and add cooled vanilla pudding. Add cheese and pineapple. Chill.

Mrs. Elmer Boehs, Isabella, Okla.

Fruit Cocktail Salad

Heat 1 can fruit cocktail, 1 cup crushed pineapple, and ¼ cup sugar to boiling point. Dissolve 1 pkg. lime jello in hot fruit. Cool until thickened. Crumble 1 pkg. cream cheese into 1 cup thick cream; whip. Mix together with the fruit, add nuts and a few diced maraschino cherries; cool until set.

Mrs. Ben Dyck, Atmore, Ala.

Jello Salad (1)

1 pkg. orange jello
2 apples, diced
1⅔ cup pineapple tidbits
1 pkg. lemon jello
2 bananas, sliced
½ cup whipping cream, whipped with sugar and vanilla added

Prepare jello in separate bowls according to directions using pineapple juice as part of liquid. Pour into flat pans and let set. Cut jello into squares, add fruits and whipped cream, toss lightly until well blended.

Mrs. Jac. H. Dyck, Hesston, Kans.

Jello Salad (2)

2 boxes jello
2 cups chunk pineapple
2 cups hot water
1 small can frozen orange juice
1 can mandarin oranges

Mix all ingredients and chill.

Mrs. Leroy Koehn, Halstead, Kans

Lime Jello Salad

Mix 1 pkg. lime jello, ¼ cup sugar and 1 cup crushed pineapple. Heat until the jello is dissolved, add 1 cup cold water. Let stand until nearly thick. Add 1 cup grated cheese, 1 cup cream, whipped and 1 cup chopped nuts. Serves about 6 to 7.

Mrs. Robert E. Koehn

Fruit Rice Salad

6 cups boiling water
1 tbsp. salt
1 cup rice
½ cup green grapes
2 cups fresh or frozen
raspberries
¼ cup maraschino cherries

1 can mandarin orange
slices
1 can pineapple tidbits
½ cup sugar
1 pkg. orange or lemon jello
¼ cup nuts

Add rice and salt to boiling water, stir occasionally. Boil rapidly for 20 min. Drain. Pour more boiling water over rice to separate kernels, (for fluffy rice, cover with cloth and set over boiling water for a few min.). Dissolve jello in 1 cup scalded juice, drained from fruits; add ¾ cup cold juice. Add sugar, fruit and rice to jello. When partially set, fold in whipped cream. Pour 1 cup raspberries in oblong pan; add rice mixture alternately with 1 cup more of berries. Garnish with fruit.

Martha Hiebert, Middleton, Mich.

Orange Cocktail Salad

2 boxes orange jello
1 small pkg. cream cheese
(Have at room temperature)

2 cups boiling water
2 cups 7-Up or Teem
2 cups fruit cocktail
1 pkg. Dream Whip

Dissolve jello in boiling water; add 7-Up. Cool until it begins to congeal; mash cream cheese with fork and add to jello. Let set. Whip and add drained fruit cocktail. Whip Dream Whip and fold into Jello.

Mrs. Alton Dean Boeckner, Hoisington, Kans.

Orange Pineapple Salad

Combine ½ cup sugar and 2½ cups crushed pineapple. Dissolve 1 pkg. orange jello in 1 cup hot water. Add pineapple mixture. Chill until almost set. Then add 1 cup whipped cream and 1 cup grated cheese. Refrigerate until ready to serve.

Mrs. Norman Koehn, Livingston, Calif.

Orange Gelatin Salad

2 pkg. orange gelatin
2 cups hot water
½ cup pineapple juice
½ cup apricot juice

1 small can crushed pineapple, drained
1 small can apricots, drained
10 chopped marshmallows

Dissolve gelatin in hot water; add juices, fruits and marshmallows. Place in refrigerator to set.

Topping

½ cup apricot juice
½ cup pineapple juice
½ cup sugar
2 tbsp. butter

1 cup heavy cream
⅓ cup grated cheese
⅓ cup nuts
1 egg
2 tbsp. flour

Mix all ingredients, except cheese, cream and nuts. Boil and stir until thickened. Cool thoroughly. Whip cream and add to topping mixture, blending well. Pour over jello mixture; top with grated cheese and chopped nuts. (1 pkg. Dream Whip may replace cream)

Mrs. Paul Becker, Halstead, Kans.
Mrs. Lincoln Koehn, Moundridge, Kans.
Mrs. Ben Dyck, Atmore, Ala.
Mrs. Donald Unruh, Greensburg, Kans.

Peach Party Salad

2 pkgs. Orange Gelatin
2 cups boiling water
1-20 oz. can Pineapple
1½ cup Pineapple Juice
1 tbsp. butter
1 cup miniature marshmallows

1 cup whipped cream
2 cups drained frozen or fresh peaches
½ cup sugar
1 egg
3 tbsp. flour
1 cup shredded Cheddar Cheese

Dissolve gelatin in boiling water. Drain pineapple. Add water or peach juice to make 1½ cups liquid. Add ¾ cup liquid to gelatin. Chill until syrupy. Spread peaches over bottom of 13x9 in. pan. Add gelatin mixture. Chill until firm. Combine sugar, flour, egg, and remaining pineapple juice. Cook over low heat stirring until thick and smooth. Stir in butter. Let mixture cool then chill. Fold pineapple, marshmallows, shredded cheese and whipped cream into mixture. Spread over gelatin. Chill several hours or overnight.

Mrs. Albert Koehn, Harrison, Mich.

Pineapple-Cheese Mold

1-3 oz. pkg. lime-flavored
    gelatin
1 cup boiling water
1 cup evaporated milk
1 cup cottage cheese
¼ cup chopped nuts

2½ cups crushed pineapple,
    well drained
½ cup mayonnaise
    (optional)
¼ cup chopped celery

Dissolve gelatin in water as directed on box. Whip mayonnaise with egg beater. Add cottage cheese, continue beating. Add evaporated milk and remaining ingredients. Pour into mold and chill until firm. Serves 8.

Mrs. John W. Toews, Livingston, Calif.

7-Up or Frosted Salad

2 pkgs. lemon jello
2 cups boiling water
1½ cups cold water or 1 large
    bottle 7-Up
2 large bananas, sliced

20 oz. can crushed pineapple,
    drained
1 cup miniature marsh-
    mallows

Dissolve jello in boiling water, stirring until jello is dissolved. Add cold water or 7-Up. Chill until partly set. Add bananas, marshmallows and pineapple (save pineapple juice for topping). Place in refrigerator to set. Spread with topping.

Topping

1 cup pineapple juice
½ cup sugar
1 egg, beaten
2 tbsp. butter

2 tbsp. flour
1 cup whipping cream
¼ cup grated cheese

Combine all ingredients except cream and cheese, in double boiler. Cook until thickened; chill. Fold in whipped cream. Spread topping over jello and sprinkle with cheese.

Mrs. Jesse Jantz, Fredonia, Kans.
Mrs. Walter Dirks, Montezuma, Kans.
Mrs. John L. Buller, Montezuma, Kans.
Mrs. Irvin Ensz, Ulysses, Kans.

Pineapple Cheese Salad (1)

I pkg. lemon gelatin dissolved in 1 cup hot water. Add 1 cup sugar and 1 tsp. vinegar. Place in refrigerator and let set until partially thickened. Whip jello mixture and add:

1 cup crushed pineapple	1 cup coarsely grated long-
1 cup cream, whipped	horn cheese

Gently combine ingredients and place in refrigerator until completely set.

Mrs. Everett Wedel, Conway, Kans.

Pineapple-Cheese Salad (2)
(Simple large salad)

2 pkgs. lime gelatin	2½ cups hot water
2 pkgs. pineapple gelatin	1 cup whipping cream
½ cup pineapple	2 cups cottage cheese
½ cup sugar	2 pkgs. strawberry gelatin

Prepare lime gelatin and let set. Combine pineapple gelatin, sugar and hot water. Dissolve and add pineapple, let set in separate bowl until partially congealed. Whip cream and fold into pineapple gelatin; add cottage cheese and pour mixture over lime jello. Let set 2 hrs. Dissolve strawberry gelatin according to directions; let cool until partially congealed then pour over first two mixtures. Chill until firm. (For smaller salad use the pineapple mixture only).

Mrs. Justina Koehn, Livingston, Calif.

Pineapple-Cheese Salad (3)

1 cup crushed pineapple	½ cup chopped nuts
¼ cup sugar	1½ cups cottage cheese
1 pkg. lemon jello	½ cup grated American
1 cup water	cheese
	1 cup whipping cream

Heat pineapple and sugar, add jello, stir until dissolved. Remove from heat, add water. Chill until partially thickened; add nuts, cottage cheese, and American cheese. Fold in whipped cream and chill.

Freda Voth, Winton, Calif.
Mrs. John Wiens, Winton, Calif.
Mrs. Lincoln Koehn, Copeland, Kans.

Pineapple-Cheese-Salad (4)

2 pkgs. lemon jello
1 cup boiling water
6 ice cubes
1 No. 2 can crushed pineapple

2 small pkgs, cream cheese
1 cup cream or evaporated milk
1 cup pecans

Add water, then ice cubes to jello. Stir until thickened. Mix cheese and milk with beater. Add cheese mixture to jello. Stir in pineapple and nuts. Pour into two molds.

Mrs. Carl Yost, Greensburg, Kans.
Mrs. Don Nightengale
Delma Friesen, Conway, Kans.

Pineapple Perfection Salad

2 pkg. lemon jello
2 cups boiling water
2 cups miniature marshmallows
1-8 oz. pkg. cream cheese

1 can crushed pineapple
1 can evaporated milk, chilled
½ cup chopped nuts

Dissolve jello in boiling water, add marshmallows and stir until melted. Add cream cheese mash with fork into small chunks. Add pineapple. Set in refrigerator until slightly firm, (about ½ hr.) Fold in beaten, chilled milk (or same amount of whipped cream) and nut meats. Return to refrigerator until firmly set. (This salad may be made in a large loaf pan as it can be cut into squares and served on lettuce).

Mrs. Viola Harms, Atmore, Ala.

Rhubarb Salad

1 pkg. Knox gelatine
2 cups diced rhubarb
2 large bananas, sliced

1 pkg. strawbery jello
3¾ cups water
1 cup sugar

Sprinkle gelatine into ⅓ cup cool water; let dissolve. Bring 2 cups water to boiling, add rhubarb, boil 1 min. Add sugar and boil 1 min. more, being careful not to overcook. Remove from heat, add gelatine and jello; stir until dissolved. Add remaining cold water, place in refrigerator. When partly congealed, add sliced bananas. Return to refrigerator; let set.

Elizabeth Frank, Copeland, Kans.

Ribbon Salad

2 pkg. lime jello
5 cups hot water
4 cups cold water
1 pkg. lemon jello
½ cup miniature marsh-
   mallows
1 cup pineapple juice

1-8 oz. pkg. cream cheese
1-1 lb 4 oz. can crushed
   pineapple
1 cup heavy cream,
   whipped
1 cup mayonnaise
2 pkg. cherry jello

Dissolve lime jello in 2 cups hot water. Add 2 cups cold water.
Pour into 14"x10" pan. Chill until partially set. Dissolve lemon
jello in 1 cup hot water. Add marshmallows and stir to melt.
Remove from heat. Add 1 cup drained pineapple juice and
cream cheese. Beat until well blended and add pineapple. Cool
slightly. Fold in whipped cream and mayonnaise. Chill until
thickened. Pour in layer over lime jello. Chill until almost set.
Dissolve cherry jello in 2 cups hot water. Add 2 cups cold
water. Chill until syrupy. Pour over pineapple layer. Chill
until firm. Makes 24 squares.

Leona Nichols, Livingston, Calif.

Salad Apple Ring

1 pkg. apple jello
⅛ tsp. salt
1 apple, sliced thin

2 tbsp. lemon juice
1-7 oz. bottle cold 7-Up
½ cup seedless grapes, cut
   in half

Disolve jello in 1 cup boiling water. Add salt and lemon juice.
Pour 7-Up slowly down inner edge of bowl. Stir gently with
up and down motion. Chill until partially set. Add apple and
grapes. Pour into 1 quart mold. Chill until set.

Mrs. Myron Koehn, Fairview, Okla.

Sweet-Heart Salad

1½ cups pineapple, crushed
½ cup sugar
1½ tbsp. plain gelatine
¼ cup cold water
1 cup hot water
6 oz. cream cheese

2 tbsp. lemon juice
2 tbsp. cherry juice
1 cup whipping cream
12 maraschino cherries
3 apples, chopped

Dissolve gelatin in cold water. Bring 1 cup water to boiling point and add gelatine. Stir, then add pineapple, sugar, lemon, and cherry juice. Cool. Mash cream cheese add chopped cherries, and apples. Combine with pineapple mixture, adding a small amount at a time. Chill, until slightly thickened. Whip cream and blend with mixture. Mold and chill. Cherries may be arranged in heart design on top.

Mrs. Robert Holdeman, Dalton, Ohio

Yum Yum Salad

Dissolve 1 pkg. orange or lemon jello in 1 cup boiling water. Let cool until partially set. Add 2 cups crushed pineapple, ¼ lb. cheese, grated, ¾ lb. marshmallows, cut into small pieces, and 1 cup grated carrots, if desired. Mix together ½ cup salad dressing and 1 cup cream, whipped. Add to jello. Place in refrigerator to chill.

Mrs. Fred Wedel, Goltry, Okla.
Anna Koehn, Galva, Kans.

Fish Salads

Salmon Salad

1 can salmon, mixed fine	1 tsp. butter
6 sweet pickles, sliced	3 tbsp. sugar
1 egg	2 tbsp. cream
1 tsp. mustard	½ cup vinegar
dash of salt and pepper	

Add pickles to salmon. Combine remaining ingredients. Cook and pour over salmon, blending well.

Mrs. Lincoln Dirks, Greensburg, Kans.

Tuna Salad

3 hard boiled eggs, diced	1 tbsp. chopped onion
1 cup cooked peas, cold	½ head of lettuce, cut into
1 small can Tuna	bite size

Toss with Miracle Whip salad dressing until well blended.

Mrs. Carl Heppner, Conway, Kans.

Salad Dressing

Found Salad Dressing

2 egg yolks
¾ cup brown sugar
2 tbsp. butter or salad oil

¾ cup vinegar
½ tsp. salt
¾ cup light cream

Beat egg yolks, sugar, vinegar and salt together. Cook in double boiler, stirring constantly until thickened. Add butter or oil. Cool, add cream, store in refrigerator.

Mrs. G. H. Dyck, Hesston, Kans.

Fruit Salad Dressing

½ cup sugar
3 tbsp. flour

1 egg, beaten
1 cup fruit juice

Cook until thickened. Remove from heat and add 2 tbsp. butter. Cool. Fold in 1 tbsp. salad dressing. Serve on fruit salad. Sprinkle with nuts.

Viola Harms, Atmore, Ala.

French Dressing (1)

1 cup sugar
1 cup catsup or tomato
  soup
1 cup salad oil

¼ cup vinegar
2 tbsp. minced onion
1 tbsp. prepared mustard

Mix well. Store in refrigerator.

Mrs. Allen Holdeman, Hesston, Kans.

French Dressing (2)

½ cup Wesson oil
½ cup vinegar
¾ cup sugar
2 tsp. salt
½ cup grated onion

1 tsp. paprika (optional)
⅔ cup catsup or 1 can (10½
  oz.) tomato soup
1 tbsp. dry mustard
1 tsp. pepper
Juice of one lemon

Mix and store in refrigerator.

Mrs. Paul Wenger, Newton, Kans.
Mrs. Alan Boehs, Fairview, Okla.

French Dressing (3)

½ cup sugar
1 cup salad oil
½ tsp. ginger
1 tsp. salt
¼ tsp. black pepper

½ cup vinegar
4 tbsp. catsup
½ tsp. paprika
1 tsp. dry mustard

Put all ingredients in jar and shake well to mix. Store in refrigerator.

Mrs. Lawrence Toews, Harrison, Mich.

French Dressing (4)

Combine:
1 cup condensed tomato soup
1½ cups salad oil
¾ cup vinegar
garlic salt to taste
1 tbsp. salt

1 tbsp. prepared mustard
1 tbsp. ground onion or
onion flakes
½ tsp. pepper

Mix all ingredients on low speed for 10 min. Keeps in refrigerator for quite some time.

Mrs. Archie Holdeman, Hesston, Kans.

Salad Dressing (1)

1 qt. buttermilk
¾ tsp. mustard
¼ tsp. garlic salt
Ground turmeric, for color

1 cup sour cream
2 tbsp. mayonnaise
Salt and pepper to taste

Mix ingredients well and store in refrigerator. Keeps well.

Mrs. John H. Schmidt, Goltry, Okla.

Salad Dressing (2)

1 cup Miracle Whip salad
dressing
½ cup sugar

¾ cup sweetened condensed
milk
3 tbsp. vinegar

Whip together.

Mrs. Paul Becker, Sedgwick, Kans.

Magic Mayonnaise

⅔ cup Eagle Brand milk
¼ cup vinegar or lemon
  juice
¼ cup salad oil or melted
  butter

⅛ tsp. cayenne
1 egg yolk
½ tsp. salt
1 tsp. dry mustard

Combine ingredients in mixing bowl. Beat until mixture thickens; chill. Makes 1¼ cups, (serve on avocado salad).

Mrs. Adam J. Schmidt, Montezuma, Kans.

Mustard

3 tsp. sugar
3 tsp. flour

1 tsp. dry mustard

Add just enough boiling water to make a thick paste. Let stand 5 min. Add vinegar to thin to desired consistency.

Mrs. John Burns, Moundridge, Kans.

SANDWICHES

Sandwiches

Barbecue Burgers

½ cup finely chopped onion
1 tbsp. butter
2 tbsp. vinegar
3 tbsp. brown sugar
1 tbsp. Worcestershire
sauce

1 tbsp. prepared mustard
1 cup catsup
¼ cup water
3 cups ground beef or pork
roast
8 to 10 hot buttered buns

Cook onion in butter until barely tender, stirring frequently. Stir in next six ingredients. Simmer 5 minutes; add meat and cook thoroughly. Spoon into buns and serve at once.

Mrs. Menno Koehn, Halstead, Kans.

Beef Hot Burgers

Fry 5 lbs. hamburger until done. Cook 4 tbsp. rice in water until done. Mix with meat and add 3 onions chopped fine, 1 large can tomato juice, salt and chili powder to taste. Simmer until right consistency. Makes 50 sandwiches.

Mrs. Harry Nickel, Hillsboro, Kans.

Chicken Sandwiches

Cook chicken with onion and salt. When done grind 2 cups chicken and 6 to 8 sweet pickles. Add ½ cup diced celery, ½ cup salad dressing, (½ cup cream, optional). Chicken broth may be added if needed. Mix well. Make sandwiches with lettuce.

Mrs. Leah Dirks, Greensburg, Kans.

Company Burgers

2 lbs. hamburger
3 tbsp. flour
Hamburger buns

1 can onion soup
Salt and pepper to taste

Brown hamburger in a heavy skillet. Sift flour lightly over browned meat stirring thoroughly. Add onion soup and seasoning. Simmer until it reaches spreading consistency. Spread on buns.

Mrs. Elton Wenger, Hesston, Kans.

Grilled Cheese Sandwiches

2 tbsp. mayonnaise
1 tsp. prepared mustard
3 tbsp. melted butter

3 slices American cheese
6 slices bread

Brush bread slices with butter; place cheese slices on bread. Combine mustard and mayonnaise, spread over cheese slices. Place remaining bread slices over cheese, cut diagonally and grill or broil sandwiches on both sides until toasted.

Bonnie Johnson, Galva, Kans.

Grilled Reubens

(Jewish Sandwich)

3 lbs. corned beef
Mild sauerkraut
Butter

Sliced Swiss cheese
Mustard
Rye bread

Cook a 3 lb. corned beef for 4 hours over a slow fire. Cool and slice in ⅛ in. thick slices. On a slice of rye bread spread mustard, add a slice of corned beef. Spread on some drained sauerkraut, place a slice of swiss cheese then a slice of rye bread. Spread butter on the outside of each slice of bread. Grill over a med. heat until brown. Serve while hot.

Oma Wiggers, Halstead, Kans.

Roast Beef Sandwich

4 hard boiled eggs
⅔ cup salad dressing
1 tsp. vinegar
½ tsp. sugar

2 cups ground cold roast
  beef
¼ cup ground onion
2 tsp mustard
  ground pickles (optional)

Mix together well. Spread on bread.

Verla Unruh, Halstead, Kans.

Fiesta Hamburgers

3 eggs	1 tbsp. Worcestershire sauce
3 lbs. ground beef	2 lbs. cooked kidney beans
2 tbsp. salt	(12 oz. dry)
¼ tsp. pepper	½ cup onion
1½ tbsp. chili powder	6 cloves garlic
⅓ cup catsup	⅓ cup salad oil
25 slices cheese	25 round buns

Beat eggs; combine with meat. Add salt, pepper, chili powder, catsup, Worcestershire sauce and beans. Mix well. Saute onion and garlic in oil until brown; combine with meat mixture. Shape into patties, and bake at 350° about 30 min. Place patties on half of buns. Top each with a slice of cheese; cover with top of buns. Place in shallow pan and heat in oven at 300° until cheese melts. Serve immediately. 25 servings.

Mrs. Adam J. Schmidt, Montezuma, Kans.

Picnic Hamburgers

8 hamburger buns, unsliced	½ tsp. salt
1 lb. hamburger	⅛ tsp. pepper
1 medium onion	2 hard-cooked eggs
1 can tomato sauce	¾ lb. American cheese

Cut slice from top of buns. Scoop out inside. Brown hamburger and onion; add tomato sauce, salt, pepper, eggs, and bun crumbs. Line inside of bun with slice of cheese and fill with hamburger mixture. Place another slice of cheese on top of meat and cover with top of bun. Wrap buns in foil and place in refrigerator. When ready to use, place in covered roaster in oven 250° for one hour.

Mrs. Richard Koehn, Halstead, Kans.

Southern Burgers

1½ lb. ground beef	¼ cup chopped onion
1 can chicken Gumbo soup	2 tbsp. catsup
1 tbsp. mustard	Salt and pepper to taste

Brown meat and onion until well done. Add remaining ingredients. Simmer over low heat 15 to 20 min. Serve on buns.

Mrs. Emerson Litwiller, Middleton, Mich.

Saucy Joes

Cook 1 lb. ground beef, ¼ cup each, chopped green pepper, chopped onion, and sliced celery together for 5 minutes. Add 1 cup barbecue sauce and simmer. Serve in buns.

Mrs. F. P. Schmidt, Chickasha, Okla.

Sloppy Joes

1½ lb. hamburger

¾ cup chopped onion

Brown in skillet then add:
1 cup chopped celery
¾ cup oatmeal
1 cup condensed milk
1 cup catsup

¾ cup water
3 tbsp. sugar
2 tbsp. vinegar
1 tbsp. Worcestershire sauce
1 tsp. salt

Bake at 300° for 1½ hours. If you use homemade catsup omit the vinegar.

Mrs. Andy N. Troyer, Uniontown, Ohio

Surprise Burgers

1 lb. ground beef
Salt and pepper
Fat for skillet

4 slices cheese
1-8 oz. can tomato sauce

Form beef into eight thin patties. Sprinkle with salt and pepper. Lay cheese on four patties; cover with remaining patties. Pinch edges together to enclose the cheese completely. Brown on one side in hot greased skillet. Turn, and pour tomato sauce over them. Simmer 8 to 10 minutes, basting occasionally. Serve piping hot with delicious pan gravy.

Mrs. Robert Jantz

Tomato Burgers

"For quick indoor barbecues!"

In skillet melt 1 tbsp. shortening
Add:
1 lb. ground beef
1 cup chopped onion
1 cup celery

1 tsp. chili powder
½ tsp. salt
Pepper

Cook until meat is browned and celery is tender. Stir to separate particles. Add 1 can tomato soup; simmer for a few minutes. Serve on toasted, split buns.

Mrs. Donald Unruh, Greensburg, Kans.

Hot Burgers

2 lbs. hamburger
1 onion
1 green pepper
2 tbsp. mustard
 chili powder

½ cup catsup
2 tbsp. brown sugar
2 tbsp. vinegar
1 tbsp. oatmeal

Fry meat and onion until done. Add chopped green pepper, salt and chili powder to taste. Add remaining ingredients. Simmer over low heat 15 to 20 minutes.

Summer Sausage

28 lbs. ground beef
7 lbs. ground pork
1½ cups salt
4 tbsp. pepper

1½ cups brown sugar
 firmly packed
4 tbsp. saltpetre

Mix together. Work with hands for 1 hr. or until real sticky. Make muslin sacks about 3 inches in diameter and stuff with meat mixture. Hang up and let dry several days. Rub outside with liquid smoke. Let dry several days again and rub smoke on again. Let hang for a week or 10 days or until quite dry. May be waxed or put in freezer. (Very good for sandwiches.)

Hurry Up Sandwich

1 can (12 oz.) corned beef, unchilled
¼ cup butter (soft)
¼ cup Catsup

6 hamburger buns, toasted
6 slices onions

Flake corned beef with fork. Combine butter and catsup, mixing well. Spread over 6 bun bottoms. Butter bun tops. Place on baking sheet and broil 3-5 min. or until meat is hot. Top with a slice of onion. Then toasted bun top. Serve hot.

Toasted Cheese Sandwich

Place slices of American cheese between two slices of bread. Butter both sides of sandwich. Place in a skillet and brown each side until cheese is melted.

SOUPS

Soups

Canned Vegetable Soup

Juice from 14 lbs. ripe tomatoes
1 qt. carrots, diced fine
2 cans peas
1 pt. lima or navy beans
2 bunches celery, cut fine

1 pkg. alphabet macaroni
1 cup sugar
1/2 cup salt
3 onions, diced
1 tbsp. paprika
3 sweet peppers, diced fine

Cook vegetables separately until well done. Combine in large kettle. Add salt, sugar, paprika and bring to boiling. Add macaroni. When done, fill jars and seal. (Butter or meat broth may be added before serving). Yield: 11 qt.
Process 30 minutes at 10 lbs. of pressure for quarts.

Mrs. Paul E. Hiebert, Hillsboro, Kans.

Chicken Borscht

1 chicken
6 med. potatoes
1 head cabbage
2 cups tomatoes

1 med. onion
1 cup sour cream
parsley, bay leaf, whole
pepper corns
and salt to taste

Cook chicken until tender. Remove meat from bones. Cook potatoes, onions, and cabbage in broth with added water until done. Add tomatoes, meat and seasonings. Simmer. Add cream before serving.

Mrs. Adin Holdeman, Hesston, Kans.

Chili Con Carne

Cook together:
1 lb. hamburger   1 finely chopped onion
Add:
1 can tomato soup   1 tsp. chili powder
1 can pork and beans
Simmer for half an hour.

Mrs. Thos. M. Wiebe, Steinbach, Man.

Bean Soup

1½ cups navy beans
3 lbs. ham bone (with meat)
½ cup tomato puree
½ tsp. pepper
⅛ tsp. nutmeg
½ cup finely chopped celery

½ cup finely chopped carrots
½ cup finely chopped onion
diced ham
1 tbsp. flour
salt to taste

Soak beans overnight in water. Cook ham and bone until done. Save ham stock and dice ham. Drain water from beans, add 2 qt. ham stock and water to beans. Boil slowly about 2 hr.; add puree, pepper, nutmeg, vegetables and diced ham. Simmer 1½ hr. or until done. Melt butter, gradually blend in flour, add ½ cup of soup liquid and stir until smooth. Add to beans and mix thoroughly. Simmer 10 min. or until slightly thickened. Serves six.

Mrs. Newell Litwiller, Carson City, Mich.

Chili Soup (1)

1 small onion
1 lb. hamburger
1 can kidney beans

1 can Campbells tomato soup
1 tsp. chili powder
1 tsp. salt or to taste

Brown onion in skillet. Add hamburger and brown slowly. Stir in tomato soup, beans, and seasonings. Simmer slowly for 10 min. (Homemade tomato soup may be used.)

Wilma Martin, Dalton, Ohio

Chili Soup (2)

1 lb. hamburger
1 onion
1 can pork and beans
1 cup egg noodles

1 pt. tomatoes or 1 can tomato soup
1 tsp. chili powder
1 tsp. salt

Boil the hamburger and onion in 1 qt. of water for about 15 min. Add pork and beans and noodles. Boil till noodles are done. Add tomatoes. Add chili powder and salt to taste.

Mrs. Thos. M. Wiebe, Steinbach, Man.

Chili Soup (3)

8 No. 2 can kidney beans
5 lbs. hamburger meat
2 bottles Heinz catsup
2 big onions
   salt and pepper to taste

½ lb. stick chili
1 No. 2 can Hi Power chili
   with beans
1 No. 2 can Hi Power chili
   without beans

Fry the meat with a little lard till done, mix together and boil till done. Fry the onions with the meat. Mash kidney beans.

Mrs. Jacob N. Yost, Durham, Kans.

Egg Plant Soup

Chip egg plant into pieces, about size of oyster. Cover with water and let boil up once. Drain. Add enough water to cook tender. When tender add milk, butter, salt and pepper. (Tastes similar to oyster soup)

Fragrant Soup

2 tbsp. butter
2 cups onion rings
3 cups water
2 beef bouillon cubes
1 tbsp. Worcestershire
   sauce

½ tsp. prepared mustard
3 diced frankfurters
1 tbsp. sugar
2½ cups cooked tomatoes
¼ cup uncooked rice

Melt sugar and butter in electric skillet. Add onion rings, fry until lightly browned. Add remaining ingredients except frankfurters. Simmer for 30 to 60 min. Add franks and simmer 10 min. more.

Hamburger and Vegetable Chowder

Brown ½ lb. hamburger.
Add:

1½ cup water
1 cup potatoes, diced
½ cup carrots, sliced
1 cup diced celery

1 No. 2 can tomatoes
2 tsp. salt
1 cup noodles
1 large onion, diced

Place in pressure pan 5 min. at 10 lb. pressure.

Mrs. Don Nightengale, Fairview, Okla.

Komst Borscht

(an old recipe brought from Russia)

Cook a bone from somewhat fat beef. Boil about 4 hr.

3 tbsp. chopped onion
2 or 3 bay leaves   ½ tsp. whole black pepper
½ tsp. dried parsley or bunch of fresh green parsley

One hr, before mealtime, chop up a small head of cabbage and add to meat and bone liquid and boil till cabbage is soft. Before serving add salt to taste and ¾ cup canned ripe tomatoes, bring to boil, and before dishing out add ½ cup sweet cream. This recipe will serve about 4 persons. Thicken or thin soup by the amount of water added, also the meat amount can be used as wished, spices put in small cloth. Cubed potatoes added too if liked that way.   Mrs. Pete Isaac, Moundridge, Kans.

Macaroni Hamburger Soup

1 med. sized cabbage head,   8 whole peppercorns
  cut fine   1 bay leaf
½ onion, chopped   1 lb. hamburger
1 tbsp. salt

Mix cabbage, onion and salt; boil until cabbage is barely done, add hamburger meat. Stir to separate meat; cook 15 min. more and remove from heat. Cook separately 1 cup macaroni or spaghetti in salted water, drain and rinse with cold water, add to soup. Make a sauce by frying: 1 tbsp. flour in 1 tbsp. butter; add 1 can tomatoes and 1 cup cream. Boil together and add to soup.   Mrs. Dora Smith, Moundridge, Kans.

Stay Abed Stew

Mix these things up in a pan that has a tight lid.

2 lbs. beef stew meat cubed   1 tsp. salt
  brown a little   ⅛ tsp. pepper
1 can tiny peas   1 can cream of tomato soup,
1 cup sliced carrots   or celery, or mushroom
1 big raw potato sliced   soup thinned with ½ cup
2 chopped onions   water

Cover with lid, then place in a 275° oven. It will cook happily all by itself in 5 hrs.   Mrs. Carl Dirks, Halstead, Kans.

Rice Goulash Soup

1½ cups chopped onion
3 tbsp. butter or
   margarine
1 lb. ground beef
1 qt. tomato juice
½ cup uncooked rice

1 tsp. salt
2 bouillon cubes (optional)
½ tsp. paprika
1 bay leaf
⅛ tsp. pepper

Cook onions, butter, and ground beef until browned. Add remaining ingredients. Bring to a boil. Stir, cover and simmer for 20 min. Makes 6 servings. (If soup is not served immediately, it will require extra broth since the rice absorbs the liquid.)

Mrs. Robert Schneider, Perrinton, Mich.
Mrs. Kenneth Litwiller, Almena, Wisc.

Russian Klops Soup

1 lb. hamburger
⅓ cup sour cream
1 egg

salt and pepper to taste
2 tbsp. chopped parsley
2 tbsp. flour

Mix all ingredients and form into small meat balls; drop into kettle with 2 qt. water and add:

1 med. size onion, chopped
5 pepper corns
1 bay leaf

5 whole allspice
salt to taste

Boil for ½ hr. Remove spices and add 4 cups of diced potatoes. Cook until potatoes are done. Make a batter of 1 cup sour cream, 3 tbsp. flour, 1 tsp. vinegar, enough water to make a thin batter, and pour into soup; stir until it reaches boiling. Remove from heat and serve.

Trudie Wiggers, Halstead, Kans.

Soup for 100 People

20 lbs. stewing meat
6 pkgs. carrots
20 lbs. potatoes
3 cans peas
3 cans green beans
3 cans green limas
1 bunch celery

6 onions
3 tall cans tomato sauce
1 bunch fresh parsley
1 tbsp. pepper corns
1 tbsp. whole allspice
salt to taste

Cook meat, onion, spices and ½ cup salt until meat is tender, (more salt may be needed). Prepare potatoes, carrots and celery. Cut into small pieces. Cook until done and add to meat. Add canned vegetables and tomato sauce. Add parsley the last few min. of cooking, remove parsley.

Mrs. Lloyd Koehn, Lehigh, Kans.

Tomato Soup (1)

1 peck tomatoes	3 mangoes
6 med. sized onions	6 whole cloves
1 large stalk celery	¼ cup salt
1 bunch parsley	

Cook together until celery is soft, put through strainer. To strained juice, add:

1 cup sugar	½ cup butter
½ cup flour or cornstarch	pepper to taste

Boil at simmering point for 45 min. or cook 15-20 min. Cold pack for 10 min. (May be used for pork and beans, spaghetti, chili soup, etc.).

Mrs. Jacob Hochstetler, Apple Creek, Ohio

Tomato Soup (2)

14 qts. ripe tomatoes	1 bay leaf
7 med. onions, chopped	4 tbsp. salt
7 sprigs parsley, chopped	8 tbsp. sugar
½ stalk celery, chopped	2 tsp. pepper

Heat tomatoes, add parsley, onion, celery, and bay leaf. Cook until done, strain. Add sugar, salt and pepper, bring to boiling; pour into jars and water bath boil for 15 min.

Alma Dyck, Livingston, Calif.

Salmon Soup

4 cups milk	salt and pepper
2 cups shredded salmon	2 tbsp. butter or butter substitute

Combine salmon, butter and milk. Season to taste. Heat thoroughly. Serve at once.

Chicken Noodle Soup

1 cooking hen, omit the liver water so chicken is well covered	1 tbsp. salt
	½ tsp. parsley
	1 small bay leaf
	pepper
2 tbsp. onion, finely chopped	
2 or 3 cups of noodles	

When chicken begins to boil, skim off the scumb, then season with salt. Boil until tender. Skim off most of fat, and remove meat from bones. Add rest of ingredients, except noodles. Boil gently for 20 min. Add noodles. Cook a few minutes until tender.

Mrs. Fannie Dyck, Hesston, Kans.

Summer Borscht

½ lb. smoked pork, chopped	1 qt. chopped beet leaves
1 qt. boiling water	3 tbsp. chopped green dill
1 tbsp. salt	1 cup chopped onion tops
1 qt. cubed potatoes vinegar to taste	½ cup cream

Put the pork into boiling water, boil ½ hr., add salt and cubed potatoes. Cook about five or ten min. Add beet leaves, onion tops, dill and vinegar. After cooking ½ hr. add the cream.

Green Bean Soup

5 cups water	salt to taste
½ lb. sausage (cut in half inch lengths)	3 bay leaves
	8 peppercorns
2 med. potatoes	4 large sprigs parsley (cut up)
1 small onion	

Boil together for 20 min.

Add: 4 cups green beans fresh or canned. Boil for 15 min. Just before serving add ¾ cup cream and 2 tbsp. butter. Serves 5 or 6.

Mrs. John Burns, Moundridge, Kans.

VEGETABLES

Vegetables

Barbecued Lima Beans

1 lb. lima beans
⅛ lb. bacon sq.
½ tsp. salt
1 large onion, chopped
2 tbsp. bacon fat
1 tbsp. sugar

2 tsp. vinegar
1 can tomato soup
⅛ tsp. chili powder
½ tsp. salt
⅛ tsp. pepper
1 lb. wieners

Wash beans and cover with water. Soak overnight. Cook until tender with bacon sq. or sliced bacon, and ½ tsp. salt. Saute onion in bacon fat, add sugar, vinegar, tomato soup, and seasonings. Simmer few min. Combine beans and wieners in baking dish, pour the sauce over top. Cover and bake 1 hr. at 300°.

Mrs. Reuben Buller, Halstead, Kans.

Baked Beans

Soak 1 qt. of navy beans overnight. Pour off water. Add fresh water and boil 15 min. with ½ tsp. soda. Drain and add:

2 cups tomatoes
1 cup chopped pork or ham
½ cup chopped onions

1 cup brown sugar
2 tsp. salt
⅛ tsp. pepper

Place in a heavy casserole with tight cover. Bake 4 hours at 325°.

Eva Koehn, Galva, Kans.

Baked Lima Beans

3 slices bacon
½ lb. ground beef
1 cup dried lima beans
salt and pepper to taste

½ small onion
1 can tomato soup
½ cup water

Soak beans over night and cook till done. Cut up bacon and brown. Add minced onion, brown ground beef, add soup and water. Put in casserole and bake 30-45 min. in 350° oven.

Mrs. John M. Jost, Hillsboro, Kans.

Asparagus Casserole

2-7 oz. cans flaked tuna or
2 lb. fresh asparagus,
  washed and cut up
2 tbsp. butter or margarine
2 tbsp. flour
1 cup milk
1 cup grated cheese
2 cups cooked diced chicken
⅛ tsp. pepper
½ tsp. salt
1 cup day old bread crumbs
2 tbsp. melted butter or
  margarine

Prepare asparagus, and cook covered 5 minutes, in ½" boiling salted water. Drain if necessary. Melt 2 tbsp. butter in saucepan. Blend in flour, remove from heat and stir in milk. Cook until sauce is med. thick, stirring constantly. Gently blend with cooked asparagus, cheese and tuna or (chicken), salt and pepper. Place into buttered baking dish. Mix bread crumbs with melted butter and sprinkle over top. Bake in preheated oven 350° for 30 to 40 minutes or until browned. Makes 8 servings.

Mrs. Aaron Boeckner, Moundridge, Kans.

Baked Mashed Sweet Potatoes and Fig Bars

4 cups mashed sweet
  potatoes
¼ cup butter
¾ cup brown sugar
10 fig bar cookies

Pare sweet potatoes and cook in slightly salted water. Leave enough water on potatoes so they are quite moist when mashed. Add butter, brown sugar, and crumbled fig bars . Mix. Place into greased baking dish. Bake at 350° for 30 to 45 minutes. Serves 6 to 8.

Mrs. Howard Baize, Livingston, Calif.

Baked Eggplant

1 med. or large eggplant
  Salt and pepper
1 medium onion
½ bell pepper
1 can cream of mushroom
  soup

Slice eggplant ½" thick and peel. Roll in flour and brown lightly in butter or oleo. Salt and pepper to taste. Place in casserole and cut pepper over top. Slice onion over top of bell pepper. Pour one can of cream of mushroom soup over top and bake at 350° about ½ hour or until a fork slips out easily.

Mrs. Orval Johnson, Walnut Hill, Fla.

Calico Beans

¼ lb. bacon	2 tbsp. vinegar
1 lb. hamburger	1 tbsp. mustard
½ cup chopped onion	1 tsp. salt
½ cup brown sugar	1 can lima beans
(packed)	1 can kidney beans
½ cup catsup	1 large can pork and beans

Brown bacon, hamburger, and chopped onion in pan. Then add remaining ingredients, and mix well. Bake at 200° for 1½ hr.

Mrs. Archie Holdeman, Hesston, Kans.

Company Vegetables

Into a 2 qt. casserole place 6 cups cooked green beans (cut into short pieces). Sprinkle with 1 cup grated cheese. Blend 1 can cream of mushroom soup with ⅔ cup Pet milk (1 small can) and pour over beans and cheese. Bake in 350° oven about 20 min. Take from oven and top with 3½ ounce can French Fried Onion Rings. Bake 8 to 10 min. more or until golden brown. Makes 8 to 10 servings. For variety use asparagus, peas or broccoli.

Mrs. Lyle Litwiller, Perrinton, Mich.

Delicious Fried Eggplant

1 cup flour	2 well-beaten eggs
¾ tsp. salt	⅔ cup milk

Mix together and make a batter. Peel eggplants and cut in ¼" slices. Dip eggplants in batter and fry in deep fat.

The secret of good, crisp golden fried eggplants is to have the fat heated to 375°. Fry 2 to 3 minutes and drain on absorbent paper.

Viola Harms, Atmore, Ala.

French Fried Onions

3 large onions	1 egg
1 cup milk	1 tbsp. melted shortening
1 cup flour	Salt and pepper to taste

Cut onions in ¼ in. slices. Separate slices into rings. Dip into flour mixture and dip in deep fat 395° for 3 min. Serves 6 to 8.

Mrs. Andy N. Troyer, Uniontown, Ohio

Barbecued Beans

1 lb. ground beef
½ tsp. salt
1 (1 lb. 12 oz.) can pork and beans
1 tbsp. Worcestershire sauce
¼ tsp. Tabasco
½ cup onion (chopped)
¼ tsp. pepper
½ cup catsup
2 tbsp. vinegar

Brown beef and onion; pour off fat. Add remaining ingredients; mix well and pour into 1½ qt. casserole dish. Bake in 350° oven for 30 minutes.

Carolyn Schultz, Neodesha, Kans.
Mrs. Manford Nickles, Sublette, Kans.

Caramel Sweet Spuds

5 med. sweet potatoes
1 tsp. salt
3 tbsp. flour
1 cup brown sugar
2 tbsp. butter
1 cup miniature marshmallows
½ cup nut meats (optional)
1 cup thin cream

Cook sweet spuds until done. Peel and cut in ½ inch slices and arrange in greased baking dish. Mix salt, flour and sugar, sprinkle over spuds. Dot with butter, and marshmallows. Pour cream over top. Bake 40-45 minutes in 350° oven.

Mrs. Paul Toews, St. Marys, Ont.

Missouri Baked Beans

2 cups dry beans
1¼ cups brown sugar
½ lb. bacon
2½ tsp. salt
¾ tsp. pepper

Soak beans overnight in cold water. Drain in the morning and add 2 pts. water, and salt. Cook until soft. Cut bacon into cubes and fry until crisp. Add pepper, brown sugar and bacon to beans. Place in covered casserole and bake 3 hr. at 325°. Keep beans covered with liquid while baking. Good hot or cold. Serves 8.

Audra Jantz, Livingston, Calif

Dakota Potato Puffs

1 cup flour	2 cups mashed potatoes
3 tsp. baking powder	4 eggs, well-beaten
½ tsp. salt	½ cup lard

Sift flour, then measure. Add baking powder and salt and sift again. Combine potatoes and eggs. Add dry ingredients and mix thoroughly. Heat lard in skillet and drop potatoes from a teaspoon. Fry to golden brown. Makes 6 servings.

Mrs. Monroe Holdeman, Harrison, Mich.

Frijoles Con Queso

(Beans with cheese)

2 cups brown beans	1 tsp. salt

Cook beans until well done
½ cup chopped onions	
2 tbsp. shortening	1 cup grated cheese

Melt shortening in skillet. Add chopped onions and brown slightly. Add cooked beans and mash well. Before serving add cheese. Stir well and serve piping hot.

Irene Buller, Cuauhtemoc, Mex.

Orange Candied Yams

8-10 med. sized yams	½ cup orange juice
1 cup brown sugar	2 tsp. salt
¼ cup butter	1 orange sectioned
	1 tsp. grated orange peel

Boil yams until tender. Drain, peel and cut in halves. Mix brown sugar, butter, orange juice and grated rind in heavy skillet. Heat slowly while stirring. Simmer yams a few at a time in mixture. Place in baking dish and put into warm oven. Simmer orange sections for 2 or 3 min. Arrange yams in serving dish and garnish with sections. (Or arrange yams in baking dish and pour mixture over yams and bake slowly for several min).

Mrs. Vernon Giesbrecht, Cimarron, Kans.

Golden Onion Rings

1 cup pancake mix
¼ cup cornmeal
¼ tsp. salt
1 cup milk
1 large Bermuda onion

Combine pancake mix, cornmeal, salt and milk; beat until smooth. Peel onion, cut into ¼ in. slices and separate into rings. Dip onion rings into batter; allow excess batter to drain off. Fry rings in deep hot fat (375°) for 2 min. or until golden brown. Drain. Sprinkle with salt; serve at once.

Mrs. Floyd Yost, Moundridge, Kans.

Green Beans with Catsup

1 No. 2 can green beans
1 small onion, chopped
3 slices bacon, cut up
⅓ cup catsup

Cut bacon into small pieces. Fry bacon and onion together untill bacon is crisp. Bring beans to boiling and cook 10 min. add catsup, bacon and onion mixture. Continue cooking a few min. more. Serve hot.

Mrs. Alpha Unruh, Cimarron, Kans.

Pork and Beans

Soak 1 qt beans overnight. Cook until done, drain.

Add:

½ cup brown sugar
½ cup sliced onion
2 tsp. salt
1 tbsp. molasses (optional)
½ cup bacon
2 cups tomatoes
½ tsp. mustard

Bake slowly for 2 hours.

Mrs. Gilbert Toews, Steinbach, Man.

Baked Fluffy Rice

1 cup uncooked rice
2½ cups water
3 tbsp. butter
1 tsp. salt

Combine ingredients in greased 1 quart casserole. Cover, bake in moderate oven (350°) for 1 hour. Remove cover. Stir rice with fork. Top with additional pat of butter.

Mrs. Paul Koehn, Halstead, Kans.

Potato Pie

1 lb. sausage
3 large potatoes, diced
1 tsp. salt

⅛ tsp. pepper
⅛ tsp. celery salt
⅛ tsp. onion salt

Bring this to a boil and cook till barely done. Leave some juice on. Meanwhile, peel skins from smoked sausages and dice. Mix with potatoes, fill into an unbaked pie crust and cover top with more pie crust and bake at 350° for 1 hr. Serve hot with cold milk.

Mrs. Elias Mininger, Winton, Calif.

Potato Scones

Mix well:
½ cup sugar
⅓ cup lard

Add:
1½ cups flour
4 tsp. baking powder

Add and mix:
1 cup mashed potatoes

¼ tsp. salt
1 egg

Mix in order given. This dough will be quite stiff. Bake at 400° till golden brown on top. Serve hot with milk or fruit. For corn bread use ½ cup corn meal instead of the ½ cup flour.

Mrs. Vesta Koehn, Wauseon, Ohio

Preaul Cumst (Sauerkraut Casserole)

1 small can (no. 303) sauerkraut
½ cup uncooked raisins or prunes, approx.
1 heaping tbsp. rice (uncooked)

⅓ cup sugar
1 cup bacon, cut in small pieces and fried
bacon drippings
pepper

Mix all ingredients and bake in moderate oven about 1½ hr. or until done. A little water can be added with other ingredients if too dry. Sausage may be used instead of bacon.

Mrs. Dayton Unruh, Durham, Kans.

Scalloped Onions

12 medium sized onions quartered
½ lb. Velveeta cheese
½ tsp. salt
2 cups buttered bread crumbs
⅛ tsp. pepper
2 tbsp. flour

Cook onions until tender, drain liquid about 1½ cup, thicken with flour, cut in cheese and bring to a boil, simmer until cheese has dissolved, pour over onions, and put in 2 qt. baking dish, cover with buttered bread crumbs. Bake in preheated oven for 30 min.

Mrs. Frieda Litwiller, Middleton, Mich.

Green Rice

2 eggs, beaten
2 cups milk
2 cups grated cheese
1 cup chopped parsley
½ tsp. cooking oil
½ onion, chopped
1 tsp. salt
¼ tsp. dry mustard
2 cups cold cooked rice

Mix well the above and put into casserole. Sprinkle with paprika for decoration. Bake. Serve with ham loaf and a green salad.

Nina Holdeman, Hesston, Kans.

Mexican Rice

2 tbsp. cooking oil
1 cup of rice, uncooked
2 cups tomato juice
2 cups water
1½ tsp. garlic salt
1 tsp. ground cumin

Brown uncooked rice in cooking oil in skillet; mix tomato juice, garlic salt, cumin and water in a bowl, add to golden brown rice. Cook slowly without stirring until light and fluffy. More water may be added if needed.

Mrs. Charles Becker, San Rafael, Mex.

Sauerkraut and Dumplings

2 cups flour
½ tsp. salt
3 tsp. baking powder
Milk for stiff batter

Sift dry ingredients 2 times. Add milk and mix. Drop by tsp. into 1 qt. juicy sauerkraut, when it is boiling. Place cover on kettle and cook 15 min.

Mrs. A. L. Yost, Moundridge, Kans.

Scalloped Potatoes (1)

6 medium red potatoes	½ small onion
½ tsp. salt	¼ lb. grated cheese
¼ tsp. pepper	½ cup heavy cream

Cook unpeeled potatoes in water until almost tender but still firm. Cool, peel and slice. Grease baking dish with butter. Cover bottom with potatoes, finely sliced onion and seasoning. Top with cheese, pour cream over top. Bake in oven at 375° for 45 minutes or until browned on top.

Mrs. William Koehn, Burns, Kans.

Scalloped Potatoes (2)
(no curdling)

3 tbsp. butter	6 cups sliced potatoes
2 tbsp. flour	2 tsp. salt
2 cups milk	

Melt 2 tbsp. butter in sauce pan, stir in flour, salt and add milk, stirring constantly until sauce boils and thickens. Add potatoes and heat, stirring until it boils again. Turn potatoes into a shallow greased casserole. Spread 1 tbsp. melted butter over top. Place on a rack above the middle of the oven and bake at 350° for 35 minutes. Onions or ham may be added.

Mrs. Gerald Wenger, Newton, Kans.

Southern Barbecued Beans

2 cups pinto beans	½ cup vinegar

Cook beans until half done. Then season with 2½ tbsp. salt and ⅛ tsp pepper. Add vinegar to the water they are cooked in, they will cook in less than usual time. When soft pour into baking dish adding their own juice.

Add:

1 cup minced bacon	4 cups tomato juice
1 cup minced onion	1 cup vinegar

More salt if needed, and sugar to sweeten well. This is the secret of good barbecued beans. (Vinegar to make them sour and sugar to sweeten them well.) Bake slowly for several hrs.

Mrs. Lee A. Holdeman, DeRidder, La.

Spinach

2 qts. fresh spinach	½ cup heavy cream
3 slices bacon	salt
3 eggs	pepper

Wash and cook spinach in covered kettle without adding water. Fry bacon crisp and remove from skillet. Fry eggs hard in bacon fat and cut into small pieces. Remove extra fat. Add cream and heat. Add spinach. Crumble bacon over top. Canned spinach may also be used. This recipe is especially tasty when served with cornbread.

Mrs. Arthur Koehn, Fairview, Okla.

Spanish String Beans

1 can string beans, drained	1 can Campbell's tomato soup

Pour tomato soup over beans and season with pepper and salt. Cook in frying pan 4 or 5 slices bacon, diced, and 1 onion, diced. Cook together and pour grease, bacon, tomato soup, and onion over beans and cook 15-20 min.

Mrs. John M. Jost, Hillsboro, Kans.

Supper Spaghetti

3 cups boiled spaghetti	1 lb. ground beef
3 cups tomato juice	1 cup carrots
½ cup fat or oil	1 cup onion
1 cup diced celery	2 tsp. salt
2 tsp. chili pepper	

Brown meat and onion. Add vegetables and juice. Put in casserole and sprinkle chopped parsley and grated cheese on top.

Yvonne Schmidt, Winton, Calif.

Sweet Potatoes

1 cup orange pop	⅓ cup white sugar
⅓ cup brown sugar	4 tbsp. butter
1 tsp. grated orange rind	¼ tsp. salt
2 tbsp. cornstarch	

Mix all ingredients and bring to boiling. Pour over boiled and sliced sweet potatoes. Bake 30 min. at 350°.

Mrs. D. G. Boeckner, Moundridge, Kans.

Squash Souffle

2 cups yellow squash	Salt and Pepper
3 tbsp. butter	2 eggs
1 cup dry bread or cracker crumbs	½ cup cooked ham, diced
2 tbsp. grated onion	½ cup buttered bread or cracker crumbs

Cook squash and mash. Melt butter and pour over bread crumbs and ham. Mix well; add squash and seasoning. Beat eggs and add to mixture; pour into buttered baking dish. Top with buttered crumbs. Bake at 300° until firm.

Mrs. Dorsey Eicher, Atmore, Ala.

Sweet Potatoes with Mincemeat

6 med. sized sweet potatoes	¾ cup apple cider
¾ cup brown sugar	1 tsp. salt
3 tbsp. light corn syrup	½ tsp. cinnamon
	1 cup prepared mincemeat

Wash and pare sweet potatoes. Cut each one in half lengthwise, and arrange in a 2 qt. casserole. Combine in a saucepan: brown sugar, corn syrup, salt, cinnamon, mincemeat and cider. Bring to boiling, stirring until sugar is dissolved and ingredients well blended. Pour hot mixture over potatoes in casserole. Cover and bake 30 min. in moderate oven (375°) or until potatoes are almost tender. Uncover and bake 10 min. more. Serves 6.

Della Rose, Atwater, Calif.

Sweet Potatoes

2 cups brown sugar	¼ cup flour
1 cup water	Large chunk of butter

Mix brown sugar and flour, add water and butter. Boil until mixture thickens like honey. Pour over cooked and sliced sweet potatoes and bake in mod. oven (350°) for 20 to 30 min.

Carol Holdeman, Hesston, Kans.

MISCELLANEOUS

Miscellaneous

Food for 50 People

Meat loaf with 3 cups crackers	10 lbs.
Oysters for stew with 10 qts. milk	5 pts.
Salmon for scallop or salad	6 lbs.
Potatoes	1⅓ pk.
Potato salad	8 qts.
Cabbage salad	6 qts.
Fruit salad	7 qts.
Baked beans	8 qts.
Creamed peas	8 cans
Pickles	2 qts.
Coffee	1 lb.
Cream for coffee	3 pts.
Cream to whip	2 pts.
Rolls	9 doz.
Ice Cream	2 gal.
Punch in 8 oz. glasses	10 qts.

Good Whitewash

This is sparkling white, dries hard, is waterproof and stays white for years.

Basement Wall Finish

4 lbs. white cement   4 lbs. lime
½ cup salt   ½ gal. water

Stir until dissolved. Let set one min., then add another half gal. of water. Let set 1 min. then apply with brush. Especially good on cement blocks or cinder blocks as it seals them and makes them moisture proof.

Granulated Soap

1 can lye

3 qts. tallow or lard (a mixture is best)

¼ cup borax

⅛ tsp. of citronella

3 qts. water

Heat water and grease until slightly warm. Add remaining ingredients and mix together. This will be granulated. Keep stirring and if it gets so you can't stir, use your hands. Keep working with it every day a little for about a week. (It will come out nice and granulated. It really is a mild soap and may be worked with your hands or a rubber glove.)

Mrs. Adam J. Schmidt, Montezuma, Kans.

Non-Cooking Hard Soap

10 lbs. luke-warm grease or tallow

2 boxes lye dissolved in 2 qts. cold water, cool to luke-warm,

6 tbsp. borax dissolved in 1 cup hot water

2 tsp. salt (not iodized)   ½ cup ammonia

4 tbsp. sugar, (dissolved)

Pour lye solution into grease slowly stirring constantly. Add other ingredients and stir until light and thick. Pour into mold which has been lined with wet cloth. Let set and cut into squares before entirely cold. Mrs. Paul Koehn, Halstead, Kans.

Household Hints

To boil cracked eggs prick the large end of egg with a needle to prevent egg from boiling out.

Before grilling a steak or hamburger in the stove broiler, put some water in the drip pan under the broiler rack. Fat drops into the water with no smoke, no sizzling fat, nor charred odor. The drip pan cleans so easy.

When cream is nearly whipped add powdered sugar to taste, plus a teaspoon of unflavored gelatine that has soaked in a tbsp. of water 5 min. Add flavoring and finish whipping. This will store in refrigerator a long time.

Add ½ to 1¼ tsp. sugar in water before adding to pie crust for a brown crust.

To avoid soggy pumpkin pie, spread a little beaten egg over the unbaked crust with a pastry brush. You can do this economically because you'll later use the rest of the egg to make the filling. Place crust in refrigerator to let egg dry before adding the filling.

When cutting dates, roll them in flour before you cut them. The slices will not cling to the knife or scissors. The flour used should be part of that called for in the recipe.

1 tsp. cream added to 2 lbs. hamburger keeps it from falling apart so easily.

When baking fresh apple pie invert pie pan over top and apples will be done in less time.

To make a smooth and creamy boiled icing, add 1 tbsp. cornstarch to each cup of sugar.

Put 1 tsp. vinegar in doughnuts. They will never be greasy.

To remove the rancid taste in liver, soak in milk for 30 min. before preparing.

Miscellaneous Hints

After cleaning chickens or cutting onions, put soda into the palm of one hand and rub your hands together. A quick rinse with soapy water removes all unpleasant odors.

After working with fruit, such as apples, peaches and cherries which turn the hands brown, the stain may be prevented if before washing your hands with soap, you take a couple of tablespoons of baking soda, dampen and wash the hands with it. It neutralizes the acid that ordinarily turns brown when hand soap hits it.

To singe chickens place one tablespoon rubbing alcohol in a small container and light. This will make a smokeless blaze.

Add 1 tbsp. baking soda to 1 gallon boiling water before putting the chicken into the water. It will make the chicken whiter and takes off pinfeathers.

Before painting walls or woodwork, make a thick paste of Bon Ami and cover windows with it. When through painting you need only to rub off the Bon Ami and the paint spatters will come off with it, leaving your windows shining and clean.

Use equal parts of turpentine and ammonia to remove paint from fabrics.

To make nut cracking and chopping easy, soak pecans in water overnight or boil 10 minutes, then crack. They will come out easy, many whole. To be chopped, place in a plastic bag and roll with rolling pin.

Home made windex for sparkling windows, mix ½ cup alcohol, 1 cup water, and a few drops of bluing.

To shorten drying cycle in drying clothes. Put a dry turkish towel in with the batch to be dried. Saves electricity and time.

Relief for burns. Castor oil gives instant relief for burns and in most cases prevents blistering.

Vinegar is an antidote to lye. Wash or rinse affected part with vinegar.

Hand Lotion (1)

2 pints soft water   ½ oz. tragacanth

Boil the 2 pts. soft water for 20 min. Cool and add tragacanth; this is for thickening. Let these two items stand overnight, then add the following.

½ oz. powdered alum   4 oz. glycerine
1 oz. boric acid   6 oz. alcohol

Perfume, if desired, or ½ pint rose water can be used and only 1½ pts. soft water. Beat well and strain. Put in small jars and seal tight. Refrigerate.

Hand Lotion (2)

Mix equal portions of bay rum and glycerine for rough hands.

Beatitudes for Homemakers

Blessed is she whose daily tasks are of love; for her willing hands and happy heart transform duty into joyous service to all her family and God.

Blessed is she who opens the door to welcome both stranger and well-loved friend; for gracious hospitality is a test of brotherly love.

Blessed is she who mends stockings and toys and broken hearts; for her understanding is a balm to her husband and children.

Blessed is she who scours and scrubs; for well she knows that cleanliness is one expression of godliness.

Blessed is she whom children love; for the love of a child is of greater value than fortune or fame.

Blessed is she who sings at her work; for music lightens the heaviest load and brightens the dullest chore.

Blessed is she who dusts away doubt and fear and sweeps out the cobwebs of confusion, for her faith will triumph over all adversity.

Blessed is she who serves laughter and smiles with every meal; for her cheerfulness is an aid to mental and physical digestion.

Blessed is she who introduces Jesus Christ to her children; for godly sons and daughters shall be her reward.

Blessed is she who preserves the sacredness of the Christian home; for hers is a divine trust that crowns her with dignity.

Mother's Influence

I took a piece of plastic clay
And idly fashioned it one day.
And as my fingers pressed it still,
It moved and yielded at my will.

I came again when days were past,
The bit of clay was hard at last;
The form I gave it still it bore,
But I could change that form no more.

I took a piece of living clay,
And gently formed it day by day,
And molded with my power and art,
A young child's soft and yielding heart.

I came again when days were gone,
It was a man I looked upon,
He still that early impress bore
And I could change it nevermore.

Recipe for a Happy New Year

Take twelve fine, full-grown months: see that these are thoroughly free from all old memories of bitterness, rancor, hate and jealousy, cleanse them completely from every clinging spite; pick off all specks of pettiness and littleness; in short see that these months are freed from all the past—have them as fresh and clean as when they first came from the great storehouse of Time.

Cut these months into thirty or thirty-one equal parts. Don't attempt to make up the whole batch at one time (so many people spoil the entire lot in this way), but prepare one day at a time as follows:

Into each day put equal parts of faith, patience, courage, work (some people omit this ingredient and so spoil the flavor of the rest), hope, fidelity, liberality, kindness, rest (leaving out this is like leaving the oil out of the salad—don't do it), prayer, meditation, and one well-selected resolution. Put in about a teaspoonful of good spirits, a dash of fun, a sprinkling of play, and a heaping cupful of good humor.

Pour love into the whole and mix with a vim. Cook thoroughly in a fervent heat; garnish with a few smiles and a sprig of joy; then serve with quietness, unselfishness, and cheerfulness.

INDEX

394   CHRISTIAN HOME COOK BOOK